COPPER CANYON

From The Sea To The Sierra

Chihuahua - Sinaloa

Cascada Piedra Volada

Barranca de Candameña

Ojo de la Reina – Eye of the Queen – Naica Mine

Crystal Cave of the Giants - Fairyland

Eye of the Crystal King

Temoris Arco Iris - Bloom of San Miguel Flowers

Témoris–an Undiscovered Jewel of the Copper Canyon

The historic borderlands between the Tarahumara of Chihuahua and the cannibalistic Acaxees of Sinaloa during early colonial era, Témoris is today one very real outpost of history. A quiet, well organized and friendly town to the casual visitor, the surrounding countryside is some of the wildest in North America. A frontier of civilization surrounded by a sometimes very hostile wilderness, the town itself is a model of tranquility. Each morning and evening a bus runs from the town, which is at a cool 5,000 feet of elevation, down to the tropical train station of the same name at about 2,000 feet above sea level. Very few people have heard of the beautiful little village that exists in an almost paradise like setting in the mountain valley above. Visitors from the outside world are a rarity, and the natives seem to be very content with their little town tucked away deep in the wild Sierra Madre of legendary times. For visitors, respect is the key to entering this mystical place.

El Fuerte

El Fuerte is becoming a world class birding hotspot with relatively common sightings of endemic and rare species including: Solitary Eagle, Rufous-bellied Chachalaca, Military Macaw, Lilac-crowned Parrot, Eared Trogon, Squirrel Cuckoo, Russet-crowned Motmot, Social Flycatcher, Happy Wren, Golden Vireo and Elegant Trogan among many others. Also of interest are the Mayo Indians, archeological sites including 200 petroglyphs, a beautiful colonial town plaza and the "fort" which is being rebuilt to house a museum for the region. Wonderful guide services, hotels and restaurants all provide a unique experience on the way to the Copper Canyon.

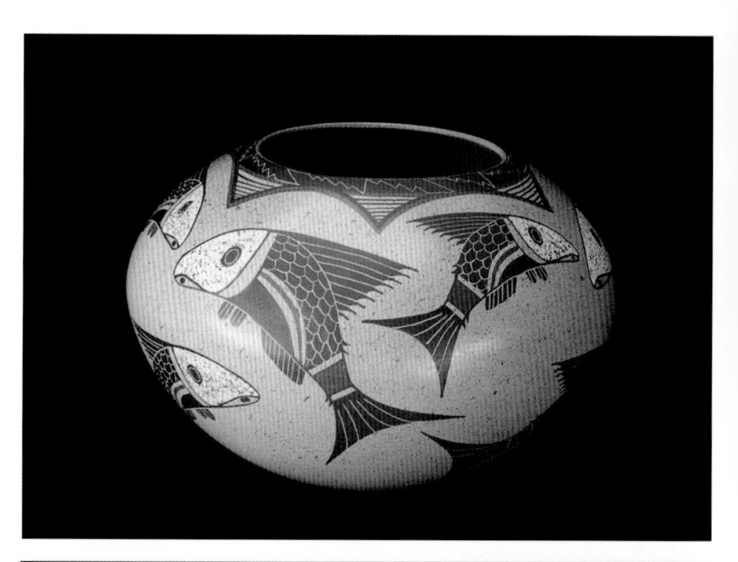

At Home in Mata Ortiz

From it's roots as a very traditional small Mexican village, Mata Ortiz has become a world class center for ceramic art. Juan Quezada, the innovator and leader of this success, has always promoted strong traditional family and village unity. As one of the leading young women artisans, Martha Martinez de Quezada is a beautiful example of how artistic and economic opportunities are passed from generation to generation throughout the entire community.

One of the unique experiences in Mata Ortiz today is that the visitor and buyer of ceramics can travel freely from home to home throughout the entire village making friends.

Hacienda San Diego - Colonia Juarez - Mata Ortiz

A Chihuahua Renaissance at the Millennium

Richard D. Fisher

INTRODUCTION

A century ago when Carl Lumholtz and Grant Shepherd rode the high Sierra Madre and walked the deep barrancas it was a completely different era. When these two explorers made their way through the rugged canyons and mountains it seemed a fresh new day, perhaps even the dawning of a new age. These two were the first to view the region from the concept of modern development and resource exploitation. Lumholtz was deeply concerned by the potential threat to the traditional Tarahumara culture, while Grant feared the effects of the Mexican Revolution.

Both of these rugged men of the frontier would perhaps be pleasantly surprised that a hundred years later several pockets of very traditional Tarahumara culture remain. They would find that transportation throughout the region is vastly "improved" and that modern services have made life much more comfortable and secure. They both might be dismayed by the neglect of beautiful buildings in Batopilas and the loss of old growth forest over much of the Sierra Madre. They would surely be surprised that many local people earn a large percentage of their income from tourism.

Carl Lumholtz would be happy to know that many of his concepts and theories concerning the mysterious pre-Colombian dwellings have proven over time to be correct. He would be very excited to learn that even today major new discoveries are being made throughout the Sierra, especially west of Madera.

Grant Shepherd would be gratified at the completion of a railroad through Copper Canyon and by thriving communities with modern amenities such as an extensive network of paved roads, electricity and even computers scattered throughout the high valleys of the Sierra. Grant would probably be very disappointed to find that silver is now being treated as a commodity and not a treasure.

ASTOUNDING DISCOVERIES 2000

In the first years of the Millennium three major discoveries have been made in Chihuahua. Lumholtz would have been exceedingly interested in major new archeological discoveries resulting in expansion of the understanding of Mesoamerican civilization in the northern Sierra. This "Puzzle of Oasis America" is the missing link between the Anasazi in the southwestern USA and the great cultures of central and southern Mexico.

Shepherd would be fascinated by the discovery of the largest known crystals on earth in the Naica Mine just south of Chihuahua City. This single event may ultimately change the entire region into one of the earth's major travel destinations.

Almost as unbelievable as these first two discoveries, are the newly recognized highest waterfalls in Mexico found in the Candameña canyon. While these incredible falls were seen previously, their true importance was not originally recognized because of the drought conditions that prevailed throughout northern Mexico during the last decade.

In 2000, major flood events have finally brought many rivers and streams back to life, and with this the waterfalls were rediscovered. The Cascada Piedra Volada (Flying Stone Waterfalls) is a jewel set in one of the most exotic, wild and rugged vistas anywhere on earth.

This planet has an incredible diversity of cultures and natural resources, but it would be almost impossible to find a single, more fascinating region and history anywhere.

THE PUZZLE OF OASIS AMERICA

"Oasis America" is how modern Mexican archeologists describe the desert oasis cultures in the southwestern USA and northern Mexico.

The origins and disappearance of the pre-Colombian Anasazi Indian culture in the American southwest has long been a mystery. It has always been a "puzzle" as to where these people came from and to where they mysteriously disappeared. Many, and perhaps even most pieces of the puzzle have been put together, but several critical links are still missing. In the last few years major new discoveries of previously unknown ruins of Indian cities have been made in the Huapoca Canyon near Madera. The most outstanding feature of these ruins is the magnificent corn storing "ollas" (jars), some of which are more than eight feet tall and four feet in diameter. These structures, which are woven from a grass rope and then plastered with fine mud, clearly show the strong connection to central Mexico. It was previously known that the Paquimé culture had an extensive trade relationship with the Anasazi of the north and with the great city states in central Mexico. Most scientists believed that these people were most closely tied to the Indian cultures of the southwestern USA. What has been discovered however, is that there are many more

"Paquimé Culture" cities, pueblos, and cliff dwellings than were known previously. It is from these more extensive archeological sites that expanded, and in some cases, new theories are being developed. More than a dozen major new sites have been documented in the last five years, and it is anticipated that at least several more major discoveries will be made in 2001-2002. What is clear is that there are many dozens of corn storage ollas found in all of the major sites. This, along with the extensive previous research, will help complete the majority of the "puzzle".

For those interested in Native American history and civilization, this will be an exciting story to follow over the next few years. There is also an undeniable connection between these canyon dwelling ancients and the canyon Tarahumara Indian culture. What has been recently learned about the Tarahumara, the newly discovered sites in the Huapoca Canyon, and what is already extensively known about the Anasazi will perhaps be the "missing link" in the "Puzzle of Oasis America". It is fortunate that in historical times the Tarahumaras inhabited the Huapoca Canyon; this was the northern limit of their territory. Today the

Pima Bajo Indians still have one major village in this canyon called Mesa Blanca. Here in northern Mexico, one can see that these cultures are undoubtedly the descendents of the Paquimé people just as the Hopi, Zuni, and the Pueblo cultures along the Rio Grande are descendents of the Anasazi.

In 1999 Carlos Lazcano, in his position as Eco-tourism Director for the State of Chihuahua, informed me of extensive new and undisturbed ruins found in the Huapoca Canyon. He very kindly gave me permission to use his photographs in this publication, as well as in my Copper Canyon guide book. He was very enthusiastic about the discoveries, but at the time I just felt it was interesting news and was not personally that excited. During the subsequent two years I had the privilege of getting to know Carlos and his family through the exploration of the Naica Crystal Cave and some explorations in Durango, Mexico. The first thing that impressed me was the very modest and unassuming personality that Carlos shared with me. What really got my attention, however, was his in-depth, scholarly approach to his explorations and his dedication to solid research. These two characteristics, in addition to his incredible mastery of technical canyon and cave

exploration skills, and a fearless nature without the usual bravado, motivated me to support his work in any way possible.

It was during an expedition with Carlos and his daughter, Anna, that we became friends. Carlos had been to these "best of the new discoveries" several times during the preceding years. He was very motivated to preserve this "sky island village" of five or six caves, as they represented a complete and unique grouping of structures with clear farming terraces literally right in front of the caves.

This is probably one of the best preserved complete village systems in the entire Paquimé cultural system. It is easily seen that the "sky island" is relatively easy to defend. In fact, there are some foundations of the "guard houses" still visible on the narrow isthmus connecting it to the main Sierra Madre Ridge. There were two small canyons on the island that had the primary cave dwellings and corn storage jars. There were perhaps another four or five smaller canyons around the rim of the island that had "out buildings" or structures where individual families lived to work and guard areas with more limited terrace structures. The corn storage jars were very complete and had a central location in the caves much like the Kivas at Mesa Verde. This clearly emphasized their importance to the village. For me, however, they highlighted the cultural connection to central Mexico. Having lived in "pure" Tarahumara canyon villages, it was very clear to me how the village actually functioned as a social unit. I could literally see this place alive with people living exactly as I had experienced Tarahumaras living in great canyons farther south.

Several other obvious environmental and cultural factors became clear as we carefully researched the sites. The leading theory for the T-shaped doorways and cave

dwellings was that their design was for defense. We can clearly see now that the T-shaped doorways were not for defensive purposes, as some were on the second story and several were inside the buildings. David Teschner pointed out that there was a very definite insulation value to the design, and that if battles were taking place inside the house, it was too late for doorway design to make much of a difference. The corn storage ollas, most valuable structures containing their irreplaceable food, were right in front of the caves and not placed in a defensive position at all. While defensive aspects are built into the site, it is clear that it was not an overriding priority.

These ancient canyon villages do not exhibit a haphazard placement. Instead, the most densely terraced areas are situated where an abrupt narrowing of the great canyon causes orographic uplift of the air which increases the likelihood of condensation and rainfall. Among the Canyon Tarahumara, traditional villages have been able to survive the ten-year drought due to their position right at the narrowing of the canyons. Even fields positioned below high west-facing cliffs get more rainfall than fields just 400 yards away.

Another factor to be researched in the upcoming years is the theory that these canyon dwelling Paquimé people primarily lived in the mountains and canyons only during the summer rainy season to grow crops and moved back to the Casas Grandes Valley during the winter season.

The methods of fertilization, number of usable years for these agricultural terraces, in addition to population demographics, will add another critical piece to the puzzle.

These important new discoveries by Carlos Lazcano should stimulate further research and theories for the Native American history in Oasis America and the Mesoamerican connection.

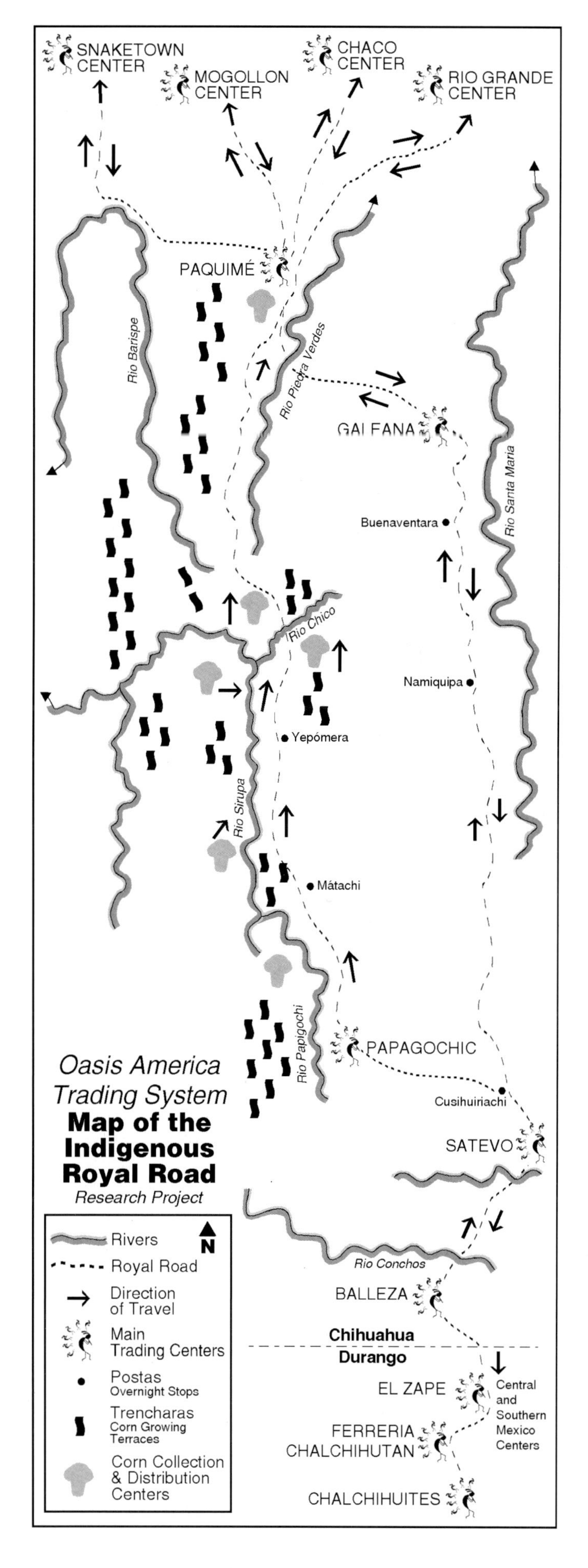

CRYSTAL CAVE OF THE GIANTS

In what has proved to be the discovery of the largest known crystals on earth, work is underway to document and preserve this historic find. While some minor damage has already occurred in the primary cave and a secondary cavern, called Cave of Dreams, iron doors have been installed by the Peñoles company to prevent damage to the giant, magnificent crystals. While investigations are underway the mine is closed, but with the newly installed lighting system, it is expected to open in the fall 2001.

Found deep in a mine in southern Chihuahua Mexico, these crystals were formed in a natural cave totally enclosed in bedrock. When I first stepped into the cavern it was like walking into the Land of the Giants. I have often admired crystal geodes held in my hand, but when photographing these unique natural structures it was almost impossible to get any sense of scale. This is a geode full of spectacular crystals as tall as pine trees, and in some cases greater in circumference. They have formed beautiful crystals that are a translucent gold and silver in color, and come in many incredible forms and shapes. Some of the largest are essentially columnar in shape and stand thirty to fifty feet high and three to four feet in diameter. Many of the smaller examples are four to six feet in circumference, have many incredible geometrical shapes, and probably weigh in excess of ten tons. The columnar pillars are at first the most striking shape, but later I noticed there were thousands of "sharks teeth" up to three feet high placed row upon row and dispersed at odd angles throughout the caverns. While some of the crystals are attached to the ceiling walls and floors of the cave as might be expected, some exist in great masses of spikes and almost float in air. These crystals seem to defy gravity, as they must weigh several tons.

The crystal cavern was discovered within the same limestone body that hosts the silver-zinc-lead ore bodies exploited by the mine. The cavern was probably dissolved by the same hydrothermal fluids that deposited the metals with the gypsum being crystallized during the waning stages of mineralization. The crystals probably grew relatively quickly to their immense size within a completely liquid-filled cavern.

As a professional photographer who specializes in environmentally difficult, narrow and wet canyons worldwide, it was almost impossible to obtain clear photographs even using every trick and technique I knew, because of the extreme ambient environment. These crystals are probably stable, as the temperature in the cave is over 150 degrees Fahrenheit with 100% humidity. In other words, these structures are enveloped in steam. As a photographer used to working in dark and dangerous environments, this experience was unique. A human can only function in this environment for six to ten minutes before severe loss of mental functions occurs. I was so excited while photographing the crystals that I really had to focus and concentrate intensely on getting back out the door, which was perhaps only thirty to forty feet away.

The Naica mine was first discovered by early prospectors in 1794 south of Chihuahua City. They struck a vein of silver at the base of a range of hills called Naica by the Tarahumara Indians. The origin in the Tarahumara language seems to mean "a shady place". Perhaps here in the small canyon there was a grove of trees tucked away by a small canyon spring.

From the discovery until about 1900, the primary interest was silver and gold. Around 1900 large-scale mining began as zinc and lead became more valuable.

During the Mexican Revolution the mine was producing a great deal of wealth. Revolutionary troops entered the town and demanded money from the owners. One of them was assassinated when he refused to pay, causing the mine to shut down from 1911 to 1922.

Just before the mine was closed, the famous Cave of Swords was discovered at a depth of 400 feet. Due to the incredible crystals, it was decided to try to preserve this cave. While many of the crystals have been collected, this is still a fascinating cave to visit. In one part there are so many crystals on one of the walls, they appear to be like an underwater reef moving in a gentle undulating motion in an ocean current.

In April 2000, brothers Juan and Pedro Sanchez were drilling a new tunnel when they made a truly spectacular discovery. While Naica miners are accustomed to finding crystals, Juan and Pedro were absolutely amazed by the cavern that they found. The brothers immediately informed the engineer in charge, Roberto Gonzalez. Ing. Gonzalez realized that they had discovered a natural treasure and quickly rerouted the tunnel. During this phase some damage was done as several miners tried to remove pieces of the mega-crystals, so the mining company soon installed an iron door to protect the find. Later, one of the workers, with the intention of stealing crystals, managed to get in through a narrow hole. He tried to take some plastic bags filled with fresh air inside, but the strategy didn't work. He lost consciousness and later was found thoroughly baked.

When entering the cave our group is issued helmets, lanterns, rubber boots, and gloves. We are then driven by truck into the main mining tunnel called Rampa Sn. Francisco. While the vertical drop is approximately 1000 feet, the drive is almost a half mile long. The heat steadily increases and the ladies could be observed to begin "glowing". The truck stops in front of a concrete wall with a steel door. I start working frantically to put the final touches on my pre-prepared camera outfit. I usually have four separate camera units, but they must be padded for the trip and then receive a last minute detail check. Every single item is preset before entering the cavern, as every moment inside is precious and concentration must be focused strictly on the crystals and people. The photographic machinery must work perfectly as the heat almost immediately begins to impair brain function.

At the end of the tunnel there are three or four steps into the aperture of the cavern itself. It is in this short tunnel that I move very quickly and concentrate on focusing my mind and that of my group on the task of photography. In this short distance the temperature and humidity goes from being uncomfortably warm to literally a blast furnace. Almost immediately our clothing is so soaked in sweat that it becomes heavy and starts to slide off our bodies. On my first trip it was really hard to keep my pants up, which was a new and unexpected experience.

Momentarily, the penetrating heat is forgotten as the crystals pop into view on the other side of the newly named "Eye of the Queen". The entire panorama is now lighted and the cavern has a depth and impressive cathedral-like appearance that was not visible on earlier trips with just our headlamps.

When inside the great cathedral of crystals, the pressure of intense heat makes my feelings run up and down the emotional scale from shear religious awe to outright panic. The ladies are no longer "glowing" and indeed are "red hot". When I'm done working after three trips into the great cavern, my friends almost have to carry me out. We want to see more, but physically cannot. When the experience is over there is a great relief, but all we can think about is when can we go back in.

When I talk to professional geologists about crystals they tell me that these natural forms are incredibly complex, yet so simple. They have a magical or metaphysical personality independent of their chemical structures. These geologists have explained to me that there is a magma chamber two to three miles below the mountain and that heat from this compressed lava travels through the faults up into the area of the mine. Super heated fluids carry the minerals the miners are seeking as well as form the crystals. The mine is ventilated; otherwise, it could not be worked. Some parts, however, are not air-conditioned, such as the Cave of the Crystals, and there you feel the heat from the magma deep below.

When describing the crystal formation the geologists' eyes light up with a special emotional fascination. They tell how the fluids travel along the Naica fault, enter voids in the bedrock, and then form entirely natural structures that are not easily explained by science.

I have been told that the mining company was afraid to tunnel through the Naica fault for fear of flooding the entire mine. In April 2000, the company became confident that the water table on the other side of the fault had been lowered sufficiently to drill. When they did this, it is almost as if a magical veil of reality was breached and an entirely new world was discovered. Two caverns filled with the Earth's largest crystals were immediately revealed. More discoveries are expected to be made in this magical kingdom of intense natural beauty.

Selenite, the gypsum crystal, named after the Greek goddess of the moon due to its soft white light, is said to have many metaphysical and healing benefits. Selenite powder has been used cosmetically for thousands of years to enhance one's natural beauty. It is believed that this crystal assists with mental focus, growth, luck, immunity, and soothes the emotions. It is unquestionably magical that the cool white rays of moonlight can originate deep underground in a black chamber that is, at least in my perception, white hot.

I thank Ing. Roberto Gonzales and Ing. Roberto Villasuso, of the Peñoles Mining Company and Sonia Estrada and Carlos Lazcano for contributions to this text and photographs.

THE SATELLITE

Relaxing in my Lazyboy chair watching the evening news in late October, I was waiting for the evening weather - one of my passions. I had just about drifted off to sleep when the satellite image of the American southwest flashed on screen. I wasn't expecting much due to the prolonged seven-year drought. What I saw made me sit bolt upright in my chair. Two huge storms were about to converge over the northern Sierra Madre.

I listened intently to the report of two unseasonable and uniquely strong fronts that were making a bull's-eye on Chihuahua's Copper Canyon region. One was a very rare October storm originating in the Gulf of Alaska and the other was a dissipating hurricane traveling almost from Hawaii. The two storms were wandering in from the north and west toward one of the most rugged and precipitous canyonlands on earth. The Northern front was cold and deep, the southern storm warm and pregnant with tropical moisture. An explosive situation.

A few years earlier my good friend, Carlos Lazcano, had told me of newly "discovered" waterfalls thought to be the highest in Mexico. Located in the Candameña Canyon near Basaseachi Falls (the previous official record holder), the newly named "Cascada Piedra Volada" (Flying Stone Waterfalls) had been dry most of the time since its discovery. I had been told that the setting of this remote waterfall was exceedingly exotic. I had always wanted to see it, and realized that this was going to be my best chance.

Carlos had told me that the falls were first spotted in 1995 when a group of Mexican climbers did the first ascent of Mexico's highest rock face called El Giante (885 meters or 2,900 feet). Shortly thereafter the falls was measured at 453 meters (1,485 feet).

The Candameña Canyon has perhaps the very best multi-day big wall climbing in Mexico, with El Giante being the premier challenge. It is from this very difficult vantage point that climbers can actually see down into the tunnel that the falls cuts deep into the bedrock and that has hidden this treasure of the Sierra Madre for so long.

I had not planned a trip to the canyons so I made a quick mental inventory of my current resources - at the moment finances meager, vehicle aged, my physical fitness sadly deficient. Oh well, so it's not a perfect world . I threw some clothes in the back of the van, bought a few supplies, and most importantly phoned up my friends at the Dept. of Tourism for some pointers. Carlos recommended a guide in the small town of Huajumar, and added that there were rudimentary hotel accommodations available.

In November 1984, I had the good fortune to be at Basaseachi Falls when another similar storm system hit the western wall of the Sierra. At the time I did not know that it was a rare and unique event. I have managed to get a photo from the 1984 flood on several book and magazine covers, and now hoped to recapture some of the drama and youthful excitement of a challenge as the millennium year was drawing to a close.

Entering the village of Huajumar, I found that Paco Camunez, the guide recommended to me, lived in the very first house I came upon. I met him walking down the one lane gravel road with a few friends just as the last rays of the sun brilliantly lit up the storm clouds racing in from the west.

Paco guided me to a rather modest concrete block hotel. We arranged to go to the falls the next morning. That night, in the small drafty hotel, I was very glad for a tepid shower and warm bed. The storm outside was blowing the rain drops like steel slivers against the outside walls. I dreamed of the falls that I had never seen, not even in a photograph. I was to see the highest falls in Mexico come morning light–in full flood, or so I imagined.

Paco came by at mid-morning. In the fog we drove the very rough 4x4 track about 10 km. (7 miles) toward the falls. It was another 2 km. walk to the overlook. When we arrived about noon the entire canyon was still shrouded in a heavy mist - a rare event. I could hear the falls booming across the gorge, but couldn't see even a few yards into what I knew was a great abyss.

We stood around in the drizzle for about an hour when Paco decided to start a fire to warm us. A little later, with a sudden rush of air, the canyon cleared. I had fantasized about photographing the falls in the mist. It was not to be. Totally obscured one moment and seconds later the air was crystal clear. I was so stunned by the sudden change of events and the vista of the falls itself, I must have fumbled with the tripods and cameras for at least ten minutes before I got off a first shot.

The scene was a shocker, even to someone used to rugged canyon panoramas. Well, as they say, it was like Peru or Nepal or this or that place, but actually it was like the most romantic and legendary Sierra Madre of my wildest imagination. Across the canyon, in addition to the waterfall, are two distinctive vertical walls accented by the falls and divided dead center by a second major side canyon filled with cascades. What a wild and magnificent view. It was like Tata Dios, the Tarahumara father god, had thrown a handful of crystals and precious stones on to the velvet green of the background forest.

Huge pine trees studded the cliffs like tiny sprigs of moss clinging to the great walls. The Candameña creek raging in the depths, almost lost and tiny to view, but very audible, lay two thousand feet directly below.

My eyes felt like a zoom lens. It was hard to focus. A close look at something and my eyes wanted to skip to another feature and zoom out to get perspective. How big was this feature? How far away was that feature? Almost no way to get a perspective. Fortunately I had my work cut out for me and I settled down to an intense five hour session of photography. No more need to try to take it all in as a whole or as details–just work the cameras.

Across the canyon the primary point of interest was booming, as waves of flood water threw themselves into thin air. At times I could follow a wave from top to bottom. Later in the afternoon the evening wind blowing up canyon would fight the falling water fiercely, trying to push the waves back toward the sky. The single thread of white water was actually a torrent falling through the air from the lip of a small incised canyon, and then entering a tube or tunnel in the side of the cliff. This tube, which is open slightly on the down stream western face, actually serves to funnel the upstream winds to confront the falling water. It creates an adversarial relationship between the air and water, unique in all the world at Cascada Piedra Volada.

It was one of those moments when life seems to happen in slow motion and yet, when it is over, it was only an instant in time. I wish I had done so much more, looked more comprehensively, experienced more intensely. Actually, for me to have done more was probably impossible; I was exhausted.

As I worked into those magical twilight hours, my mind unconsciously began singing the Moody Blues song "Nights in White Satin". It was one of those things that you aren't conscious of when it happens; it's just there, in your mind over and over again.

Shadows on the ground,
Never make a sound,
Fading away in the sunset...
I can see it all, from this great height,
I can feel the sun, slipping out of sight.
And the world goes on, through the night.
Twilight time to dream awhile,
Unveils the deepening blue.
As fantasy strides, over colorful skies,
The form disappearing from view.
In twilight time, dream with me awhile.
A nightingale plays a dark mellow phrase,
Of notes that are so rich and true.
An aerial display by the firefly brigade,
Dancing to tunes no one knew.
In twilight time, dream with me awhile.
Nights in white satin, never reaching the end,
Letters I've written, never meaning to send.
Beauty I'd always missed, with these eyes before,
Just what the truth is, I can't say anymore.
'Cos I love you, yes I love you,
Oh how I love you, oh how I love you.
Breathe deep the gathering gloom,
Watch lights fade from every room...
Impassioned lovers wrestle as one,
Lonely man cries for love and has none...
Cold hearted orb that rules the night,
Removes the colours from our sight.
Red is grey and yellow white,
But we decide which is right.
And which is an illusion???

As I emerged from my working dream state, Paco was very patiently waiting. We talked a bit in my broken Spanish. I didn't know the Spanish word for satellite. I explained that a machine high in the sky had forecast this rare event three days in advance. When he understood what I was trying to communicate, he became very animated. Normally Paco is a quiet and reserved man, but clearly intelligent. "Satelite tres dias antes?" he inquired. "Mas o meno (more or less)," I replied. He was flabbergasted that anyone would be interested in weather events in this canyon, much less put the information to practical use.

The next day I headed out to meet Carlos and explore the Naica Mine Crystals. I reflected, I'll never get rich living this way. My vehicle just got a lot older on those Sierra Madre roads and one three mile hike during a week of tough driving will never get me in physical shape. It's a rough life, but I suppose somebody's gotta live it!

I express my gratitude to Carlos Lazcano for inviting me to participate in exploring three areas described in this millennium chapter: the ruins of the Huapoca Canyon, the Naica Crystal Cave and the Piedra Volada Waterfalls. I would also like to thank David Teschner for his extensive support, both material and personal, enabling the successful completion of this work .

Juan Quezada's boyhood fascination with prehistoric pottery shards has led to a contemporary ceramic art movement now recognized in art circles from Mexico City to museums and galleries throughout the United States. Two generations of potters from the village of Mata Ortiz on the high plains of northern Chihuahua look to Juan as the originator and inspiration of their art form.

At twelve or thirteen Juan began supplementing his family income by cutting wood in the mountains and hauling it back to Mata Ortiz on burros. As he crossed the plains, he picked up shards from the mounds left by people of the prehistoric Casas Grandes culture. Intrigued by the beautiful designs and by the thought that the ancients had made such pottery, he began to search for clay and to experiment. Over a period of 15 years, he taught himself to make thin-walled pieces painted with intricate fine-lined designs. Through trial and error, using his artistic skills, he recreated all of the steps of ceramic technology without any outside instruction or inspiration other than the shards. His work became a model for his relatives, then neighbors and friends of neighbors, until now, 23 years after his discovery by an north American art historian, over 400 potters support their families by selling their wares to an ever-increasing number of traders and tourists.

To learn more about Juan Quezada and the potters of Mata Ortiz, read the "Miracle of Mata Ortiz" by Walter P. Parks which can be ordered from The Coulter Press • 6154 Hawarden Dr. • Riverside, CA 92506 • (909) 684-4224 for $19.95.

$19.95

History of Copper Canyon and the Tarahumara Indians

Contemporary Photography
Richard D. Fisher
David L. Teschner
Carlos Lazcano Sahagún

Unknown Mexico
Carl Lumholtz

Silver Magnet
Grant Shepherd

A Letter from the Publisher and Editor, Richard D. Fisher

For many years the classic text and history of Copper Canyon and the Tarahumara Indians has been out of print. Due to a deep commitment to the region, its peoples, and its history, the publisher is seeking to help perpetuate and make available the two most important books on the Copper Canyon and the Tarahumara culture in this new anthology of *Unknown Mexico* by Carl Lumholtz and the *Silver Magnet* by Grant Shepherd. It should be noted that only the chapters that apply to the Northern Sierra Madre, Copper Canyon, and the Tarahumara Indians in *Unknown Mexico* (Chapters 4-22) are reprinted in this collection.

The publisher is very excited to present, in the color photography section, a modern look at this incredibly diverse region. Up until 1990 very little had changed since 1890. In fact, in some respects the northern Sierra Madre was even farther off the beaten track in modern times than a century ago. Of course, since 1990 the rate of modernization has accelerated dramatically. The outstanding photography of Carlos Lazcano in the Cliff Dwellings near Madera and the publisher's photographs of the Sierra Madre and its diverse cultures will bring the reader back in time to the experiences of Lumholtz and Shepherd. The publisher is pleased to present this new work in conjunction with the outstanding history of the region.

In this second edition we would like to thank a new photographic talent, David L. Teschner, for his contributions of photographs and efforts in research. The publisher is sure his talents will be appreciated by the readers.

This 2001 edition of the History of Copper Canyon also includes a wonderful new section that highlights with color photography and text the new discoveries of the millennium in Chihuahua and throughout the northern Sierra Madre region.

The publisher hopes that you, the public, will support this publication and associated cultural preservation efforts. Those who know the personal style of the publisher over the years know his deepest satisfaction is working with dedicated people, from many cultures, on productive, technically challenging, and mutually beneficial cultural projects. With this goal in mind, the publisher invites you to make any possible contribution to improving the quality of this book, especially in helping to find more historical photographs for the next edition.

Thank you for your support.

Very sincerely yours,

Richard Fisher

Richard D. Fisher
Publisher – Sunracer Publications

History of Copper Canyon and the Tarahumara Indians

Anthology

Contents

SUNRACER PUBLICATIONS
P.O. Box 86492
Tucson, AZ 85754
Phone: (520) 882-5341
Fax: (520) 882-4454
email: sunracer@theriver.com
www.coppercanyon.org
www.canyonsworldwide.com

Edited by
Richard D. Fisher

Photography
Richard D. Fisher
David L. Teschner
Carlos Lazcano Sahagún

Typesetting
Koala-t Type

Proofreading
Audrey Lowenthal
Kirsteen Anderson
Elizabeth McKindley
Dorothy Taylor

All contemporary photographs of cave dwellings in the Carl Lumholtz text are printed with the permission of Carlos Lazcano Sahagún.

ISBN Number 0-9619170-9-1

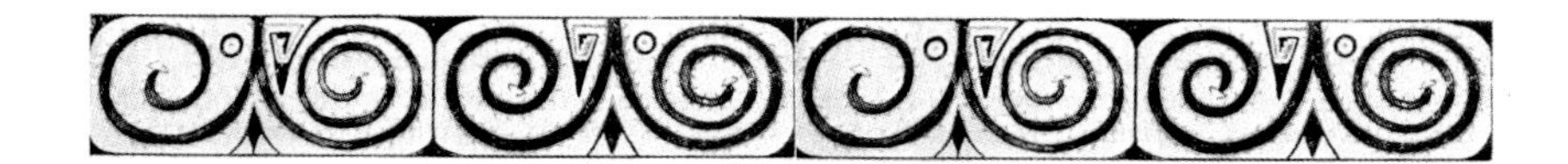

Unknown Mexico

Carl Lumholtz

Chapter 4

A Splendid Field Prepared for Us by the Ancient Agriculturists of Cave Valley—House Groups in Caves along a Pretty Stream—Well-preserved Mummies Found in Caves—More Trincheras—Our Excavations in Caves and Mounds Confirm to the Mormons Their Sacred Stories—We Move to the Plains of San Diego—Visit to Casas Grandes and the Watch-tower—Successful Excavations of the Mounds near San Diego.

Finding the locality so inviting for research, I decided to remain here, returning to Pacheco only to dispatch the rest of my party to make excavations at the ranch of San Diego, thirty miles to the east, down on the plains of Chihuahua. The ranch was temporarily leased by an American, Mr. Galvin, who received my expedition hospitably, and invited the members to remain as long as they pleased and to make excavations wherever they wanted.

Cave Valley is the widening of a long, low-walled cañon through which the Piedras Verdes River flows. As its name implies, it contains many caves in the felsitic conglomerate overlying the region. It is from one-quarter to half a mile wide, and has a fine, rich, loamy soil. The stream is ten to twenty feet wide and from one to three feet deep. Fine forests of pine, oak, cedar, and maple surround it, and make it an ideal dwelling-place for a peaceful, primitive people.

The little knoll on which we were encamped rises on the north side of a brook which empties itself in the river. It was in equally close proximity to the dwellings of the living and the dwellings of the dead.

Up the main stream, on the western wall of the cañon, and about a mile from our camp, is a large cave containing the curious cupola-shaped structure already mentioned. The cave is easy of approach up a sloping bank from its south side, and arriving at it we found it quite commodious and snug. It is about eighty feet wide at its mouth, and about a hundred feet deep. In the central part it is almost eighteen feet high, but the roof gradually slopes down in the rear to half that height.

A little village, or cluster of houses, lies at its back and sides. The interior of most of the rooms must have been quite dark, though the light reaches the outside of all the houses. The walls are still standing about six feet high. The compartments, though small, are seldom kennel-like. Some of the houses have shallow cellars. The roof of the cave was thickly smoked over its entire surface. From traces of walls still remaining on it, we may infer that a second story had been built toward the centre of the cave, though this could only have been five feet high. These traces of walls on the roof further prove the important fact that this second story had been built in terrace-fashion, receding about four feet back from the front of the ground story.

The cave had evidently been occupied for a very long time, the houses showing many alterations and additions, and on the walls I counted as many as twelve coatings of plaster and whitewash. The conventional design of the ear of corn is well preserved in every doorway. Rude scrawlings of soot and water cover nearly all the front walls, mixed here and there with a few traces of red ochre. There are meander designs, lightning, and drawings of cows and horses; but the latter were doubtless put on after the walls were demolished, and their general appearance denotes recentness.

Several of the cyclopean riffles lead from the cave cliff to the stream.

The houses here, as well as in all other caves we examined, were built entirely of a powdery substance, the decomposed material of the cave itself. Great quantities of it were found on the floors of caves which had not been occupied by man. It is not a sandy nature, and its colour is light brown, sometimes almost grey, or even white. The ancient builders simply had to mix it with water and mould it into bricks, which, through fairly uniform in thickness, were very irregular in size. There were no marks of implements on the walls; all the work seems to have been done by hand and smoothed over with some wetted fabric. In one cave of this valley the walls show finger-marks on the plaster. Occasionally we found a small boulder of hard stone embedded in the wall.

The most unique feature of this cave, however, is the cupola-shaped structure which stands in an open space in front of the house group, near the mouth of the cave, but still under its roof. Its height, measured inside, is twelve feet, and its widest inside diameter is eleven feet.[1] Its walls average eight inches in thickness. It has one aperture three feet wide at the top, another one of the same dimension near the base, and there are several others nearly opposite each other. In the two upper ones are seen distinct impressions of timber in the plaster.

The building was made by twisting long grass into a compact cable and laying it up, one round upon another. As the coil proceeded, thick coats of plaster were laid on inside and outside. This plaster, which is the same material as that of which the houses are constructed, got thoroughly mixed with the straw during the process of building, and the entire structure was finished without any opening except the one at the top. The other apertures were undoubtedly cut out afterward. There is no trace of withes or other binding material to hold the straw cables in place. They are kept in position only by the plaster, which here, as in the houses, is almost as hard as the conglomerate of the surrounding rocks.

My Mexicans from Sonora called it *olla,* a jar, and insisted that it was a vessel used for keeping water; but this is entirely improbable, for several reasons, mainly because the river is in close proximity and easy of access. It was without the slightest doubt a granary. Similar structures, used for that purpose to the present day, may be seen in the States of Vera Cruz and Tlaxcala. In a cave only a short distance away, the rear portion of which also contained a group of houses, we found between the mouth of the cave and the house walls the remains of five of these peculiar buildings which I call granaries. They, too, were made of straw and plaster, similar to the one described, but the walls here were only two inches thick. The remains showed that they had not been set up in any special arrangement, nor were all five alike. Two of them were deeply sunken into the floor of the cave, and inside of them we found, between the rubbish and debris that filled them, several grains of corn and some beans.

The other caves which we examined in this valley were of the same general character as these two, although we found no granaries in them. On this page is shown the ground plan of a cave on the east side of the river, and attention is drawn to the singular concrete seats or blocks against the wall in the house on the west side of the cave. A floor of concrete had been made in this cave extending inward and fairly level.

Evidence of two-storeyed groups of houses was clearly noticeable in many caves; but our investigations were somewhat impeded by the destruction wrought by some Mormon relic-hunter, who had carried off almost everything removable. He had even taken away many of the door lintels and hand-grips, in fact, most of the woodwork, from the houses.

In the rear of some of the caves it was so dark that we had to light a candle to find our way, crawling from house to house. In one instance we found a stone stairway of three steps.

In spite of the tremendous dust which is raised by digging into the ground, and which makes the work very arduous, we searched diligently and succeeded in bringing to light a number of objects which fairly well illustrate the culture of the ancient people. Among them were needles and awls of bone; a complete fire drill with a stick showing drilling, basketry work covered with piñon pith, mats and girdles, threads of fibre or hair, and sandals plaited of yucca leaves. Wads of cotton and pieces of pottery were found in many places; and an interesting find was a "boomerang" similar to that used to this day by the Moqui Indians for killing rabbits. The handle is plainly seen, but the top is broken. The implement, which is made of very hard, reddish wood, has but a slight curve. We discovered many smooth pieces of iron ore that had probably been used for ceremonial purposes, and a bow that had been hidden away on a ledge.

That the ancient cave-dwellers were agriculturists is evident from the numerous corncobs, as well as grain of corn and beans, that we came upon. Datems, a green, sweet fruit still eaten by the Mexicans, were identified everywhere in the cave-dwellings.

Having effectually started the work of investigation here, I went to look after the second section of my expedition, which had been sent to San Diego. I covered the thirty-five miles with four pack mules in one day. There is a charming view of the brow of the sierra over the plains of San Diego, which are fully ten miles wide; but after descending to them I found a hard, cold wind blowing. The weather here is not at all as pleasant as in the sheltered Cave Valley up in the mountains.

I went to Casas Grandes, a village of 1,200 souls, six miles north of San Diego, and succeeded in getting a draft cashed. On learning that Mr. Moses Thatcher, a prominent Mormon apostle from Utah, was on a tour of inspection of the colonies, I proceeded to Colonia Juarez, a prosperous Mormon settlement on the Piedras Verdes River, ten miles from Casas Grandes and six miles from San Diego. It was only four years old, but had already a number of well laid-out broad streets, set on both side with cottonwood trees, and all the houses were surrounded by gardens. I explained to Mr. Thatcher that I desired to make excavations in Cave Valley, and he courteously acceded to my wishes, adding that I might take away anything of interest to science.

To reduce expenses, I paid off many of my Mexican men, who then returned to their homes in Sonora, going over the sierra by the trial we had made in coming east. A few months later several of them returned, bringing others with them, and asked to work again in the camp, which remained in San Diego for about nine months longer — long enough for us to see quite a little trade in oranges, sugar, tobacco, etc., developing between Sonora and Chihuahua by way of the road cut out by us, and called, after me, *el camino del doctor.*

Excavations in Cave Valley were continued, and the burial caves gave even better results that the cave-dwellings. They were located in the eastern side of the cañon, which is rarely touched by the sun's rays. With one exception the ceilings and sides of these caves were much blackened by smoke. There was not the slightest trace of house walls, and no other sign that the place had ever been inhabited; therefore, a fire here could have had no other purpose than a religious one, just as the Tarahumaras to this day make a fire in the cave in which they bury their dead. Indeed, the first sight there was nothing in the cave to indicate that they had every been utilised by man; but below the dust we came upon a hard, concrete floor, and after digging through this to a depth of three feet, we fortunately struck a skull, and then came upon the body of a man. After this we disinterred that of a mother holding a child in her arms, and two other bodies, all lying on their left sides, their knees half drawn up, and their faces turned toward the setting sun. All were in a marvellous state of preservation, owing to the presence of saltpetre in the dust. This imparted to the dead a mummy-like appearance, but there was nothing to suggest that embalming or other artificial means of preservation of the bodies had been used. The entire system was simply desiccated intact, merely shrunken, with the skin on most of the bodies almost unbroken. The features, and even the expression of the countenance, were in many cases quite distinct. Some had retained their eyebrows and part of their hair, and even their intestines had not all disappeared.

The hair of these people was very slightly wavy, and softer than that of the modern Indian; in fact, almost silky. The statures were quite low, and in general appearance these ancients bear a curious resemblance to the Moqui Indians, who have a tradition that their ancestors came from the south, and who, to this day, speak of their "southern brethren"; but it would be very rash to conclude from this that the cave-dwellers of northwestern Chihuahua are identical with the Moqui ancestors. I afterwards brought to light several other bodies which had been interred under similar conditions. The bottom of the burial caves seems to have always been overlaid with a roughly level, concrete floor. There was no trace here of cysts, or other formal sepulture.

None of the remains wore ornaments of metal, but various shell ornaments, anklets and bracelets of beautifully plaited straw, which, however, crumbled into dust when touched. Their clothing consisted of three layers of wrappings around the loins. Next to the body was placed a coarse cotton cloth; then a piece of matting, and over that another cotton cloth. Between the legs was a large wad of cotton mixed with feathers of the turkey, the large woodpecker, and the bluejay. In a few instances, the cotton cloth was dyed red or indigo. Near the head of each body stood a small earthenware jar of simple design; in some cases we also found drinking gourds placed at the head, though in one instance the latter had been put on the breast of the dead. Buried with the person we found a bundle of "devil's claws" *(Martynia).* These were used by the Mexicans of today for mending pottery. They drill holes through the fragments to be joined and pass into them one of these claws, just as we would a rivet. The claw is elastic and strong, and answers the purpose very well. My Mexicans understood at once to what use they had been put.

As already alluded to, trincheras were also found in Cave Valley, where they were quite numerous. There was one or more in every ravine and gully, and what was a new feature, some were built across shallow drainages on the very summit of a hill. This summit was a bald conglomerate, about 150 feet above the valley. In one place we observed eight trincheras within 150 feet of each other, all built of large stones in the cyclopean style of masonry. The blocks were lava and hard felsite, measuring one and a half to three feet. As a rule, these trincheras had a lateral extent of thirty feet, and in the central part they were fifteen feet high. After all the great labour expended in their construction, the builders of these terraces had secured in each only a space thirty feet long and fifteen feet wide; in other worlds, these eight terraces yielded together barely 3,000 square feet, which means space enough for planting five or six hundred hills of corn. People who do not know the Indians would consider this too small a result to favour the theory that these terraces were erected for agricultural purposes. But the Indian's farming is, in proportion to his wants, conducted on a small scale, and he never thinks of raising more corn than he actually needs; in fact, many tribes, as for instance the Tarahumares, seldom raise enough to last the family all the year through.

Further groups of cave-dwellings were found some ten miles higher up the river, in what is called the "Strawberry Valley," probably through the prevalence of the strawberry tree, of which several beautiful specimens were seen. The largest cave there contained fourteen houses. Unlike the dwellings in the Cave Valley, here a gallery ran in front of the houses. The woodwork here was fresher than that of the Cave Valley houses, and as the walls had only three coats of plaster and whitewash, and the corners did not show much wear, these dwellings were undoubtedly of more recent origin. But the general character of the structures was similar to those we first investigated. No implements were found in these caves. In the same locality were quite a number of smaller caves containing houses in demolition. In one of them the walls were composed of stones and mud, and here we also saw the first circular-shaped house in a cave.

By digging below the concrete floor of one of the rooms, we came upon the skeletons of five adults. This was a singular fact, showing that these ancient cave-dwellers observed the custom of burying their dead under the floors of their houses when conditions permitted it. Cave-dwellings compromising twenty rooms were also seen by the Mormons at the head of Bavispe River.

My relations with the Mormons continued to be friendly, and in my dealings with them I found them honest and business-like. While thriftily providing for the material requirements of this life, they leave all their enjoyment of existence for the future state. Their life is hard, but they live up to their convictions, though these, in some points, date from a by-gone stage in the development of the human race.

They were much interested in our work, never doubting but that it could only be to their advantage to have light thrown upon the mysteries buried in their caves, as, in their opinion, our researches would only confirm the statements made in the "Book of Mormon," which mentions the prehistoric races of America. They told me that the book speaks of the arrival of three races in America. The first landing was made at Guaymas in Sonora, the people being fugitives from the divine wrath that destroyed the Tower of Babel. They were killed. The second race landed in New England, coming from Jerusalem; and the third, also coming from Jerusalem, landed in Chile.

We spent altogether about six weeks in Cave Valley, and the weather, as far as our experience went, was pleasant enough, although in February, for several days, a strong, cold wind was blowing, so as to interfere with our work in the mounds at daytime and with our sleep at night. In addition to the discomforting feeling that at any moment my tent might be blown down, I was worried by the possibility of its falling on the results of our excavations, the pottery and skeletons, which, for safety's sake, I kept in my tent. The situation was not improved by some indiscreet burro (donkey), who would stray into the camp and get himself entangled in the tent ropes.

On January 30th nearly seven inches of snow fell. One day a flock of twenty-five turkeys was observed near our camp, but our efforts to get within shooting distance proved futile, as these cunning birds, who apparently move about so unconcernedly, always disappeared as if they had vanished into the ground, whenever one of us, no matter how cautiously, tried to approach them.

News of Apaches was again afloat, and one day a Mexican officer called at the camp obviously in pursuit of Apaches from whom he had recently taken twelve horses; but unfortunately the men had escaped. The presidente of Casas Grandes had been advised of the killing of two Americans near San Bernardino by some Apaches, and had also ordered some men to look for the miscreants in the sierra.

Having thoroughly investigated the caves, we turned our attention to the mounds, which are very numerous in this part of the country. They are always covered with grass, and sometimes even trees grow on them. When excavated they disclosed the remains of houses of a type similar to that of the cave-dwellings. Some of the mounds were high enough to justify the supposition that the houses had two stories, each six or seven feet high, and containing a number of rooms. From the locality in which the mounds were found it becomes at once evident that the houses which once stood there were not destroyed by inundations and covered by diluvial deposits. The mounds are composed of gravelly cement and fine debris of house walls, and the rooms left are completely filled with this material. It is easy to imagine how the mounds were formed by the gradual demolition of the ceilings, plastering, and roofs, forming a heal which to-day appears as shapely as if it had been made by man for some definite purpose.

The houses were communal dwellings, each consisting of one room, which generally was not quite ten feet square. The walls, eight to nine inches thick, built of a mixture of clay and earth, were fairly well preserved in places. In one house, which had unusually solid compartments, the walls were twenty, and in some places even thirty-three inches thick. Here nothing could be found, either in the rooms or by excavating below the floor. The same conventional doorways were met with in all the mound houses, but there was hardly any trace of woodwork.

Excavations in one of the mounds near our camp disclosed very interesting composite structures. One part of the walls consisted of large posts set in the ground and plastered over, forming a stuccoed palisade. At right angles with this was a wall of cobblestones, and among the buried debris were fragments of adobe bricks. In one room of this group, at a depth of less than five feet, we struck a floor of trodden concrete. Breaking through we found a huddle of six or seven skeletons, which, however, were not entire.

Rarely if ever was any object found in these rooms, except, perhaps, some stray axe, or some metates and grinding stones, and in one case a square stone painted pot. But by digging below the concrete floors we came upon skeletons which seemed to have been laid down without regard to any rule, and with them were invariably buried some household utensils, such as earthenware jars and bowls, beautifully decorated; axes, and mauls, fairly carved and polished. One very rare object was secured; a doubled-grooved axe. The skeletons were badly preserved, but we were able to gather several skulls and some of the larger bones.

The floor material was so hard that only by means of heavy iron bars could we break through it. As it was impracticable for us to make complete excavations, the number of rooms each mound contained cannot be stated. There were in the immediate neighbourhood of Cave Valley at least ten or twelve separate groups, each of which had from four to eight rooms on the ground floor. The entire district is richly studded with mounds. On an excursion three or four miles down Piedras Verdes River I saw several groups of mounds, some of which, no doubt, contained many objects of antiquity. On top of one low hill was a large group, and half a mile north of this another, 160 paces long and containing two oblong mounds. Some of the mounds were ten or twelve feet high.

A very trustworthy Mormon informed me that there were no ruins, in caves or otherwise, along the river between this settlement and Colonia Juarez; nor were there any, he said, for a hundred miles south of Pacheco, though mounds could be seen in several places. Therefore when I at last departed from Cave Valley, I took his advice and did not follow the course of the Piedras Verdes River down to San Diego, but led the pack train the safer, though longer, way over the regular road. The country along the river was afterward explored by members of my expedition. They came upon several small caves high up on the side of the cañon, some of which had once been inhabited, to judge from the many potsherds and the smoky roofs; but no cave-houses were found until higher up the river, where some were seen in the sandstone cliffs.

I broke camp in Cave Valley on March 11th, and arrived on the same day at Old Juarez, a few miles from my camp at San Diego. Now the weather was warm; the grass was sprouting, and I noticed a flock of wild geese going northward.

The plains of San Diego used to swarm with antelopes, and even at the time of my visit herds of them could be seen now and then. One old hunter near Casas Grandes resorted to an ingenious device for decoying them. He disguised himself as an antelope, by means of a cloak of cotton cloth (manta) painted to resemble the colouring of the animal. This covered his body, arms, and legs. On his head he placed the antlers of a stag, and by creeping on all fours he could approach the antelopes quite closely and thus successfully shoot them. The Apaches, according to the Mexicans, were experts at hunting antelopes in this manner.

We excavated a mound near Old Juarez and found in it a small basin of black ware. There were twelve or fifteen other mounds, all containing house groups. The largest among them was 100 feet long, fifty feet wide, and ten feet high; others, while covering about the same space, were only three or four to six feet high. They were surrounded, in an irregular way, by numerous stone heaps, some quite small, others large and rectangular, inclosing a space thirty by ten feet.

From an archaeological point of view, the district we now found ourselves in is exceedingly rich, and I determined to explore it as thoroughly as circumstances permitted. One can easily count, in the vicinity of San Diego, over fifty mounds, and there are also rock carvings and paintings in various places. Some twenty miles further south there are communal cave-dwellings, resembling those in Cave Valley, which were examined by members of the expedition at the San Miguel River, about eight miles above the point at which the river enters the plains. Inside of one large cave numerous houses were found. They had all been destroyed, yet it was plainly evident that some of them had originally been three stories high.

But the center of interest is Casas Grandes, the famous ruin situated about a mile south of the town which took its name, and we soon went over to investigate it.

The venerable pile of fairly well preserved ruins has already been described by John Russell Bartlett, in 1854, and more recently by A.F. Bandelier; a detailed description is therefore here superfluous. Suffice it to say that the Casas Grandes, or Great Houses, are a mass of ruined houses, huddled together on the western bank of the river. Most of the buildings have fallen in and form six or eight large mounds, the highest of which is about twenty feet above the ground. Low mesquite bushes have taken root along the mounds and between the ruins. The remaining walls are sufficiently well preserved to give us an idea of the mode of building employed by the ancients. At the outskirts of the ruined village the houses are lower and have only one story, while in its central part they must have been at one time at least four stories high. They were not palaces, but simply dwellings, and the whole village, which probably once housed 3,000 or 4,000 people, resembles, in its general characteristics, the pueblos in the Southwest, and, for that matter, the houses we excavated from the mounds. The only features that distinguish these from either of the other structures are the immense thickness of the walls, which reaches as much as five feet, and the great height of the buildings. The material, too, is different, consisting of enormous bricks made of mud mixed with coarse gravel, and formed in baskets or boxes.

A striking fact is that the houses apparently are not arranged in accordance with any laid-out plan or regularity. Nevertheless they looked extremely picturesque, viewed from the east as the sun was setting. I camped for a few days on top of the highest mound, between the ruined walls.

No circular building, nor any trace of a place of worship, could be found. The Mexicans, some of whom have nestled on the eastern part of the ruins, have from time to time come upon beautiful jars and bowls, which they sold to relic hunters or used themselves. Such pottery is far superior in quality and decoration to anything now made in Mexico. The ancient metates of Casas Grandes, which are much appreciated by the present inhabitants of the valley, are decidedly the finest I have ever seen. They are square in shape, resting on four legs, and well finished. There have also been taken out some stone axes and arrowheads, which are much like those found in the Southwest of the United States.

Some years ago a large meteorite was unearthed in a small room on the first floor of one of the highest of the buildings. When discovered it was found carefully put away and covered with cotton wrappings. No doubt it once had served some religious purpose. On account of its glittering appearance, the Mexicans thought it was silver, and everybody wanted to get a piece of it. But it was taken to Chihuahua, and the gentlemen who sent it to Germany told me that it weighed 2,000 pounds.

There are still traces of well-constructed irrigation ditches to be seen approaching the ruins from the northwest. There are also several artificial accumulations of stones three to fifteen feet high and of various shapes. One of them has the form of a Latin cross measuring nineteen feet along its greatest extent. Others are rectangular, and still others circular. About three miles off, toward the west, are found pictures pecked on large stones, one representing a bird, another one the sun.

An interesting relic of the population that once prospered in Casas Grandes Valley is a watch tower, plainly visible on a mountain to the southwest, and about five miles, in a straight line, from the ruins. Well-defined tracks lead up to it from all directions, especially from the east and west. On the western side three such trails were noticed, and several join at the lower part of the ridge, which runs southward and culminates in the promontory on which the watch tower stands 1,500 feet above the plains.

The western side of the ridge is in some places quite precipitous, but there is a fairly good track running along its entire extent to the top. Sometimes the road is protected with stones, and in other places even with walls, on the outer side. Although the ascent is, at times, steep, the top can be reached on horseback.

The path strikes a natural terrace, and on this is seen a ruined house group built of undressed stones on the bare rock. Some of the walls are twenty-four inches thick. And a little to the south of it is a large mound, from which a Mormon has excavated two rooms. A very well-built stone wall runs for more than 100 paces from north to south on the western, or most easily accessible, side of the pueblo.

After leaving this ancient little village, we made a pleasant ascent to the top, where a strikingly beautiful panorama opened up before us on all sides. The summit commands a view of fertile valleys for miles around in every direction. To the west is the valley of the Piedras Verdes River, and to the east the valley of the Casas Grandes; and in the plains to the south the snakelike windings of the San Miguel River glitter in the sun. Toward the north the view is immense, and fine mountains form a fitting frame for the landscape all around the horizon.

What a pre-eminently fine position for a look-out! As I contemplated the vast stretches of land commanded from this point, I pondered for how many centuries sentinels from this spot may have scanned the horizon with their eagle eyes to warn their people of any enemy approaching to disturb their peaceful occupations.

The fort is circular and about forty feet in diameter. The surrounding wall is on one side about eleven feet high and very broad, while in other places it is much lower and narrower. There are four clearly outlined chambers in the centre; but by excavations nothing could be found in them, except that the flooring was one inch thick.

It was quite warm here. Some birds were about, and there were a few flowers out. Wild white currant bushes were growing inside of the fortress, breathing delicious fragrance. But aside from the top, the mountain was all but barren of vegetation.

A few days afterward I went on an excursion up the Casas Grandes Valley, as far as the Mormon colony Dublan. This valley, which is about fifteen miles long and equally as broad, is very fertile where properly irrigated, and maize and wheat fields delight the eye. Naturally, the country is well populated, and the mounds which are met with everywhere prove that this was already the case in ancient times. In fact, mounds, in groups or isolated, are numerous as far north as Ascension.

How richly the apparently poor soil repays the labour which man expends on it many be seen in the flourishing colony the Mormons have here. Wherever they go, the Mormons transform waste land into scenes of prosperity, so much so that the Mexicans attribute the success of these indefatigable developers to a gold mine, which they are supposed to work secretly at night.

As I found it imperative to return to the United States in the interest of the expedition, I considered it expedient to reduce my scientific corps to three. My camp at San Diego I left in charge of Mr. H. White, who later on was relieved by Mr. C.V. Hartman. During my absence they conducted excavations of the mounds along the southern bank of the Piedras Verdes River, near its junction with San Miguel River, and in convenient neighbourhood to the camp. Neither the mounds themselves nor the houses inside of them differ much from those already described on the upper part of the river, except that some of the mounds here were somewhat larger. Judging from the beams left, they probably contained a few three-story houses. However, in either locality most of the mound houses were only one story high, and where second or third stories were indicated, they were never found intact. In neither place were circular houses observed. The mounds here were located on a rich, alluvial clay soil.

Here, as on the upper part of the river, the treasures we secured were taken from underneath the floors of the houses, where they had been buried with the dead. Here, as there, they consisted of beautifully decorated earthenware jars and bowls, some of them in bizarre representations of animal and human forms, besides stone implements, shell beads, pieces of pyrites and turquoise, all being generally unearthed intact.

The things were found alongside of skeletons, which were huddled together in groups of from two to five in one of the corners. The jars, bowls, etc. had generally been deposited close to the body, as a rule near the head. The skulls of the skeletons were mostly crushed, and crumbled to dust when exposed to the air. There was no trace of charring on the bones, although in some cases charcoal was found close to the skeletons.

To excavate such mounds is slow and tedious work, requiring much patience. Sometimes nothing was found for weeks. Small mounds gave results as good as, if not better than, some large ones. In shape they are more or less conical, flattened at the top; some are oblong, a few even rectangular. The highest among them rose to twenty to twenty-five feet, but the majority varied from five to twelve feet. The house walls inside of them were from eight to sixteen inches thick.

The pottery which was excavated here may be judged by the accompanying plates. It is superior in quality, as well as in decoration, to that produced by the Pueblos of the Southwest of the United States. The clay is fine in texture and has often a slight surface gloss, the result of mechanical polishing. Though the designs in general remind one of those of the Southwestern Pueblos, as, for instance, the cloud terraces, scrolls, etc., still most of the decorations in question show more delicacy, taste, and feeling, and are richer in colouring.

This kind of pottery is known only from excavations in the valleys of San Diego and of Piedras Verdes River, as well as from Casas Grandes Valley. It forms a transition from the culture of the Pueblos of Arizona and New Mexico to that of the Valley of Mexico, a thousand miles farther south.

Chapter 5

SECOND EXPEDITION—RETURN TO THE SIERRA—PARROTS IN THE SNOW—CAVE-DWELLINGS AT GARABATO, THE MOST BEAUTIFUL IN NORTHERN MEXICO—A SUPERB VIEW OF THE SIERRA MADRE—THE DEVIL'S SPINE RIDGE—GUAYNOPA, THE FAMOUS OLD SILVER MINE—ARROS RIVER—ON OLD TRAILS—ADVENTURES OF "EL CHINO"—CURE FOR POISON IVY.

When in the middle of January 1892, I resumed my explorations, my party was only about one-third as large as it had been the year before. In pursuance of my plan, I again entered the Sierra Madre, returning to it, as far as Pacheco, by the road on which we had come down to San Diego. We travelled over freshly-fallen snow a few inches deep, and encountered a party of eight revolutionists from Ascension, among whom I perceived the hardest looking faces I had ever laid eyes on. All questions regarding their affairs they answered evasively, and I could not help feeling some anxiety for three of the men, who with a Mexican guide, had for some weeks been exploring the country around Chuhuichupa, a discarded cattle range some forty miles south of Pacheco. Next day I sent a man ahead to warn them against the political fugitives. The Mormons told me that for more than a fortnight they had been keeping track of these suspicious-looking characters who had been camping in the neighbourhood.

There were repeated falls of snow, and the sierra assumed a thoroughly northern aspect. Only the multitude of green parrots with pretty red and yellow heads, chattering in the tree-tops and feasting on pine cones reminded us that we were in southern latitudes. As all tracks had been obliterated by the snow, I secured a Mormon to guide us southward.

About ten miles south of Pacheco we passed Mound Valley, or "Los Montezumas," so named after the extraordinary number of montezumas, or mounds, found in the locality, probably not far from a thousand. Looking at them from a distance, there seemed to be some plan in their arrangement, inasmuch as they formed rows running from north to south. They are small, and nearly all of them are on the south side of a sloping plain which spread itself over about 500 acres in the midst of densely pine-covered highlands.

On making camp a few miles south of this plateau we found that one of the mules had strayed off. My dismay over the loss of the animal was not alleviated by the news that the mule was the one that carried my blankets and tent, and that I had a good prospect of passing at least one uncomfortable night on the snow. The American who had been intrusted with keeping count of the animals on the road immediately went back to look for the lost one; but not until next day did a Mexican, who had been sent along with him, bring back the pack, which the mule had managed to get rid of. The animal itself and its aparejo were never recovered by us.

On my arrival at Chuhuichupa I found everything satisfactory. There are extensive grass-lands here, and a few years after our visit the Mormons established a colony. The name Chuhuichupa is interesting, as it is the first one we came upon that was of undoubted Tarahumare origin, "chuhui" being the Spanish corruption of "Chu-i," which means "dead." The name signifies "the place of the dead," possibly alluding to burial caves.

Here Mr. Taylor had discovered very interesting cave-dwellings, fifteen miles southeast to east in a straight line from the camp, but fully twenty-five miles by the track he had followed. The Mexicans called the cave Garabato, a Spanish word, which in Mexico is used in the sense of "decorative designs," and refers here to ancient paintings or scrawlings on the house walls. The cave is situated in a gorge on the northern slope of the Arroyo Garabato, which drains into the Rio Chico. It is in conglomerate formation, faces east, and lies about 215 feet above the bottom of the gorge. The ascent is steep and somewhat difficult. At a little distance the high, regular walls of the house, with their many door and window openings, presented a most striking contrast to their surroundings of snow-covered jagged cliffs, in the lonely wilderness of pine woods. Some of the walls had succumbed to the weight of ages, but, on the whole, the ruins are in a good state of preservation, and although I found cave-dwellings as far south as Zapuri, Chihuahua, none of them were nearly as well preserved nor on such an extensive scale. Time would not allow me to visit the cave myself, and the following description is based on notes taken by Mr. Taylor on the spot, as well as on his photographs and his verbal explanations.

The space covered by the houses and fallen walls was 125 feet from side to side, and at the central part the dwellings were thirty-five feet deep. The roof of the cave, or rather, the overhanging cliff, was at the highest point eighty feet above the floor. The houses were arranged in an arc of a circle so large as hardly to deviate from a straight line. The front row seems to have been of but one story, while the adjoining row back of it had two stories. The roof of the houses at no place reached the roof of the cave. Each room was about twelve feet square, and the walls, which showed no evidence of blocks or bricks, varied in thickness form fifteen inches at the base to seven inches at the top of the highest. At some places large stones were built into the walls; in another wall wooden posts and horizontal sticks or lathes were found. The surface of the walls, which were protected against he weather, was smooth and even, and the interior walls showed seven or eight coatings of plaster. The floors, where they could be examined, were smoothly cemented and so hard as to effectively resist the spade. The pine poles which formed the roof were smooth, but hot squared; they were three to four inches in diameter, and some of them were twenty-four feet long. According to all appearances, they had been hewn with a blunt instrument, as they were more hacked than cut. Many of them were nicely rounded off at the ends, and several inches from the ends a groove was cut all around the pole.

In the centre of the back rooms of the ground floor there was usually a pine pole, about ten inches in diameter, set up like a rude pillar. Resting on this and the side walls of the rooms in a slight curve was a similar pole, also rounded, and running parallel to the front of the houses; and crossing it from the front to the rear walls were laid similar poles or rafters about four inches in diameter. The ends of these were set directly into the walls, and covering them was a roofing of mud, some three inches thick, hard, and on the upper surface smooth. The second story, where it had not caved in, was covered in the same manner. None of the lower story rooms had an outlet to the apartments above, and the evidence tended to prove that the second story houses were reached from the bottom of the cave over the roofs of the front row of houses by means of ladders.

Most of the rooms were well supplied with apertures of the usual conventional form; sometimes there were as many as three in one room, each one large enough to serve as a door. But there were also several small circular openings, which to civilised man might appear to have served as exits for the smoke; but to the Indian the house, as everything else, is alive, and must have openings through which it can draw breath, as otherwise it would be choked. These holes were three or four inches in diameter, and many of them were blocked up and plastered over. A large number of what seemed to have been doorways were also found to be blocked up, no doubt from some ulterior religious reason.

A peculiar feature of the architecture was a hall not less than forty feet long, and from floor to rafters seven feet high. Six beams were used in the roof, laid between the north and south walls. There were rafters of two different lengths, being set in an angle of about ten degrees to each other. The west wall contained twelve pockets, doubtless the cavities in which the rafters had rested. They were, on an average, three inches in diameter, and ran in some six inches, slanting downward in the interior. The east wall was found to contain upright poles and horizontal slats, forming a framework for the building material. The interior was bare, with the exception of a ledge running along the southern side and made from the same material as the house walls. It was squared up in front and formed a convenient settee.

At the end of this hall, but in the upper story, was found a house that was distinguished from the others by a peculiar decoration in red, while the space around the door was painted in a delicate shade of lavender.

There seems to have been still another hall of nearly the same length as the one described, but which most have been at least one foot and a half higher. It is now almost entirely caved in.

No objects of interest were found that could throw any light on the culture of the builders of these dwellings, except the fragment of a stone axe and a piece of matting.

The day after my arrival at Chuhuichupa I continued my journey, now accompanied by Mr. Taylor and Mr. Meeds. We had as a guide an old Mexican soldier, who had been recommended to us as a man who knew the Sierra Madre better than anyone else. He had, no doubt, lived a wild life; had taken part in many a "scrap" with the Apaches, as his body showed marks of bullets in several places, and he had prospected for gold and silver, traversing a good deal of ground in the mountains at one time or another. But topographical knowledge *per se* does not necessarily make a good guide. Although "Don Teodoro," by something like instinct, always knew where he was, it did not take us long to discover that he had not judgement enough to guide a pack-train, and his fatuous recklessness caused us a good deal of annoyance, and even loss.

After leaving the grass-lands of Chuhuichupa, we passed through extensive pine regions, full of arroyos and cordons, and it struck me how silent the forest was here. No animal life could be seen or heard. About ten miles south we caught sight of Sierra de Candelaria, which suddenly loomed up in the southeast, while the Arroyo de Guaynopa yawned at our left. We slowly ascended a beautiful cordon running toward the southwest. The track we followed, our guide assured us, was *el camino de los antiguos,* but it probably was only an Apache trail. The cordon was rather narrow, and from time to time gave us sweeping views of the stupendous landscape in one direction or another, as the animals slowly made their way up and finally reached the summit. A grandly beautiful sight awaited us; we went a little out of our way to gain a promontory, which, our guide said, was designated "Punto Magnifico." It was at an elevation of 8,200 feet, and gave us certainly the most strikingly magnificent view of the Sierra Madre we yet had enjoyed.

An ocean of mountains spread out before and below us. In the midst of it, right in front of us, were imposing pine-clad mesas and two weathered pinnacles of reddish conglomerate, while further on there followed range after range, peak after peak; the most distant ones, toward the south, seeming at least as far as eighty miles away. The course of the rivers, as they flow deep down between the mountains, was pointed out to us. The principal one is the Arros River, which from the west embraces most of the mesas, and then, turning south, receives its tributaries, the Tutuhuaca and the Mulatos, the latter just behind a pinnacle. West of the Arros River stretches out the immense Mesa de los Apaches, once a stronghold of these marauders, reaching as far as the Rio Bonito. The plateau is also called "The Devil's Spine Mesa," after a high and very narrow ridge, which rises conspicuously from the mesa's western edge and runs in a northerly and southerly direction, like the edge of a gigantic saw. To our amazement, the guide here indicated to us where the camino real from Nacori passes east over a gap in the "Devil's Spine" ridge, and then over several sharp buttes that descend toward the mesa. An odd-looking mesa lay between Rio Bonito and Rio Satachi. Farthest to the west were the big hogbacks near Nacori, standing out ominously, like a perpetuated flash of lightning. The sun was nearing the horizon; the air was translucent, and the entire panorama steeped in a dusky blue.

Immediately below us, to our left, lay Guaynopa. The mountainside looked so steep that it seemed impossible for us to descend from where we were. But we had already heard the voices of our muleteers singing out to the animals 1,000 feet below, and that reminded us that we also had better reach camp before darkness should overtake us. We descended 2,500 feet, and, leaving the pines behind, found ourselves in a warmer climate. It never snows here, according to our guide. That the precipitation took the shape of rain we learned when we were impeded by it for two days.

There were yet eighteen miles between us and the deserted mines of Guaynopa. It was a laborious journey over the hills, mostly ascent. Finally we came to a steep slope covered with oaks, along which there was a continuous descent toward Guaynopa. While zigzagging our way down, we caught sight of a large cave with houses and some white cone-shaped structures staring at us across an arroyo midway up the opposite side, which was at least two thousand feet deep. Through my field glasses I could make out very distinctly a group of houses of the usual pattern; and the large, white structures could without difficulty be recognised as granaries, similar to those observed in Cave Valley. It was my intention to go back and examine this cave more closely, as soon as I had found a camping place; but circumstances interfered. Several years later the cave was visited by Mr. G. P. Ramsey, to whom I owe the following brief description.

The cave is situated about twenty-five miles in a straight line south of the Mormon colony of Chuhuichupa. There are indications of a spring in the cave, and there is another one in the arroyo itself. The buildings are in very bad condition, owing to the action of the elements and animals; but fifty-three rooms could be counted. They were located on a rocky terrace extending from the extreme right to the rear centre of the cave. This extreme right extended slightly beyond the overhanging cliff, and contained groups of two-storied houses. In the central part of the cave were a number of small structures, built of the same material and in a similar manner as those I described as granaries in Cave Valley. They were still in excellent condition, and, as will be seen at a glance, they are almost identical with the granaries used to the present day in some southern States of Mexico.

We continued our descent, and, having dropped altogether some 2,000 feet, at last found ourselves along-side some lonely and unattractive old adobe houses. They were built by the Spaniards and are reputed to have once been the smelter of the now abandoned silver mine of Guaynopa. Only the naked walls remain standing on a decline, which was too steep to give us sufficient camping ground. So we went still a little further, to the top of a hill near by, where we made a tolerably good camp.

This then was the famous locality of Guaynopa, credited with hiding such fabulous wealth. There was still another mine here of the same repute, called Tayopa, and both of them are said to have been worked once by the Jesuits, who before their expulsion from Mexico were in possession of nearly all the mines in the country. According to tradition, the Apaches killed everybody here, and the mines were forgotten until recent times, when ancient church records and other Spanish documents revealed their existence. Several expeditions have been sent out, one, I believe, by the Government for the purpose of locating them; but being situated in the roughest and most inaccessible part of the Sierra Madre, they are still awaiting their rediscovery, unless, contrary to my knowledge, they have been found in recent years. There is no doubt that the country carries very rich silver ore, and we ourselves found specimens of that kind; but the region is so difficult of access that it probably would require too great a capital to work the mines.

There was now a plain track leading along the hillside down toward the Rio Arros, which is scarcely two miles off; but the country was so wild and rugged that the greatest care had to be exercised with the animals to prevent them from coming to grief. The path runs along the upper part of a steep slope, which from a perpendicular weathered cliff drops some 400 feet down into a gorge. As the declivity of the slope is about forty-five degrees, and the track in some places only about a foot wide, there is no saving it if an animal loses its foothold, or if its pack slips. All went well, however, until we reached a point where the track commenced to descend, when our villain of a guide tried to drive some burros back on the track, instead of leading each one carefully. The result was that one of the poor beasts tumbled down, making immense bounds, a hundred feet at a time, and, of course, was killed.

We had no difficulty in fording the Guaynopa Creek near its junction with the Arros River, and selected a camping place on a terrace 200 feet above it. The stream, which is the one that passes the cave-dwellings, carries a good deal of limpid water, and there are abundant signs that at times it runs very high. The elevation of the ford, which is here about the same as that of Arros River, 3,400 feet, was the lowest point we reached in our crossing of the Sierra Madre between Chuhuichupa and Temosachic. It took us almost the entire day to move the animals the one mile and a half to this camp. On the way we had found some good quartz crystals in the baryte, about four inches high and one inch in width.

The country before us looked more forbidding than ever, as if it did not want us to penetrate any further into its mysteries, but our guide seemed to be quite at home here.

Our march toward Rio Chico was about thirty miles of ups and downs, ascending to a height of 7,600 feet and descending again some 3,000 feet. In the beginning it was almost impossible to make out the track; where it did not lead over bare rocks, it was nearly obliterated by overgrown grass.

The first ascent was over a mile long in a straight line; then, after a little while, came the most arduous climbing I had until then ever attempted. Following the slope of the mountain, the track rose higher and higher in long zigzags, without any chance for the animals to rest, for at least three-quarters of a mile. It was necessary to push them on, as otherwise the train would unavoidably have upset, and one or the other rolled down the declivity. One large white mule, El Chino, after it had almost climbed to the top, turned giddy at the "glory-crowned height" it had reached, and, sinking on its hind legs, fell backward and rolled heels over head down, with its two large canvas-covered boxes, like a big wheel. As luck would have it, it bumped against a low-stemmed old oak that cropped out of the hillside in an obtuse angle to it, some ninety feet below. Making one more turn up the stem, the mule was nicely caught between the forked branches, which broke the momentum, loosened the cargo, and caused the animal to fall back into the high grass. One box landed close by, the other, containing our library, pursued its course downward 200 feet further, bursting open on the way and scattering the wisdom of the ages to the winds, while the mule escaped without a scratch.

The burros came into camp three hours after us, and the drivers explained how they had succeeded in bringing them up the long slope only by constantly punching them to prevent them from "falling asleep."

As we continued our journey toward Rio Chico the panorama of the sierra changed continuously. We got a side view of the big Mesa de los Apaches, and many weathered pinnacles of eroded conglomerate were seen standing out like church spires in this desert of rock, varying in colour from red to lead gray. Once we caught sight of a stretch of the Rio Arros deep down in a narrow, desolate valley, some 3,000 feet below us. The geographical formation of the region is mostly volcanic; then follows conglomerate, and on the high points porphyry appears.

We camped on the crest of the eastern side of the Rio Cañon, in an ideal place with bracing air. A fine, sloping meadow afforded quite an arcadian view of the animals peacefully grazing and resting; but looking westward, the eye revelled in the grand panorama of the sierra. The two sides of the Rio Chico Valley rise here evenly from the bottom of the gorge so as to suggest the letter V. In many places its brow is overhung by precipitous cliffs, and further down still more steeply walled chasms yawn up from the river bed.

My chief packer now became ill from the effects of poison ivy. He was one of those unfortunate individuals who are specially susceptible to it. According to his own statement it sufficed for him to pass anywhere near the plant, even without touching it, to become afflicted with the disease. In this case he did not even know where he had contracted it, until the cook showed him some specimens of the plant near the oak tree close by the kitchen tent. The poor fellow's lips were badly swollen; he had acute pains in his eyes, and felt unable to move. Sometimes, he said, the disease would last ten days, and his skin become so tender that he could not endure the weight or contact of his clothes. But by applying to the afflicted parts of his body a solution of baking soda and water, I was able not only to relieve his suffering, but to enable him, after two days, to continue with us on our journey.

In the meantime we had investigated some caves in the conglomerate of the steep cañon side, about 250 feet above the bottom of the gorge, and rather difficult of access. The house group occupied the entire width of the cave, which was eighty feet across, and there was a foundation wall made of stone and timber underneath the front part. The walls were made of stone, with mortar of disintegrated rock that lined parts of the cave and were plastered inside and out with the same material. Lintels of wood were seen in the windows, and rows of sticks standing in a perpendicular position were found in two of the walls inside of the plastering. On one side of the cave, some two feet off, was a small tower, also in ruins, measuring inside four feet in diameter, while the walls were about six inches thick.

Pinnacles of eroded conglomerate are a prominent characteristic of the landscape west of the Rio Chico; further on, the usual volcanic formation appears again. After fully twenty miles of travel we found ourselves again in pine forests and at an altitude of 7,400 feet. Here we were overtaken, in the middle of February, by a rain and sleet storm, which was quite severe, although we were sheltered by tall pine trees in a little valley. It turned to snow and grew very cold, and then the storm was over. Here a titmouse and a woodpecker were shot, and the bluebirds were singing in the snow.

Travelling again eleven miles further brought us to the plains of Naverachic, where we camped. It was quite a treat to travel again on comparatively level land, but, strange to say, I felt the cold so much that I had to walk on foot a good deal in order to keep warm. The word Naverachic is of Tarahumare origin; nãvé means "move," and ráchi refers to the disintegrated trachyte formation in the caves.

We had just emerged from a district which at that time was traversed by few people; perhaps only by some illiterate Mexican adventurers, though it had once been settled by a thrifty people whose stage of culture was that of the Pueblo Indians of today, and who had vanished, nobody knows how many centuries ago. Over it all hovered a distinct atmosphere of antiquity and the solemnity of a graveyard.

Chapter 6

Fossils, and one way of utilizing them—Temosachic—The First Tarahumares—Ploughs with Wooden Shares—Visit to the Southern Pimas—Aboriginal Hat Factories—Pinos Altos—The Waterfalls near Jesus Maria—An Adventure with Ladrones.

About thirty miles from the village of Temosachic (in the Tarahumare tongue Remosachic means Stone Heap) we entered the plain of Yepomera, and came upon an entirely different formation, limestone appearing in an almost horizontal layer some thirty feet deep. In this bed the Mexicans frequently find fossils, and at one place four large fossil bones have been utilized as the corner posts of a corral or inclosure. We were told that teeth and bones were accidentally found at a depth of from twenty to thirty feet and some bones were crystallised inside. This formation, which stretches itself out toward the east of Temosachic, but lies mainly to the north of this place, has an extent of about fifteen miles from north to south, and from three to four miles from east to west.

Fossils picked up by Mr. Meeds in the cutting of a creek near Yepomera consisted of some fragmentary teeth and pieces of bone from some small animal. They were found in the hard clay that underlies the lime-stone. Large fossil bones also are said to have been gathered near the town of Guerrero, Chihuahua, quite recently. It seems to be a custom with the common people to make a concoction of these "giants' bones" as a strengthening medicine; we heard of a woman who, being weak after childbirth, used it as an invigorating tonic.

Here in Temosachic we were joined by Mr. Hartman, who had brought part of our baggage from San Diego by wagon in order to enable us to travel as unencumbered as possible.

From now on, until as far as the southern border of the State of Chihuahua, the country is occupied by the large Indian tribe of the Tarahumares. They are now confined to the Sierra Madre, but in former times they also occupied the entire plain of Chihuahua, as far west as the present capital of that State, and in a narrow strip they may have reached as far as 100 miles north of Temosachic. They were the main tribe found in possession of the vast country which is now the State of Chihuahua, and although there are still some 25,000 left, the greater part of them have become Mexicanised, adopting the language and the customs of the whites, together with their dress and religion. Father Ribas, in the seventeenth century, speaks of them as very docile and easily converted to Christianity.

The high plateau of the Sierra Madre for a couple of hundred miles southward is not difficult to follow. Most of it is hilly and clad in oaks and pines; but there are also extensive tracts of fine arable land, partly under cultivation, and fairly good tracks connect the solitary villages and ranches scattered over the district. The country of the aborigines has been invaded and most of the descendants of the former sovereigns of the realm have been reduced to earning a precarious living by working for the white and mixed-breed usurpers on their ranches or in their mines. The native language, religious customs, and dress are being modified gradually in accordance with the new régime. Only in the less desirable localities have the Tarahumares been able to hold their own against the conquerors.

There is not much interest attached to the study of half-civilised natives, but the first pure-blooded Tarahumares I met on their little ranch about ten miles south of Temosachic were distinctly Indian and very different from the ordinary Mexican family. There was a kind of noble bearing and reserve about them which even the long contact with condescending whites and half-breeds had not been able to destroy. The father of the family, who, by the way, was very deaf, was a man of some importance among the native ranchers here. When I approached the house, mother and daughter were combing each other's hair, and did not allow themselves to be disturbed by my arrival. The younger woman wore her long glossy tresses plaited in Mexican fashion. She evidently was in robust health and had well-moulded shapely arms and an attractive face, with an eagle nose. She was beautiful, but I could not help thinking of how much better she would have looked in her native costume.

On the road we had several times overtaken donkey trains carrying corn to the mines of Pinos Altos. In the small Rio Verde we caught three kinds of fish: suckers, catfish, and Gila trout, which grow from one to three feet long, and, according to Tarahumare belief, change into otters when they are old.

The name of the village of Tosanachic is a Spanish corruption of the Tarahumare Rosanachic, which means "Where there is White," and alludes to a number of white rocks or cliffs of solidified volcanic ash, which rise to a height of some fifty feet and give to the little valley quite a striking appearance. There are caves in these rocks, and three poor families of Pima Indians lived in some of them.

In the village we noticed the first Tarahumare plough, the share of which was made of a section of oak. In its general appearance it is an imitation of the ordinary Mexican plough, in other words, is simply a tree stem with a branch as a handle. But, however primitive in design and construction, the civilised man's implement always has an iron share. Of course, such among the Tarahumares as can afford iron shares, never fail to get them; but in several parts of their country ploughs made entirely of wood, that is to say, ploughs with wooden shares, are seen. The foremost part of such a plough is cut to a point, and into a groove made for the purpose a section of tough oak is inserted, to serve as a share. It is held in place by the tapering of the groove, and some wedges or plugs. The share has naturally to be renewed quite frequently, but it serves its purpose where the ground is not stony. Later on, in Cusarare, Nararachic and other places, I found plough-shares of stone applied in the same manner as were the wooden ones.

Here at an elevation of 7,600 feet, and at the end of February, I saw the first flowers of the year, some very fresh-looking yellow *Ranunculus.* On crossing the ridge to Piedras Azules, sixty-odd miles south of Temosachic, a decided change of climate and vegetation was noticeable. I found another kind of *Ranunculus,* as well as various other flowers, and as we passed through a small but gorgeous cañon, with the sun shining against us through the fresh leaves of the trees, everything in Nature made the impression of spring. All was green except the ground, which was gray. The road was stony, and bad for the feet of the animals; altogether the country presented a new aspect with its small volcanic hills, many of them forming cones.

A few Indian hamlets surrounded by peach trees in full bloom were found here. The Indians here are Pimas, who, in their general characteristics, resemble the Tarahumare, although they impress you as being less timid and suspicious, and more energetic, perhaps also more intelligent than the latter. We had no difficulty in taking some photographs. Among those who agreed to have their picture taken was a dignified, courteous old man, who thought he was a hundred years old, but was probably only eighty. He showed me some scars on his body, which were a souvenir from a fight he had once with a bear.

In order to see more of the Southern Pimas I went to the near-by village of Yepachic, which I think is also a Tarahumare name, yêpá meaning snow. There are, however, more Mexicans than Pimas in the village, and the presidente was a half-caste Tarahumare; he was once a shepherd, but had made money by trading mescal to the natives — six bottles for a cow.

Although the Pimas whom I visited in the neighbourhood, were very reserved and even more Indian-like than the Tarahumares I had seen so far, still in their dress they showed more traces of advancing civilisation than the latter tribe. Everything here betrays the nearness of the mines, with the characteristic accompaniment of cheap clothes, cheap, tawdry jewelry, and a slight influx of iron cooking utensils. The Pimas, like the Tarahumares, use pine cones for combs; and we picked up several discarded ones near their houses.

I went still fifteen miles further northward, but found that most of the Indians there had gone to the Pinos Altos mines to look for work. That "March comes in like a lion" I realised even here in the sierra, when, on this excursion, on which I had not taken my tent along, I was overtaken by a snow-storm. We had gone to bed with the stars for a canopy, clear and beautiful; we woke up under a blanket of snow, which turned to rain, drenching us to the skin and making us shiver with cold.

I saw several small, shallow caves, and learned that many of them were utilised by the Pimas during the wet season. I also passed a rock-shelter, which served as a permanent home. The housewife was busy making straw hats. She was very shy, as her husband was away; but I elicited the information that she gets two reales (25 cents) for each hat. The making of straw hats and mats is quite an industry among the Pimas. In the houses they have a cellar-like dug-out outside of the dwelling and covered with a conical roof of dry grass. These cellars, in many cases, serve not only as the workrooms, but also as store-rooms for their stock in trade.

In one or two instances I found Pima families living in open inclosures, a kind of corral, made from cut-down brushwood. I noticed two small caves that had been transformed into storehouses, by planting poles along the edge and plastering these over with mud, to make a solid wall, behind which corn was stored.

In Yepachic I estimated there were about twenty Pima families. I had some difficulty in inducing them to pose before the camera; the presidente himself was afraid of the instrument, thinking it was a diabolo (devil).

There are probably not more than sixty Pima families within the State of Chihuahua, unless there are more than I think near Dolores. Some twenty-odd families of these five live in caves during the wet season, and a few of them are permanent cave-dwellers. I understand that the Pimas in Sonora utilise caves in the same way.

I made an excursion from the mine of Pinos Altos (elevation 7,100 feet) to Rio Moris, about ten miles west, where there are some burial caves; but they had already been much disturbed by treasure seekers, and I could secure only a couple of skulls. An interesting feature of the landscape near Rio Moris is a row of large reddish pinnacles, which rise perpendicularly from the river-bed up along the hillside, and form a truly imposing spectacle. An excited imagination may see in them so many giants suddenly petrified while walking up the mountain. Around Pinos Altos and Jesus Maria the rock is of blue porphyry, quite hard in places, and speckled with little white patches. It is in this rock that the gold- and silver-bearing quartz occurs.

Through the courtesy of the bullion-convoy I was enabled to dispatch some of my collections via Chihuahua to the museum at New York, among other things eight fine specimens of the giant woodpecker.

Then, sending my train ahead, I made with a guide a little detour to visit the beautiful waterfall near Jesus Maria. It is formed by the River Basasiachic, which, except during the wet season, is small and insignificant. Before the fall the stream for more than a hundred yards runs in a narrow but deep channel, which in the course of ages it has worn into the hard conglomerate rock. The channel itself is full of erosions and hollowed-out places formed by the constant grinding and milling action of the rapidly rushing water, and the many large pebbles it carries. Just at the very brink of the rock, a low natural arch has been eroded, and over this the stream leaps almost perpendicularly into the deep straight-walled cañon below. The height of the cascade has been measured by a mining expert at Pinos Altos, and found to be 980 feet. Set in the most picturesque, noble environments, the fall is certainly worth a visit.

I arrived at its head just as the last rays of the setting sun were gilding the tops of the mountains all around. The scenery was beautiful beyond description. Above and around towered silent, solemn old pine-trees, while the chasm deep down was suffused with a purple glow. About midway down the water turns into spray and reaches the bottom as silently as an evening shower, but as it recovers itself forms numerous whirlpools and rapids, rushing through the narrow gorge with an incessant roar. When the river is full, during the wet season, the cascade must present a splendid sight.

I wanted to see the fall from below. The guide, an elderly man, reminded me that the sun was setting, and warned me that the distance was greater than it seemed. We should stumble and fall, he said, in the dark. But as I insisted on going, he put me on the track, and I started on a rapid run, jumping from stone to stone, zigzagging my way down the mountainside. The entire scenery, the wild, precipitous rocks, the stony, crooked path, the roaring stream below—everything reminded me of mountains in Norway, where I had run along many a *säter* path through the twilight, alone, just as I was running now.

As luck would have it, I met an Indian boy coming up from the river, where he had been trout fishing, and I asked him to accompany me, which he did. About halfway down we arrived at a little promontory from which the fall could be seen very well. The rock seemed to be here the same as on top, showing no sign of stratification. A few yards from the point we had reached was a spring, and here we made a fire and waited for the moon to rise. To make him more talkative, I gave the boy a cigarette. He spoke only Spanish, and he told me that he had neither father nor mother, and when his uncle died he was quite alone in the world; but a Mexican family brought him up, and he seemed to have been treated well. At present he was paying two dollars a month for his board, earning the money by selling grass in Pinos Altos.

At nine o'clock we began to ascend through the moonlit landscape. I had left my mule some hundred yards from the fall, and here I also found the guide. At two o'clock in the morning I arrived at my camp.

The road continued through rather monotonous country, the altitude varying from 6,300 to 7,700 feet. Grass began to be scarce, and the animals suffered accordingly. It is the custom with Mexican muleteers to select from among themselves a few, whose business throughout the journey it is to guard the animals at night. These men, immediately after having their supper, drive the animals to a place where suitable pasture is found, never very far from the camp, and bring them back in the morning. They constitute what is called la sabana. Comparatively few men suffice for this duty, even with a large herd, as long as they have with them a leader of the mules, a mare, preferably a white one. She may be taken along solely for this purpose, as she is often too old for any other work. The mules not infrequently show something like a fanatic attachment for their yegua, and follow blindly where they hear the tinkling of the bell, which is invariably attached to her neck. She leads the pack-train, and where she stops the mules gather around her while waiting for the men to come and relieve them of their burdens. Sometimes a horse may serve as a leader, but a mare is surer of gaining the affection of all the mules in the train. This is an important fact for travellers to bear in mind if they use mules at all. In daytime the train will move smoothly, all the mules, of their own accord, following their leader, and at night keeping close to her. In this way she prevents them from scattering and becomes indispensable to the train.

But in spite of the vigilance of the sabana and the advantage of a good yegua, it may happen, under favourable topographical and weather conditions, that robbers succeed in driving the animals away. While giving the pack-train a much-needed rest of a day in a grassy spot, we woke next morning to find five of our animals missing. As three of the lot were the property of my men, they were most eagerly looked for. The track led up a steep ridge, over very rough country, which the Mexicans followed, however, until it suddenly ran up against a mountain wall; and there the mules were found in something of a natural corral.

Not until then did our guide inform us that there lived at Calaveras (skulls), only three miles from where we were stopping, a band of seven robbers and their chief, Pedro Chaparro, who was at that time well-known throughout this part of the Tarahumare country. I had no further experience with him, but later heard much of this man, who was one of a type now rapidly disappearing in Mexico. He did not confine his exploits to the Mexicans, but victimised also the Indians whenever he got an opportunity, and there are many stories in circulation about him.

On one occasion he masqueraded as a padre, a black mackintosh serving as his priestly garb. Thus attired he went to the unsophisticated Tarahumares in the more remote valleys and made them send out messengers to advise the people that he had come to baptise them, and that they were all to gather at a certain place to receive his blessings. For each baptism he charged one goat, and by the time he thought it wise to retire he had quite a respectable herd to drive home. When the Indians found out that they had been swindled, they caught him and put him into jail, intending to kill him; but unfortunately some of his Mexican confrères heard of his plight and came to his rescue. However, a few years later, this notorious highwayman, who had several murders to answer for, was caught by the government authorities and shot.

On the road, as we travelled on, we met many Tarahumares carrying on their backs trays *(huacales)* with apples, which they were taking to market. The price per tray was $2, and the apples were delicious.

At night it was very cold, the thermometer falling to 13° below the freezing point. I was sorry to learn from my men that the prospects of grass further south were small.

At the village of Bocoyna (elevation 7,100 feet) we were 400 miles from San Diego by the track we had made. Bocoyna is a corruption of the Tarahumare Ocoina (ôcó=pine; ína=drips; meaning Dripping Pine, or Turpentine). Here I had to stop for two days, because no less than six of us, including myself, were suffering from the grippe, which a piercing, dry, cold wind did not tend to alleviate. However, as the worst cases did not last more than five days, we soon were all well again, though the Mexicans were almost overcome by the effects of the disease.

The presidente here was a powerful-looking half-caste and very original. After I had read to him twice my letter from the governor of the state; in which the people were told, among other things, to promote the success of the expedition in every way, especially by selling us what provisions we needed and not to overcharge us, he, by way of obeying the orders of his superior, immediately ordered that not more than $6 should be charged for a fanega of corn. He also had at once four nice, fat hens killed and sold them to us at the market price.

After we passed Bocoyna, the country for ten miles was flat, but fertile. It was gratifying to observe that here the Indians had some ranches with considerable land still left to them. We passed several such homesteads lying close together, and as many as four yokes of oxen were ploughing, each attended by a Tarahumare, whose entire clothing consisted of a breech-cloth. The Indians here are very numerous and they are still struggling to resist the encroachments of the whites upon their land, though the ultimate result is in all cases the same.

Chapter 7

The Uncontaminated Tarahumares—A Tarahumare Court in Session—The Power of the Staff—Justice has its Course—Barrancas—Excursion to the Gentiles—Tarahumare Costumes Simple and Inexpensive—Trincheras in Use Among the Tarahumares.

We were lucky enough to secure a guide who spoke the Tarahumare language very well, and our next stop was at the pueblo of Cusarare (a Spanish corruption of Usarare, usáka = eagle), an Indian village situated in a rather rough country full of weathered porphyry rocks. We made camp a few miles outside of the village and sent the guide to prepare the people for our coming. There had recently been considerable talk among the Mexicans of the wild people in the deep gorges, called barrancas, and it was with no little anticipation that I approached the country now immediately before us. There were no Mexicans living in Cusarare, nor in the country ahead of us; in fact, with the exception of the small mining camp in Barranca de Cobre, there were none within fifty miles to the south, and almost an equal distance from east to west.

Indian pueblos throughout Mexico are almost abandoned for the greater part of the year. I refer, of course, only to those which have not yet become Mexican settlements. The first thing the missionaries in the early times had to do was to force the Indians to leave their scattered ranches and form a pueblo. To make a place a pueblo they had to build a church. The Indians were pressed into service to erect the building, and kept at work, if necessary, by a troop of soldiers who often accompanied the missionaries and in this way assisted them in spreading the gospel.

From the missionaries' point of view this was a very practical arrangement; but the purpose of having the Indians remain in the villages has not been accomplished to this day. Only the native-chosen authorities, who are obliged to reside there during their term of office, form something like a permanent population in the pueblos. The natives come together only on the occasion of feasts, and on Sundays, to worship in the way they understand it. Someone who knows the short prayer, generally the gobernador, mumbles it, while the congregation cross themselves from time to time. If no one present knows the prayer, the Indians stand for a while silently, then cross themselves, and the service is over.

After church they meet outside for the second purpose that brings them to the village, namely, the transaction of whatever judicial business may be on hand, generally the adjustment of a theft, a marriage, etc.

I arrived in the pueblo on a Sunday, and a great many Indians had come in. Easter was approaching, and every Sunday during Lent, according to early missionaries' custom, the so-called "Pharisees" make their appearance. These are men who play an important part in the Easter festival, which always lasts several days. They paint their faces hideously, tog themselves up with feathers on their sombreros, and carry wooden swords painted with red figures. Such ceremonies were a clever device of the Jesuits and Franciscan missionaries to wean the Indians from their native feasts by offering them something equally attractive in the new religion they were teaching. The feasts are still observed, while the teachings are forgotten.

I found the people assembled before the old adobe church, where they had just finished their service. The gobernador at once attracted my attention as he stood with his large white blanket wrapped around him, Indian fashion, up to his chin—a fine, almost noble personality, with a benign expression on his eagle face.

The Indian never allows anything to interfere with whatever business he may have on hand, be it public or private. Presently all rose, and eight men, the authorities of the pueblo, marched in two rows to the court house, followed by the rest of the people. There is always found near the church a commodious building, called La Comunidad, originally intended as city hall, court house, and hotel. In this case it was so dilapidated that the judges and officers of the court about to be held took seats outside on the lawn in front of one of the walls. They were preparing to administer justice to a couple of offenders, and as this is the only occasion on which I have seen the details of Indian judicial procedure carried out so minutely as to suggest early missionary times, I am happy to record the affair here in full.

The gobernador and four of the judges seated themselves, white man's fashion, on a bench erected for the purpose, where they looked more grand than comfortable. Two of them held in their right hands canes of red Brazil wood, the symbol of their dignity. The idea of the staff of command, sceptre, or wand, is wide spread among the Indians of Mexico; therefore, when the Spaniards conquered the various tribes, they had little difficulty in introducing their batons *(la vara)*, as emblems of authority, which to this day are used by the gobernadors and other officials. They are made much in the same way as the ancient staffs, and of the same material, the heavy, red Brazil wood. Below the head of these canes there is always a hole bored, and through this a leather thong is passed, by which the staff is hung up on the wall when not in use. Those of the highest authorities are ornamented with silver caps; the lesser officers have smaller canes, in proportion to the degrees of their dignity, while the lowest officials have only a thin stick, about a foot and a half long, through the hole of which a red ribbon is passed. The small canes are not carried in the hand, but stuck in the girdle on the left side. Nobody summoned before the judges by a messenger carrying a staff of red Brazil wood dares to disobey the command. The most desperate criminal meekly goes to his doom, following often a mere boy, if the latter has only a toy vara stuck in his belt with the red ribbons hanging down. It is the vara the Indians respect, not the man who carries it.

No supreme court in any civilised community is so highly respected and so implicitly obeyed as were the simple, grave men sitting in front of the crumbling adobe wall and holding on to their canes with a solemnity that would have been ridiculous, if it had not been sublime.

Four "soldiers" formed a line on each side. There was nothing to distinguish them from ordinary civilians, except their "lances," or bamboo sticks to which bayonet points had been fastened. These lances they planted in the ground and seated themselves. Presently the two culprits, a man and a woman, came forward, with never a suggestion in their placid faces that they were the chief actors in the drama about to be enacted. They seated themselves in front of the judges, while the witnesses took their places behind them. The mother of the woman sat close by her guilty daughter, but there was not other exhibition of sentiment. The judges did most of the talking, addressing questions to the defendants, who made a few short answers; the rest of the assemblage observed a decorous silence. There were neither clerks nor lawyers.

I was, of course, not able to follow the testimony, but it was very short, and it was explained to me that the woman had run away with a married man. They had provided themselves with plenty of corn from the man's former home, and furthermore had stolen some beans, and lived very happy in a cave for one year. The man could not be captured, even though on several occasions he visited his family. But they frequently made native beer, and got drunk, and while in this condition they were caught and brought before this tribunal.

While the trial was going on, one of the "soldiers" got up and went some twenty yards off, dug a hole in the ground and planted a thick pole or post in it. No sooner had he completed his task, when the accused man rose with a queer smile on his face, half-chagrined, half-sarcastic. Dropping his blanket, he walked deliberately up to the pole, flanked by two soldiers, each of whom took hold of his hands, and by putting them crosswise on the further side of the pole, made the culprit hug the pole very tightly. Now another man, wrapped closely in his blanket, stepped briskly up, drew as quick as a flash a leather whip from under his garment, and dealt four lashes over the shoulders of the prisoner, who was then released, and stolidly walked back to his seat, as if nothing had happened.

Now came the woman's turn to be punished for her part in the thefts. They took off her blanket, but left on a little white undergarment. She was marched to the pole and held in the same manner as the man; but another man acted as executioner. She, too, received four lashes, and wept a little when they struck her; but neither she nor her fellow-sufferer made any attempt at, or sign of, revolt against the sentence of the court. While the chastising went on, the audience rose and stood reverently. After returning to her seat, the woman knelt down, and both delinquents shook hands with the chief judge.

There still remained the second part of the accusation to be dealt with, the one relating to the marital complications. The man asked permission to leave his first wife, as he wanted to marry the woman with whom he ran away. But no divorce was granted to him. He was ordered to return to his legitimate spouse, who was present at the proceedings with her child in her arms. Evidently disappointed, he slowly stepped over to where she was standing and greeting him with a happy smile.

But the woman with whom he had been living had now to be provided with another husband. Who would take her? The judge addressed the question to a young man, a mere boy, standing near by, and he replied that he would marry her, if she were willing. She said yes, so he sat down beside her. Their hands were placed together, the gobernador said a few admonishing words to them, and they rose, man and wife, duly married. How was this for rapid transit to matrimonial bliss?

The next day the guide took us up along some higher ridges, and after ten or twelve miles of slow ascent, we arrived at the summit of Barranca de Cobre, where we made a comfortable camp about half a mile back of the point at which the track descends into the cañon. Here we had an inspiring view; deep gorges and ravines, the result of prolonged weathering and erosion, gashing the country and forming high ridges, especially toward the south and west. In other words, here we observed for the first time barrancas, which from now on form an exceedingly characteristic feature of the topography of the Sierra Madres. These precipitous abysses, which traverse the mighty mass of the sierra like huge cracks, run, as far as Sierra Madre del Norte is concerned, mainly from east to west. In the country of the Tarahumare, that is to say, the State of Chihuahua, there are three very large barrancas. They are designated as Barranca de Cobre, Barranca de Batopilas, and Barranca de San Carlos. The Sierra Madre del Norte runs at an altitude of from 7,000 to 8,000 feet, at some points reaching even as high as 9,000 feet. It rises so gradually in the east, for instance, when entered from the direction of the city of Chihuahua, that one is surprised to be suddenly almost on top of it. The western side, however, falls off more or less abruptly, and presents the appearance of a towering, ragged wall. In accordance with this general trait of the mountain system, the beginnings of the barrancas in the east are generally slight, but they quickly grow deeper, and before they disappear in the lowlands of Sinaloa they sometimes reach a depth of from 4,000 to 5,000 feet. Of course, they do not continue equally narrow throughout their entire length, but open up gradually and become wider and less steep.

Besides these large barrancas, which impede the traveller in the highlands and necessitate a course toward the east, there are innumerable smaller ones, especially in the western part of the range, where large portions of the country are broken up into a mass of stupendous, rock-walled ridges and all but bottomless chasms. A river generally flows in the barrancas between the narrow banks, which occasionally disappear altogether, leaving the water to rush between abruptly ascending mountain sides.

As far as the first of the large barrancas was concerned, near the top of which we were standing, we could for some little distance follow its windings toward the west, and its several tributaries could be made out in the landscape by the contours of the ridges. Barranca de Cobre is known in its course by different names. Near the mine of Urique (the Tarahumare word for Barranca), it is called Barranca de Urique, and here its yawning chasm is over 4,000 feet deep. Even the intrepid Jesuit missionaries at first gave up the idea of descending into it, and the Indians told them that only the birds knew how deep it was. The traveller as he stands at the edge of such gaps wonders whether it is possible to get across them. They can in a few places be crossed, even with animals if these are lightly loaded, but it is a task hard upon flesh and blood.

It was in these barrancas, that I was to find the gentile (pagan) Indians I was so anxious to meet. From where I stood looking at it the country seemed forgotten, lonely, untouched by human hand. Shrubs and trees were clinging to the rocky brows of the barrancas, and vegetation could be seen wherever there was sufficient earth on the mountain and the sides of the ravines; but, on the whole, the country looked rather barren and lifeless.

Still, it did not take us long to find traces of human beings. Our tents were pitched on an old trinchera. Cut deep into a rough ledge not far off was the rough carving of a serpent, sixty feet long, that must have been left here by a race antecedent to the Tarahumares. And a little further off we came upon the ruins of a modern Tarahumare house. It seems as if the Indians must extract a living out of the rocks and stones; though when we got down into the barranca and into the ravines we came upon patches of land that could be cultivated; and there were some small areas of pasture, although extremely precipitous.

The first thing to do was to despatch the guide into the valleys and gorges below, which from our camping place could not be seen, only surmised, that he might persuade some Tarahumares to act as carriers on an excursion I contemplated making through the region. In a couple of days a party was made up, consisting, besides myself, of Mr. Taylor, the guide, two Mexicans, and five Tarahumares with their gobernador. Bundles weighing from forty to seventy-five pounds were placed on the backs of the Indians and the Mexicans; even the guide took a small pack, though it would have been beneath the dignity of the gobernador to take a load upon himself. But his company was valuable on account of his great influence with his people.

It was an exceedingly interesting excursion of several days' duration. Owing to the presence of the gobernador the Indians received us well. Nobody ran away, though all were extremely shy and bashful, and the women turned their backs towards us. But after a while they would offer us beans from a pot cooking over the fire. They served them in earthenware bowls with a couple of tortillas (corn cakes). In another vessel, which they passed around among us, they offered the flavouring, course salt and some small chile (Spanish peppers), which vegetable is cultivated and much relished by the Tarahumares.

But the most interesting dish was iskiate, which I now tasted for the first time. It is made from toasted corn, which is mixed with water while being ground on the metate until it assumes the consistency of a thick soup. Owing to certain fresh herbs that are often added to the corn, it may be of a greenish color, but it is always cool and tempting. After having tramped for several days over many miles of exceedingly rough country, I arrived late one afternoon at a cave where a woman was just making this drink. I was very tired and at a loss how to climb the mountain-side to my camp, some 2,000 feet above; but after satisfying my hunger and thirst with some iskiate, offered by the hospitable Indians, I at once felt new strength, and, to my own astonishment, climbed the great height without much effort. After this I always found iskiate a friend in need, so strengthening and refreshing that I may almost claim it as a discovery, interesting to mountain climbers and others exposed to great physical exertions. The preparation does not, however, agree with a sedentary life, as it is rather indigestible.

The dress of the Tarahumare is always very scanty, even where he comes in contact with the whites. One may see the Indians in the mining camps, and even in the streets of the city of Chihuahua, walking about naked, except for a breech-cloth of coarse, home-spun woollen material, held up around the waist with a girdle woven in characteristic designs. Some may supplement this national costume with a tunic, or short poncho; and it is only right to add that most of the men are provided with well-made blankets, which their women weave for them, and in which they wrap themselves when they go to feasts and dances. The hair, when not worn loose, is held together with a home-woven ribbon, or a piece of cotton cloth rolled into a band; or with a strip of palm leaf. Often men and women gather the hair in the back of the head, and men may also make a braid of it.

The women's toilet is just as simple. A scrimpy woollen skirt is tied around the waist with a girdle, and over the shoulders is worn a short tunic, with which, however, many dispense when at home in the barranca. The women, too, have blankets, though with them they are not so much the rule as with the men. Still, mothers with babies always wear blankets, to support the little ones in an upright position on their backs, the blanket being tightly wrapped around mother and child. The women nowadays generally wear sandals of the usual Mexican cowhide pattern, like the men; but there is ample evidence to prove that such was not the case in former times.

The people are, for Indians, not especially fond of ornaments, and it is a peculiar fact that mirrors have no special attraction for them. They do not like to look at themselves. The women often wear ear-ornaments made of triangular pieces of shell attached to bead strings, or deck themselves with strings of glass beads, of which the large red and blue ones are favourites; and necklaces made from the seed of the *Coix Lachryma-Jobi* are used by both sexes, chiefly for medicinal purposes. The men wear only single strings of these seeds, while the necklaces of the women are wound several times around the neck. The shaman, or medicine-man—a priest and doctor combined—is never without such a necklace when officiating at a feast. The seed is believed to possess many medicinal qualities, and for this reason children, too, often wear it.

Peasant women in Italy and Spain use the same seed as a protection against evil, and even American women have been known to put strings of them on teething children as a soothing remedy.

An important fact I established is that the Indians in the barrancas, in this part of the country, use something like trincheras for the cultivation of their little crops. To obtain arable land on the mountain slopes the stones are cleared from a convenient spot and utilised in the construction of a wall below the field thus made. The soil is apt to be washed away by heavy rains, and the wall not only prevents what little earth there is on the place from being carried off, but also catches what may come from above, and in this way secures sufficient ground to yield a small crop. Fields thus made can even be ploughed. On the slopes of one arroyo I counted six such terraces, and in the mountainous country on the Rio Fuerte, toward the State of Sinaloa, chile, beans, squashes, Coix Lachryma-Jobi, and bananas are raised on trincheras placed across the arroyos that run down the hills. There they have the form of small terraces, and remind one of similar ones found farther north as ancient ruins, to such an extent that one might suppose that the Tarahumares have made use of the relics of antiquity. Mr. Hartman in one long arroyo thereabouts observed four at some distance from one another. They were from four to ten feet high, and as broad as the little arroyo itself, some eight to sixteen feet.

Chapter 8

The Houses of the Tarahumares—American Cave-dwellings of Today—Frequent Changes of Abode by the Tarahumare—The Patio or Dancing Place—The Original Cross of America—Tarahumare Store-Houses.

The houses we saw on this excursion were of remarkable uniformity, and as the people have had very little, if any, contact with the whites, it is reasonable to infer that these structures are original with them. On a sloping mesa six families were living in such buildings not far from one another.

These houses have a frame of four forked poles, planted firmly into the ground, to form a square or rectangle. Two joists are laid over them parallel to each other. Under one of them, in the front of the house, is the doorway. The joists support the flat roof of loose pine boards, laid sometimes in a double layer. The rear joist is often a foot or so lower than the front one, which causes the roof to slant towards the back. The boards may simply be logs split in two and with the bark taken off. The walls are made by leaning boards, ends up, against the roof, while the door consists of a number of boards, which are removed or replaced according to convenience. In most instances the doorway is protected from the outside against wind and weather by a lean-to. Access to the house is gained sideways, even where a small vestibule is built, extra poles being driven in the ground to support the porch-roof boards.

While this style of architecture may be said to be typical throughout the Tarahumare country, there are many variations. Generally attempts are made to construct a more solid wall, boards or poles being laid lengthwise, one on top of the other, and kept in place by sliding the ends between double uprights at the corners. Or they may be placed ends up along the side of the house; or regular stone walls may be built, with or without mud for mortar. Even in one and the same house all these kinds of walls may be observed. A type of house seen throughout the Tarahumare country, as well as among the pagan Tarahumares in the Barranca de Cobre, is shown in this illustration.

It is also quite common to see a frame work of only two upright poles connected with a horizontal beam, against which boards are leaning from both sides, making the house look like a gable roof set on the ground. There are, however, always one or more logs laid horizontally and overhung by the low eaves of the roof, while the front and rear are carelessly filled in with boards or logs, either horizontally or standing on ends. In the hot country this style of house may be seen thatched with palm-leaves, or with grass.

The dwelling may also consist only of a roof resting on four uprights *(jacal);* or it may be a mere shed. There are also regular log-cabins encountered with locked corners, especially among the southern Tarahumares. Finally, when a Tarahumare becomes civilised, he builds himself a house of stone and mud, with a roof of boards, or thatch, or earth.

It is hardly possible to find within the Tarahumare country two houses exactly alike, although the main idea is always easily recognised. The dwellings though very airy, afford sufficient protection to people who are by no means sensitive to the drafts and climatic changes. The Tarahumares do not expect their houses to be dry during the wet season, but are content when there is some dry spot inside. If the cold troubles them too much, they move into a cave. Many of the people do not build houses at all, but are permanent or transient cave-dwellers. This fact I thoroughly investigated in subsequent researches, extending over a year and a half, and covering the entire width and breadth of the Tarahumare country.

In this land of weather-worn porphyry and interstratified sandstone, natural caves are met with everywhere, in which the people find a convenient and safe shelter. Although it may be said that houses are their main habitations, still the Tarahumares live in caves to such an extent that they may be fitly called the American cave-dwellers of the present age.

Caves were man's first abode, and they are found in certain geological formations in all parts of the globe. Human imagination always peopled the deep, dark caverns with terrible monsters guarding treasures, and legends and fairy tales still cling about many of them. Shallow caves, however, have from the earliest time attracted man to seek shelter in them, just as the animals took refuge in them against the inclemency of the weather. Prehistoric man in Europe was a cave-dweller, and modern investigations have given us a clear and vivid picture of the life of the ancient race, who existed in France while the mammoth and the reindeer were roaming over the plains of western Europe.

As civilisation advanced, under changing climatic conditions, and as man began to improve his tools and implements, he deserted the caves and preferred to live in houses of his own building. But a long time after the caves had been abandoned as abodes of the living, they were still used for interring the dead. Do we not remember the story told in Genesis, how Abraham bought for 400 shekels a cave from Ephron that he might bury Sarah there and have a family tomb?

The cave-dwellers of France vanished many thousand years ago; but here are yet in several parts of the globe, for instance, in Tunis and in Central Africa, races who still adhere to the custom of living in caves, although their condition of life is different from that of the antediluvian cave-dwellers.

In Mexico the cave-dwellers are in a transitory state, most of them having adopted houses and sheds; but many of them are still unable to perceive why they should give up their safe and comfortable natural shelters for rickety abodes of their own making. Padre Juan Fonte, the pioneer missionary of the Tarahumares, who penetrated into their country eighteen leagues from San Pablo, toward Guachochic, speaks of the numerous caves in that country and relates that many of them were divided into small houses. Other records, too, allude to the existence of cave-dwellers in that part of the Sierra Madre. Still, the fact of there being cave-dwellers today in Mexico was until recently known only to the Mexicans living in their neighbourhood, who regard this condition of things as a matter of course.

While most of the Tarahumares live permanently on the highlands, a great many of them move for the winter down into the barranca, on account of its warmer temperature, and, if they have no house, they live wherever they find a convenient shelter, preferably a cave; but for want of better accommodations they content themselves with a rock shelter, or even a spreading tree. This would suit them well enough were it not that, at least in recent years, there has not been rain enough in the barrancas to enable the people to raise there the corn they need. They therefore go back to the highlands in March, because in the higher altitudes rainfall can be depended upon with more certainty. The general custom among the Indians living near to a barranca is to plant two crops of corn; one in early March on the crest, and the other one in June, at the beginning of the rainy season, down in the barranca, and after having harvested at both places they retire to their winter quarters to enjoy themselves. Sometimes the cave of a family is not more than half a mile from their house, and they live alternatively in one or the other abode, because the Tarahumares still retain their nomadic instincts, and even those living permanently on the highlands change their domicile very frequently. One reason is that they follow their cattle; another that they improve the land by living on it for a while; but there are still other reasons for moving so much about, which are known only to themselves. In summer many people leave their caves on account of the scorpions, tarantulas, and other pests that infest them.

In front of the entrance to the cave there is generally a wall of stone, or of stone and mud, raised to the height of a man's chest, as a protection against wind and weather, wild beasts, etc. The cave is fitted up just like the houses, with grinding stone, earthen jars and bowls, baskets, gourds, etc. The fire is always in the middle, without hearth or chimney, and the jars in which the food is cooked rest on three stones. A portion of the ground is levelled and made smooth for the family to sleep on. As often as not there are skins spread out on the floor. Sometimes the floor space is extended by an artificial terrace in front of the cave. In a few cases the floor is plastered with adobe, and I have seen one cave in which the sides, too, were dressed in the same way. Generally there are one or two store-houses in the caves, and these constitute the chief improvement. Of course, there are a good many caves where there are no store-houses; still they are the striking feature of the cave. A few times I found walls of stone and mud erected inside of the cave, breast high, to partition off one or two rooms for the use of the family, as well as for the goats and sheep. Often, inclosures are built of wood fences for the domesticated animals and occupy the greater part of the cave.

The largest inhabited cave I have seen was nearly a hundred feet in width and from twenty to forty feet in depth. If caves are at all deep, the Indians live near the mouth. They never excavate caves, nor do they live in dug-outs. I heard of one arroyo, where six inhabited caves, only thirty or fifty yards apart, can be seen at one time; but this is a rare case. Generally they are farther apart, maybe a hundred yards to a mile, or more; and that suits the Tarahumares very well, each family preferring to live by itself.

In one place I saw a cave, or rather a shelter under a big boulder, utilised as a dwelling; and here a kind of parapet had been built of stone gravel, terrace fashion, to enlarge the area of the cave floor.

Inhabited caves are never found in inaccessible places, as is the case with cave-dwellings in the southwestern part of the United States. Where caves are difficult to access, the Indians may place a wooden ladder, or rather, a notched tree trunk, which is the national style of staircase. Once I saw steps cut into the soft "rock" (solidified volcanic ash), leading up to a dwelling. There was also a kind of settee cut out of the cave-wall.

Many of the caves are remarkably symmetrical in shape, and naturally quite comfortable. Caves may be found in the arroyos in the highlands, as well as in the barrancas. If I were to designate a region where they are more plentiful than elsewhere, I should mention the country from Carichic towards Urique, and also to the north and west of Norogachic. Many caves have within memory of man been permanently abandoned, owing to the occupancy of the land by the Mexicans, as the Indians dislike to be near the whites.

The Tarahumares are not the only tribe still clinging to caves. As we have seen, the Pimas, too, are, to a limited extent, cave-dwellers, and the same is the case with the northern Tepehuanes, as well as with the allied Huarogios in their small area.

Are these cave-dwellers related to the ancient cliff-dwellers in the southwestern part of the United States and northern Mexico? Decidedly not. Their very aversion to living more than one family in a cave and their lack of sociability mark a strong contrast with the ancient cliff-dwellers, who were by nature gregarious. The fact that the people lived in caves is in itself extremely interesting, but this alone does not prove any connection between them and the ancient cliff-dwellers. Although the Tarahumare is very intelligent, he is backward in the arts and industries. It is true that the women weave admirable designs in girdles and blankets, but this seems to be the utmost limit of their capabilities. In the caves they sometimes draw with ochre clumsy figures of animals and women, and on some rock may be seen outlines of feet scratched with stone "in order to leave their imprint in this world when they die." Tarahumare pottery is exceedingly crude as compared with the work found in the old cliff-dwellings, and its decoration is infantile as contrasted with the cliff-dwellers' work. The cliff-dwellers brought the art of decoration to a comparatively high state, as shown in the relics found in their dwellings. But the cave-dweller of today shows no suggestion of such skill. Moreover, he is utterly devoid of the architectural gift which resulted in the remarkable rock structures of the early cliff-dwellers. These people as far as concerns their cave-dwelling habits cannot be ranked above troglodytes.

The Tarahumare never lives all his life in one house or cave; nor will he, on the other hand, leave it forever. He rarely stays away from it more than two or three years. A family, after inhabiting a house for a time may suddenly decide to move it, even if it is built of stone. The reason is not always easy to tell. One man moved his house because he found the sun did not strike it enough. After a death has occurred in a dwelling, even though it was that of a distant relative incidentally staying with the family, the house is destroyed, or the cave permanently abandoned; and many other superstitious apprehensions of one kind or another may thus influence the people. Very often a man moves for the sake of benefiting the land, and after tearing down his house he immediately plants corn in the spot on which the house stood. A family may thus change its abode several times a year, or once a year, or every other year. The richest man in the Tarahumare country, now dead, had five caves, and moved as often as ten times in one year.

A never absent feature of the Tarahumare habitation, be it house or cave, is a level, smooth place in front of it. This is the dancing place, or patio, on which he performs his religious exercises, and he may have more than one. The formation of the land may even oblige him to build terraces to obtain space enough for his religious dances.

On this patio, which measures generally about ten yards in every direction, one, two, or three crosses are planted, as the central object of all ceremonies (except those in the cult of the sacred cactus híkuli). The cross is generally about a foot high; sometimes it stands two feet above ground. It is made of two sticks of unequal length, preferably sticks of pine wood, tied together in the form of the Latin cross. I saw two crosses raised outside of a man's house, which were formed by the natural growth of small pine trees, and these were four feet high. The shamans, for their curing, use small crosses—three or four inches long.

It is a well-known fact that on their arrival in America the Spaniards to their amazement found Indians in possession of the cross. Omitting here the cross of Palenque, the symbol of a tree, the tree of life, it is safe to say that the original cross of most Mexican tribes is the Greek cross, though the Latin was also used. To them the former is of fundamental religious moment, as indicating the four corners of the world; but a word for cross, or anything corresponding to it, does not occur in the language of any of the tribes known to me. Nevertheless the cross (the Greek), to the Indian the symbol of a cosmic idea, is pecked on the rocks, or drawn on the sand, or made in corresponding strokes with medicine over the patient's body.

With the Tarahumare the cross is the pivot around which all his ceremonies and festivals move. He always dances to the cross, and on certain occasions he attaches strings of beads, ears of corn, and other offerings to it. It is used by the heathen as well as by the Christian Tarahumares. The question is whether this tribe has changed its form since its contact with the whites or whether the cross was originally like the one in use today. From many of the Tarahumares' utterances I incline to think that their cross represents a human figure with arms outstretched, and is an embodiment of Father Sun, the Perfect Man. When two crosses are placed on the patio, the smaller stands for the moon. This conception also explains the custom of setting up three crosses at the principal dance, the rutubúri, the third cross representing probably the Morning Star. Among Christianised natives the three crosses may come gradually to mean the Trinity.

On one occasion I saw a cross at least ten feet high with a cross beam only one foot long, raised next to two crosses of ordinary size, all standing on the patio of a well-to-do Indian, and the inference was easily drawn that the high cross was meant for Father Sun. The Northern Tepehuanes say that the cross *is* Tata Dios, the Christianised Indian's usual designation of God.

The impression that the cross represents a human figure gains further probability by the fact that a cross is erected on the special patio of the dead, and I have noticed that this cross is moved in the course of the ceremonies to the principal dancing place "to see the dancing and drink tesvino," as the Indians explained it. Surely, this cross represented the dead.

Here is seen the front and rear view of a cross which is of great interest, although its shape is evidently an exaggerated imitation of a Catholic cross or crucifix. I came upon it in the mountainous country east of Morelos, and the Tarahumares near the Ranch of Colorados presented it to me. It had apparently not been made long ago, and was painted with red ochre. The arms have been tied on in the usual fashion with twine of fibre, the mode of fastening it appearing most distinctly on the back of the cross.

Seen from the front the designs on the head, or the uppermost part, represent the Morning Star, the dots being his companions, the other stars. But it is significant that this constellation is also called the "eyes" of the cross. The dots on the other side of the cross are also meant for stars, in order that, as the Indian explained to me, Tata Dios may see the stars where they are dancing; he lives in the stars—a belief evidently arising from Catholic influences. The human figures painted on the cross are intended to emphasise its meaning. The most important of these human-like contours are those directly below the junction of the arms with the vertical stem. They are evidently repetitions of the main cross, the arms being expressed in the crude carvings. What the various pairs of curved side lines mean, I am unable to say.

What is of more importance to the Tarahumare than his dwelling is his store-house, which he always builds before his domicile. In fact, his personal comfort is made secondary even to that of his domestic animals. As a survival of the time when he had no house at all may be noted the fact that husband and wife, after having been away on a journey for several days or longer, do not on the first night after their return sleep in the house or cave, but at some convenient place near the store-house.

These store-houses are always well put together, though many of them are not large enough to accommodate a medium-sized dog, the Tarahumares preferring number to size. In them he stores what little property he has beyond that in actual use, chiefly corn and beans, some spare clothing and cotton cloth, hikuli, herbs, etc. The door of the house is made from one or more short boards of pine wood, and is either provided with an ingeniously constructed wood lock, or the boards are simply plastered up with mud along the four edges. The Tarahumare rarely locks his house on leaving it, but he is ever careful to fasten the door of his store-house securely, and to break open a store-house sealed up in the manner described is considered the most heinous crime known to the tribe. Mexicans have committed it and have had to pay for it with their lives.

The most common kind of store-house is from four to six feet high, round, and built of stones and mud, with a roof of pine boards, weighed down with earth and stones. Other store-houses of similar size are square and built of boards with corners interlocked. They, too, are covered with boards. These diminutive buildings are often seen inside of caves; or else they are erected in places difficult of access, on tops of boulders, for instance. Sometimes they are seen in lonely places, more often, however, near the dwellings; and the little round structures make a curious effect when erected on boulders in the vicinity of some hut, looking, as they do, like so many diminutive factory chimneys. They proclaim more clearly than anything else the fact that when the people reach that stage in their development in which they begin to till the soil, they soon become careful of the little property they have, in marked distinction to the savage and nomadic tribes, who are always lavish and improvident. I have seen as many as ten store-houses of the kind described, and once even fourteen near one dwelling, but generally one or two only are found near by.

Small caves, especially when difficult to reach and hidden from view, may be utilised as store-houses, and are then sealed up in the same way as the other variations are. Sometimes regular log-houses are used.

Chapter 9

Arrival at Batopilas—Ascent from Batopilas to the Highlands of the Sierra—A Tarahumare who had been in Chicago—An Old-timer—Flight of our Native Guide and Its Disastrous Consequences—Indians Burn the Grass All Over the Country—Travelling Becomes too Difficult for the Animals—Mr. Taylor and I go to Zapuri—Its Surroundings—The Pithaya in Season.

We continued our way toward the south, crossing Barranca de Cobre where it is 3,300 feet deep. The track we followed was fairly good, but led along several dangerous precipices, over which two burros rolled and were killed. The highest point we reached on the track over the highlands south of the barranca was 8,300 feet. There seemed to be a divide here, the climate being cool and moist, and the farthest ranges toward the south and west enveloped in mist and fog. Although Barranca de Batopilas is not as narrow and impressive as the barranca we had just left, still the mighty gap, as we looked into its hazy bottom from the highlands, presented an imposing, awe-inspiring sight.

Following the windings of the well-laid-out road we descended into the cañon and made camp a few miles this side of the town of Batopilas. The silver mines here, which are old and famous, were discovered in the seventeenth century. I was cordially received by Mr. A. R. Shepherd, the well-known mining expert, whose courtesy and kindness were much appreciated by the members of the expedition.

My recent experience had convinced me that the only way to study the natives properly was to live among them for a length of time, and as such a thing was out of the question with so large a party as I still had with me, I made up my mind to discharge as soon as possible everybody and to remain alone.

The country was now suffering from a relentlessly scorching sun. The heat increased as the wet season approached, and, as the animals were getting weaker and weaker, I disposed here of about half of them, and the number of attendants and the amount of baggage were correspondingly reduced. On continuing the journey with the weak and hungry mules, we found the ascent of the southern side of Barranca de Batopilas quite laborious; but on the crest we enjoyed the fresh breeze, the more gratefully after the enervating heat in the bottom of the cañon.

Thus we arrived at the village of Yoquibo (yōkí = bluebird; īvo = mesa: bluebird on the mesa). Here I had to stop for a few days to reconnoitre the road. I was told that the grass had been burned by the Indians almost as far as the ranches of Guachochic, our main objective point. The Indians at that time (May) always burn the grass, and the entire country is wrapped in smoke. This, they think, is necessary to produce rain; smoke-clouds and rain-clouds, in their opinion, bringing about the same ultimate result. But it is exceedingly trying for travellers, man and beast. Only by accident is some little spot of grass spared here and there, and progress becomes almost an impossibility.

Immediately upon our arrival I went to see the gobernador, and, strange to say, I found him engaged in teaching his young wife how to weave. Three months ago his first wife had died of smallpox. Old bachelors and widowers have a hard time in getting wives, because the Tarahumare belles have a decided preference for young men. But the wifeless Indian feels very unhappy, as it means that he has to do all the woman's housework, which is very laborious, and therefore thoroughly distasteful to him. By way of fascinating this young girl, the gobernador had to exert himself to the extent of teaching her how to make girdles and wearing apparel.

The next day this gentleman returned my call, carrying his bow and arrow. I had already learned in Batopilas that the party of Indians who, about two years ago, had been exhibited by a now deceased traveller as representative cave-dwellers, had been gathered mainly in the neighbourhood of Yoquibo. My visitor had been one of the troupe, and I was eager to find out what impression the civilised world had made on this child of nature, who had never known anything but his woods and his mountains. Therefore, almost my first question was, "How did you like Chicago?" "It looks very much like here," was the unexpected reply. What most impressed him, it seemed, was neither the size of the city nor its sky-scrapers, though he remembered these, but the big water near which those people dwelt. He had liked riding in the railroad cars, but complained that he had not had enough to eat on the journey.

His experience on this trip had familiarised him with the white man and his queer, incomprehensible ways, and made him something of a philosopher. I wanted him to accompany me on my visits to the few houses here, as the people were very shy and timid. Although he was very much engaged, as I could see, having to look after his animals as well as his wife, he obligingly went with me to two houses. We saw a woman with twins; one of them a miserable-looking specimen, suffering from lack of food.

There were also some cave-dwellings near Yoquibo, one or two of which were occupied. In the afternoon when I went out alone, the people all disappeared the moment they saw me approaching, except one group of strangers who had come to beg and did not pay any attention to me. They were too busily engaged in making ready for the pot a certain kind of larvae, by extracting them from the cocoon, a small white sac of silky texture found on the strawberry tree.

The guide told me that Indians like these, who beg for food, always return to those who give them alms, the amount of the gift, as soon as their circumstances allow.

Here in Yoquibo I met one of those Mexican adventurers who under one pretext or another manage to get into the Indian villages and cannot be routed out again. Certain of them ply some little trade, generally that of a blacksmith, others act as "secretaries," writing what few communications the Indians may have to send to the government authorities; some conduct a little barter trade, exchanging cheap cotton cloth, beads, etc., for sheep and cattle; but most of them supply the Indians with Mexican brandy, mescal. The one in Yoquibo had established himself in the only room left intact in the old dilapidated vicarage, and eked out a living by selling mescal to the Indians.

This fellow's appearance, especially his unsteady, lurking eyes, suggested the bandit. No doubt, like most of his class, he was in hiding from the government authorities. He was something of a hypochondriac, and among other ailments he thought he had an animal in his stomach, which he got in there by way of a knife-stab he had received some time ago. When he came to me to get some remedy, he carried a rather fine rifle, and in spite of all his suffering, real or imaginary, the bandit nature asserted itself, when I made some complimentary remark regarding his weapon. His half-closed eyes slurred in a crafty, guileful manner from side to side as he drawled: *"Despues de Dios, mi rifle!"* ("Next to God, my rifle!")

After considerable looking about, I at last found an Indian willing to act as guide for the next stage of our journey. He was an elderly man, and at dusk he was quietly sitting near the campfire, eating his supper, when the tall figure of Mr. Hartman appeared on the scene, wrapped in a military overcoat. He probably looked to the Indian very martial and threatening as he approached through the twilight. At any rate, his appearance had a most unexpected effect on our guide. I suddenly heard a noise behind me, and on looking around, I saw him running as fast as his legs would carry him, leaving his supper, dropping his blanket, splashing through the creek, and disappearing in the night, never to be seen again by us. He imagined that a soldier was coming to seize and kill him; that the meat-pot in which he was to be cooked was already on the fire, while the skulls of other unfortunates that had been eaten were lying in a heap near one of the tents. He alluded apparently to four skulls which I had taken out of an ancient burial cave. In explanation I will say that some time ago he had been arrested for some crime and had broken away from jail; soldiers, or rather, the police, were after him, and he mistook Mr. Hartman for one of his pursuers and ran for safety.

The incident proved somewhat unfortunate for us. In consequence of the wild stories he told about us, the Indians, of a suspicious nature anyway, sent messengers all over the sierra, warning the people against the man-eaters that were coming. Our strange proceedings in Cusarare, namely, the photographing, had already been reported and made the Indians uneasy. The terrible experience of our runaway guide seemed to confirm their wildest apprehensions, and the alarm spread like wildfire, growing in terror, like an avalanche, the farther it went. We found the ranches deserted on every hand, women and children hiding and screaming whenever they caught a glimpse of us. At every turn our progress was impeded. Wherever I came I was abhorred as the man who subsisted on babies and green corn, and the prospect of my ever gaining the confidence of the Indians was exceedingly discouraging for the next four or five months.

Though it was impossible to secure a new guide, I still made a start the next day, following a fairly good track which leads south toward Guachochic. Yet further obstacles presented themselves. The animals began to give out. It was the season of the year when they change their coats, and are in poor condition even under the best circumstances, and mine were exhausted from lack of food. They would not eat the dry grass, and the green pasture was still too scanty to suffice for their maintenance. The information that the natives had burned all the grass proved correct to its fullest extent, so there was nothing for me to do but to establish a camp, scarcely a day's journey off, at Tasajisa, where there was some pasture along the ridges that had as yet escaped the fire of the Indians. Leaving the larger part of my outfit and about half of my mules in charge of my chief packer, Mr. Taylor and I continued the journey with the best and strongest of the animals, making a circuitous tour to the little mining town of Zapuri, in the neighbourhood of which were some caves I wanted to investigate.

After a day's journey we turned westward and got beyond the range of the fires. Turkeys were seen close to our camp and appeared plentiful; I also saw a giant woodpecker, but just as I got ready to shoot, it flew away with a great whirr of its wings. We soon began to descend, and after a long and fatiguing day's travel over cordons and sierras, and through a wide barranca surrounded by magnificent towering mountains, we arrived, late in the afternoon, at Zapuri. The superintendent of the mine, to whom I brought a letter of introduction from the owner of the property, received us with cordial hospitality. Here the climate was splendid; the nights were just pleasantly cool, the mornings deliciously calm; they were all the more enjoyed after the windy weather of the sierra.

Immediately upon my arrival here I had a chance, through the courtesy of the superintendent, to secure a Mexican and some strong mules, which took Mr. Taylor over to Parral on his way back to the United States. Mr.

Hartman remained with the expedition two months longer, to join me again the following year for a few months. I also got a guide for myself and made an excursion to the caves in the neighbouring barrancas. After we had gone some ten miles, over very bad roads, we came to the home of an old Tarahumare woman, who was reputed to be very rich. Knowing Mexican exaggeration in this regard, I computed that the twelve bushels of pesos she was supposed to have hidden might amount, perhaps, to $50 or $100 Mexican money. Whatever her wealth was, she showed it only in a lavish display of glass beads around her scrawny neck; they must have weighed at least six or eight pounds. But, then, her homestead was composed mainly of four or five substantial circular store-houses.

The wealth of the Tarahumare consists in his cattle. He is well off when he has three or four head of cattle and a dozen sheep and goats. There is one instance where a man had as many as forty head of cattle, but this was a rare exception. They rarely keep horses, and never pigs, which destroy their cornfields; and are believed, besides, to be Spaniards *(Gachupines)*. Pork, though sometimes eaten, is never sacrificed. No tame turkeys are kept, but occasionally the people have some hens, and in rare cases a family may keep a turtle dove or a tame quail. When a man has oxen, he is able to plough a large piece of land and raise enough corn to sell some. But corn is seldom converted into money.

Here we packed the most necessary things on our best mule, and with the guide and two Indians, who carried bundles, we descended to the river. The road was fairly good, but as we approached the river we came to several bad places. In one of these the mule's aparejo struck a rock, which caused the animal to lose its foothold. Unresistingly it slid down the steep slope for about seven yards and came against a tree, forefeet on one side, hindfeet on the other. The boy who led it, eager to do something, managed to get the halter off, so that there was nothing by which to hold the animal except its ears. I held fast to one of these, steadying myself on the loose soil by grabbing a root sticking out of the ground. The intelligent animal lay perfectly still over the trunk. Finally I managed to get out my bowie-knife and cut the ropes off the pack, which rolled down the hill, while the mule, relieved of its bulky burden, scrambled to its feet and climbed up. It was born and bred in the barranca, otherwise if would never have been able to accomplish this feat.

Toward evening we arrived at the section of a barranca called Ohuivo (Ōví = return, or "the place to which they returned") on the Rio Fuerte. The Indians here, although many of them have been affected by the nearness of the mines, are reticent and distrustful, and our guide evidently had not much influence with them. They refused to be photographed, and even the gobernador ran away from the terrible ordeal.

During the several days I remained in this valley the heat never varied from 100°, day and night, which was rather trying and made doing anything an exertion. The country looked scorched, except for the evergreen cacti, the most prominent of which was the towering pithaya. Its dark-green branches stand immovable to wind and storm. It has the best wild fruit growing in the northwestern part of Mexico, and as this was just the season when it ripens, the Indians from all around had come to gather it. It is as large as an egg and its flesh soft, sweet, and nourishing. As the plant grows to a height of twenty to thirty-five feet, the Indians get the fruit down with a long reed, one end of which has four prongs, and gather it in little crates of split bamboo, which they carry by straps on their backs. It is a sight to see men, women, and children start out gaily at day-break, armed with slender sticks, climbing rugged heights with grace and agility, to get the pithaya, which tastes better when plucked at dawn, fresh and cool, than when gathered during the heat of the day. The fruit, which lasts about a month, comes when it is most needed, at the height of the dry season (June), when the people have a regular feasting-time of it. Mexicans also appreciate the pithaya, and servants frequently abscond at that time, in order to get the fruit. The beautiful white flowers of the plant are never found growing on the north side of the stem.

With the Indians, the pithaya enters, of course, into religion, and the beautiful macaw (guacamaya), which revels in the fruit, is associated with it in their beliefs. The bird arrives from its migration to southern latitudes when the pithaya is in bloom, and the Indians think that it comes to see whether there will be much fruit; then it flies off again to the coast, to return in June, when the fruit is ripe. The following gives the trend of one of the guacamaya songs: "The pithaya is ripe, let us go and get it. Cut off the reeds!* The guacamaya comes from the Tierra Caliente to eat the first fruits. From far away, from the hot country, I come when the men are cutting the reeds, and I eat the first fruits. Why do you wish to take the first fruits from me? They are my fruits. I eat the fruit, and I throw away the skin. I get filled with the fruit, and I go home singing. Remain behind, little tree, waving as I alight from you! I am going to fly in the wind, and some day I will return and eat your pithayas, little tree!"

*With which the fruit is brought down.

Chapter 10

Nice-looking Natives—Albinos—Ancient Remains in Ohuivo—Local Traditions, the Cocoyomes, etc.—Guachochic—Don Miguel and "The Postmaster"—A Variety of Curious Cures—Gauchochic Becomes my Head-quarters—The Difficulty of Getting an Honest Interpreter—False Truffles—The Country Suffering From a Prolonged Drought—A Start in a North-westerly Direction—Arrival at the Pueblo of Norogachic.

I followed the river a day's journey up and noticed some small tobacco plantations on the banks. I met some good-looking people, who had come from Tierras Verdes, the locality adjoining on the south. Their movements were full of action and energy. Their skins showed a tinge of delicate yellow, and as the men wore their hair in a braid, they had a curious, oriental appearance. The women looked well in black woollen skirts and white tunics. The people from that part of the country are known for their pretty, white, home-made blankets, and it was evident that in those inaccessible parts the Indians had still something for the white man to take away.

The natives of this valley had a curious habit, when they were made to dive for fish, of afterward throwing themselves in a row on the sun-heated sand to warm their stomachs for a minute or two.

Near Ohuivo, in the mountains toward Morelos, there used to live a family of ten albinos. When I was there only two survived, smallpox having made havoc among them. Their skin was so delicate that even the contact of their clothing irritated it. Mr. Harman visited one of them, an old woman who lived in a cave with her husband, a small, dark-skinned fellow, and the two certainly were "mated, but not matched." Her features were entirely Indian, but her complexion was unique in Mexico, even among the white population. She reminded one of a very blond type of Scandinavian or Irish peasantry. Her hair was yellowish-white, but her eyebrows and -lashes were snow-white. The face and body were white, but disfigured with large red spots and small freckles. She kept her eyes more than half shut, as she was very shy it was not possible to ascertain the color of the iris; but Mr. Hartman was assured by the husband that it was bluish.

Most of the Indians in Ohuivo live in houses. The few caves that are occupied are not improved in any way. One cave contained ancient habitations, and tradition says that there the Tubares had once established themselves. The cave is nothing but a nearly horizontal crack in the rock, situated on the southern side of the river, some 300 feet above the bottom of the valley. It runs from south-east to north-west to a length of about 200 feet, interrupted perpendicularly by a crevice. Entering the cave at the southernmost end I found twelve low-walled rooms, standing singly, but closely side by side. They were square with rounded corners. The walls were built of stone and mud and one foot thick, and the floors were hard and smooth. A store-room, in a good state of preservation, resembled in every detail the store-houses used by the Tarahumares of the present day, being square and built of stone and mud. In none of these rooms was it possible for me to stand upright. Apart from this group, a few yards higher up in the cave, were two small houses. The floor of the cave was getting higher and higher. I had to crawl on my stomach for about ten yards and suddenly came to the edge of a precipice; but a track led around it to the other side, where I found a main portion of the houses, eighteen in all, the largest having a side thirteen feet long, though the others were considerably smaller. They were arranged just like those of the first section, in one row, and were made of the same material, except a few, which were built of adobe. In these the walls were only eight inches thick. One of the rooms was still complete, had square openings, and may have been a store-room. The others seem to have had the conventional Indian apertures. In two chambers I noticed circular spaces sunk into the floor six inches deep and about fourteen inches in diameter. What I took to be an estufa, nineteen feet in diameter, was found in the lowest section. Behind it was only a small cluster of five houses higher up in the cave.

Though this is the only ancient cave-dwelling I visited in Ohuivo, I was assured that there were several others in the neighbourhood. The broken country around Zapuri is interesting on account of the various traditions which, still living on the lips of the natives, refer to a mysterious people called the Cocoyomes, regarded by some Tarahumares as their ancient enemies, by others as their ancestors. They were the first people in the world, were short of stature and did not eat corn. They subsisted mainly on herbs, especially a small agave called tshāwí. They were also cannibals, devouring each other as well as the Tarahumare. The Cocoyomes lived in caves on the high cliffs of the sierra, and in the afternoon came down, like deer, to drink in the rivers. As they had no axes of iron they could not cut any large trees, and were unable to clear much of the land for the planting of corn. They could only burn the grass in the arroyos in order to get the fields ready. Long ago, when the Cocoyomes were very bad, the sun came down to the earth and burned nearly all of them; only a few escaped into the big caves.

Here in Zapuri the Cocoyomes had four large caves inside of which they had built square houses of very hard adobe; in one of the caves they had a spring. The Tarahumares often fought with them, and once, when the Cocoyomes were together in the largest cave, which had no spring, the Tarahumares besieged them for eight days, until all the Cocoyomes had perished from hunger. From such an event the name of Zapuri may have been derived.

Intelligent Mexicans, whom I consulted, agree that it means "fight" or "contest" (Spanish, *desafio*).

From a place called Tuaripa, some thirty miles farther south, near the border of the Tepehuane country, and in the same mountainous region, I have the following legend, about the Cocoyomes and the serpents:

> Two large serpents used to ascend from the river and go up on the highlands to a little plain between Huerachic and Tuaripa, and they killed and ate the Cocoyomes, returning each time to the river. Whenever they were hungry they used to come up again. At last an old man brought together all the people at the place where the serpents used to ascend. Here they dug a big hole and filled it with wood and large stones, and made a fire and heated the stones until they became red hot. When the serpents were seen to make their ascent on the mountainside, the men took hold of the stones with sticks, and threw them into the big, wide-open mouths of the serpents, until the monsters were so full with stones that they burst and fell dead into the river. Even to this day may be seen the marks on the rocks where the serpents used to ascend the mountain-side.

Once having again ascended to the highlands, I found rather level country as far as Guachochic, some forty-five miles off the track I followed. The name of the place signifies "blue herons," and the fine water-course, which originates in the many springs here, was formerly the abode of many water-birds. The locality thus designated is to-day a cluster of Mexican ranches, most of them belonging to one family. There is an old church, but at present no independent Indians live in Guachochic; the aborigines found about the place are servants of the Mexicans.

Guachochic lies at an elevation of 7,775 feet and at the southern end of a mesa, the largest one in the Sierra Madre del Norte, being twelve miles long and three miles wide. Except on the southern end this plateau is bordered with stately pine forests. Many Indians live on the mesa and in the numerous valleys adjoining it, but they are all "civilised"; that is, contaminated with many Mexico-Christian notions, and have lost their pristine simplicity.

I had a letter of introduction to the principal personage in Guachochic, Don Miguel, who enjoys the rare reputation of being just and helpful toward the Indians; and, being a large land-owner, he is a man of considerable influence also with his fellow-countrymen. To those in need he lends money on liberal terms out of the pile of silver dollars buried under the floor of his house. Robbers know from sad experience that he is not to be trifled with. Once, when a band of marauders had taken possession of the old adobe church and were helping themselves to the buried cash of the inhabitants of the ranches, he rallied the terrorised people, gave the robbers battle and routed them effectually. He upholds authority against lawlessness, and wants justice to have its course, except when one of his own relatives has done the shooting—I was sorry to learn that in this regard he was probably not beyond rebuke; but his many good deeds to the needy and oppressed, whether Mexican or Indian, should make us lenient toward this failing. The Indians appeal to him of their own accord. Three ruffians once went to the house of a well-to-do Indian, recently deceased, and told his mourning relatives that they had come to see to the division of the property among the heirs, and that they must have good things to eat and plenty to drink while thus occupied; calling upon the relatives to brew plenty of beer and kill an ox. Their orders were promptly obeyed; but in addition they charged the heirs a fee of three oxen, one fanega of corn, and some silver money. This struck the simple and patient Indians as rather excessive, for what would then be left to divide between themselves? So they took their grievance to Don Miguel to be settled. I do not know of any white man in those parts who would have taken the trouble, as he did, to protect the poor Indians' rights against the wily schemers.

The old gentleman was not at home when I arrived at his ranch, but I met one of his sons, who lives at Guachochic.

"I am the postmaster," he said proudly, stepping forward and showing me, at the same time, his credentials, which he evidently carried in his pocket. The mail from the lowlands to the mining towns passes over this place, and the mail-carrier sleeps in this house. In the course of the year he may also bring a few letters to the inhabitants of this part of the country. We soon entered into a conversation about postal matters, which naturally interested me greatly, as I was anxious to communicate as often as possible with the outside world. In spite of the great pride this man took in his office, his notions regarding his duties were rather vague. Being desirous of knowing what was going on among his neighbours, he had no compunction about opening the few letters they got; not that he destroyed them after reading them—he very coolly handed them over opened. The people did not like this, and considered it rather high-handed on his part; but then, what was there for them to do about it?

He said he had heard that I could cure people. When a man is called Doctor, the Mexican peasantry expect him to possess comprehensively all useful knowledge in the world. Looking at me for a moment, this healthy, ruddy-checked man suddenly, without saying a word, took hold of my hand and pressed it against his forehead for a little while; then, all the time, in silence, he carried it backward until my fingers touched a small excrescence on his back. Now was the chance to find out whatever was the matter with him!

On my next visit to his office he received me with a queer, hesitating expression on his face, and suddenly blurted out, "Can you cut out trousers?" For some time he had had a piece of cloth in his house, and he said he would pay me well if I could help him to have it made into trousers. To cure people, mend watches, repair sewing-machines, make applejack, do tailoring, prognosticate the weather—everything is expected from a man who comes from far away. And the good people here are astonished at a confession of ignorance of such matters, and take it rather personally as a lack of good-will toward them. It is the old belief in the medicine man that still survives in the minds of the people, and they therefore look upon doctors with much greater respect than on other persons.

People who live outside of civilisation are thrown upon their own resources in cases of sickness. The daughter of my Mexican guide was confined and the coming of the afterbirth was delayed. I give here, for curiosity's sake, a list of the various remedies applied in the case:

1. The carapace of the armadillo, ground and taken in a little water. This is a Tarahumare remedy, said to be very effective for the trouble mentioned.
2. The skunkwort (the herb of the skunk).
3. The patient to hold her own hair in her mouth for half an hour.
4. The wood of *Palo hediondo,* boiled.
5. *Urina viri,* half a cup. This remedy is also externally used for cuts and bruises.
6. Fresh excrement from a black horse. A small quantity of water is mixed with it, then pressed out through a piece of cloth and taken internally.
7. Perspiration from a black horse. A saddlecloth, after having been used on the horse, is put over the abdomen of the woman.
8. A decoction of the bark of the elm.
9. Pork fat.

After a number of days the patient recovered. Whether it was *propter hoc* or merely *post hoc* is a matter of conjecture.

Guachochic served admirably as a central point from which excursions in various directions could be made, as it lies in the very midst of the Tarahumare country. It is true that the Mexicans have appropriated all the best land round about, and their extensive and fertile ranches lie all around Guachochic. Toward the east, in the direction of the pueblos of Tonachic and Lagunitas, the broad strip of good arable and pasture land as far as Parral is owned exclusively by Mexicans.

But in the immediate neighbourhood of Guachochic toward the west and south lie the ridges and barrancas that run toward Sinaloa, and these are inhabited by pagan Tarahumares. Toward the north the Indians hold undisputed sway over the extensive region of mountains, pine-covered plateaus and well-watered arroyos around the pueblos of Norogachic, Pamachic, and Nararachic, and here are found the most independent Tarahumares that are left, who still defy the whites to take their land away from them. They are more valiant than the rest and not easily intimidated.

The first thing for me to do, after establishing camp near Guachochic, was to secure strong mules and the necessary men to bring up the outfit that had been left behind in Tasajisa, and after a week's absence they returned with all the animals and goods intact.

Guachochic is an uninteresting place at its best, and at this season it seemed especially dreary, on account of the crop failure from which the sierra had been suffering for the last two years. There is never much to get here, but now even corn and beans could hardly be bought. It was therefore quite a treat to have a square meal with Don Miguel, whose wife was a clever cook, and who, considering all circumstances, kept a fair Mexican table. He could also give me some general information about the Indians; not only here, but in many other parts of Mexico, I was often astonished at the ignorance of the Mexican settlers concerning the Indians living at their very doors. Aside from certain conspicuous practices, even intelligent Mexicans know little of the customs, much less of the beliefs, of the aborigines. Regarding the pagans in the barrancas, I could get absolutely no information beyond a general depreciation of them as savages, *bravos* (fierce men) and *broncos* (wild ones). One Mexican whom I interviewed about certain caves thought that the only thing I could be looking for was the silver possibly hidden in them, and therefore told me that there were 12,000,000 pesos buried in a cave near the mining town Guadalupe y Calvo, waiting to be recovered. Thus it was exceedingly difficult in the beginning to determine just which would be the best way to start my investigations, and all that was left for me to do was to find out for myself where my best field was by making extensive excursions into the domains of the Tarahumare in company with an intelligent interpreter. And there was the rub! There are in this part of the sierra a certain number of men who make a living by dealing with the Indians, and who, having been born and bred in the country, speak the difficult language of the Tarahumares as well as the Indians themselves. But as each man operates in a certain district and has a monopoly of the trade with the Indians within its confines, the temptation to cheat the unsophisticated natives out of their little property is naturally very great, and by far the greater number of the dealers succumb to it. As soon, however, as one of them is found out, he loses his influence with the Indians, and to go with a man of that stamp would have been disastrous to my purpose. The duty of the *lenguaraz,* as the interpreter is called, is to smooth the traveller's way among the distrustful Indians with skillful words, to get provisions, make bargains, and explain to the Indians the purpose of his visit. Last but not least, he must obtain all possible information from them. This may mean one day's hard work, and the trying of his patience with many apparently futile questions which are made to get at the Indian's real meaning. Thus it may be understood how one is completely at the mercy of one's lenguaraz, and how important it is for the success of an expedition to find the right man. There is nothing else to do but to try and try again, one after another.

The Indians near Guachochic seemed all to be depressed, poor, and hungry. Most of their animals had died from lack of food, and the few that had not succumbed to starvation had to be sold in exchange for corn. A couple of Indians who were on their way to Parral to buy wheat died of starvation before they reached their destination. The Indians ascribed the hard times to the presence of the whites, who had deprived them of their lands as well as of their liberty. The gods, as they put it, were angry with the whites and refused to send rain.

In the summer, especially in July, a false truffle is found on the highlands of Guachochic, which serves as a food to the Indians. It grows abundantly a couple of inches below the ground, raising the earth a little; and is found also under the limb of a fallen tree. The dogs help in finding this fungus, and they are so fond of it that they go on their own accord to look for it. Pigs grow fat on this food, and coyotes, bears, and grey foxes also eat it. It is considered by Professor W. G. Farlow as a variety of *Melanogaster variegatus*, which he calls *Mexicanus*. It tastes like an over-ripe pear, with a flavour of onion when one first bites into it. The ordinary *Melanogaster variegatus* is eaten in Europe, and esteemed for its pleasant taste.

It was disagreeable to travel during the dry season, on account of the difficulty in getting provisions and finding pastures for the animals. But I made up my mind to start under any circumstances on an excursion toward the north-east, knowing that the fresh grass would come up quickly after a few of the thunder-storms not infrequent at that season. Toward the end of June I selected a few of my strongest animals, and, leaving one of my Mexicans to take care of the remainder, started out with two. As luck would have it, a heavy storm drenched our first camp, and afterward the rain seemed almost to pursue me, much to the delight of the Indians I visited, who had been praying and dancing for rain for a long time. One day I had the imposing spectacle of three thunder-storms coming up from different directions. The one in the south sent flashes of lightning out of its mass of dark clouds over the clear sky; but after all, not much rain resulted.

There was no difficulty in finding one's way from Guachochic to Norogachic. At one place I noticed an Indian trail leading up a ridge apparently consisting of volcanic tuff. To facilitate the ascent, steps, now worn and old, had been cut for a distance of a couple of hundred feet. I made my way among the Indian ranches to Norogachic, the residence of the only priest living at present in the Tarahumare country. The name of the place contains an allusion to a certain rock in the vicinity. There is another priest who pays some attention to the Tarahumares, but he lives in Nonoava, and makes only annual visits to baptise infants or marry their elders who wish for the blessings of the Church.

Chapter 11

A Priest and His Family Make the Wilderness Comfortable for Us—Ancient Remains Similar to Those Seen in Sonora—The Climate of the Sierra—Flora and Fauna—Tarahumare Agriculture—Ceremonies Connected with the Planting of Corn—Deterioration of Domestic Animals—Native Dogs of Mexico.

I called on the padre and found him to be a very social, nice, energetic-looking person with a tinge of the "red man" in his veins.

He complained to me that the Indians were lazy about coming to mass. None of them paid taxes, and there was no way of forcing them. Nearly all of them he considered heathens, and only about a thousand came to the feasts. They arrive in the village on the evening before, and hear vespers. Then they give themselves up to drinking, and on the feast day proper are not in a condition to go to church.

He thinks there are some great men among the Tarahumares, but that, their mental faculties being entirely uncultivated, they are, as it were, rough diamonds. In the padre's opinion not only all the Indians, but also the Mexicans living among them, will soon relapse into paganism altogether.

Living under rough conditions as he does, it is a lucky thing for the padre that his physique is equal to emergencies. Once at the neighbouring village of Tonachic (=where there are pillars) he admonished the people, in a powerful sermon, to mend their ways. As they were coming out of church, a scoundrel who resented the charges attacked him with a stick, but the padre managed to disarm him and gave him such a sound thrashing with his assailant's own weapon that the latter had to keep his bed for a fortnight.

He showed me his stately old adobe church, built in missionary times. The ceiling, however, was infested with myriad of bats, the smell of which was quite sickening, and I was glad to get out again. With him in this uttermost outpost of Christendom lived his aged mother and six sisters, and they treated us with all the hospitality their very limited means permitted. We especially enjoyed their home-made macaroni.

In the family of the good priest lived a little Indian orphan girl, about five years old, as nice and sweet a child as one might wish to see. He was teaching her how to read and write, and she had learned her letters in two months.

The padre, good-natured to officiousness, helped me to get Indians to be photographed. He also would insist upon arranging them before the camera. His efforts, however, were directed more toward achieving artistic triumph than scientific truth, and he wanted, for instance, to decorate the Indians with peacock feathers. He yielded, however, to my suggestion that turkey feathers would be more appropriate, and straightway ordered one of his turkeys to be caught and deprived of some of its tail feathers. The only way in which I could show my appreciation of the disinterested kindness of the family was by photographing them, too. It was a new sensation to them, and the ladies asked to have it done next day, as they wanted to arrange their hair and prepare themselves properly.

After them it was the turn of the presidence of the village "to look pleasant," but at this juncture the camera met with an accident. The ring holding the lens broke and fell out. This happening miles away from civilisation was decidedly annoying. But the sisters proved themselves equal to the occasion. Their father having been a tinsmith, they had picked up the trade and had tools; and the ring was soldered on so well that it lasted until I returned to the United States the following year.

Norogachic is situated in the most populous part of the Tarahumare country, and its presidente exercises authority over the large surrounding district. He told me that his municipality counted 4,168 souls, among them about 300 Mexicans. With the help of a very intelligent Mexican I made a rough calculation of the number of Indians belonging to Tonachic and Guachochic, next neighbours of Norogachic, and estimated in the former 350, and in the latter 250 families. Counting each family as consisting of eight members, this would give us a population of 4,800. Thus the most populous part of the Tarahumare country, including the three municipalities of Norgachic, Tonachic, and Guachochic, would contain a population of about 8,500 Indians.

As the presidente of Norogachic is an honourable man and speaks the native language, he exercised great influence over them, and on one occasion, when they had gathered in large numbers and threatened to avenge some abuse, he was able to avert disaster. Nature had endowed him with the doubtful blessing of bloodshot eyes, a feature generally attributed to powerful sorcerers, and this was perhaps more a point in his favour than otherwise with the Indians.

One day he took us to the top of a hill where there were some stones set in circles, about one foot above and half a foot under the ground. They reminded us of similar stone arrangements we had come upon in Sonora, but these were larger and more primitive. Altogether there were nine circles, varying in size from nine to thirteen feet in diameter. One, however, measured only five feet across, and the stones forming it were fully two feet above the ground. Close by was another similar small circle, and some little distance off still another. On a small mesa, I found a flint arrow-point. There were also some potsherds there, but of the same kind as those used by the people to-day.

The natives rightly counted only three seasons—the dry, the rainy, and the winter. The first lasts from March till June, and is very warm and windy. Throughout July and August one can generally count on thunder-storms and heavy rains, while the mornings are bright. The rains then rarely extend over a large territory, but are confined to local showers, a circumstance very annoying to the agricultural inhabitants, who often see dark clouds rolling up, apparently full of moisture, yet resulting in nothing but gusts of wind. A ridge may change the course of the clouds. Sometimes one valley may be flooded with rain, while not far away the heat is drying up everything. During September and October more constant rains occur, and may last more or less for a week at a time.

In the beginning of the wet season (July and August) the rains come from the south-west, but later on north-eastern winds bring rain. In winter there are constant winds from the south-east to the north, somewhat trying until one gets used to them. Snow is by no means unknown, and Indians have been known to freeze to death when caught out intoxicated.

The climate in the sierra, although not so pleasant on account of the constant winds, is extremely salubrious, the heat never exceeding 97° F., while the nights are deliciously cool. Lung diseases are here unknown. When I asked an old American doctor in Guadalupe y Calvo about his experience in regard to the health of the people, he said, "Well, here in the mountains they are distressingly healthy. Despite a complete defiance of every sanitary arrangement, with the graveyards, the sewers, and a tannery at the river's edge, no diseases originate here. When cholera reached the mountains some years ago, nobody died from it. The people simply took a bath in Mexican fashion, and recovered." Down in the barrancas, however, where the heat often becomes excessive, the climate is far from healthy, and I have seen even Indians ill with fever and ague, contracted generally during the rainy season.

Between these two extremes, on the slopes of the sierra, toward the warm country, at an elevation of 5,000 feet, I found the most delightful climate I ever knew. It was like eternal spring, the air pure and the temperature remarkably even. There is a story of a Mexican woman, who, settling in this part of the country, broke her thermometer because the mercury never moved and therefore she concluded that it was out of order. The pleasantness of the climate struck me particularly on one occasion, after a prolonged stay in this invigorating though windy climate of the sierra. I had caught a cold the night before, and was not feeling very well as I dozed on the back of my mule while it worked its way down the mountain-side, but the sleep and the delightful balmy air made me soon feel well again. At times a mild zephyr played around us, but invariably died out about sunset. The night was delightfully calm, toward morning turning slightly cooler, and there was nothing to disturb my sleep under a big fig-tree but the bits of figs that were thrown down by the multitudes of bats in its branches. They were gorging themselves on the fruit, just as we had done the afternoon before.

Journeying on the pine-clad highlands, the traveller finds nothing to remind him that he is in the southern latitudes, except an occasional glimpse of an agave between rocks and the fantastic cacti, which, although so characteristic of Mexican vegetation, are comparatively scarce in the high sierra. The nopal cactus, whose juicy fruit, called tuna, and flat leaf-like joints are an important article of food among the Indians, is found here and there, and is often planted near the dwellings of the natives. There are also a few species of *Echinocactus* and *Mammilaria,* but on the whole the cacti form no conspicuous feature in the higher altitudes of the sierra.

Along the streamlets which may be found in the numerous small valleys we met with the slender ash trees, beside alders, shrubs, *Euonymus* with brilliant red capsules, willows, etc. Conspicuous in the landscape was still the madroña, with its pretty, strawberry-like, edible berries.

Flowers on the whole are not abundant in the sierra. The modest yellow *Mimulus* along the water-courses is the first tom come and the last to go. Various forms of columbine *(Aquilegia)* and meadow rue *(Thalictrum)* should also be remembered. In August and September I have seen the sloping hills of the sierra north-west of the pueblo of Panalachic (Banalachic; banalá=face, i.e., the outline of a prominent rock near by), covered with large crimson flowers, and also certain yellow ones, called *baguis,* making the country appear like a garden. I noticed in the same locality two kinds of lovely lilies, one yellow and one containing a single large red flower. The Tarahumare have names for all these plants.

Before all, however, should be mentioned the carmine-red *Amaryllis.* Like the crocus and the snowdrops of northern climates it appears before the grass is green. It is a perfect treat to the eye to meet now and then in this dry and sandy country, and at such a chilly elevation, this exquisitely beautiful flower, which is here appreciated only by the humming-birds. Edible plants, species of *Mentha, Chenopodium, Cirsium,* for instance, and the common water-cress, are, at a certain time of the year, numerous; but fruits and berries are rare, blackberries being the most common ones.

Animal life is not particularly plentiful in the sierra. Still, deer, bears, and mountain lions are fairly common, and there are many kinds of squirrels and rats. The jaguar *(felis onza)* is found now and then on the summits of the barrancas. Eagles, hawks, turkeys, blackbirds, and crows are the most noticeable birds. The turkey is called by the Tarahumare, tshīví; by the Mexicans of the sierra of Chihuahua, *guajolote;* while farther south he is designated *cocono.* Now and then the brilliant green trogon is met with.

There are many species of woodpecker, all familiar to and named by the Tarahumares. The giant woodpecker is seen in the more remote parts, but it is on the point of being exterminated, because the Tarahumares consider his one or two young such a delicacy that they do not hesitate to cut down even large trees to get at the nests. The Mexicans shoot them because their plumage is thought to be beneficial to health. It is held close to the ears and the head in order to impart its supposed magnetism and keep out the maleficent effects of the wind. In the pairing season these birds keep up a chattering noise, which to my ears was far from disagreeable, but very irritating to the Mexican whom I employed. He used to shoot the birds because they annoyed him.

Corn is the most important agricultural product of the Tarahumares. The average crop of a family may be estimated at six or twelve fanegas. One exceptionally rich Tarahumare, now dead, is said to have raised as much as four hundred fanegas a year, but this was a fact unique in the history of the tribe. The people also raise beans, squashes, chile, and tobacco, all on an exceedingly small scale. On the highlands, the primitive plough already described is still used sometimes, though it is rapidly being superseded by ploughs of Mexican pattern. In the arroyos and barrancas, where the condition of the land makes ploughing impossible, the Indians use the ancient mode of agriculture, still in vogue among remote natives of Mexico and called *coamillar.* They cut down the trees, clear a piece of land from brushwood, and leave it in this condition until just before the wet season set sin. Then they burn the wood, which by that time is well dried up, and plant the corn in the ashes. They simply make a hole in the earth with a stick, drop a few grains of corn into it, and close it up with the foot. Of the usual number of grains I am not aware. The Tepehuanes use four. Their hoes are generally bought from the Mexicans or else home-made, the natural knotted growths of tree limbs being utilised. Women never assist in ploughing, though they may be seen helping in the fields with the weeding and hoeing, and even with the harvesting.

In the sierra a piece of land may yield good crops for three years in succession without manure, but in the broad mountain valleys and on the mesas a family can use the same field year after year for twenty or thirty seasons. On the other hand, down in the barrancas, a field cannot be used more than two years in succession, because the corn-plants in that time are already suffocated with weeds. The planting is done from the middle of April to the first week in July, and the harvest begins about the first week in October and lasts until the beginning of December.

Communal principles prevail in clearing the fields, in ploughing—each furrow in a field is ploughed by a different man—in corn planting, in hoeing, weeding, harvesting, gathering wood for feasts, in fishing and in hunting.

If a man wants to have his field attended to, the first thing he has to do is to prepare a good quantity of the national stimulant, a kind of beer called tesvino. The more of this he has, the larger the piece of land he can cultivate, for the only payment his helpers expect and receive is tesvino.

The master of the house and his sons always do first one day's work alone, before their friends and neighbours come to help them. Then they begin in earnest to clear the field of stones, carrying them in their arms or blankets, and cut down the brushwood. Tesvino is brought out into the field, and iskiate, and the men, all very much under the influence of the liquor, work with the animation of a heap of disturbed ants.

When the work of hoeing and weeding is finished, the workers seize the master of the field, and, tying his arms crosswise behind him, load all the implements, that is to say, the hoes, upon his back, fastening them with ropes. Then they form two single columns, the landlord in the middle between them, and all facing the house. Thus they start homeward. Simultaneously the two men at the heads of the columns begin to run rapidly forward some thirty yards, cross each other, then turn back, run along the two columns, cross each other again at the rear and take their places each at the end of his row. As they pass each other ahead and in the rear of the columns they beat their mouths with the hollow of their hands and yell. As soon as they reach their places at the foot, the next pair in front of the columns starts off, running in the same way, and thus pair after pair performs the tour, the procession all the time advancing toward the house.

A short distance in front of it they come to a halt, and are met by two young men who carry red handkerchiefs tied to sticks like flags. The father of the family, still tied up and loaded with the hoes, steps forward alone and kneels down in front of his house-door. The flagbearers wave their banners over him, and the women of the household come out and kneel on their left knees, first toward the east, and after a little while toward each of the other cardinal points, west, south, and north.

In conclusion the flags are waved in front of the house. The father then rises and the people untie him, whereupon he first salutes the women with the usual greeting, "Kwīra!" or "Kwirevá!" Now they all go into the house, and the man makes a short speech thanking them all for the assistance they have given him, for how could he have gotten through his work without them? They have provided him with a year's life (that is, with the wherewithal to sustain it), and now he is going to give them tesvino. He gives a drinking-gourd full to each one in the assembly, and assembly, and appoints one man among them to distribute more to all.

The same ceremony is performed after the ploughing and after the harvesting. On the first occasion the tied man may be made to carry the yoke of the oxen, on the second he does not carry anything.

The southern Tarahumares, as well as the northern Tepehuanes, at harvest time, tie together some ears of corn by the husks, two and two. The ears are selected from plants which have at least three or four ears, and after a while tesvino is made from them. At the harvesting feast, the stalks of these plants, and over them the people dance kuvála.

The Tarahumare takes good care of his domestic animals and never kills one of them, unless it be for a sacrifice. Sheep and goats are kept at night in enclosures or caves. The shepherd follows his flock wherever the animals choose to find their food, and there are not better herdsmen than the Tarahumares, who wisely trust to the natural instinct of the beasts. They do not pride themselves on breeds. It is astonishing to notice the number of rams with two pairs of horn among the tribe. In every flock two or three specimens may be observed, one pair bending forward the other to the side. I have seen some with three pairs of horns. Near Nonoava, where the Indians are much Mexicanised, they make butter and cheese, using the rennets from the cow, sheep, and deer, but they do not drink milk, saying that it makes them stupid, and they are watchful to prevent their children from drinking it. Dogs are not much liked except for hunting. A great number of them hang around the houses, but they have to make their own living as best they can. They are of the same mongrel class found everywhere among the Indians of to-day. They are generally of a brownish color and not large, but some of them are yellow and with ears erect.

The so-called dogs of Chihuahua, which command quite a price among dog-fanciers, are found only in the capital of the state. They are small pet dogs and very timid, with large ears and prominent eyes. I understand that the yellowish-brown are considered the purest breed, but they are found in many different colors, from snow-white and black-and-white to dark-brown. They are said to have a small cavity on the top of the head, though according to some authorities this is not an unfailing mark of the breed, which seems to be indigenous. The illiterate Mexican, in his tendency to connect everything good with Montezuma, thinks that the pure dogs of Chihuahua are descendants of those which were left behind by that regent near Casas Grandes at the time when he started south, which afterward became wild and degenerated into the prairie-dogs of to-day.

Another dog indigenous to Mexico is the hairless dog, also a pet, found throughout the republic among the Mexicans. It is credited with possessing curative properties, for which reason people keep them in their beds with them at night.

Chapter 12

The Tarahumares Still Afraid of Me—Don Andres Madrid to the Rescue—Mexican Robbers Among the Tarahumares—Mode of Burial in Ancient Caves—Visit to Nonoava—The Indians Change Their Minds About Me, and Regard Me as a Rain-god—What the Tarahumares Eat—A Pretty Church in the Wilderness—I Find at Last a Reliable Interpreter and Proceed to Live À L'indienne.

As I travelled along I found the natives unobliging and afraid of me. One man who had hid himself, but was after a while forced to reappear, bluntly asked, "Are you not the man who kills the fat girls and the children?" At another time I was taken for Pedro Chaparro, the famous robber, who had notoriously deceived the Indians. The guide took only a half-hearted interest in me, as he feared that by being seen with me he was ruining his trade with the natives, who were especially suspicious about my writing in my note-book, taking it as a proof of my design to take their land away from them. Still, I accomplished a good deal and made interesting observations, though the difficulties under which I had to labour were quite exasperating.

It was a positive relief, when in the beginning of August, six weeks after my start from Guachochic, I arrived at Guajochic (guajo = *sancudo,* a small mosquito), one of the stations where the bullion trains stop on their travels between Batopilas and Carichic. The man then in charge of this rather lonely looking place, Andres Madrid, turned out be very interesting. Born of Tarahumare parents, in the town of Carichic, he had received quite a liberal Mexican education and was virtually a Mexican, though in hearty sympathy with his native tribe. His grandfather had been a noted shaman, or medicine man, whom Don Andres, as a boy, had accompanied on his travels. He was intelligent, lively and imaginative, of a strong humourous vein, and very entertaining. Generous in giving information about the Indians, and speaking the native language, he would have made an ideal interpreter, except for the fact that he grew tired too easily. Only by piecemeal and when having an abundance of time could an ethnologist expect to take advantage of his accomplishments. As he was honest, and helpful to the Indians, and besides was a representative of the Mexican authorities, the Indians had unlimited respect, nay, adoration, for him.

Knowing all that happens in the sierra, he had already heard of me some time ago, and laughed at the cannibalistic propensities attributed to me. He immediately sent a messenger to el capitan at Nararachic, to advise him of my arrival, and to request him to tell the Indians to present themselves to be photographed by a man who came from Porfirio Diaz, a name to conjure with in Mexico, who wanted to know all about the Tarahumares. Nararachic is an insignificant pueblo, to which the Indians of this locality belong. The name means "where one was weeping."

Being taken under the wing of Don Andres benefitted me in many ways. When the Indians from the hills all around could see my white tent close by his little home, they understood that I could not be so bad, or else the good Don Andres would not have anything to do with me.

The Indians in the vicinity had recently gone through the sensation of fighting with four real robbers, who had several times succeeded in plundering store-houses while the owners were off at some feast. At last the Indians had caught them. The thieves travelled on foot, but had a pack-horse which carried all the blankets and handkerchiefs stolen, the total value of which ran up to $112. Sixty-five Tarahumares had banded together in the course of four or five hours, and obliged the robbers to take refuge in a cave, from which they defended themselves with rifles for several hours. The Tarahumare first threw stones at them, as they did not want to waste their arrows. Finally, Don Andres, who had been sent for, arrived at the place, and induced the robbers to surrender; but only with difficulty could he prevent the Tarahumares from attacking them. "What does it matter," they said, "if one or two of us are killed?" Cowards as the Tarahumares are when few in number, they do not know fear when many of them are together. They are harmless when not interfered with, but neither forget nor forgive an injury. On several occasions they have killed white men who abused their hospitality, and they even threatened once, when exasperated by abuses, to exterminate all the whites in some sections of their domain.

The robbers were taken by an escort of Indians to the little town of Carichic, and from there sent to Cusihuiriachic ("where upright pole is") to be tried. This place is about a hundred miles from Nararachic, and as the Indians during the next weeks were called to be present at the trial as witnesses, it annoyed them not a little. They were sorry they had not killed the evil-doers; and it would even have been better, they said, to have let them go on stealing.

In the fight the gobernador had got a bullet through his lung. I saw him a fortnight afterward, smoking a cigarette and on the way to recovery, and after some days, he, too, walked to Cusihuiriachic. A few months later the robbers managed to dig themselves out of the prison.

On an excursion of about ten miles through the picturesque Arroyo de las Iglesias, I passed seventeen caves, of which only one was at present inhabited. All of them, however, had been utilised as dwellings before the construction of the road to Batopilas had driven the Indians off.

I saw also a few ancient cave-dwellings. Of considerable interest were some burial-caves near Nararachic, especially one called Narajerachic (= where the dead are dancing). A Mexican had been for six years engaged there in digging out saltpetre, with which he made powder, and the cave was much spoiled for research when I visited it. But I was able to take away some thirty well-preserved skulls and a few complete skeletons, the bodies having dried up in the saltpetre. Some clothing with feathers woven in, and some bits of obsidian and of blue thread were found, but no weapons or utensils. According to the miner, who appeared to be trustworthy, he had excavated more than a hundred corpses. They were generally found two and a half feet below the surface, and sometimes there were others underneath these. With many of them he found ear ornaments made of shells, such as the Tarahumares of to-day use, besides some textile made of plant fibre, and a jar with beans.

A few months later at Aboreachic (Tarahumare: Aoreachic = where there is mountain cedar) I examined a burial-cave in which the dead were interred in a different manner from that described before. The cave is somewhat difficult of access. The ascent of 300 feet has to be made over a track at some places so steep that holes have been cut for the feet, to enable a person to climb up. On reaching the top I found a spacious cave, which had been used as a kind of cemetery, but unfortunately the peculiarity of the cave had attracted treasure-seekers, whose destructive work was everywhere to be seen. Still I could see that the corpses had been placed each by itself in a grave in the floor of the cave. The graves were oblong or circular basins lined with a coating of grass and mud and about three feet deep. Apparently no earth had been placed immediately over the body, only boards all around it laid lengthwise in a kind of box. The bodies were bent up and laid on their sides. Over the top boards was spread a layer of pine bark about an inch thick, which in turn was covered with earth and rubbish three inches deep, and this was overlaid with the coating of grass and mud so as to form a solid disk four or five inches thick. The edge of the basin was slightly raised, thus making the disk a little higher than the level of the floor. I secured four skulls from here, besides a piece of excellently woven cloth of plant fibre, another piece interwoven with turkey feathers, and a fragment of a wooden needle.

Don Andres told me that he had observed similar modes of burial in the neighbourhood of Nararachic. It may be worth mentioning that the miner who excavated in the burial-cave near Nararachic mentioned above, told me of having met with somewhat similar structures in his cave; the material was the same, but they were of different sizes, not larger than two feet, and he found them empty.

The ancient modes of burial that I have come upon in the Tarahumare country are either like those in Nararachic or in Aboreachic. There scarcely seems any doubt that the bodies buried here were Tarahumares. The Indians of today consider the dead in the ancient burial-caves their brethren, and call them Anayáuli, the ancients.

From Guajochic I went to Nonoava (in Tarahumare: Nona, nõnó = father), although this town is outside of the Tarahumare country proper. The natives here, as may be expected, are pretty well Mexicanised, and losing their customs, religion, and language. The Apache raids were well remembered here, as they were in Carichic, Cusarare, and Bocoyna.

I came upon a Mexican here who had married a Tarahumare woman. His predilection for her tribe was also attested by his dress, which was exactly like that worn by the natives. He had a dark, almost swarthy complexion, but otherwise he did not resemble an Indian. His big stomach and short arms and legs betrayed his real race, and contrasted strangely with the slender limbs and graceful movements of the Tarahumares.

Near Nonoava I photographed a magnificent fig-tree of the kind called *beyota,* the fruit of which is appreciated even by the Mexicans. It was 116 feet across, and the leaves, as in other trees of the species, were very small. There are larger trees of this kind to be found, but they are rare. In the wet season, when the figs are ripe, the Tarahumares have a habit of singing under the trees while gathering the fruit.

I noticed some beautiful mezquites in the bed of a creek, the bottom of which was clayish. Although the season for it was late, Indians were gathering the fruit. The proper season is before the rain sets in. The Indians throw the seeds away, but boil the fruit, grinding it between stones and mixing it with water. This drink is also used through Sonora and Chihuahua by the Mexicans.

On my return I again spent some time in Guajochic. The Indians came to visit me every day, and following my rule of giving to every visitor something to eat, I was making satisfactory progress in cultivating their friendship. Some of them after eating from my plates and cups, went to the river to rinse their mouths and wash their hands carefully, to get rid of any evil that might lurk in the white man's implements. To be generous is the first step toward gaining the confidence of both the Indians and the Mexicans, and a gift of food is more eloquent than a long speech. The Indian, however, before he knows you, always wants to see you eat first.

I interviewed many of the shamans, and began to gain some little knowledge of their songs, which helped to bring me nearer to them. Shortly after my first arrival here it happened that rain fell, and precipitations continued quite frequently during my stay. The Indians, who are intensely interested in rain, to obtain which they make so many exertions and sacrifices, evidently began to connect my presence with it. Before my departure they confided to Don Andres that "It was not good that that man went away; it might happen that he carried the rain with him." They even seemed to delight now in posing before my mysterious camera, which they imagined to be a powerful rain-maker. I heard no more excuses for not wanting to be photographed. They no longer told me that it would cause their death, and that their god would be angry with them; nor was there any more of that unwillingness expressed by one Indian who told me that, inasmuch as he did not owe me anything, he did not want to be photographed. Thus, almost without knowing it, I established friendly relations with the people.

However, it must not be thought that all my troubles were ended yet. The Indians are very clannish, and, although my damaged prestige was now almost restored, and, no doubt, favourable rumours heralded me wherever I went, still the good-will of each district had in a way to be won. Many months later, when I found myself among the pagans farther south, I was interpellated quite persistently on the subject of the skulls in Yoquibo. They wanted to know why I had dug them up. My Mexican interpreter, whom they took to task on the subject, advanced an explanation, which was no doubt strictly in accordance with his best knowledge and belief. He declared that my object had been to find out whether those people had been properly baptised—a reason which apparently perfectly satisfied the Indians.

I travelled in a southeasterly direction, making my way back to Guachochic, over the highlands of Humarisa (húmashi = to run). This locality is of considerable elevation, with the Indian ranches lying about here and there on strips of level land, which run in among the rocky hills like *fjords.* Bears are quite common here, and the Indians have difficulty in guarding their fields against them. They are not even to be frightened by stones, and at night they will eat corn until they have enough, and then walk away.

The time of the year in which it is most difficult for the Indians to subsist had passed, and the copious rains of the past months had developed ears of corn. Rarely or never do the Indians plant corn enough to last them all the year round, and they have, therefore, during the summer to depend for support mainly on herbs, roots, fruits, etc. The leaves and flowers of the ash-tree are cooked and eaten, and the flowers of the pine-tree. They never suffer from hunger when living near a river, where they can fish, but in the highlands they have been known to die of starvation.

These natives are fonder of corn than of any other food, and when working for the whites would leave without a word if no more corn or flour were forthcoming. They like, too, to have meat most every day, though they cannot always get it. They rarely, if ever, kill any of their domestic animals for food, as, according to their views, man is only the manager for the gods to whom these creatures really belong, and cows, sheep, and the like can be killed only as sacrifices and eaten at the feasts. But any kind of animal in the forest and field, in the air and the water, is acceptable. I once asked a strong and healthy-looking Indian how he managed to keep in such good condition, when food was so scarce, and he said that he ate meat. "What kind of meat?" I asked, and he replied, "Mice, gophers, and small birds." Their favourite meat, however, is deer, mice, and skunks.

Chunks of meat are simply laid upon the coals to roast, or turned before the fire on a wooden spit, the ends of which rest on stones. This, by the way, is the universal method of cooking meat in Mexico. These Indians often eat their meat almost raw, nor have they any repugnance to blood, but boil and eat it. Fish and frogs are boiled by being placed between two thin sticks tied together at the ends to do duty as a gridiron.

The flowers of the maize are dried in the sun, ground and mixed with water; if not required for immediate consumption they are put in jars and kept for the winter. Many herbs are very palatable, as, for instance, the makvásari (of the *Cruciferae*), which is also kept for winter use after having been properly dried. In the autumn the Indians sometimes eat potatoes, which, when cultivated at all, are planted between the corn, but grow no larger than pigeon eggs. The people eat three kinds of fungi, and they have an extensive knowledge of the poisonous ones. Salt and chile are used as relishes.

A peculiar delicacy is ārí, the secretion of a scale insect, *Carteria mexicana.* In the months of July and August it is gathered from the branches of certain trees in the barrancas, rolled by hand into thick brown sticks, and thus preserved for the winter. A small portion is boiled in water and eaten as a sauce with the corn porridge. Its taste is sweetish acid, not particularly pleasant to the palate, but very refreshing in effect, and it is said to be efficacious in allaying fever. The Indians prize it highly, and the Mexicans also buy it.

Just a few miles before reaching Guachochic, one passes the pueblo of Tonachic, from whence the Indians have been more or less driven off by the whites. In missionary times the village appears to have been of some importance, to judge from the church, which is quite pretty, considering its location in the middle of the sierra. In the sacristy I saw lying about three empty cases, but the silver crucifixes and chalices they once contained had been carried off by Mexican thieves. The man in charge of the building showed me three immense drawers full of gold- and silver-embroidered silken robes of exquisite fineness and great variety. There were at least several dozens of them.

The altar-piece was arranged and painted very tastefully in red and gold. Several oil paintings were hanging in the church, but so darkened by the hand of time that it was impossible to make out whether they were of any artistic merit. Wonderful men those early missionaries, who brought such valuables into this wilderness, over hundreds and thousands of miles, on the backs of mules and Indians. It was rather anomalous to see the poor, naked Indians outside the door, for whose benefit all this had been done. A woman was sweeping away the dirt from the swarms of bats that nested in the ceiling.

The richest and most prominent man in the village enjoyed the reputation of being a great ladron. When I called on him I found him in bed suffering from a toothache. He had his head wrapped up and was completely unnerved, and many people came to sympathise with him in his affliction. When I told him that I liked the Tarahumares, he answered, "Well, take them with you, every one of them." All he cared for was their land, and he had already acquired a considerable portion of it. His wife was the only person in the village who knew how to recite the prayers in the church. This made the husband feel proud of her, and he evidently considered her piety great enough to suffice for the family.

On my return to Guachochic I discharged the Mexicans who had been with me since my travels through Sonora; they were here of little use to me, as they did not know the country. I also disposed of the greater number of my mules, keeping only about a half a dozen.

With the kind permission of Don Miguel I installed most of my baggage in one of his houses, and considered his ranch a kind of headquarters from which I made several long excursions in various directions. Thanks to my pack and riding mules I could take along, as barter, corn, glass beads, tobacco, and cotton cloth, and bring back collections made on the road. I was accompanied by a couple of Mexicans from this part of the country and some Indians who acted as carriers. Of course, whenever I went down into the barrancas, I had to leave my mules and cargo in some safe place on the highlands and take along only the most necessary stores as we proceeded on foot. On such trips I had to depend entirely on the natives; they secured the food, and selected the cave or rock shelter, or the tree under which we slept.

Our bill of fare was made up mainly of corn and beans, with an occasional sheep or goat, and some herbs and roots as relishes. Corn was prepared in the styles known to the Indians, either as corn cakes (tortillas) or, more often, by simply toasting the grains on a piece of crockery over the fire. The dish is easy enough to prepare and does not taste at all bad, but it is hard work for one's teeth to make a meal of it, as the kernels assume the consistency of little pebbles, and many months of such a diet lengthens your dentist's bill at about the same ratio as that in which it shortens your molars. You will ask why I did not carry provisions along with me. Simply because preserved food is, as a rule, heavy to carry, to say nothing of its being next to impossible to secure more when the supply is exhausted. Some chocolate and condensed milk which I ordered from Chihuahua did not reach me until several months after the date of the order. Besides, the Indians are not complaisant carriers, least of all in this exceedingly rough country.

For over a year I thus continued to travel around among the Tarahumares, visiting them on their ranches and in their caves, on the highlands and in the barrancas. There are few valleys into which I did not go in this central part of the Tarahumare country, that is, from the Barranca de Batopilas and Carichic in the north toward the regions of the mining place Guadalupe y Calvo in the south. By and by I also found a suitable lenguaraz, Don Nabor, who lived a day's journey from Guachochic. He was a tall, lank, healthy-looking fellow, some fifty years old, very poor and blessed with a large family of sons and daughters, some of them full grown. All his life he had been intimate with the Indians; he spoke their language as well as he did Spanish, and really liked the Tarahumares better than his fellow Mexicans. Being a great hunter but a poor shot he brought home but little game, and made his living chiefly by trading with the Indians. He was the picture of good-nature, laughing with the Indians at their jokes, and weeping with them at their sorrows. Among them he passed as a wit, and being very honest was a general favourite. He never took anything without asking, but was not backward about that. Of his teeth he had hardly any but two of his upper incisors left, which was rather hard for a man of his ravenous appetite; but he utilised them with such squirrel-like dexterity as almost to keep pace with others.

Chapter 13

The Tarahumares Physique—Bodily Movements—Not as Sensitive to pain as White Men—Their Phenomenal Endurance—Health—Honesty—Dexterity and Ingenuity—Good Observers of the Celestial Bodies and Weather-forecasters—Hunting and Shooting—Home Industries—Tesvino, the Great National Drink of the Tribe—Other Alcoholic Drinks.

The Tarahumare of to-day is of medium size and more muscular than his North American cousin, but his cheek-bones are equally prominent. His colour is light chocolate-brown. I was rather surprised often to find the faces of the people living in the warm barrancas lighter in colour than the rest of their bodies. The darkest complexions, strange to say, I encountered on the highlands near Guachochic. In the higher altitudes the people also develop higher statures and are more muscular than in the lower portions of the country.

Both men and women wear long, flowing, straight black hair, which in rare cases is a little wavy. When a woman marries, I am told, she cuts her hair once. When the hair is cut because it has grown too long and troublesome, they place it under a stone or hang it in a tree. A shaman once cut his hair short to get new thoughts with the new hair, and while it was growing he kept his head tied up in a piece of cotton cloth to keep his thoughts from escaping. When the people are very old, the hair turns gray; but they never grow bald. Beards are rare, and if they appear the Indians pull them out. Their devil is always represented with a beard, and they call the Mexicans derisively shabótshi, "the bearded ones." Much as they enjoy tobacco, an Indian would not accept some from me, because he feared that coming from a white man it would cause a beard to grow on his face.

There are more women in the tribe than men. They are smaller, but generally just as strong as the other sex, and when angered, for instance by jealousy, the wife may be able to beat her husband. Hands and feet are small. Many of the women have surprisingly small and well-shaped bones, while the men are more powerfully built. The corner teeth differ from the front teeth in that they are thicker, and, in spite of exceptionally fine teeth, tooth-ache is not unknown in the tribe. Men, even those who are well nourished, are never stout. The women are more inclined to corpulency.

Eight people with hair-lip, seven hunchbacks, six men and four women with six toes to their feet, and one or two cases of squint-eyes came under my notice. One boy had a club-foot with toes turned inside, and I saw one man who had only stumps of arms with two or three finger-marks on each. I have observed one case of insanity among these Indians.

Pediculi (lice) from the head and clothing of the Tarahumare are blackish in colour, but the claw is not different from that of the white men's parasites.

When at ease, the Tarahumare stands on both legs, without stiffness. In micturition he stands, while the Tepehuane sits down. The body is well balanced. The gait is energetic. He swings his arms and plants his foot firmly, with the toes generally in, gliding along smoothly with quick steps and without swaying to and fro, the body bent slightly forward. The palm of the hand is turned to the rear. Tarahumares climb trees by embracing the tree as we do; but the ascent is made in jumps, the legs accordingly not embracing the tree as much as is the case with us. In swimming they throw their arms ahead from one side to another. They point with the open hand or by protruding the lips and raising the head at the same time in the desired direction. Like the Mexicans they beckon with their hands by making downward movements with their fingers.

To the casual observer the native appears dull and heavy, so much so that at first it would seem hopeless to get any intelligent information out of him; but on better acquaintance it will be found that their faces, like those of Mexican Indians in general, have more variety of feature and expression than those of the whites. At the same time it is true that the individual does not show his emotion very perceptibly in his face. One has to look into his eyes for an expression of what passes in his mind, as his face is not mobile; nor does he betray his feelings by involuntary actions. If he blushes, as he sometimes does, the colour extends down the neck and is visible in spite of his dusky skin. Laughter is never immoderate enough to bring tears to the eyes. The head is nodded vertically in affirmation and shaken laterally in negation only by the civilised Tarahumares.

There is a slight though undefinable odour about the Tarahumare. He is not aware of it; yet he will tell you that the Mexican smells like a pig, and the American like coffee, both offensive odours to Tarahumares. They all love to feel warm, and may often be seen lying in the sun on their backs or stomachs. Heat never seems to trouble them. Young babies sleep on their mothers' back without any covering on their heads to protect them from the fierce rays of the summer sun. On the other hand, the Tarahumare endures cold unflinchingly. On an icy winter morning, when there are six inches of snow on the ground, many a man may be seen with nothing on but his blanket fastened around his waist, pursuing rabbits.

While their senses are keen, I do not consider them superior to those of any well-endowed white man. To test eyesight, Sir Francis Galton directs us to cut out a square piece of paper one and a half inches a side, paste it on a larger piece of black paper, and mark how far a person can distinguish whether the square is held straight or diagonally. None of the Indians could distinguish the different positions until they were within seven hundred and ten feet. On another occasion, however, when I tested six individuals, four men could tell the position of the square at a distance of nine hundred and five feet. One of these had syphilis. They certainly do not feel pain in the same degree as we do. On this point any collector of hair could have reason to satisfy himself. Scientists consider the hair a particularly distinguishing feature among the races of men, not only in regard to its colour, but also as to its texture. In fact, the human race is by some classified according to the character of the hair of the head. Compared under the microscope a section of the hair of a Chinaman or an American Indian is found to be circular, that of a European oval in shape. As a rule, the flatter the hair the more readily it curls, the perfectly cylindrical hair hanging down stiff and straight. A section of the straight hair of a Japanese, for instance, forms a perfect circle. So much importance being attached to the structure of the hair, I made a collection from different individuals. They were willing enough to let me have all the samples I wanted for a material consideration, of course, but the indifferent manner in which they pulled the hair from their heads, just as we should tear out hairs from the tail of a horse, convinced me that inferior races feel pain to a less extent than civilised man. I once pulled six hairs at a time from the head of a sleeping child without disturbing it at all; I asked for more, and when twenty-three hairs were pulled out in one stroke, the child only scratched its head a little and slept on.

They are not so powerful at lifting as they are in carrying burdens. Out of twelve natives, ten of whom were eighteen and twenty years old, while two owned to fifty years, five lifted a burden weighing 226²/₅ pounds (102 kilograms). I was able to lift this myself. The same five lifted 288³/₅ pounds (130 kilograms), as also did two strong Mexicans present, aged respectively eighteen and thirty years. In order to test their carrying capacity, I had them walk for a distance of 500 feet on a pretty even track. One very poor and starved-looking Tarahumare carried 226²/₅ pounds (102 kilograms) on his back, though tottering along with some difficulty; two others carried it with ease, and might have taken it farther. All three were young men.

Their endurance is truly phenomenal. A strong young man carried a burden of over 100 pounds from Carichic to Batopilas, a distance of about 110 miles, in seventy hours. While travelling with such burdens they eat nothing but pinole, a little at frequent intervals.

The wonderful health these people enjoy is really their most attractive trait. They are healthy and look it. It could hardly be otherwise in this delightful mountain air, laden with the invigorating odour of the pines combined with the electrifying effect of being close to nature's heart. In the highlands, where the people live longer than in the barrancas, it is not infrequent to meet persons who are at least a hundred years old. Long life is what they all pray for.

They suffer sometimes from rheumatism, but the most common disease is pleurisy *(dolor de costado),* which generally proves fatal. Syphilis rages in some parts of the country. There was at the time of my visit to Pino Gordo hardly a native there who had not, at one time or another, been afflicted with it; but the victims get quickly over it without special treatment, sometimes within a year. Children of syphilitic parents show the symptoms soon after birth. Small-pox, too, plays havoc among the population. I have seen some people suffering with cataract in the eyes, and some foot-runners complained that their sight sometimes became impaired during or after a race. The Tarahumares have not any cases of tape-worm, although their sheep have it; probably the large quantities of tesvino drunk during the winter may have something to do with this.

Medicine takes remarkably strong hold of the Indians. One man suffered for two weeks from fever and ague, lost his appetite, and seemed a general wreck; but after a two-grain quinine pill became at once himself again, and a few days later was able to take a message for me to a place forty miles off and return the same day.

The natives do not bathe except in the wet season. When they go to feasts, they wash their hands and faces, and the women comb their hair. Sometimes they may wash their feet, but more frequently they clean their heads. In fact, the regular way of taking a bath is to wash the head. For this purpose they use an agave called sõké. Occasionally they use a white earth from Cusarare, called *javoncillo;* it is very soft and it is also used as white colour in decorating pottery. When the men go into deep water to bathe they smear fat all over their bodies to guard against all kinds of bad animals in the water; women do not usually take this precaution.

A Tarahumare does not commit homicide unless he is drunk. There are only isolated exceptions. A *jefe politico* (prefect) told me that in forty years he had heard of only two murders. In both of these cases a drunken husband had killed his wife at a feast, and knew nothing of the crime after he became sober. I have been told that in some rare instances a Tarahumare woman will sit on her child right after its birth and crush it, in order to save herself the trouble of bringing it up. The Tepehuanes are reputed to do the same thing, and for the same purpose. Still with both tribes crimes of this kind are exceedingly rare.

Suicide is never committed unless a person is drunk and angered by some slight or by jealousy. At one time there was a veritable epidemic of suicides among the Indians near Guachochic, the men hanging themselves with their girdles; one of them even suspended himself by the feet. But it is doubtful whether a pagan Tarahumare ever killed himself.

As a rule, the Tarahumare is not a thief. Only when he thinks himself entirely unobserved, he may appropriate some trifle that particularly strikes his fancy, but the indications are that he learned the art from the Mexicans. Once on our travels we passed a man who was weeding his field. We tried to induce him to give us some information, but he was too busy to talk, and we went on. Soon he noticed that we had accidentally dropped our large axe, and immediately he interrupted his pressing work and came running after us with it. I wanted to compensate him for the trouble he had put himself to, but he would not accept the money I offered, saying that he had not had to go far, and, anyway, he did not bring the axe to get payment for it.

As long as he is in his native state, a Tarahumare never cheats at bargains. He does not like to sell anything that is in any way defective. He always draws attention to be the flaw, and if a jar has any imperfection, it requires much persuasion to make him part with it. He shows honesty also in other ways. Often I trusted Indians with a silver dollar or two for corn to be delivered a few days later, and never was I disappointed by them. On the other hand, they are chary of selling anything to a stranger. When a Mexican wants to buy a sheep, or some corn, or a girdle, the Tarahumare will first deny that he has anything to sell. What little he has he likes to keep for himself, and he considers it a favour to part with any of his belongings for money. A purchase, however, establishes a kind of brotherhood between the two negotiants, who afterward call each other "naragua," and a confidence is established between them almost of the same character as that which exists between compadres among the Mexicans.

From outsiders they accept silver coins, but not paper money, because they have been cheated with wrappers from cigarette boxes, and besides, they have no means of keeping such money safe and sound from mice, moisture, etc. Among themselves a little trading goes on, the highlands obtaining from the barrancas in the west copal, chile, ari, ear ornaments made from shells, and goats, in exchange for corn and beans. The Indians from Nararachic go to Rio Concho for the shells from which they make their ear pendants. The powder produced in working the shells is saved and mixed with salt to be used as a remedy for eye troubles.

The tribe had undeniably a certain gift for mechanics. The people are deft with their fingers and do everything neatly. This shows itself in their ingeniously constructed wooden locks and in the niceness with which they stuff animals. They are also very clever in following tracks, and even recognise the hoof-prints of particular horses among others in the same trail. They will also tell you that a tired deer keeps its toes more closely together than an animal just aroused from its lair. And never do they lose their way in the forest, not even when drunk. They love to sit among their corn plants, and will hide among them when strangers approach.

The Tarahumares are inquisitive, and will stand for a long time looking at you from a distance, if anything unusual attracts their attention. They are very critical and there is much gossip going on among them. They also laugh at the Mexicans, and say that the hair on their faces is like the fur on a bear. Squint-eyes also afford them much amusement. They are smart, attentive and patient. They have no qualms of conscience about telling an untruth, but my experience with them shows appreciation and gratitude for benefits received. An Indian whom I had occasion to treat to a good meal, many months afterward at a feast came up and said to me, "You were good to me when I was very hungry," and he proved his thankfulness by assisting me in various ways in establishing friendly relations with his people, which otherwise would have been very difficult to bring about.

Children are bright, and when sent to school learn Spanish quickly. They also master reading and writing without difficulty. They are diligent, eager to learn, and very religious, docile, and easily converted to Christianity.

There is a story about a padre who asked a Tarahumare boy, "What is God doing in Heaven?" The boy said, "The same as the macaw does in the tree." The padre asked, "What does the macaw do in the tree?" and the boy replied, "He eats the good seeds and lets the bad ones drop." A Mexican asked me if God was going to walk on earth again, and my Tarahumare attendant remarked, "No, he is now afraid to come, because people have too many rifles."

When they learn something their ambition runs high, and the boys always want to become generals and presidents of the republic.

The Tarahumares are careful observers of the celestial bodies, and know the Pleiades, the Belt of Orion, and the Morning and the Evening Star. The Great Dipper is of no special interest to them. Near Guachochic the Tarahumares plant corn in accordance with the positions of the stars with reference to the sun. They say if the sun and the stars are not equal the year will be bad; but when the stars last long the year will be good. In 1891, the sun "traveled slowly," and the stars "travelled quickly," and in June they had already "disappeared." Therefore the Tarahumares predicted that their crops would be below the average, which came true. On June 3rd I asked an Indian how much longer the sun would travel on, and he told me that it ought not to be more than fifteen days. The Tarahumares are reputed to be good weather prophets among the Mexicans, who frequently consult them upon the prospects of rain. The Indians judge from the colour of the sun when he rises as to whether there will be rain that day. If the crescent of the moon is lying horizontally, it is carrying much water; but when it stands up straight, it brings nothing. This belief is shared by the Mexicans. When the moon is full and has "a ring around," she is dancing on her patio. At the period of the dark moon she is dead, but will return after three days. Eclipses are explained as collisions between the sun and the moon on the road, when they fight.

The Tarahumare men make bows and arrows, and in the central part of the country are great hunters and clever at shooting. The fore-shaft of their arrows is made of palo hediondo, a wood used also in the making of needles. But the people living near the pueblo of Panalachic and the Barranca de Cobre are poor shots, and their favourite weapon is the axe. The boys still play with slings, which not so long ago were used for killing squirrels. A club with a stone (Spanish, *macana*) is said to have been formerly in common use. The grandfathers of the present generation of Nararachic had flint-tipped arrows. The Indians also know how to prepare excellent buckskin. They peg the hide on the ground and leave it for three days, and when it is sufficiently dry the hair is scraped off with a knife. It is then smeared over with the brain of the animal and hung up in the sun for four days. The next step is to wash it well in warm water in a wooden trough. Then it is well kneaded, and two people taking hold of it draw it out of the water and stretch it well between them. It is dried again and is then tanned with the crushed bark of the big-leaved oak-tree. A natural cavity in a rock is chosen for a vat, in which the skin is left for two days. After this it is well rinsed and squeezed until no water remains in it. Two persons are required for the operation, which is always performed in a place on which the sun beats strongly, while at the same time it is sheltered from the wind by surrounding rocks.

Deer are caught in snares fastened to a bent tree, so that the animal's foot is held, while the tree when released hoists the quarry up. The Indians also chase deer with dogs toward some narrow passage in the track where they have placed sharp-pointed pine sticks, two feet long, against which the deer runs and hurts itself. Blackbirds are decoyed by kernels of corn threaded on a snare of pita fibre hidden under the ground. The bird swallows the kernel, which becomes entangled in its oesophagus and is caught. Small birds are also shot with bow and arrows, or killed with stones.

The Tarahumare is ingenious in devising many kinds of traps for birds and animals. Into the burrow of the gopher he places a small upright frame cut from a piece of bark. There is a groove inside of the frame, and in this the snare runs; and a string is attached to a bough above ground. Another string, on which some grains of corn are threaded, keeps the snare set and obstructs the gopher's passage through the frame. When trying to get at the kernels the gopher cuts the string, the snare is released, and he is caught in his own burrow.

Squirrels are hunted in the most primitive way—by cutting down the tree on which the animal is discovered. Sometimes it will escape when the tree falls, and then the man has to cut down another tree, and thus he may go on felling as many as ten trees before he can bag his game, not a very substantial reward for a whole day's work.

The women make girdles and blankets on primitive looms, inserting characteristic designs in the weaving. It takes four days of constant work to make a girdle, but no woman weaves more than one blanket a year, and it is almost an event when it is finished. The weaving frame consists simply of four sticks—placed on the ground tied together in a rectangle or triangle, and pieces of reed on which the thread is wound, one for each colour, are used as shuttles. Textiles from Pamachic are especially highly valued. The blankets from that locality are sold all over the Tarahumare country and are the finest made by the tribe.

The Tarahumares are not far advanced in the art of making pottery. Their work is crude and not very substantial. The industry is practised only by the women, and the degree of ability varies considerably. The art is often hereditary. The nicest pottery I found in the neighbourhood of Panalachic, where it is decorated with certain designs in red and white. One woman in a western barranca cultivated a specialty of making large jars for holding tesvino.

Women when making pottery taste a little of the clay before commencing work, ascertaining whether it is the right kind or not. Some of the clay is acid and not good. The clay which is serviceable is a little sweet and a pale yellow colour. The clay is dried and ground, and then mixed with ground pieces of old pottery instead of sand. To make a piece of pottery, a lump of clay is hollowed out in the shape of a cup, and on this foundation the jar is built up, thin layers of clay being placed on successively, and smoothed carefully over with wet hands, making the walls thinner and thinner. The vessel is built up standing on a bowl filled with ashes and covered with a piece of cotton cloth.

I saw a clever woman make a medium-sized jar in twenty-seven minutes. She was seated in the sun, and finished four vessels in one afternoon. Then, assisted by her husband, she began to even them on the outside with a small, smooth, oblong piece of a gourd. The vessels were then put into the house in order that they might not dry too quickly. After an interval of fifteen minutes, during which she nursed her infant, which had been bother her all the while, she began work again. First, with the edge of a sharpened stick she removed all irregularities on the outside and on the brim, and then with a stone she polished the vessel. To polish the jars seemed to take the longest time, for each of the workers engaged on a vessel for over an hour, and even then had not completed the task. They polished outside and a little way inside below the brim. Finally they painted decorations with ochre, and polished again for a long time, but only the outside. Now the jars were again put into the house to dry a little more before the polishing was finished.

To burn the jars, they must first be thoroughly dried, as otherwise the fire would crack them. When the weather is nice the fire may be made outside the house; but usually it is built inside on the ordinary fireplace. Each vessel, one at a time, is turned upside down over charcoal, and pieces of pine bark are built up all around and over it like a square little hut, then ignited. Care is taken that no piece of bark comes so near to the jar as to touch and injure it. Where the bark cannot be readily procured, wood is used. The heat first turns the clay dark, and afterward a pretty yellow colour.

There is one industry which has a peculiar bearing on the whole life of the Tarahumares, namely, the making of native beer.

Nothing is so close to the heart of the Tarahumare as this liquor, called in Mexican Spanish *tesvino.* It looks like milky water, and has quite an agreeable taste, reminding one of kumyss. To make it, the moist corn is allowed to sprout; then it is boiled and ground, and the seed of a grass resembling wheat is added as a ferment. The liquor is poured into large earthen jars made solely for the purpose, and it should now stand for at least twenty-four hours; but inasmuch as the jars are only poorly made, they are not able to hold it very long, and the people take this responsibility on themselves. A row of beer jars turned upside down in front of a house is a characteristic sight in the Tarahumare region.

The tesvino forms an integral part of the Tarahumare religion. It is used at all its celebrations, dances, and ceremonies. It is given with the mother's milk to the infant to keep it from sickness. In "curing" the new-born babe the shaman sprinkles some over it to make it strong. Beer is applied internally and externally as a remedy for all diseases Tarahumare flesh is heir to. No man could get his field attended to if he did not first make ready a good supply of tesvino, because beer is the only remuneration his assistants receive. Drinking tesvino at the feast marks the turning-point in a person's life. A boy begins to drink tesvino because now he feels himself a man; and when a girl is seen at feasts, it is a sign that she is looking for a husband. No marriage is legitimate without a liberal consumption of tesvino by all parties present at the wedding. Hunting and fishing expeditions are accompanied by beer-drinking to insure luck. No matter how many times the Tarahumare changes his abode in the course of his life, he always makes tesvino when moving into a new house or cave. Even the dead would not get any rest, but come back and harm the survivors, if a quantity of tesvino were not set aside for them. In fact, there is absolutely no act of importance that is not, in one way or another, connected with the drinking of this beer. Never is a jar commenced unless some of the liquor is sacrificed before the cross, for the gods are believed to be as fond of the beer as are mortals. Rain cannot be obtained without tesvino; tesvino cannot be made without corn; and corn cannot grow without rain. This, in a nutshell, is the Tarahumare's view of life.

There are many occasions during the year, especially during the winter time, when regular symposiums are held, generally inside of the house; but the people never drink tesvino unless there is some purpose to be attained, be it luck in some undertaking, or good crops, or the health of the family, or some similar benefit. They man dance yúmari for a little while at any of these functions.

It is the custom to appoint one man to distribute the liquor among the guests. In doing this the host offers to the chosen one three drinking-gourds full of tesvino, which the latter empties, and he enters upon his duty by giving to every man present three gourds in succession and to every woman four. The guests, although from politeness hesitating between each gourdful, are only too delighted to comply with this inviolable rule, which speaks eloquently for their constitutions.

The seat beside the distributer is the most coveted. I, too, was always glad to get it, because it gave me the best chance to observe the behaviour of the Indians at the feasts. The dispenser establishes himself close to the big jar, and being immensely popular with everybody he is never left alone. The geniality of the Tarahumares, their courteousness and politeness toward each other in the beginning of a feast, is, to say the least, equal to that of many a civilised gentleman. When the cup is offered to anyone, he most urgently protests and insists that the distributer shall drink; often this remonstrance is heeded, but the gourd is never emptied; something is always left in it, and this the guest has to take, and a second gourdful is immediately held out to him. Though he again refuses, he generally allows himself to be persuaded to drink it, and this mock refusing and urging goes on as long as they have their wits together.

To my knowledge, this beer is not known outside of the Tarahumare tribe and their immediate neighbours, the northern Tepehuanes, the Tubars, and some Mexicans in Chihuahua who have also adopted it. It must not be confounded with the well-known Mexican drink, pulque, to which it is superior in flavour. It is very nourishing, and the Indians as well as the Mexicans are in the habit of abstaining from food before partaking of the beer, which they assert would otherwise not agree with them. But, food or no food, at all feasts and dances they drink such incredibly large quantities that they are invariably completely overpowered by it, though when taken in moderation tesvino is only mildly stimulating.

Another national beverage, maguey wine, is made from a favourite sweet food of many Indian tribes, which a white man's stomach can hardly digest, namely, the baked stalk of the maguey plant, or that of other agaves. To prepare the liquor, the leaves are cut from the bulb-shaped stalk or heart, which looks like a hard white head of cabbage. These hearts contain a great deal of saccharine matter, and are baked between hot stones in earth mounds, being protected against contact with earth by layers of grass.

When the Tarahumares want to make maguey wine they leave the baked stalks in water in natural hollows or pockets in rocks, without any covering. The root of a certain plant called frijolillo is added as ferment, and after two days the juice is wrung out with a blanket.

An intoxicating drink is also made from another agave, called tshãwí, which, though, common on the higher slopes of the barrancas, has only recently become known to science. According to tradition it is the first plant God created, and the liquor made from it is considered by the pagan Tarahumares as indispensable to certain ceremonies.

The Tepehuanes, too, put much importance on this brew, and say that the plant is so sensitive that if one passes a jar in which it is being boiled the liquid will not ferment.

Finally it should be mentioned that an intoxicating, though extremely distasteful, drink is made from the stalk of the maize plant *(caña),* by pounding this material into a pulp, then allowing it to soak in water for three days, when it is fermented, whereupon the liquor is prepared in the same way as the maguey wine.

Inside of Bowl. Diameter, 17 ctm.

Height, 14.5 ctm. Height, 16.5 ctm.

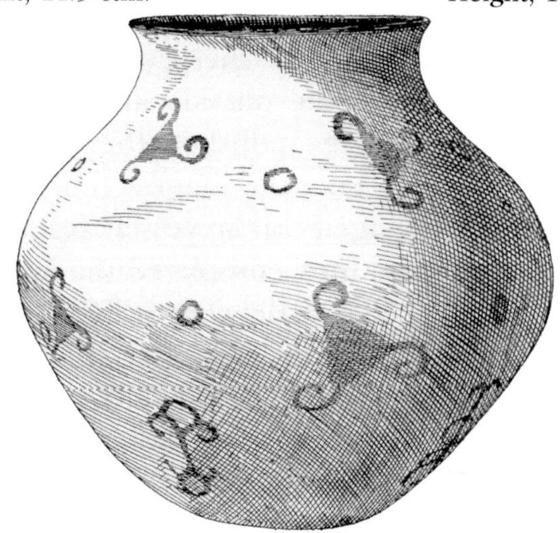

Height, 19 ctm.

Tarahumare Pottery from Panalachic. Decorations in red ochre and white *javoncillo.*

Chapter 14

Politeness, and the Demands of Etiquette—The Daily Life of the Tarahumare—The Woman's Position is High - Standard of Beauty—Woman Do the Courting—Love's Young Dream—Marriage Ceremonies, Primitive and Civilized—Childbirth—Childhood.

For a barbarian, the Tarahumare is a very polite personage. In his language he even has a word "rēkó" which is the equivalent of the English "please," and which he uses constantly. When passing a stranger, or leaving a person, he draws attention to his action by saying, "I am going." As he grows civilized, however, he loses his good manners.

In spite of this he is not hospitable; the guest gets food, but there is no room for him in the house of a Tarahumare. A visitor never thinks of entering a house without first giving the family ample time to get ready to receive him. When he approaches a friend's home, good manners require him to stop sometimes as far as twenty or thirty yards off. If he is on more intimate terms with the family, he may come nearer, and make his presence known by coughing; then he sits down, selecting generally some little knoll from which he can be readily seen. In order not to embarrass his friends he does not even look at the house, but remains sitting there gazing into vacancy, his back or side turned toward the homestead. Should the host be absent the visitor may thus sit for a couple of hours; then he will rise and go slowly away again. But under no circumstances will he enter the home, unless formally invited, "because," he says, "only the dogs enter houses uninvited." Never will the lady of the house commit such a gross breach of etiquette as to go out and inform him of her husband's absence, to save the caller the trouble of waiting, nor will she if alone at home, make any statements as to that gentleman's whereabouts.

The Tarahumare never does anything without due deliberation; therefore he may, for a quarter of an hour, discuss with his wife the possible purport of the visit, before he goes out to see the man. They peep through the cracks in the wall at him, and if they happen to be eating or doing anything, they may keep the visitor waiting for half an hour. Finally the host shakes out the blanket on which he has been sitting, throws it around himself, and, casting a rapid glance to the right and left as he passes through the door, goes to take a seat a few yards distant from the caller. After some meditation on either side, the conversation, as in more civilized society, opens with remarks about the weather and the prospects for rain. When this subject is exhausted, and the host's curiosity as to where the man came from, what he is doing, and where he is going to, is satisfied, the former may go back to the house and fetch some pinole and meat for the traveller. The object of the visit not infrequently is an invitation to take part in some game or foot-race; and as the men are sure to remain undisturbed, they generally reach some understanding. A friend of the family is, of course, finally invited to enter the house, and the customary salutation is "Assagá!" (" Sit down!") In this connection it may be noted that the Tarahumares in conversation look sidewise, or even turn their backs toward the person they speak to.

After having eaten, the guest will carefully return every vessel in which food was given to him, and when he rises he hands back the skin on which he was seated. Should occasion require, the host will say: "It is getting late, and you cannot return to your home to-night. Where are you going to sleep? There is a good cave over yonder." With this he may indicate where the visitor may remain over night. He will also tell him where he may find wood for the fire, and he will bring him food; but not unless the weather is very tempestuous will he invite an outsider to sleep in the house.

When at home the Tarahumare keeps regular hours, rising and retiring with the sun. Having slept on a skin on the floor, rolled up in his blanket, without anything for a pillow except perhaps a stone or a chunk of wood, he sits for a while near the fire, which is kept up most of the year at night in the house or cave. His wife brings him his breakfast of pinole. While combing out his long black hair with a pine cone, he may ask the boys and girls whether they have attended to the traps he told them to set on the night before. They run out and soon they come in with some mice. "Here they are," they say, "but they are very poor!" The father, however, may consider them fat and nice, and the mother affably adds: "Of course, they are fat, since they have eaten so much corn." They go about to roast them, while the husband looks on. Generally the Tarahumares have a number of traps set to catch mice. They are so fond of this "game" that, when civilised, they have been known to ask permission from Mexican acquaintances to go through their houses to hunt for them. The mice are skinned and threaded on a thin stick, which is stuck through their necks and serves as a spit.

Having enjoyed the dainty morsel thus set before him, the husband now tells his wife what he is going to do to-day. He will run deer or hunt squirrels, and accordingly takes his bow and arrows or his axe with him. In spring-time he may go to the field. The wife also tells of her plans for the day. The work that engages most of the time of the housewives in Mexico is the grinding of the corn, on the metate, for corn-cakes; and if she has any time to spare she boils beans, looks for herbs, or works on her weaving-frame; but she never sits about idle. She looks as conscientiously after her duties as any white woman; she has always something to do, and many things to take care of in her small way.

About sunset the husband returns, bringing a squirrel or rabbit, which he carries concealed in his blanket, that no neighbour may see it and expect an invitation to help to eat it. As he goes and comes he never salutes his wife or children. He enters in silence and takes his seat near the fire. The animal he caught he throws toward her where she is kneeling before the metate, so that it falls on her skirt. She ejaculates "Sssssssssss!" in approval and admiration, and, picking it up, praises its good points extravagantly: "What a big mouth! What large claws!" etc. He tells her how hard he worked to get that squirrel, how it had run up the tree, and he had to cut down that tree, till finally the dog caught it. "The dog is beginning to be very good at hunting," he says. "And now I am very tired." She spreads before him a generous supper of beans, herbs, and maize porridge, which she has ready for him. And while he eats she goes industriously to work removing the fur from the game, but leaving on the skin, not only because it keeps the meat together while it is boiling, but mainly because she thinks there is a good deal of nourishment in it, which it would be a shame to waste.

When the man is at home, and neither sleeping nor eating, he may sit down and make a bow or some arrows; or, stretched out on his back, he may resort to his favourite amusement, playing his home-made violin. Like all Indians of Mexico, the Tarahumares are fond of music and have a good ear for it. When the Spaniards first came, they found no musical instruments among the Tarahumares except the short reed flute, so common to many Mexican tribes, the shaman's rattle, and the rasping stick. But they soon introduced the violin and even the guitar, and throughout Mexico the Indians now make these instruments themselves, using pine wood and other indigenous material in their construction, sometimes with remarkable skill and ingenuity, and for glue the juice of a certain lily root. Having no idea of the value of money, they frequently sell a tolerably good instrument for fifty or even twenty-five cents.

Toward evening the Tarahumare father of a family gets more talkative and chats with his wife, and then:

"The day is done, and the darkness
Drops from the wings of night
As a feather is wafted downward
from an eagle in his flight."

And as the shadows deepen, he wraps himself closer in his blanket, and before he knows it childlike slumber enfolds him. Frequently he grows hungry in the middle of the night, and reaches out for food, as well as for his violin, devoting himself to music for half an hour, before he drops off to sleep again.

There are more women in the tribe than men, and they are looked upon as of less importance. There is a saying among the people that one man is as good as five women. Her prayers are not of as much value as his, because she prays only to the moon, and her deity is not as big as his, the sun. For this reason her place is behind the man in all dances. Yet she occupies a comparatively high position in the family, and no bargain is ever concluded until the husband has consulted his wife in the matter. I am bound to say, however, that on such occasions every member of the household, even the youngest and smallest child, is asked to give an opinion, and, if one of the little tots objects, the sale will not be closed. In such cases there is nothing for the customer to do but to try to influence the young business man who raised the objection, not directly, but through his parents. This accounts for a good deal of the frightful loss of time incurred in dealing with these Indians. The purchase of a sheep may require two days, and the negotiations concerning an ox may extend over an entire week.

That a woman of intelligence and character is appreciated even among barbarians is proven by the fact that once a woman was made gobernador, or chief, because "she knew more than men." She did not assume the title, but she is said to have ruled with more wisdom and justice than many of her predecessors and successors.

Husband and wife never show their affection in public except when drunk. Parents kiss their little ones on the mouth and on the stomach, and the youngsters express their love for each other in the same way. On some occasions I have seen lovers sitting closely together, she holding on to his forefinger. The women are of a jealous disposition.

The Tarahumare standard of beauty is not in accordance with the classic ideal as we perceive it, nor is it altogether in conformity with modern views on the subject. Large, fat thighs are the first requisite, and a good-looking person is called a "beautiful thigh." Erect carriage is another essential to beauty. In the face, the eyes attract more notice than any other feature, and the most admired ones are "the eyes like those of a mouse." This is the highest praise that can be bestowed upon anyone's personal appearance. They all like straight hair, and consider hair very ugly when it has a curl at the end. I once asked a bright young Tarahumare how the man must look who is most admired by women, whether his mouth and nose should be large or small, etc, and he replied, "They must be similar to mine!" Aside from good looks, the women like best men who work well, just as in civilized countries a woman may look out for a good *parti*.

But wealth does not make the possessor more attractive to the girls. In Nararachic was an elderly man who owned forty head of cattle and eighteen horses. When he became a widower, he had to live with an elderly woman of bad reputation, as he could not get another woman to marry him.

The young women enjoy absolute liberty, except as regards Mexicans, against whom they are always warned. They are told that they become sick from contact with such men. Never are they forced to contract what would turn out to be a loveless marriage. A beautiful Indian girl was much sought for by a Mexican. He spoke the Tarahumare language very well, and offered to give her a good house and fine clothes and a whole handful of silver dollars. Her brother, who was half civilized, and therefore more corrupt than the ordinary Indian, also tried to persuade her to accept the rich suitor. But she tossed up her head and exclaimed, "Tshíne awláma negalé" which, freely translated, means: "I do not like that fellow; love goes where it chooses."

The custom of the country requires the girl to do all the courting. She is just as bashful as the young swain whom she wishes to fascinate, but she has to take the initiative in love affairs. The young people meet only at the feasts, and after she has gotten mildly under the influence of the native beer that is liberally consumed by all, she tries to attract his attention by dancing before him in a clumsy way up and down on the same spot. But so bashful is she that she persistently keeps her back turned toward him. She may also sit down near him and pull his blanket and sing to him in a gentle low voice a simple love-song:

If occasion requires, the parents of the girl may say to the parents of the boy, "Our daughter wants to marry your son." Then they send the girl to the boy's home, that the young people may become acquainted. For two or three days, perhaps, they do not speak to each other, but finally she playfully begins to throw pebbles at him. If he does not return them, she understands that he does not care for her. If he throws them back at her, she knows that she has won him. She lets her blanket drop and runs off into the woods, and he is not long in following her.

Sometimes the boy, when he likes a girl very much, may make the first advances, but even then he has to wait until she throws the first pebbles and drops the blanket, for, among the Indians, it is the woman who seeks the man, and the fair who deserve the brave.

Next day they come home together, and after this they do not hide themselves any more. The parents of the girl are advised to make tesvino, as the young couple should not be separated any more, and word is sent out to a few friends and relatives to come to the wedding.

The guests arrive in the afternoon and most of the people remain outside of the house during the ceremony, but the bridegroom and his parents go inside, where they seat themselves on skins spread out on the floor. The mother of the girl has placed a large skin next to a big jar of tesvino, and on this the father of the boy sits down. As soon as he has taken his place, the host offers him three gourds full of the drink and requests him to accept the office of honour, the distribution of tesvino to all present, and he immediately enters upon his duties. He first gives four gourds full to the mother of the bride, as the mistress of the tesvino, and three gourds full to the host, the master; then four gourds full to his own wife. The bridal couple have been called in and told to sit down side by side, and all the rest of the people come in and stand around the pair. There is no special place assigned to anyone; but the father of the boy stands up and his mother sits down, while the girl's father sits down and her mother stands up. The boy's father now makes a speech, telling the bridal couple that they must remain together, and never separate nor fight. He specially tells the young man that he has to kill deer and take care always to bring some animal home to his wife, even if it be only a chipmunk or a mouse. He also has to plough and to sow corn and to raise crops, that he and she may always have enough to eat and not go hungry.

The father of the girl next takes the word, addressing himself mostly to the bride. Now that she is united to the man of her choice, she should always comply with her wifely duties. She must make blankets for her husband, and be industrious, make tesvino and iskiate, pinole, tortillas, gather herbs, etc., that her husband may always have something to eat and not go hungry. He names all the herbs singly. She must also help him, in her way, with ploughing and sowing, so that he may raise plenty of corn to make tesvino that others may help him. She never must be lazy.

The father of the girl now gives tesvino to his future son-in-law, whose father in turn gives some to the bride. The bridal couple are covered with blankets, and in some cases his and her right hands are tied together. There is no other marriage ceremony. But all the guests partake of the liberally flowing bowl, and the festivities end in general and complete intoxication.

About two weeks later, the parents of the bridegroom make a feast exactly the same in character, but now the father of the girl occupies the seat of honour next to the big tesvino jar and acts as distributer. He also makes the first speech. The bridegroom gives to his brother-in-law a flint for striking fire, and six arrows. No matter how many brothers the bride has, they all get this present. It is considered an exchange for the girl. The shamans avail themselves *jus prima noctis.*

After the marriage the bridal couple separate, each staying in the old home for several weeks, after which the young man comes to live with his father-in-law for half a year or a year, until he has time to make a house for himself. In the meantime the young couple are fed, but they receive nothing else. The young man has his own animals, which he got when he was small, and now his father gives him a piece of land.

Among the Christian Tarahumares the fiscal is advised of any contemplated marriage. This functionary has charge of the church edifice and the teaching of the children. It is his duty to take the young couples to the padre to be married. But the padre is far away and comes around only once a year, and sometimes even less frequently, and then the fiscal, so to say, rounds up all the matrimonially inclined. On account of the innate ardour to comply with all religious requirements the Tarahumares are willing to go through the ceremony, though to them it has no significance beyond the payment of one dollar. On this account they do not mind waiting for the padre's blessing for a couple of years, until they get ready to part with one dollar, thereby generally saving an extra trip for baptizing.

As the padre's visits are so few and far between, the fiscal even considers it incumbent upon himself to make up matches on his own account, telling the people that when the padre comes they should be ready to get married. But so independent are the Tarahumare girls that it has happened that when the padre asks the portentous question, they cry, "Kaeke, kaeke" ("No, no"), and run away.

In my time there was a padre (now removed) who emulated the example of the shamans and was frequently in his cups. On one occasion he was unable to perform the marriage ceremonies, and the sacristan accompanying him had to take his place. All this man knew about the rite was to ask the man and the woman whether they would have each other. On hearing their "Yes" he would say, "Where is the dollar?" and pocketing it send the couple off with, "Now you are all right."

When an addition is expected in the family the chief preparation of the woman is to get ready a quantity of beer, calling on her friends to help her, while the husband goes to look for the shaman. When she feels her time is approaching, she retires to some lonely spot, as she is too bashful to bear her child while others are about. She tightens her girdle around her waist, and bears her child sitting up, holding on to something above her, like the branch of a tree. After the little stranger has arrived the husband may bring her a jar with warm water from which she occasionally drinks. He also digs a hole, in which, after he has gone, she buries the placenta, placing stones on top of the place on account of the dogs. The umbilical cord is cut with a sharp reed or a sharp-edged piece of obsidian, but never with a knife, for in that case the child would become a murderer and could never be a shaman. I once asked a Tarahumare where he was born, expecting him to give me the name of some ranch; I was rather amused when he pointed to a big stone a little farther on along a slope. That was his birthplace.

The mother may lie down for that day, but the following morning she works as usual, as if nothing had been the matter with her. The husband does not work for three days, because he thinks his axe would break or the horns of his ox would fall off, or he would break a leg. The third day he takes a bath.

When the baby is three days old the shaman comes to cure it. A big fire is made of corn-cobs, the little one is placed on a blanket, and with the father's assistance the shaman carries it, if it is a boy, three times through the smoke to the four cardinal points, making the ceremonial circuit and finally raising it upward. This is done that the child may grow well and be successful in life, that is, in raising corn. Then the shaman takes a burning corn-cob from the fire and with the charred end makes three parallel lines lengthwise over the child's head and three across them. He also sprinkles tesvino on the head and other vital parts of the body to make them strong, and cures the umbilical cord. He may, too, anoint the child with the fat of the rattlesnake mixed with herbs, and leave it in the sun, that the light may enter his heart. For his services the shaman gets a little maize, beans, salt, etc.

On the fourth day the mother goes down to the river to bathe, and while bathing leaves the little one naked, exposed to the sun for at least an hour, in spite of all wailing, that Father Sun may see and know his new child. The baby is not washed until it is a year old. Then it is cured again, by the shaman, who on various occasions throughout its life repeats his curing, that the child may grow well and that no sickness or bad accidents may befall it. To protect it still further, pieces of palo hediondo or the chuchupate root, the strong smell of which is supposed to avail against disease, are wrapped in a piece of cloth and tied around the child's neck.

The mother nurses the child until it is three years old. In some instances she begins to give it once in a while a little pinole when it is only six months old. When two years of age a child begins to walk and to talk. Sometimes when the mother is busy, for instance at the metate, and will not stop to nurse him, the little rascal may take a stick and in his way try to beat her.

The Tarahumare woman is a faithful mother, and takes good care of her children. She generally has from six to eight, often more. While small the children play with primitive dolls. They dress up corn-cobs with scraps of textiles and put them upright in the sand, saying that they are matachines and drunken women. The also play, like other children, with beans and acorns, or with young chickens with their legs tied together. Of course the youngsters maltreat these. Sometimes they play, too, with stuffed squirrels, but there are no special children's games. The father makes bows and arrows for the boys, and instructs them in hunting and agricultural work. As the girls grow up, the mother teaches them how to spin yarn and weave blankets, "for," she tells them, "otherwise they will become men." She also tells them not to have children too rapidly in succession, for there is no one to carry them for her. Women cannot eat the tenderloin until they are very old, because if they did they could have no children. For the same reason they must not eat the pancreas. The women who fear lest they may have difficulty in giving birth to a child make soup of an opossum and eat it. Girls must not touch deer antlers, or their breasts would fall off.

A characteristic custom is that the children, no matter how old they get, and even after they are married and have families of their own, never help themselves to anything in the parents' house. The mother has to give all the food, etc., and she gives as long as she has anything.

Parents never inflict corporal punishment upon the young people. If a boy does not behave himself, he gets scolded, and his father's friends may also remonstrate with him at a feast. Otherwise, the children grow up entirely independent, and if angry a boy may even strike his father. A girl will never go so far, but when scolded will pout and weep and complain that she is unjustly treated. How different is this from the way in which, for instance, Chinese children treat their parents! It does not favour much the theory that the American Indians originally came from Asia.

Chapter 15

Many Kinds of Games Among the Tarahumares—Betting and Gambling—Foot-races the National Sport—The Tarahumares are the Greatest Runners in the World—Divinations for the Race—Mountains of Betting Stakes—Women's Races.

To my knowledge there is no tribe so fond of games as the Tarahumares. There are few days in the year when a man has not a game of some kind to play. Even when they become civilized and demoralized, in spite of their depression and poverty this passion of theirs still clings to them. While it is true that there is always something of value, however insignificant, put at stake, their gambling spirit is not vicious. They have some curious practices in their play: when going to run a race, or when intending to play *cuatro* or *quinze*, they do not eat chile. Where holes in the ground are required for a game, as in cuatro and quinze, they are generally made in the level space on a rock.

Very common is it to see two young men amusing themselves with shooting-matches, shooting arrows at an arrow which has been shot out into the ground some fifty yards off as a mark. This arrow, as well as the game itself, is called in Mexican Spanish *lechuguilla.* In Tarahumare the game is called chogírali, and the target-arrow chogira. The arrow coming nearest the chogira counts one point; and if it comes within four fingers' width of the aim, it counts as four. The game is for twelve points. The distance is not measured from the points of the arrows, but from the winged parts, one man measuring for all. If a shot arrow strikes so as to form a cross with the chogira, it counts as four. If it only touches the point of the latter in the ground it counts two. It two arrows happen to form crosses, neither counts.

Instead of arrows, three sticks may be employed. One is thrown out at a distance and is the chogira, and the other two sticks are thrown toward it, and count in a similar way as the arrows. Often while traveling, the Tarahumares play this game, in either form, as they go along the road, perhaps for the entire distance. Two and three pairs may play together.

There is also a game very similar to quoits, played with stone disks, flat on one side and convex on the other. It is called rixiwátali (rixíwala = disk), and two and two play against each other. First one stone is moistened with spittle on one side to make it "heads or tails" and tossed up. The player who wins the toss plays first. Each has three stones, which are thrown toward a hole in the ground, perhaps twenty yards off. One of each party throws first, then goes to the hole and looks at it, while the other players make their throws. The stone falling nearest to the hole counts one point; if it falls into the hole, it counts as four; if the stone of the second player falls on top of the first stone in the hole, it "kills" the first stone. The game is out at twelve. To measure distances, they break off small sticks. Lookers-on may stand around and bet which of the players will win.

Another game is called tákwari, "to beat the ball"; in Spanish, *palillo*. It is played only by women. Two play at a time. One knocks a small wooden ball toward the goal, while her opponent tries to get it to another. This game is also played by the northern Tepehuane women, who sometimes use two short sticks tied together in the middle, instead of the ball. The sticks are thrown ahead from their places on the ground with a kind of quick, prying movement, with the aid of a longer stick.

Civilised Tarahumares, as well as the Mexicans, play with knuckle-bones as dice. The game is called *la taba*, and the bones are taken from either the deer, the sheep, or the goat. Only one bone is used by the two players. Twelve points make a game, and each player has twelve grains of corn with which he keeps count. He makes two rings in the sand, and puts his twelve grains in one ring, and as the game progresses he transfers them into the second ring until the game is out.

Their greatest gambling game, at which they may play even when tipsy, is quinze; in Tarahumare, romavóa. It is played with four sticks of equal length, called romálaka and inscribed with certain marks to indicate their value. Practically they serve the same purpose as dice, but they are thrown in a different way. The player grasps them in his left hand, levels their ends carefully, lifts his bundle, and strikes the ends against a flat or square little stone in front of him, from which they rebound toward his opponent. The sticks count in accordance with the way they fall. The point of the game is to pass through a figure outlined by small holes in the ground between the two players. The movements, of course, depend upon the points gained in throwing the sticks, and the count is kept by means of a little stone, which is placed in the respective hole after each throw. Many accidents may impede its progress; for instance, it may happen to be in the hole into which the adversary comes from the opposite direction, In this case he is "killed," and he has to begin again from the starting-point. The advance is regulated by a number of ingenious by-laws, which make the game highly intellectual and entertaining. If he has the wherewithal to pay his losses, a Tarahumare may go on playing for a fortnight or a month, until he has lost everything he has in this world, except his wife and children; he draws the line at that. He scrupulously pays all his gambling debts.

The northern Tepehuanes also know this game, and play with sticks eighteen to twenty inches long. As these larger sticks fly quite a distance off when rebounding, the players sit rather far apart.

Wrestling also may be observed, but what may be termed the national sport, of which the Tarahumares are inordinately fond, is foot-racing, which goes all the year round, even when the people are weakened from scarcity of food. The interest centers almost entirely in the betting that goes with it; in fact, it is only another way of gambling. It is called ralá hípa ("which the foot throw"), the word alluding to a ball used at the race.

No doubt the Tarahumares are the greatest runners in the world, not in regard to speed, but endurance. A Tarahumare will easily run 170 miles without stopping. When an Indian is sent out as a messenger, he goes along at a slow trot, running steadily and constantly. A man has been known to carry a letter in five days from Guazapares to Chihuahua and back, a distance of nearly 600 miles by the road. Even considering shortcuts, which he, no doubt, knew, it was quite a feat of endurance; for he must have lived, as the Indians always do while traveling, on pinole and water only.

Where the Indians serve the Mexicans they are often employed to run wild horses into the corral. It may take them two or three days, but they will bring them in, the horses thoroughly exhausted, while the men, who, of course, economise their strength, and sleep, and eat pinole, are comparatively fresh. In the same way they will run down a deer, following it for days through snow and rain, until the animal is cornered and easily shot with arrows, or until it is overtaken utterly jaded and its hoofs dropping off.

This propensity for running is so great that the name of the tribe alludes to it. Tarahumare is a Spanish corruption of ralámari, the meaning of which, though somewhat obscure, may doubtless best be given as "foot-runners," because ralá certainly means "foot."

The race is always between two localities, each side being represented by from four to twenty runners. The two parties show in their apparel some distinctive mark; for instance, all of one troop have red head-bands, while the others may wear white ones.

A peculiar feature is that the men toss along a small ball as they run, each party having one of their own. These balls are about two and a half inches in diameter and carved from the root of the oak. The foremost runner kicks it with the toes of his right foot, so as to make it bound along as far as 100 yards, and he and all the men behind him follow in the same trot as before. The first man reaching it again kicks it onward. It must never be touched by the hand, unless it happens to fall in some awkward place, as between stones or in a water-pool, when it is picked up and kicked on.

There is never any laid-out track, but the circuit is determined in a general way by crosses cut in trees. There are certain favourite places always used as race-courses. The runners seem to have a preference for the level tops of low ridges lying in a circle, wherever this is possible. If this is not feasible, they may run forward and back on a ridge, starting always near the middle, from some little plane or other convenient place, where the people gather for the occasion.

There is a manager for each party, and the two arrange the time and place for the race to be held, also the number and length of the circuits to be made. A circuit may measure from three to twelve miles in extent, and when the circuits are short as many as twenty may be agreed upon. At one race-course near Carichic, the circuit is about fourteen miles long, and twelve circuits may be run here without stopping. Runners of equal ability are matched against each other, each side being, of course, anxious to secure the best. The managers take care of their men until the race comes off. The training consists mainly in abstinence from tesvino for two or five days before the event. When preparing for a big race the runners may practice; not that they need training in running, for that comes to them as naturally as swimming to the duck; but only that they practice kicking the ball and try the ground.

Much more important are the magical devices by means of which they endeavour to secure their own success and to defeat their opponents. A daring manager may go to a burial cave, taking two balls with him. He digs out a bone, preferably the tibia from the right leg, and sets it on the floor of the cave in which it has been found. In front of it he places a jar with tesvino and some vessels containing food. On either side of these he lays one of his balls, and in front of all he plants the cross. The food and the beer are the payment to the dead that he may help to win the race by weakening the adversaries.

As human bones are supposed to induce fatigue, some may be brought to the race-track and secreted there in such a way that the competing runners have to pass over the spot, while the manager's own crew are advised of the danger, to avoid it. The man uses the utmost care not to touch the bones with his fingers, lest he should dry up; instead, he uses sticks in handling and carrying them.

Scores of remedies are brought to the scene, either to strengthen friends or to weaken opponents. Certain herbs are thrown into the air or shaken before the runners to enervate them. Some enterprising Mexican may bring a white powder or similar substance, declaring that it is very efficacious, and get a Tarahumare to pay a high price for it. But whatever means are employed, one way or the other, there is always a counter-remedy to offset its effect. Specially potent is the blood of the turtle and the bat, stirred together, dried, and mixed with a little tobacco, which is then rolled into a cigar and smoked. Hikuli and the dried head of an eagle or a crow may be worn under the girdle as a protection.

The services of the shaman are indispensable for the foot-runners. He helps the manager, himself often a shaman, to rub the men with herbs and smooth stones to make them strong. He also makes passes over them to guard them against sorcery. On the day before the race he "cures" them. Food and remedies are placed on a blanket beneath the cross, together with many magical things. The herbs are very powerful and have to be tied up in bags of buckskin or cotton cloth, as otherwise they might break away. The water for the runners to drink is also placed underneath the cross, and candles are set on either side of the pile. The runners bring their balls and stand in a row around the cross. Then the shaman, taking his position in front of the latter, smokes incense of copal over them, and sings of the tail of the grey fox, and other songs. He also makes a speech, warning them not to accept pinole or water in other people's houses. All their food and drink must come from their relatives as a guard against witchcraft and illness. The runners drink three times from the water and the strengthening remedies; then the principal runner leads the others in a ceremonial circuit around the cross, walking as many times around it as there are circuits to be run in the race. The men sleep near the cross, to watch the remedies on the blanket. With them they have some old man, for old men see even when they sleep, and watch against sorcery.

After the ceremony the shaman takes each runner aside and subjects him to a rigid examination in regard to his recent food and his relations with women. Fat, potatoes, eggs, and anything sweet are prohibited, because all these things make the men heavy; but rabbits, deer, rats, turkeys, and chaparral-cocks are wholesome, and such nourishment enables them to win.

An augury as to which side will win is also taken. Water is poured into a large wooden tray, and the two balls are started simultaneously and rolled through the water over the tray. The party whose ball first reaches the other end will surely win. This test is gone through as many times as there are to be circuits in the race.

A race is never won by natural means. The losers always say that they have been bewitched by the others. Once I was talking the temperature of some foot-runners before they started, and their opponents, seeing this, lost heart, thinking that I had made their contestants strong to win the race. Often one of the principal runners becomes disheartened, and may simulate illness and declare that their rivals have bewitched him. Then the whole affair may come to nothing and the race be declared off. There are stories about injurious herbs that have been given in pinole or water, and actually made some racers sick. It may even happen that some dishonest fellow will pay to the best runner of one party a cow if he lets the other party win. But, as a rule, everything goes on straightforwardly. No one will, however, wonder that there are six watchmen appointed by each side to guard the runners from any possible peradventure, and to see that everything goes on in a proper, formal way. Tipsy persons are not admitted, and women in a delicate condition are carefully kept away, as the runners become heavy even by touching such a woman's blanket.

On the day of the race the forenoon is spent in making bets, the managers acting as stakeholders. These people, poor as they are, wager their bows and arrows, girdles, head-bands, clothes, blankets, beads, ari, balls of yarn, corn, and even sheep, goats, and cattle. The stakes of whatever nature are tied together—a blanket against so many balls of yarn, a stick of ari against so many arrows, etc. At big races the wagers may amount to considerable heaps of such articles, and the position of manager requires a man of decision and memory, for he has to carry all the bets in his head and makes no written record of them. The total value of the wager may reach a thousand dollars, and what to the Indians are fortunes may change hands in accordance with the result of the race. One man on one occasion had $50 worth of property at stake.

The scene is one of great animation. As many as two hundred people may assemble, among them women and children. At the gathering-point, which is called in Tarahumare "the betting-place," all the bets are made, and here the race is started and concluded. Here the managers also place a row of stones, one stone for each circuit to be run, and whenever a circuit is completed one stone is taken away. In this way the count is kept. The runners walk about wrapped in their blankets like the rest of the people. They have had nothing to eat all day but pinole and tepid water, and their legs have been rubbed with warm water in the morning by the managers.

When finally all the people have arranged their stakes the gobernador steps forward and makes a speech, in which he specially exhorts the runners not to throw the ball with their hands; if they do, they certainly will go to hell! He also warns them against cheating of any kind.

At the given signal, quick as lightning, the runners throw off their blankets, and one man in each party, previously selected, throws his ball as far as he can, and all the runners start after it. A second ball is always kept in reserve, in case the first should be lost.

The racers wear rattles of deer-hoofs and bits of reeds tied together on a strip of leather, which they stick in the backs of their girdle or hang over their backs. The magic rattling keeps them from falling asleep while running, so they say; besides, the deer-hoofs lend them the swiftness of the stag. Some runners adorn themselves with leathers from various birds, preferably the macaw and the peacock, tying them to short sticks. The few Tarahumares who have ever seen a peacock think a good deal of this bird, because it is considered light footed and mystic, being foreign to their country. Some runners may be seen who paint their faces and legs with white chalk, near Batopilas, for instance.

They do not run at an extraordinary speed, but very steadily, hour after hour, mile after mile. Good runners make forty miles in six or eight hours. At one race, when they covered according to calculation twenty-one miles in two hours, I timed the leading runner and found that he made 290 feet in nineteen seconds on the first circuit, and the next in twenty-four seconds. At a race rehearsal I saw them cover four miles in half an hour.

The public follows the race with great enthusiasm from beginning to end, the interest growing with each circuit. Many begin to follow the runners, shouting to them and urging them on. They also help them by pointing out the ball so that they can kick it without stopping to look for it. The wives of the contestants heat water and prepare pinole, which they hold out in drinking-gourds to the men as they pass. The latter stop for a few seconds to partake of this their favourite dish; and if this cannot be done, the tepid water is thrown over the shoulders of the runners, by way of refreshing them. As darkness comes on, torches of resinous pine wood are lighted and carried along to illuminate the path for the runners, that they may not stumble, making the scene one of extreme picturesqueness, as these torch-bearers, demon-like, hurry through the forest.

One contestant after another drops out. The excitement becomes wilder; more and more people join accompanying the few runners left, their principal motive being to shout encouraging words to the runners and urge them to exert themselves to the utmost. And at last the best man comes in, generally alone, the others having either given up the contest or being far behind.

The race usually commences at midday; but often the bets are not finished until late in the afternoon. It may last four hours and even longer. A famous runner, now dead, could run from midday until sunrise. There is no prize for the winner himself, except the golden opinions he earns among the women; and his father may accept presents from lucky bettors. A man who wins a cow is expected to give two pesos to the victorious runner; in case he wins a goat he gives half a real.

The race over, the wagers are immediately paid and the Indians quickly disperse, soon to arrange for another contest.

Sometimes there is an old man's race preceding that of the young men, the latter being always the principal event of the day. Races are also run by women, and the betting and excitement that prevail on these occasions run as high as the men's races, though on a smaller scale. Instead of tossing the ball with their toes, they use a large wooden fork, with two of three prongs, to pitch it forward. Sometimes they have a ring of twisted strips of yucca leaves instead of the ball, but more often two interlocked rings which they throw ahead with a stick curved at the end. This game, which is called rowémala (rōwé signifies a ring), must be very ancient, for rings of this kind have sometimes been found in ancient cliff-dwellings. It is certainly a strange sight to see these sturdy amazons race heavily along with astonishing perseverance, when creeks and water-holes come in their way, simply lifting their skirts *á la Diane* and making short work of the crossing.

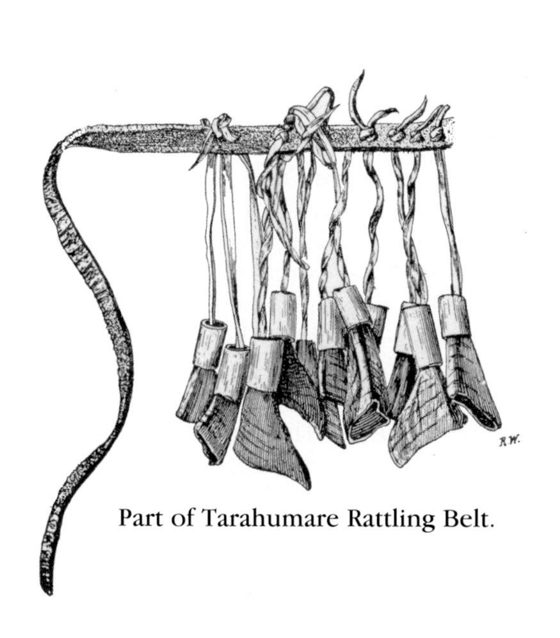

Part of Tarahumare Rattling Belt.

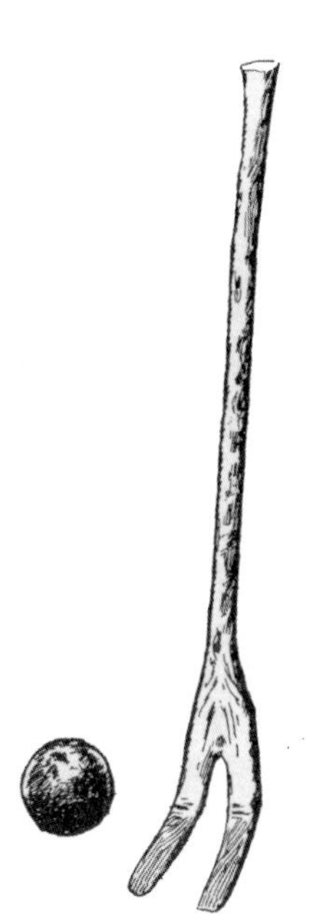

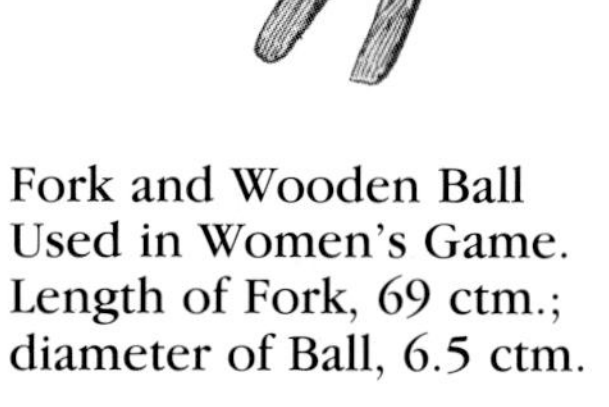

Fork and Wooden Ball Used in Women's Game. Length of Fork, 69 ctm.; diameter of Ball, 6.5 ctm.

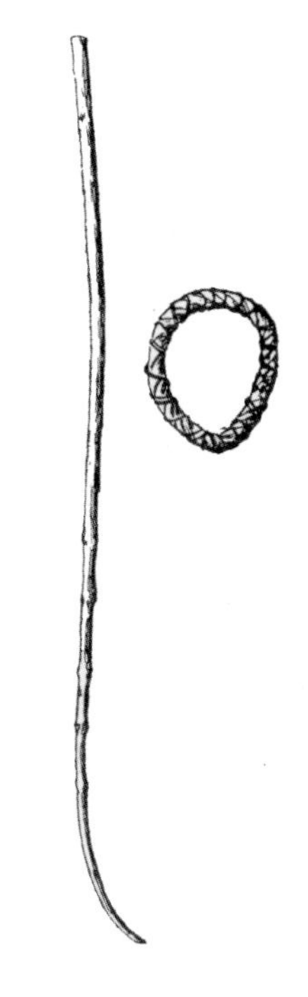

Stick and Ring Used in Women's Game. Length of Stick, 85 ctm.; diameter of Ring, 11 ctm.

Chapter 16

Religion—Mother Moon Becomes the Virgin Mary—Myths—The Creation—The Deluge—Folk-lore—The Crow's Story to the Parrot—Brother Coyote—Beliefs about Animals.

The pagans or *gentiles* in the barrancas say that they have two gods, but no devil. These gods are Father Sun (Nonorúgami) and Mother Moon (Yerúgami). The Sun guards the men in the daytime; therefore the Tarahumares do not transact business after sunset. He also makes the animals sleep. The Moon watches at night, and is the special deity of the women. In her nightly vigils she is assisted by her son, the Morning Star, who commands all the other stars, because they are his sons and they are Tarahumares. The Stars advise their brothers on earth when thieves are entering their houses. When the Tarahumares affirm anything solemnly, they say, "By those above!" meaning the Sun, Moon, and the Stars.

But the greater part of the Tarahumares are nominally Christians, though all that they know of Christianity are the words *Señor San José and Maria Santisima.* Moreover, they have adopted the words *Tata* (Father) *Dios* (God) for their Father Sun; and the Virgin Mary becomes with them a substitute for Mother Moon, and in natural sequence the wife of Tata Dios. They celebrate in their own peculiar way all the Christian feasts they know, with as much pleasure and as elaborately as their own native ceremonies.

Next in importance is the Devil, whom they fear even more than their own sorcerers. He is always represented with a big beard, such as the Mexicans wear. He is old and has only one eye, and the shamans have seen him often. He plays the guitar, but never the violin, because the bow and the strings form a cross. He would like very much to go to heaven, and the shamans have to work hard to keep him from doing so. There is also a female devil, his wife, who bears many children, always twins, who are the original Mexicans.

Their paradise consists in big ranches, where they will get all the animals which in this life they sacrificed to Tata Dios. The occupation of Tata Dios in heaven is to run foot-races with the angels, while the Devil vies with the sorcerers in making the lives of the Tarahumares uncomfortable, he being the chief sorcerer of all.

The Tarahumares are the sons of God, and the Mexicans the sons of the Devil. For this reason the Tarahumares say that it is no crime to eat the cows of the Mexicans; they think the cows do not really belong to the Shabotshi anyway. Neither do they tell when a Tarahumare steals anything from a Mexican, while they are very quick to find out if one Tarahumare steals from another.

I give here some of the myths and traditions of the tribe. Those which Christian ideas have entered into will easily be recognized, and it is not necessary to draw special attention to them.

CREATION MYTHS

In the beginning there were many worlds before this, but one after the other came to an end. Just before the world was destroyed for the last time, all the rivers flowed toward the place where the sun rises. But now the waters also flow toward the other side, where the sun sets.*

The bears put the world into shape. Before their time it was nothing but a waste of sand.

In ancient times there were plenty of lagoons around Guachochic; but the land was put in order, when the people came and began to dance yūmarí.

The rocks were at first soft and small; but they grew until they became large and hard. They have life inside.

The people grew up from the soil, while the earth was as level as a field ready for sowing. But in those days they lived to be only one year old, and then they died like the flowers.

According to another tradition they descended from heaven with corn and potatoes in their ears, and were led by Tata Dios into these mountains, the middle of the world, having originally come from the north-east or east.

THE SUN AND THE MOON IN THE BEGINNING OF THE WORLD

In the beginning the Sun and the Moon were alone, and they were children. They wore dresses made of palm-leaves, and they lived in a house thatched with palm-leaves. They had neither cattle nor sheep. Both the Sun and the Moon were dark, and the Morning Star was the only one that shed any light on the earth. The Moon was eating lice from the hair of the Sun, and Morning Star was watching at night. There were 600 Tarahumares at that time, and they were much hampered by the darkness. They could not do their work, and they had to hold each other's hands, and they were stumbling all the time. Then they cured the Sun and the Moon by dipping small crosses into tesvino, and touching the Sun and the Moon on the chest, on the head, and on the back. Then the Sun and the Moon began to shine and to shed light.

STAR LEGEND

A man lived with three women. He was making arrows while they went to look for squirrels and woodchucks,

*The Rio Fuerte, the only large water-course in the Tarahumare country, empties into the Pacific Ocean.

away." When the man saw them running away he shot arrows after them. The women were ascending to heaven, holding each other's hands, and he transfixed them to the sky, where they can still be seen just as they rose, as three bright stars in the belt of Orion. The three women remained in heaven but the man remained in the world and was changed into a coyote.

DELUGE LEGENDS

When the world became full of water, a little girl and a little boy climbed up on a mountain, called Lavàchi (gourd), which is south of Panalachic, and when the waters subsided they came down again. They brought three grains of corn and three beans with them. The rocks were soft after the flood, and the footprints of the little boy and the little girl may still be seen. They planted the corn and went to sleep and had a dream that night; then they harvested, and all the Tarahumares are descended from them.

The Tarahumares were fighting among themselves, and Tata Dios sent much rain, and all the people perished. After the flood he sent three men and three women to people the earth. They planted corn at once, bringing three kinds, the same varieties still found here—soft corn, hard corn, and yellow corn.

GIANTS

On the heights once lived giants. They were as big as pine-trees and had heads as big as bowlders. They taught the Tarahumares how to plant corn, by cutting down trees and burning them, but they ate children.

A woman bore a giant in a cave, which was situated very high up on the side of a valley. She died, because the child was so large, and he was taken care of by his grandmother. Once when she was asleep, she turned over and crushed him.

From Wasivori (near Cusarare) came giants to Nararachic to ask alms. Tesvino they liked very much. They worked very fast, and the Tarahumares put them to hoe and weed the corn, and gave them food and tesvino. But the giants were fierce, and ravished the women while the latter were under the influence of the Moon; therefore the Tarahumares got very angry and they mixed a decoction made from the chilicote-tree with the corn that they gave the giants to eat, and the giants died.

TATA DIOS AND THE DEVIL—THE SHEEP AND THE DEER—WHY THE COCKS CROW IN THE MORNING*

Tata Dios came down into the world, and he had in his house many large jars filled with strong tesvino. On the other side of the river Huerachic, in the big arroyos, lived the Devil. He was very poor, and he had only one small jar with tesvino, and that was bad. The Devil and his brother invited Tata Dios to come and drink tesvino with them. Tata Dios went to the Devil's house, and they gave him the jar and the drinking-gourd, and he sat down to drink; but he did not get intoxicated because there was not enough tesvino. When he had emptied the jar, Tata Dios said: "Now we will go to my house and drink tesvino; I have some, too." They accepted the invitation, and all went away together, and Tata Dios gave them a large jar full of tesvino and the drinking-gourd. They drank much, and the Devil and his brother sang like Mexicans, until they lay down on the ground completely overcome. Later in the night the Devil rose, and he went to the wife of Tata Dios. And when she awoke, she was very angry, and roused her husband, and he fought with the Devil, until Tata Dios got killed. But after a while he rose and said to the Devil, "Now go away, go below." "I am going home to get my weapons," said the Devil. But first he went into the house of Tata Dios and robbed him of his money, and [noticing the reporter's book] of his books and everything. He hid all the things in his house and Tata Dios came to look for them. Tata Dios again was very angry, and they fought until he was killed. But this time, too, he rose and said to the Devil, "Go below," and the Devil went below and remained there, and Tata Dios went home.

One day at dawn the people saw the lands full with sheep everywhere. On a flat stone Tata Dios drew figures like the tracks of the deer, and from them all the deer originated.

When Tata Dios returned to heaven, he carried in his right hand a rooster, which he placed on top of a palm-tree. The cock crowed three times while Tata Dios ascended to heaven. After this, whenever the sun rises in the morning, the cocks on earth respond when they hear the cocks in heaven crow.

After Tata Dios had gone to heaven he never came back. He is angry with the Tarahumares, and he wants to destroy the world, but the Virgin says: "Let the people alone; I pity the family we left behind." This is the reason why the world stands.

When Tata Dios went away, he said, "I will leave two crosses here." He then put up a cross where the sun sets at the end of the world, and another where the sun rises. The cross in the east he uses when he rises to heaven and when he comes to visit the Tarahumares, and the cross in the west is for the Tarahumares when they die and go to heaven. Between these two crosses the Tarahumares live. They would like to go to the crosses and worship before them, but they are prevented from doing so by large bodies of water. They therefore set up small crosses in front of their houses, and before them they hold their dances, and God comes to eat near these crosses. He only eats the soul or substance of the food, and leaves the rest for the people.

THE GIANTS, THE CROW, AND THE BLACKBIRD

The Crow, who is very knowing, told the following story to the Parrot, who told it to the poagans:

The Blackbird and the Crow, long, long ago, saw a contest between two giants, who made a bet as to which of them could throw a stone the farthest. The stakes were four deer. One giant, called Gōlí, carried a bird in his hand and threw it instead of the stone; so he won; then he returned to where the Blackbird and the Crow were standing. The Blackbird said to the Crow, "They will not do us any harm until they stoop to pick up a stone." But the Crow replied,

*As related by an old "Christian" Tarahumare woman in Huerachic, on the upper Rio Fuerte.

"Maybe they bring the stone in their hands." So they flew away, and while they were flying the Crow said, "I am going to the mountain to look for my wife and my son. They went away and have been lost for six days."

THE DEER, THE TOAD, AND THE CROW

The Crow set out for the mountain, where the Deer and the Toad were making a bet. "Let us try," they said, "who can see the sun first in the morning." The stakes were twenty-five Gadflies, and they asked the Crow to be a witness to the contest. In the morning they were ready to watch for the sun. The Toad was looking westward from the highest mountain, but the Deer looked to the east. The Toad said, "Look here, Brother Crow, I have already seen the sun starting," and the Crow said to the Deer: "Brother Deer, you have lost. Give him the twenty-five Gadflies." The Deer asked one day's time to catch the Gadflies, but the Toad thought he was not going to pay him, and said to the Deer, "Let us have a race, that you may settle your bet." The Deer readily consented to this, and a stone was put up as the goal. The Toad went away to call many other toads, and placed them at intervals toward the goal, and when the Deer arrived at the stone the Toad was already sitting on it, and said, "Brother Deer, you have lost." And the Deer went away.

Then the Toad said to the Gadflies: "Go and sting the Deer much, that he may have to run quickly. If you will sting him much, I will never eat you." The Gadflies were vexed with the Deer, because he had put them up on a bet, therefore they were very willing to sting the Deer, and they have been stinging him ever since.

STORY OF THE COYOTE

The Coyote asked permission from Tata Dios to come into the world, and Tata Dios asked him what he would do there. The Coyote replied that he would steal the animals and the corn from the Tarahumares. Then Tata Dios gave him permission to go and make a living in this way, because the Coyote did not know how to work.

THE MOUNTAIN LION, THE COYOTE, AND THE GREY FOX

The Coyote challenged the Mountain Lion to a contest, that they might see which of them had the better eyesight and was the smarter. The Lion said, "Let us see who can first shoot an animal." Then he proposed that they should go to a water-hole, and to this the Coyote agreed; so they started out on the hunt. The Lion climbed up on a tree, but the Coyote remained below on the ground, and paid no attention to what the Lion was doing. A deer came, and the Lion struck it dead. The Coyote saw this from where he was hunting, and by and by he found a dead mare. When they met again the Lion said to the Coyote, "Well, how did you get on?" The Coyote replied: "Very well; I killed a mare." But the mare had been dead so long that she was smelling. Therefore the Lion said to the Coyote, "Don't be a liar," and he chased him off, and the Coyote was ashamed of himself.

The Coyote next met the Grey Fox, and told him to go and challenge the Lion. The Grey Fox went to the Lion and said: "How do you do, Brother Lion? I hear you got the best of Brother Coyote." The Lion replied: "No Brother Grey Fox; the Coyote made a fool of himself." Then the Grey Fox said: "Let us see whether you can get the best of me, and which of us can catch a rabbit first." So they went to the mountain to look for rabbits. At sunrise the Lion took a position facing the north, and the Grey Fox faced south, and both of them watched for rabbits. After spying for a while, the Lion saw one, but by that time the Grey Fox was asleep alongside of him. So the Lion said to the rabbit: "Pass right between us, and then go to the hole in the oak-tree on the rock, and act as if you wanted to go into the hole, but go away to one side." Then the Lion woke up the Grey Fox and said: "Over there is a rabbit. He went into a small hole into which I cannot follow him; but you are small, and you can catch him." The Grey Fox just saw the rabbit's tail disappearing behind the rock, but the rabbit hid himself, and did not enter the hole, as the Lion had told him. "All right," said the Grey Fox, "I will go; but, as you saw the rabbit first, you have won the bet." But the Lion said: "No; you go into the hole, and fetch the rabbit out and eat him." Then the Grey Fox entered the hole, and the Lion made a fire in front of it, and when the Grey Fox came out again he was burned, and his feet were sore from the fire. That is why the Grey Fox always walks so lightly. And he reproached the Lion, saying that he was very bad, and begged him to let him go and not to kill him. He cried and went to hide himself in a cave, because he was afraid of the Lion. Then the Humming-bird who lived in the cave stung him in the face with his bill and in the eyes, and he went away and never came back again.

THE HENS, THE GREY FOX, AND THE COYOTE

The Woodpecker made a guitar and gave it to the Butterfly to play on, and the Cock danced a pascual, and the Cricket danced with the Locust, and the Hen was singing. While the dance was going on, the Coyote came to see what he could get from the feast, and the Grey Fox also came, and he brought some tunas (fruit of the nopal cactus). They were very nice and sweet, and he gave one to the Coyote, and said, "Here, Brother Coyote, take this nice mouthful." He had well rubbed off the spines, and the fruit tasted well to the Coyote. It made his heart glad, and he wanted more. The Grey Fox said to the Coyote, "I will give you more tunes, but you must eat them with your eyes shut." He gave him some tunas from which he had not cleaned off the spines, and as the spines hurt the Coyote he became very angry and wanted to eat the Grey Fox. But the Fox said to him: "Don't be angry, Brother Coyote: I will give you a drink; and don't howl, because there are dogs around." He went to the Cock and to the Hen, and asked them for tesvino, and he brought it to the Coyote and said, "Here, Brother Coyote, drink this." The Coyote drank two gourdsful, and then a third one, and when he had finished this he began to howl, because he was very drunk, and he asked the Grey Fox, "Why are they all dancing?" The Grey Fox replied: "They dance, because Miss Cricket married Mister Locust; therefore the Butterfly is playing on the guitar, and the Cock dances with delight, and the Hen is singing." But the Coyote said: "I don't want the Hen to sing; I want to eat her." Then the Grey Fox took the Coyote into the arroyo and told him to remain there, while he went to fetch the Hen. But instead of the Hen he got two very fierce dogs and put them in a bag, and carried them into the arroyo, where the Coyote was waiting. He was very drunk and very angry, and he said to the Grey Fox, "Why did you keep me waiting so long, you cursed old Grey Fox!" The Grey Fox replied: "Don't be angry, Brother Coyote; here I bring you some very nice Hens. I was looking for many of them that is why I remained away so long. Now, shall I let them out one by one, or do you want them all at once?" The Coyote replied, "Let them out all at once, that I may have a good old time with them." Then the Grey Fox opened the bag, and out came the two fierce dogs; and they caught the Coyote and bit him and tore him to pieces. The Grey Fox ran away and hid himself, but afterward he came and got the paws of the Coyote and threw them into a water-pool.

THE MOUNTAIN LION AND THE BEAR

The Mountain Lion killed a deer, and the Bear wanted to take it away from him. They fought, and the Lion won, and the Bear asked his pardon, because the Lion is more powerful than the Bear.

THE FROG AND THE COYOTE

The Frog and the Coyote made a wager as to which of them would gain in a foot-race. They were to run along a ridge, and return to a point close by the starting-point. The Coyote lost, because the Frog jumped directly over to the finishing-point. This happened twice, and the Coyote wanted to kill the Frog, but the Frog dived into a water-hole, where the Coyote could not catch him.

The Bears, whose skin is of the same color as the Tarahumares, are called "grandfathers," ūmúli, and are so to speak their forebears. In ancient times they danced on top of the mountains, where they have roads yet.

Often the bears are sorcerers, who, after death, assumed the shape of these animals. In fact, there are two kinds of bears, one that is real, and another one that is a dead Tarahumare. The people do not know which is which. Only the shamans can make the distinction, and it is useless to try and kill the man-bear, because he has a very hard skin, and arrows cannot pierce it. He is the very devil.

The following curious incident happened near Nararachic a few years ago: A bear had done much damage to a Tarahumare's corn-field. Some forty Indians with over fifty dogs gathered together to kill the bear. In order to make the dogs ferocious, the Indians set them to fight among each other, by way of preparing them for the hunt. The Indians now divided themselves into several parties, and presently one lot encountered the bear. They asked the shaman who was with them whether the creature was a bear or something else, and he replied, "Let the dogs on and see." As the dogs had never seen a bear, they were timid, and did not bark or attack the beast; therefore the shaman said: "This is not a bear. All is lost. The dogs do not know him, and the bear does not see the dogs with his eyes. He is from hell, and he is a devil, who came here in the shape of a bear, because he wants to eat us. Let him alone and let us all go away." And they all retreated.

The mountain lion is a good animal and watches over the people. When he sees an animal such as the bear or the coyote approach a man, he roars to warn the man; and if the man pays no attention, the lion attacks the animal to save the man; therefore strips of his skin are worn around the ankles and the neck as a protection.

The grey fox is considered an astute animal and is feared. If he passes by a house in which there is a sick person, and calls three times, the patient will die. One of my Indian men related the following story: One night he and another man were sleeping in a house when he heard the grey fox whistle. At first he did not know what it was, and he said to his companion, "Listen, what is that?" The other one said, "This is a very bad thing, very ugly." He was a man who knew something, and he said, "If this grey fox returns for two nights more and whistles outside of the house of our sick neighbour, that man will die." My informant did not believe this at the time; but the next night the grey fox returned and whistled very uncannily, and on the third night he did it again. And on the following morning a man came and asked the Indian to help him to bury the neighbour who had died during the night. They went to the house of the dead man, and "then," the narrator concluded, "I knew that the grey fox had said the truth, for the grey fox never tells a lie."

The grey fox and the rabbit in ancient times danced rutubúri.

The horned toad holds the world. It says: "Don't tread on me! I am the colour of the earth and I hold the world; therefore walk carefully, that you do not tread on me."

The master of the deer lives inside of the mountains, in the earth; therefore the Tarahumares place small quantities of corn and beans, or three arrows in a jar, on top of the highest mountain to buy the deer from the one below.

The brown ground squirrel (chipawíki), which lives among rocks and seldom ascends trees, is thought to become a serpent. This belief is also current among certain classes of Mexicans. A Mexican told me that a man once smashed the head of a chipawíki in the hollow of a tree, and when he wanted to take his game out, he found that the rest of the animal had the body of a serpent. It cannot be used for sacrifices.

Rats become bats.

The owl is very bad. Whenever it comes to a house and screeches, somebody falls ill. If it calls three times, in three consecutive nights, the sick person will die. The owl is also very smart. It knows when the Tarahumare's blanket (in which he is wrapped when sleeping along the fire) is going to be burned. When the owl hoots near a home it says, "Chu-i, chu-i, chu-i,"—"dead, dead, dead." Owls are killed but not eaten.

The goat sucker makes darts through the air and calls down rain. It has two nice fat young, which the Tarahumares consider a great delicacy.

The crow is much in disfavour because it eats the corn. Only the young crows are eaten.

The large swifts (olamáka) are thought to be witches, who pierce the souls of people and eat them. They are used by the sorcerers, whom they obey like dogs. Once a woman was sitting in a corn-field watching it by the side of a fire, and making yarn, when a swift settled on her skirt. She told a girl to bring a large basket, with which she covered the bird up, caught it and had it for many years. Every night the bird flew away, and then returned in the morning. Once, when the woman was absent at a tesvino feast, the girl killed the bird and roasted it. She could not eat it, however, because it had such a bad smell, and the woman found it on her return in the basket, dead and roasted. The girl ran away and the raccoons ate the corn the woman was watching.

The giant woodpecker during the wet season rises high up toward the sun; that is why he gets his tail burned.

When the Tarahumares handle any kind of fish they take care not to touch their hair, for fear that it may turn grey and they become old.

The rattlesnakes are the companions of the sorcerers and watch to meet them and then talk with them. A Mexican once killed a rattlesnake, and the Indian grew very angry and said that the snake had protected his house; now he had no one to guard it.

Large serpents, which only the shamans can see, are thought to live in the rivers. They have horns and very big eyes.

The dragon-fly has no song; it flies about without making a noise.

Tata Dios put sheep into the world; they are good animals because they give wool from which people can weave blankets, and their meat is good, and they do not weep when they are killed. But goats were put into the world by the Devil; their hair is of no use, their meat is bad, and they howl much when they are killed.

Chapter 17

The Shamans or Wise Men of the Tribe—Healers and Priests in One—Disease Caused by Looks and Thoughts—Everybody and Everything Has to Be Cured—Nobody Feels Well without His "Doctor"—Sorcery—The Powers of Evil Are As Great As Those of Good—Remarkable Cure for Snake Bite—Trepanning among the Ancient Tarahumares.

Without his shaman the Tarahumare would feel lost, both in this life and after death. The shaman is his priest and physician. He performs all the ceremonies and conducts all the dances and feasts by which the gods are propitiated and evil is averted, doing all the singing, praying, and sacrificing. By this means, and by instructing the people what to do to make it rain and secure other benefits, he maintains good terms for them with their deities, who are jealous of man and bear him ill-will. He is also on the alert to keep those under his care from sorcery, illness, and other evil that may befall them. Even when asleep he watches and works just as if his body were awake. Though real illness is the exception with him, the Tarahumare believes that an ounce of prevention is better than a pound of cure, and for this reason he keeps his doctor busy curing him, not only to make his body strong to resist illness, but chiefly to ward off sorcery, the main source of trouble in the Indian's life. The demand for shamans is therefore great, but the supply is quite equal to it. For instance, in the little village of Nararachic and the neighbouring ranches, where there are about 180 households, twenty-five shamans are living, each of whom takes care of about twenty souls, though only about ten of them enjoy great reputation in the community.

Before a man is allowed to consider himself a shaman, he is examined by a "board" of recognized members of the profession, who pass upon his fitness to enter their ranks.

These priest-doctors have their specialties. Some sing only at rutuburi or yumari dances, others only at hikuli-feasts. A few of them do not sing at all, but are merely healers, although far the greater number also sing at the feasts. Those who make a specialty of the hikuli cult are considered the greatest healers. They all conscientiously fast and pray. Complying with the demands of the gods, which impose restrictions and abstinence, and they are therefore called "righteous men" (owirúami). They are the wise men of the tribe; and as rainmakers, healers, and keepers of the heritage of tribal wisdom and traditions, their influence is powerful.

Their services are never rendered gratuitously; in fact, what with the payments they receive from singing at feasts and curing the sick, they generally manage to live better than the rest of the people. Whenever a shaman is hungry, he goes to the house of some of his well-to-do clients and cures the family, receiving all the food he wants in payment for his efforts, for what would become of the people if the shaman should die? The Devil would surely take them away at once. Therefore the best parts of the meat from the animal killed for the feast is given to the shamans, and they generally get all the tesvino they can hold. In winter time, when numerous feasts are being held, the shamans are nearly all the time under the influence of their native stimulants. Yet this does not seem to harm them, nor does it in the estimation of the people detract from the efficacy of their singing; the curing is no less potent, even though the doctor can hardly keep from falling all over his patient. It is always incumbent on the shamans to be peaceful, and they never fight at the feasts.

The singing shamans invariably have a primitive musical instrument, the rattle, with which they beat time to their singing and dancing. Ordinarily it is made from a gourd filled with pebbles and mounted on a short stick which serves as a handle. Another kind is made from coarse shavings glued together. The latter variety is not infrequently decorated with daubs of red or some similar painting. Sometimes at the feast the shaman, even nowadays, may be seen wearing a head-dress made of the plumes of birds. Through the plumes the birds are thought to impart all that they know. Besides, the plumes are supposed to keep the wind from entering the shaman's body, and thus prevent him from falling ill.

When curing, the shamans may sometimes use rational means. There is in existence around Norogachic for instance, a kind of sweating-bath, made by placing in a hole in the ground, just large enough for a man to sit in, several hot stones, pouring water on them, and covering them up with branches of the fragrant mountain cedar. The steam passing through the latter is credited with curative power.

The Indians know several excellent medicinal herbs. Palo amarillo is a kind of household remedy used extensively in every family. There are many other highly valued herbs and trees, some of which have a wonderfully refreshing and invigorating aromatic scent. Headache is cured by a green herb called pachoco, of which they smell until they begin to sneeze. To cure constipation they boil ari with a grain of salt, or they heat stones and pour water over them and sit over the steam.

Both the sacred little cactus called híkuli and the maguey have undoubtedly medicinal properties, but the administration of these remedies, especially of the former, is connected with so many rites and ceremonies that their therapeutic value becomes obscured. The curative power of tesvino is absolutely magical, and this is the remedy to which recourse is most commonly had. In administering it the shaman makes his customary passes, and exhales over the patient to blow away the disease. He also dips a small cross into the liquor, and with the wetted end taps the sick man on the head, neck, shoulders, and back, and draws crosses over his arms. Finally the patient is given three spoonfuls of the liquor while all the members of the family stand around and murmur approvingly, "Thank you, thank you." Occasionally tesvino is exclusively used for curing, with the aid of two small crosses, one of red Brazil wood, the other of white pine. If he chooses, a shaman may provoke illness as well as cure it, but he cannot cure the person he made ill.

When a shaman is asked to cure a person of any complaint, real or imaginary, his first move is to find the cause of the trouble. According to his opinion illness is brought on either by the wind or by sorcery. From the former kind of disease nobody dies, although the heart, the liver, or the head may be attacked; but the other kind is serious. Sorcerers may put snakes into the legs, and such animals as centipedes, toads, larvae, scorpions, or even small bears into the body of some unfortunate person, and these disturbers have to be drawn out at once or else they will eat the sick man's heart. The shaman therefore first feels the patient all over, to find if something—in other words, the disease-bringing animal—is moving underneath the skin. Illness may also result from small stones, or the spine of the nopal placed in the body by the same agency.

A person suspected of having been bewitched is told to hold his mouth open to the sun, that the shaman may see whether the evil entered the body through this aperture. People become bewitched at night through the openings of the body, and the shaman also examines the nostrils, ears, etc. It is also the shaman's business to find out who caused the trouble, and since he can see more than ordinary people he is able to track the offender.

Some people by their mere looks or thoughts are liable to make a person ill. Such illness may be brought on in retaliation for some slight or offence, and may even result in death. The first thoughts of a person falling ill are: Whom have I offended? What have I taken that I should have left alone, and what have I kept that I should have given? Then the shaman may tell him to find the person to whom he had refused to give food, and the sick one and his wife go from house to house asking the people: "Was it you whom I refused food? Someone has made me ill, and I want him to make me well again." If he can find the person whom he had offended, and arrange matters with him, he will recover.

The doctor may find that the person's heart is on the wrong side, and prescribe a liberal allowance of tesvino to get it back to its proper place. But generally the skill of the shaman is taxed more severely and he resorts to the more direct and powerful methods of magic. A common occurrence is that of illness caused by maggots, which the shaman has to extract from the patient by means of a sucking-tube, a short piece of reed about three inches long, cut from a kind of reed different from that of the arrow-shaft. He places it on the afflicted spot, and after sucking vigorously for a minute or so empties from his mouth into his hand or into a corn-leaf, what purports to be the maggots. I never had an opportunity of examining closely the small white bits of something or other that he spit out, but they seemed to me to be tiny pieces of buckskin which the man had secreted in his mouth and which swelled up when saturated with saliva. To the shaman they represent maggots; that is, the embodiment of the disease, and all the people firmly believe that they are maggots. The corn-leaf and its contents are buried; a cross is made on the ground over the spot and a ceremonial circuit run around it. When resting between operations, the shaman places his sucking-tube into a bowl of water in which some herbs are soaking.

The mode of curing, however, varies. A common way in use near Guachochic is to make the patient stand on all fours and bathe him well with water; then to place him on a blanket and carry him over a fire toward the cross and the four corners of the world. When put down on the ground again he lies or kneels on the blanket, and the shaman places his tube against the afflicted part and begins to suck forcibly, while the rest of the people stand around with sticks, ready to kill the disease so as to prevent it from returning and doing harm to others. Presently the shaman produces from his mouth a small stone, which he asserts was the cause of the disease. While the people are furiously beating the air, he proceeds at once to bury it in the earth, or in the bottom of the river, into which he dives. He may suck out as many as eight stones, but generally contents himself with four; and for treating a man in this way he receives four almuds of maize.

On one occasion, when I had taken a little cold, I asked a shaman friend whether he could cure me. "Certainly I can," was the confident reply. He took from a little basket, in which he kept his hikuli or sacred cacti and probably similar valuables, three black stones and said that he would sell one of these to me; if I put it into warm water it would cure me. This was not quite to my liking, as I wanted him to perform the magical feat of sucking maggots out of the skin. He complied with my request, and told me to go ahead to my camp, whither he would follow me soon. On his arrival I offered him some food, as my case was not urgent, but he declined, and proceeded to cure me. A saddle blanket was spread out for me to kneel on, and my Mexican and Indian attendants were told to retire, while he made his examination. Having ascertained that I had a headache, he took my head between his dirty hands, pressed it, applied his lips to my right ear, and commenced to suck very energetically. This was rather trying to my nerves, though not unendurably so. Presently he let go his hold, and spit out quite a lot of blood into a cup an Indian boy was holding out to him. He repeated the operation on my left ear with the same result. "More pain?" he asked.

"Yes," I said, "In my right hand." He immediately grabbed that member in his mouth, by biting almost through the skin over the pulse, and after having sucked for a little while, deposited contents, of a similar nature, into the cup from his mouth. It was afterward found that the blood was mixed with a considerable number of grass seeds, which had been the cause of my illness. I had not known that I was so "seedy."

The curing is often performed at dances, during the night, as the family who give the feast expect to receive, in return for all their trouble and expense, the benefit of the shaman's magic powers, whether any of them are ill or not. Once a man, his wife, and his child had been cured with tesvino, but nevertheless they still anxiously looked to the shaman for more treatment, apparently feeling that they needed more strength against coming evil. The woman said: "Yesterday I fell into the water and got wet and felt ill, and in the night I dreamed that I was dead and that you cured me." To this the doctor replied, "Yes, that is why I came to cure you." Then, yielding to their beseeching glances, he daubed them again, this time holding their hands and with a little cross in his left hand. Then he said; "Now you need not be afraid; I have cured you well. Do not walk about any more like fools and do not get wet again." And they were content.

There is a shaman near Baqueachic (bākā́ = bamboo reed) who has a great reputation for curing cattle, or rather for keeping them in health. Every year he makes a tour of the different ranches, and the Indians bring their animals to him to be treated. A large hole is dug in the ground and a fire kindled in it. Then some green branches of the mountain cedar and some copal are thrown in and burned, and the animals driven one by one through the smoke. Since the veterinary gets one animal for each ceremony, he becomes quite rich.

The shamans also undertake to cure the sun and the moon, because these, too, are often ill and have to be righted. Not a feast is held in which some spoonfuls from the jars containing the remedies are not thrown up for the benefit of the sun and the moon. Occasionally, however, special ceremonies have to be performed to cure the celestial bodies, particularly the moon, because from her all the stars receive their light. At the period of the dark moon she is considered to be sick and tied up by the Devil, and the world is sad. Then the shamans assemble to consult about her ailment and the means of curing her. An ox may be killed and tesvino made. In killing the animal, care is taken not to injure the heart, which is treated with great ceremony. The people always avoid touching it, and at sacrifices they hang it with the lungs to a stick raised near the cross. The shamans stand near, with small earthenware dishes containing copal incense; while the oldest cuts with his knife four crosses on four diametrically opposite points of the heart, and from the upper part all but slices off a piece, which is left hanging down beside the main part. All the blood the heart contained is sacrificed to the four cardinal points with much singing. Then the shaman asks for an earthen bowl which has never been used before, and in this he places the heart and burns it without adding fat or anything else. The ashes he rubs between his fingers until reduced to a fine dust, which he mixes with water and some medicinal herbs. The shamans stand in the middle, and the people around them, and all are unanimous in their prayer that they may see the moon. Each shaman takes three spoonfuls of medicine, the rest of which is thrown on the cross, and the shamans watch all night.

The Christian Tarahumares even feel called upon to cure the church when those buried in and around it have been noisily dancing and damaging the building to make the people give them tesvino. The principal shaman heads the procession, carrying a jar of liquor. His assistant holds in one hand a bowl containing water mixed with the crushed leaves of the maguey, and in the other some fresh maguey leaves. The tesvino, as well as the green water, is liberally thrown upon the walls and the floor of the church to lay the perturbed spirits.

How to cure smallpox is beyond the ken of the shamans, but they try to keep off the dread enemy by making fences of thorny branches of different trees across the paths leading to the houses; and snake-skins, the tail of the grey fox, and other powerful protectors or charms, are hung around the doors of their dwellings to frighten the disease away. The same purpose is accomplished through the pungent smell produced by burning in the house the horns of cows, sheep, and goats.

The shamans also profess to produce springs by sowing water. They make a hole one yard deep in the rocky ground. Water is brought in a gourd and poured into it, together with half an almud of salt. The hole is then covered up with earth, and after three years a spring forms.

High as the shamans stand in the estimation of the people, they are by no means exempt from the instability of mundane conditions, and the higher a man rises the less secure is his position. The power to see everything, to guard against evil, and to cure illness issues from the light of his heart, which was given him by Tata Dios. It enables him to see Tata Dios himself, to talk to him, to travel through space at will, for the shamans are as bright as the sun. But all this supposed great power to do good may at any moment be turned to evil purposes. There are indeed some shamans whose kindly, sweet-tempered manners and gentle ways enable them to retain their good reputation to the end; but few go through life who can keep themselves always above suspicion, especially when they grow older; and innocent persons have on this account been cruelly persecuted. Such a fate is all the more liable to befall them on account of the recognized ability of a shaman to both cure and produce disease.

No doubt the great quantity of stimulants taken by shamans in the course of their career causes them to go periodically through a state of excitement, which, combined with the enthusiasm which they work themselves up to, gradually gives to these men, who frequently are richly endowed with animal magnetism, a supernatural appearance. Advancing years have their share in making such a man look odd and uncanny, not only on account of his grey hair, wrinkled face, and shaggy eyebrows, but still more by his reserved bearing and distinctive personality. Women shamans, too, may turn bad and become witches.

Much as in cases of heresy among Christian ministers, the other shamans hold a consultation regarding a suspected colleague, and may decide that the light of his heart has failed him and that he is no longer one of them. From that time on, good people avoid him; they no longer give him food, and do not tolerate him about their homes; they are afraid of him; and the better a shaman he was before, the more terrible a sorcerer he is now supposed to have become. Soon every accident that happens in the locality is laid at the accused man's door.

There are, on the other hand, many evil-minded persons who pretend to possess supernatural powers to do harm, and accept payment for services of that kind; in short, who make it a business to be sorcerers. The power of the sorcerer to do evil is as great as the ability of the good shaman to cure it. The sorcerer may rasp on his notched stick, and sing death and destruction to a person or to attain his ends he may use hikuli, smooth stones, the corpse or the foreleg of some highly venerated animal and powerful rainmaker, as the toad, which is never killed except by bad persons. A terrible thing in the hands of a sorcerer is a humming-bird stripped of its feathers, dried, and wrapped in pochote wool. To the Tarahumares the brilliant little bird, often mentioned in their songs, is a good and mighty hero-god, but the sorcerer perverts his great power to his own evil purposes. The sorcerer is feared by all; pregnant women, especially, go out of his way, as he may hinder them from giving birth to their children. When Tarahumares see a shooting star they think it is a dead sorcerer coming to kill a man who did him harm in life, and they huddle together and scream with terror. When the star has passed, they know that somewhere a man has been killed, and that now the sorcerer is taking out his heart.

If a man does any harm to a powerful sorcerer, the latter, after death, enters into a mountain lion or jaguar or bear, and watches by the wayside until the offender comes, when he kills him.

Sorcerers are also believed to prevent rain from falling, and therefore the people were once much pleased when they saw me photographing a sorcerer. The camera was considered a powerful rain-maker, and was thought to make the bad man clean. The people may chastise a man suspected of sorcery, to frighten him from doing further mischief. A sick person also is supposed to improve when the sorcerer who made him ill is punished; but if accidents and misfortune continue to happen, the accused man may be killed. Such extreme measures have been resorted to even in recent years, though rarely.

The magical powers of a sorcerer are appalling. When a Tarahumare walks with a sorcerer in the forest and they meet a bear, the sorcerer may say: "Don't kill him; it is I; don't do him any harm!" or if an owl screeches at night, the sorcerer may say: "Don't you hear me? It is I who am calling."

The sorcerer dies a terrible death. Many dogs bark and run away and come back; they look like fire, but they are not; they are the evil thoughts of the sorcerer. The river, too, makes a greater noise as it flows, as if somebody were dipping up water and pouring it out again. Uncanny, weird noises come from every part of the house, and all the people in it are much frightened. Hardly anyone goes to talk to the dying man, and no one bids him good-bye. The Christian Tarahumares do not bury him in the churchyard with other people, but alone in a remote cave, and they bury all his things with him—his machete his axe, and heavy things that other people never take along, but which the sorcerer, because he is very powerful, can carry with him when he goes to heaven.

As we have seen, the medical education of the shamans is extremely limited. Their rational *materia medica* is confined to the hikuli cactus and a few roots and plants. Aside from this they have a cure for snake-bites which is really remarkable. The injured man kills the reptile, cuts out its liver and gall, and smears the latter over the wound; he may also eat a piece of the liver, but it must be taken from the animal that inflicted the injury, then he will be well again in three days. If people die of snake-bites, it is because the reptile escaped. The gall of a rattlesnake has a sickening smell; even my dogs were repulsed by it when I once killed a four-foot rattler. The method may be considered as in accord with the modern theory that the bile of many animals contains strong antitoxins.

However, there is nothing new under the sun. In the Talmud we find recommended as a cure for hydrophobia to eat the liver of the dog that bites one; and in the Apocrypha we read that Tobias was cured of blindness by the gall of a fish.

Most surprising of all is the fact that this tribe, which to-day shows but very slight knowledge of surgery, should in former times have practiced trepanning. That the Tarahumares understood this art is evident from two skulls which I brought back from their country. The skulls were found under the following circumstances:

In 1894 I stayed for a fortnight in a remote part of the Sierra Madre, called Pino Gordo on account of its magnificent pine-trees. The district is separated on the north from the central part of the Tarahumare country by the deep Barranca de San Carlos, and there are no Mexicans living within its confines. The place in which I found one of the skulls is twenty miles north of the mining town of Guadalupe y Calvo. A lonely trail leads through it on which, only occasionally, perhaps once in the course of a month, a Mexican from the ranches at Guachochic may journey to Guadalupe y Calvo.

One day the principal man of the locality, who had been very friendly to me, showed me a burial-cave. I had persuaded him that it was better for me to take away the bones contained in it, in order to keep them in a good house, than to let them remain where they were, "killing sheep and making people sick." "But why do you want them?" he asked. Having been satisfied on this point, he one day led the way to a wild, steep arroyo, pointed at its head, and having thus indicated where the cave was, at once left me. I made my way as best I could up the steep little gorge, accompanied by one of my men. On arriving at the top I found the entrance to the cave completely covered with stones plastered together with mud. A heap of stones was also piled outside against the wall.

The cave I found very small, and, contrary to the exaggerated reports of the Indians, it contained only three skeletons. According to the custom prevailing throughout part of the country of the Tarahumares, these remains had not been buried. The skeletons were simply lying on their backs, from east to west, as if looking toward the setting sun. A few crudely made clay vessels of the ordinary Tarahumare type were found alongside of them. On gathering the three skulls I was at once struck by a circular hole in the right parietal bone of one of them. As they undoubtedly belonged to the Tarahumares, the question at once occurred to me: Can it be possible that this barbaric tribe, not particularly advanced in the arts, was capable of trepanning? The remoteness of the place entirely negatives the suggestion that a civilized surgeon could have had anything to do with it.

The skull, the lower jaw of which is missing, is that of a Tarahumare woman over fifty years of age. The age of the specimen itself is impossible to arrive at, on account of the peculiar circumstances in which it was preserved. However, the cranial walls still contained some animal matter, were still somewhat fatty to the touch, and retained some odour. A spindle provided with a whorl made from a piece of pine-bark, which was lying among the bones in the cave, indicates that the body of this female had not been put there in recent times. This variety of whorl, so far as I can ascertain, has not been observed among the Tarahumares of the present day. It is, indeed, possible that the skeleton may be pre-Columbian.

The skull does not present any deformities or fractures, and the singular aperture is almost exactly round, measuring two centimeters in diametre. A careful examination shows that the cut was made a long time, several years in fact, before death. The regularity of the hole indicates beyond doubt that it is artificial.

Another skull taken from a burial-cave near Nararachic is also that of a female, and the opening here, too, is in the parietal bone, and in almost the same place as the opening in the first skull described. In this second specimen the cavity is almost filled in with new bone, and as in this instance the edges are very regular and uniform, and distinctly beveled, they show that the operation was performed by scraping. This cannot be said of the first specimen found; the almost circular form of the opening, and its perpendicular walls, prove conclusively that in this instance the surgeon did not employ the simple method of scraping the bone. I have never found among the Tarahumares any implement with which such an operation could have been performed. Possibly it was done with a kind of flint wimble with three teeth, much like the instrument used to-day in trepanning by the Berbers in L'Aurés, who cure even headaches by this method. It is, of course, impossible to say now whether the ancients performed the operation simply to relieve the patient of bone splinters, pus, blood, etc., pressing on the brain, or whether it was done to let out an evil spirit. It is the first time that cases of trepanning have been found in Mexico.

Chapter 18

Relation of Man to Nature—Dancing As a Form of Worship learned from the Animals—Tarahumare Sacrifices—The Rutuburi Dance Taught by the Turkey—The Yumari Learned from the Deer--Tarahumare Rain Songs—Greeting the Sun—Tarahumare Oratory—The Flowing Bowl—The National Importance of Tesvino—Homeward Bound.

Since the people obtain their subsistence from the products of the soil, they naturally are deeply concerned in the weather upon which their crops depend. Rain, therefore, is the focal point from which all their thoughts radiate. Even the plough is dipped into water before it is put to use, in order that it may draw rain. The people may try to force the moon and the sun to give them rain. In times of drought they reproach especially the moon for making the people live on the leaves of the ash-tree and what other poor stuff they can find; on her account they are getting so thin that they can no longer recognize themselves. They scold her, and threaten to denounce her to the sun. The sun himself may be rebuked for lack of rain. At other times they may throw up water to heaven with many ceremonies, that Tata Dios may replenish his supply. Generally, however, their relations with the gods, as with men, are based on the business principle of give and take.

Sacrifices of food, the meat of domestic animals or of game, and of tesvino, are needed to induce Father Sun and Mother Moon to let it rain. The favour of the gods may be won by what for want of a better term may be called dancing, but what in reality is a series of monotonous movements, a kind of rhythmical exercise, kept up sometimes for two nights. By dint of such hard work they think to prevail upon the gods to grant their prayers. The dancing is accompanied by the song of the shaman, in which he communicates his wishes to the unseen world, describing the beautiful effect of the rain, the fog, and the mist on the vegetable world. He invokes the aid of all the animals, mentioning each by name and also calls on them, especially the deer and the rabbit, to multiply that the people may have plenty to eat.

As a matter of fact, the Tarahumares assert that the dances have been taught them by the animals. Like all primitive people, they are close observers of nature. To them the animals are by no means inferior creatures; they understand magic and are possessed of much knowledge, and may assist the Tarahumares in making rain. In spring, the singing of the birds, the cooing of the dove, the croaking of the frog, the chirping of the cricket, all the sounds uttered by the denizens of the greensward, are to the Indian appeals to the deities for rain. For what other reason should they sing or call? For the strange behaviour of many animals in the early spring the Tarahumares can find no other explanation but that these creatures, too, are interested in rain. And as the gods grant the prayers of the deer expressed in its antics and dances, and of the turkey in its curious playing, by sending the rain, they easily infer that to please the gods they, too, must dance as the deer and play as the turkey.

From this it will be understood that dance with these people is a very serious and ceremonious matter, a kind of worship and incantation rather than amusement. Never do man and woman dance together, as in the waltz and polka of civilised people. The very word for dancing, "nolávoa," means literally "to work." The wise old man may reproach laggard, inexperienced younger ones, saying, "Why do you not go to work?" meaning that they should go to the dance and not stand idly about while the feast is going on. If the Tarahumares did not comply with the commands of Father Sun and dance, the latter would come down and burn up the whole world.

The Indian never asks his god to forgive whatever sin he may have committed; all he asks for is rain, which to him means something to eat, and to be free of evil. The only wrong toward the gods of which he may consider himself guilty is that he does not dance enough. For this offence he asks pardon. Whatever bad thoughts or actions toward man he may have on his conscience are settled between himself and the person offended. I once asked a prominent heathen shaman why the people were not baptised, and he said: "Because Tata Dios made us as we are. We have always been as you see us. People do not need to be baptised, because there is no devil here. Tata Dios is not angry with us; why should he be? Only when people do bad things does he get angry. We make much beer and dance much, in order that he may remain content; but when people talk much, and go around fighting, then he gets angry and does not give us rain."

Dancing not only expresses prayers for rain and life, but also petitions the gods to ward off evil in any shape, as diseases of man, beast, or crops. The people may dance also in case too much rain is falling, or for luck in field work, hunting, despatching the dead, etc.; and in this way they also give thanks for the harvest. By dancing and with tesvino they express all their wants to the gods, or, as a Tarahumare told me, "We pray by dancing and the gourd."

With the dances is always connected the sacrifice of an animal; the greater portion of the meat is eaten by the people themselves, who, beside, bring forth all kinds of nice food, the best they have. Such dancing festivals, as a matter of course, are given either by individuals or by the community. It is thought that Tata Dios himself comes down each time to make his demands on the

Tarahumares for dancing and sacrificing. He communicates his wishes in a dream to someone, not necessarily a shaman; and in the dry season, when the Indians begin to prepare their fields, most of these notices come and are generally made known to all at a race, where many people always come together. During all these months hardly a day passes without a messenger being sent out from some place in the country to advise one or the other of the principal shamans that God has come down and demanded a feast. Sometimes Tata Dios asks for an ox to be killed; at other times he wants only a sheep. Frequently he indicates that the animal must be white; on other occasions he is not particular about the colour. The threat is added that if the sacrifice is not forthcoming, and the people do not dance soon, all the corn will be burned up, and they will have to die of hunger. Or, if there has been too much rain, the notice may say that, unless they sacrifice and dance at once, all will be drowned, because it is going to rain tremendously. Occasionally it is directed that they dance only a little while, then rest, then dance again; or else they have to keep on dancing for a night and a day, or two nights in succession. When a great many sacrifices have been made and animals begin to be scarce, Tata Dios may have to content himself with iskiate and tortillas. The people may continue to make feasts and to dance, and yet get no other results but fresh messages, ordering still more sacrifices. Then the Indians begin to argue with Tata Dios that he must not be so greedy; he has filled himself up with oxen and sheep and tesvino, and they cannot give him any more. When such revolt seems imminent the shaman may throw out an ominous hint that the sacrifices have to be made; for what would the Tarahumares say if Tata Dios wanted one of them to be killed?

Among the reasons given by the Christian Tarahumares for continued dry weather are the following: The Devil has made Tata Dios sick and has tied him up; or the Moon (Virgin Mary) is sick; or the people have not given Tata Dios enough food and he is very hungry; or the railroad engines of the Americans are making so much smoke that Tata Dios is angry; or, finally, someone at a feast has infringed upon the law of decorum, and thereby annulled its value.

At present domestic animals are considered more valuable at sacrifices than the beasts of the field and the forest; yet squirrels (chipawiki), turkeys, deer, rabbits, and fish are still used to some extent, especially by those who do not possess domestic animals. Twenty men may go out to hunt a deer, or from six to ten men try to bring in four or five squirrels for a communal feast, to which all contribute the corn necessary for the tesvino, say, half an almud, more or less, according to the means of each householder. Never does any onr man give all the corn required for a tribal feast, though he may donate all the meat, in the shape of an ox, a cow, or a sheep. Goats are sacrificed only at burial functions. If the people do not give the best they have for the sacrifice, they will obtain only poor results.

The dances are always held in the open air, that Father Sun and Mother Moon may look upon the efforts of their children to please them. They dance on the level space in front of the dwelling, preferably each danced on its own patio. Some people have as many as three such dancing-places, but most of them have content themselves with one. If a Tarahumare could afford it, he would have ten patios to accommodate more people and dances near his house.

To my knowledge there are six different dances, but of these I will describe only two, the rutuburi and the yumari, as these are the most important and the two almost exclusively used in the central part of the country. The other four I saw only among the southern Tarahumares.

The rutuburi was taught to the people by the turkey. Generally three crosses are put up, and there are three shamans, the principal one being in the middle, his assistants need not be shamans, but the master of the house and his son, or some trusted friend, may officiate. When the dancing is about to begin, these men take a position in a line before the crosses, facing east, and shake their rattles continuously for two or three minutes from side to side, holding the instruments high up in the air, as the rattling is meant to attract the attention of the gods. Then, with the singing and shaking of the rattles—now down and up—they move forward in a manner similar to that of a schoolgirl skipping over a rope, passing the crosses to a point as far east as the starting-point was to the west, altogether about eighteen yards. Then they turn around and move back to the starting-point. In this way they keep on dancing forward and back three times, always in an easterly and westerly direction, swinging their rattles down and up, while passing from one point to the other, and from side to side whenever they reach it. The down-and-up movement of the rattle is not a simple down and up, but the down stroke is always followed by a short after-clap before the arm rises for the new swing, producing thus a three-part rhythm. They sing the following stanza, repeating it over and over again:

Introduction to Rutuburi

Ru – tu – bú – ri váe – ye – na Ru – tu – bú – ri váe – ye – na
Rutuburi, from one side to the other moving! Rutuburi, from one side to, etc.
Ó – ma wáe – ka xá – ru si. Ó – ma wáe – ka xá – ru – si.
All! many! Arms crossed! All! many! Arms crossed!

This is the introduction and prelude to the whole dance. After this formal opening the men take their places in line to the right of the shamans, and the women to the left. They stand for a few minutes while the shamans sing and swing their rattles, the men silently holding their arms folded over their breasts, as described in the song. This crossing of the arms I take to mean a salutation to the gods. While the Tarahumares of to-day never salute each other by shaking hands, neither is there any trace at present of their ever having saluted each other by crossing arms over the breast, which form was probably never used except with the gods, at ceremonies.

All the people are closely wrapped in their blankets, which they wear throughout the dance. In its general traits, the dance is performed in the same way as the opening ceremony. The shamans, or sometimes only the leader, jumps along as described, but the men just walk to and fro, and have to take long steps in order to keep abreast with the leaders. The women follow the men after the latter have gone several yards ahead, skipping in the same way as the shamans, though less pronounced. They stamp the hard ground with the right foot and run without regard to time, so that the pattering of their naked feet reminds one of a drove of mules stampeding. They overtake the men, so as to turn around simultaneously with them and wait again for a few seconds for the men to get ahead of them. Thus the dance is continued without interruption for hours and hours. This may sound as if the spectacle was monotonous; but such is not the case. On the contrary, there is a certain fascination in the regular, rhythmical movement from side to side—like the double pendulum of some gigantic, unseen clock. The shaman specially captivates the attention of the observer, being the very incarnation of enthusiasm. He swings his rattle with energy and conviction, as if bent on rousing the gods out of their indifference, while he stamps his right foot on the ground to add weight to the words, which he pours forth in a loud, resonant voice from his wide-open mouth. Although the Tarahumare, as a rule, has a harsh and not very powerful singing voice, still there are some noteworthy exceptions, and the airs of the rutuburi songs are quite pleasing to the ear. These, as all their dancing-songs, are of great antiquity and strangely enchanting.

*A kind of tomato

The water is near;
Fog is resting on the mountain and on the mesa.
The Bluebird sings and whirs in the trees, and
The Male Woodpecker is calling on the llano,
Where the fog is rising.
The large Swift is making his dashes through the evening air;
The rains are close at hand.
When the Swift is darting through the air he makes his whizzing, humming noise.
The Blue Squirrel ascends the tree and whistles,
The plants will be growing and the fruit will be ripening,
And when it is ripe it falls to the ground.
It falls because it is so ripe.
The flowers are standing up, waving in the wind.
The Turkey is playing, and the Eagle is calling;
Therefore, the time of rains will soon set in.

In the wet season, when the rabbits are about, the shamans sing of the rabbit. In the winter time they sing of the giant woodpecker, and in harvest time, when the people begin to make merry, they sing of the blackbird.

The yumari was learned from the deer. According to tradition it is the oldest dance. At the hour appointed, the shaman, facing the cross and the east, here, too, opens the proceedings by shaking his rattle to both sides to notify the gods. Then he begins to walk around the cross, humming a song and marching in time to the rattle, which he now swings down and up. He makes the ceremonial circuit, stopping at each cardinal point for a few seconds. After this he begins his dance, and the rest of the assemblage gradually join in. The dance consists in short walks, forward and backward, with lock-step, the men being arrayed in line on both sides of the shaman, their eyes fixed on the ground, their elbows touching. In this way they swing to and fro, generally describing a curve around the cross, or, sometimes, forming a circle against the apparent movement of the sun. The women dance in a similar way, in a course of their own behind the men; but they frequently break ranks, jumping forward and backward with movements wholly devoid of grace. When the dance goes in a circle, the women move with the sun.

[The tones marked with the accent > in each of the following Yumari songs are grunts.]

The yumari songs tell that the Cricket wants to dance; the Frog wants to dance and jump; and the Blue Heron wants to fish; the Goatsucker is dancing, so is the Turtle, and the Grey Fox is whistling. But it is characteristic of the yumari songs that they generally consist only of an unintelligible jargon, or, rather, of a mere succession of vocables, which the dancers murmur.

Unlike the rutuburi, the yumari soon becomes tiresome, in spite of its greater animation. Yet the spectacle has something weird in it, especially when seen by the fitful flicker of the fire, which throws a fantastic light upon the grotesque figures, like goblins moving about on the same space. Many mothers carry their sleeping infants on their backs. Sometimes, the blanket which supports the baby loosens, and the little thing hangs half out of it, following every movement of the parent.

At most feasts both these dances are performed, and the Indians themselves consider them to have the same general purpose. It is, therefore, not easy to see the relation of the two dances to each other. Rutuburi is the more serious dance, and is more efficacious than yumari, though the latter, of course, has its own special value; for instance, it expresses a prayer that the shaman may have strength to cure. In yumari, all sing and dance, and very frequently all the performers are drunk, while during the former dance absolute decorum is observed. Both dances are for the sun and the moon—rutuburi, in order to call them down; yumari, to despatch them. Therefore, the usual dancing-feasts commence with rutuburi. When the function is about to be concluded, an hour or two before sunrise, yumari is commenced, and leads over to the second part of the festival, the eating and drinking. After this, yumari may be continued throughout the day, while the Indians get drunk. Rutuburi is also danced at thanksgiving for the harvest, while on such occasions yumari asks for a good year to come. Then, again, rutuburi may be danced throughout the day, and yumari at night; but generally the former dance commences soon after sunset. On one occasion, while I was waiting for the performance to begin, the son of the house, in answer to my query, pointed to the sky, and told me that the dance would not commence until the Pleiades reached a certain spot in the heavens, which I calculated to mean about eleven o'clock. This indicated that the stars have some connection with the dancing.

At the break of dawn busy hands begin to get everything ready for the great ceremony of the sacrifice. For several days the women of the household and their friends have been making tortillas and boiling beans and *tamales* (small quantities of unsalted ground corn, wrapped and boiled in corn-husks). An animal was killed on the preceding day, and the meat has been boiling (without salt) in large jars all day and all night. Tata Dios does not like bones; therefore no bones are cooked with this meat. Several of the women have been dividing their time between dancing and watching the food-supply, to guard it against mishap from any source. A blanket is spread underneath, just to the west of the cross, or the three crosses, as the case may be, and on it in a line they place the jars of tesvino; behind these are set three small earthenware bowls filled with the stringy mass of the meat; then come three baskets of tortillas; and finally three little jars with wooden spoons in each are brought on and put in their proper places, behind the rest of the food. The latter vessels contain medicines to be taken, for the welfare of the people is looked after from every point of view.

In the meantime the dancing goes on with undiminished force. Nearly every night during the dry season, for nobody knows how many centuries, the Morning Star has been looking down upon his sons, the Tarahumares, as they dance in the heart of the sierra, casting his last rays upon the weird scene around their dying fires before he flees from the approaching keeper of the day. Just before the first beam of the rosy light announces the coming of Father Sun, the dancing ceases, and the rattles are added to the sacrificial offerings on the blanket. Everybody now is ready to do homage to the deity about to appear above the horizon. The shaman greets him with the words, "Behold, Nonorugami is coming!" and then solemnly proceeds toward the cross, while the people form a line behind him and preserve a respectful silence throughout the ensuing ceremony. He fills a large drinking-gourd with tesvino, and, holding it in his left hand, throws a small dipperful of the liquor with his right hand into the air, three times to each cardinal point, making the ceremonial circuit. Then the meat and the tortillas are sacrificed in the following way: The shaman takes up from the ground the vessel in front of him, and lifts it three times toward heaven. Then with his fingers he takes up a little meat, offers it to the cross with the word "Koá!" (Eat), and throws it up into the air. Next he breaks off a small piece of tortilla, and repeats the same ceremony. Thus he sacrifices to all the cardinal points. The two assistants of the shaman follow their principal in every act he performs.

The solemnity of the scene is by no means impaired by the numerous dogs, which are gathering to see what they can snatch up. Of course, the people drive them away, but in the end they always get Nonorugami's share of the food, while the god is supposed to eat only the nourishing substance.

What is left in the jars or bowls after the sacrifice is placed back on the blanket under the cross. The broth of the meat, too, is sacrificed, and so is the blood of the animal that has been killed for the feast.

Whenever the shaman returns to the people after performing the sacrifice, he says, "This was done on behalf of Nonrugami," and all the people respond: "Matetravá! Matetravá! Kalahúpo!" (Thank you! Thank you! It is all right!)

When the gods have had their share of the tesvino and the food, the curing begins. The medicines are cold infusions of different medicinal plants, the shaman standing directly in front of the middle cross, takes up the jar containing the chief medicine, palo hediondo; his assistant to the north takes up the bowl containing a root called ohnoa; and the one on the south maguey water. After having duly sacrificed to the gods, the great shaman himself takes three spoonfuls of the medicine, and gives the same quantity to his assistant to the north, who in turn first takes his remedy and then gives some to the shaman. In the same way the latter exchanges with his assistant to the south, and then the two assistants exchange remedies. The bowls are then handed by the shaman to the owner of the house, who in turn passes them on to the first man in the row, and from him they go from hand to hand to the last man in the line, each man taking three spoonfuls out of each bowl, while each of the women gets four. The man who drinks last gives the bowls back to the owner of the house, who in turn hands them to the shaman, who puts them back on the blanket underneath the cross. Meanwhile the incense-burners have been filled with hot coals, on which the shaman now throws some copal, the smoke of which he waves over all the people. He, as well as the other men, open their blankets a little to get the smoke on their bodies. This finishes the curing act, and now a speech is made. At private festivals the shaman is the orator of the occasion, but at communal or tribal festivals the gobernador is expected to, and generally does, perform this part of the proceedings. Rhetoric is one of the accomplishments of the Tarahumares, though it is not to be judged in accordance with the white man's standard. Here is a speech made by the gobernador at the end of one of the feasts I witnessed:

Listen to me! Stand up in a row and listen to what I have to tell you. All of you stand up in line, men, women, and children, because I am going to give you my words, to present to you the words which the One Above bids me to tell you. Now all is over! We have done something good to Tata Dios, and he has given you life to dance; and now he is giving you life for another year. All of you will have to make feasts like this. You have no experience; therefore listen to me and hear what I have to tell you. If you do not believe what I am telling you, the Devil will carry you off. You all are inexperienced, all of you who are standing here in a row around. Be quiet, and do all your business quietly. Drink quietly, talk quietly, sing quietly. And do not fight, because if in the fight you kill somebody, what will you have afterward? Nothing but sorrow and sadness! The One who is above us bids me to tell you, to say to all of you, men, women, and children, that this water, this tesvino that we are drinking is what makes us lose our heads. You know it all, and the One Above knows that this is the truth that I am telling you. Don't fight, don't pull each other's hair, don't beat anyone in the face until he bleeds. For the blood and the hair belong to Tata Dios, and you pull his hair and shed his blood. Drink tesvino to your hearts' content, get much drunk, but then lie down and sleep, and in the morning you return to your homes without coming to blows with anyone.

All the time the speech is punctuated with expressions of approval, and at the end they all say: "Matetravá! Matetravá! Kalahúpo!" (Thank you! Thank you! It is all right!)

A speech is also often made in the beginning of the feast, when much the same sentiments are expressed. The orator tells the people to follow the good example of the host, that sacrificing and dancing may go on here, there, and everywhere, so that the gods will get plenty to eat and grant the prayers of the Tarahumares.

He strongly admonishes them to keep away from women, as otherwise the value of the feast would be lost. This day belongs to Tata Dios, and nothing else is to be thought of. If anyone transgresses this command, he will have to give an ox or a sheep and tesvino, to make the feast all over again.

While the dancing and singing, sacrificing and speechmaking, are going on, the people behave with decorous solemnity and formality. The ceremonies are never interrupted by unseemly conduct; everybody deports himself with grave sobriety, and refrains from loud talking and laughing and from making any disrespectful noise. But after the gods have been given their share, the people go in, no less energetically, for enjoying themselves.

Food and tesvino are never distributed by the same man, nor are men and women waited on by the same functionary; in other words, one man is appointed for each sex, to dispense the tesvino, and two others to serve the food.

They eat but little of the solids, as it is customary for the guests to take home their portions, the women bringing jars and baskets along for the purpose. Little or nothing of the tesvino is spared, and it is the avowed intention and aim of everybody to get "a beautiful intoxication." They all like to get drunk. An Indian explained to me that the drunken people weep with delight, because they are so perfectly happy. Every Tarahumare has in his heart a cross which Tata Dios placed there long, long ago, and this cross they respect. When drunk they remember Tata Dios better. At their feasts they sit alongside of him and drink with him. The women sit alongside of the Moon and remember ancient times.

But unfortunately this blissful stage of their intoxication does not last long, and then the animal nature in them manifests itself. Under the influence of the liquor, men and women rapidly lose that bashfulness and modesty which in ordinary life are such characteristic traits of their deportment. Furthermore, whatever grudge one man may have against another now crops out, and very likely a fight will ensue, in which the two opponents recklessly pull each other's hair and punch each other's faces. Sometimes in such an outbreak of unreasoning animalism one of the combatants will seize a stone and batter the other one's head to crush it. Afterward, when sober again, the murderer may deeply deplore his deed—if he remembers it at all.

Mothers, when overcome by the spirit of the feast, may unawares allow their babies to fall out of the blankets and into the fire. Children may frequently be seen with bruises and scars which they carry as mementos of some tesvino feast. I know one man who had no hair on one side of his head, having when a child been a victim of such an accident. But seldom, if ever, is a child allowed to become fatally injured.

Taking it all in all, it is a good-natured, jolly, silly crowd, out for a good time and enjoying themselves. All are good friends, and familiarity becomes unlimited. Late in the afternoon those still able to walk start on their way home. Rarely, however, can they reach their domiciles, if these are any distance off, before nature enforces her rights; and the track is strewn with men and women, who, overcome with the effects of their spree, have lain down wherever they happened to be, to sleep themselves sober. Tarahumare society has not yet advanced far enough to see anything disgraceful in debauches of this kind, which, if viewed from their standpoint, are *pro bono publico*; and we ourselves need go back only to our grandfathers' and great-grandfathers' time to find that inebriety was not at all inconsistent with good morals and high standing. Moreover, no matter how often the Tarahumares indulge in such saturnalia, as soon as they recover their senses they are as decorous and solemn as ever. Their native stimulant does not seem to affect either their physical or their mental faculties, and, all scientific theories to the contrary, their children are strong, healthy, and bright.

Aside from social and religious considerations, the drinking of tesvino is a vital factor on the national life of the tribe. Incredible as it may sound, yet, after prolonged and careful research into this interesting psychological problem, I do not hesitate to state that in the ordinary course of his existence the uncivilized Tarahumare is too bashful and modest to enforce his matrimonial rights and privileges; and that by means of tesvino chiefly the race is kept alive and increasing. It is especially at the feasts connected with the agricultural work that sexual promiscuity takes place.

A large gathering is not necessary in order to pray to the gods by dancing. Sometimes the family dances alone, the father teaching the boys. While doing agricultural work, the Indians often depute one man to dance yumari near the house, while the others attend to the work in the fields. It is a curious sight to see a lone man taking his devotional exercise to the tune of his rattle in front of an apparently deserted dwelling. The lonely worshipper is doing his share of the general work by bringing down the fructifying rain and by warding off disaster, while the rest of the family and their friends plant, hoe, weed, or harvest. In the evening, when they return from the field, they may join him for a little while; but often he goes on alone, dancing all night, and singing himself hoarse, and the Indians told me that this is the very hardest kind of work, and exhausting even to them.

Solitary worship is also observed by men who go out hunting deer or squirrels for a communal feast. Every one of them dances yumari alone in front of his house for two hours to insure success on the hunt; and when putting corn to sprout for the making of tesvino the owner of the house dances for a while, that the corn may sprout well.

In certain parts of the country, near Aboreachic, for instance, a dance called valixíwami is in vogue. Here the line of the women faces that of the men, and the two rows dance backward and forward, following each other all the time.

In a dance called cuváli, which is found still further south, the movements are the same as in the dance just mentioned, but the steps are different. It is danced for the same reason as rutuburi is, and it makes the grass and the fungi grow and the deer and the rabbits multiply. This is the only dance known to the Tepehuanes.

In the winter they dance for snow, a dance called yohé; and finally there is a dance called ayéna, which calls the clouds from the north and south that they may clash and produce rain.

I was present at feasts in which four of these dances were performed, and the order in which they followed each other was: Rutuburi, yumari, valixiwami, cuvali.

According to one version of the tradition, both yumari and rutuburi were once men who taught the Tarahumares to dance and sing. They live with Father Sun. Valixiwami and cuvali were also men and companions of the former, but much younger.

At certain feasts for the benefit of the moon, three cigarettes are offered under the cross. The shaman takes one of them, gives a puff, raising the cigarette at the same time upward toward the moon and saying: "Suá" (rise) "vamí" (yonder) "repá" (upward). This is repeated three times. The master of the house and his wife do the same. The ceremony is performed in order to help the moon to make clouds. Now all present may smoke. The Tarahumare never smokes in the middle of the day; he would offend the sun by so doing. He indulges in the "weed" mostly at feasts when drunk. When an Indian offers another man tobacco and a dry corn-leaf to roll his cigarette it is a sign that everything is well between them.

Every year between March and May a large performance takes place on a special patio in the woods. Its purpose is to cure or prevent disease, and much tesvino is consumed. A straw-man, about two feet high, dressed in cotton drawers, and with a handkerchief tied around its head is set up next to the cross. It represents Father Sun, and the cross is his wife, the Moon. Sometimes a stuffed recamúchi (cacomistle, *bassariscus*) is used either in the place of a straw-man or in addition to it. After the feast is over, the manikin is taken to the place from which the straw was obtained, in order to make the grass grow. The Christian Tarahumares keep it in the sacristy of their church.

The latter also celebrate Christmas, and on this occasion some of them, the so-called *muchachitos,* paint their faces and carry on their backs stuffed animals, such as the grey fox, squirrel, or opossum, while dancing to the music of the violin. They jokingly call the skins their *matachitos*, and hold them as women carry their babies. At present the only object is to make the beholder laugh; but of course the play is a remnant of some ancient custom, the meaning of which is now forgotten through the new associations with which the missionaries of old imbued the ceremonies and rites found among the pagans.

A similar suggestion of antiquity is unmistakably embodied in the deer masks, as well as in the heads with antlers attached, which the same men also may wear.

During Easter week live rattlesnakes are carried about, but the heads of the reptiles are tied together so that they can do no harm. One man may have as many as four serpents with him.

Chapter 19

PLANT-WORSHIP—HIKULI—INTERNAL AND EXTERNAL EFFECTS—HIKULI BOTH MAN AND GOD—HOW THE TARAHUMARES OBTAIN THE PLANT, AND WHERE THEY KEEP IT—THE TARAHUMARE HIKULI FEAST—MUSICAL INSTRUMENTS—HIKULI LIKES NOISE—THE DANCE—HIKULI'S DEPARTURE IN THE MORNING--OTHER KINDS OF CACTI WORSHIPPED—"DOCTOR" RUBIO, THE GREAT HIKULI EXPERT—THE AGE OF HIKULI WORSHIP.

To the Indian, everything in nature is alive. Plants, like human beings, have souls, otherwise they could not live and grow. Many are supposed to talk and sing and to feel joy and pain. For instance, when in winter the pine-trees are stiff with cold, they weep and pray to the sun to shine and make them warm. When angered or insulted, the plants take their revenge. Those that are supposed to possess curative powers are venerated. This fact, however, does not save them from being cut into pieces and steeped in water, which the people afterward drink or use in washing themselves. The mere fragrance of the lily is supposed to cure sickness and to drive off sorcery. In invoking the lily's help the shaman utters a prayer like this:

"Sūmatí okiliveá saevá rākó cheeneserová
waminámela ke usugitúami cheeotshéloaya
cheelivéva tesola chapimélava otshéloa rimivélava
Matetravá Sevaxóa wilieóva!"

"Beautiful this morning in bloom lily thou guard me!
Drive them away (those who) make sorcery! Thou make me grow old!
Thou give me walking-stick (to) take up (in) old age
(that I may) find! Thanks exhale fragrance standing!"

("Beautiful lily, in bloom this morning, guard me! Drive away sorcery! Make me grow old! Let me reach the age at which I have to take up a walking-stick! I thank thee for exhaling thy fragrance there, where thou art standing!")

High mental qualities are ascribed especially to all species of *Mammillaria* and *Echinocactus,* small cacti, for which a regular cult is instituted. The Tarahumares designate several varieties as hikuli, though the name belongs properly only to the kind most commonly used by them. These plants live for months after they have been rooted up, and the eating of them causes a state of ecstasy. They are therefore considered demi-gods, who have to be treated with great reverence, and to whom sacrifices have to be offered.

The principal kinds thus distinguished are known to science *as Lophophora Williamsii* and *Lophophora Williamsii,* var. *Lewinii.* In the United States they are called mescal buttons, and in Mexico *peyote.* The Tarahumares speak of them as the superior hikuli (hikuli wanamé), or simply hikuli, they being the hikuli *par excellence.*

The Huichol Indians, who live many hundred miles south of the Tarahumares, also have a hikuli cult, and it is a curious and interesting fact that with them the plant has even the same name, although the two tribes are neither related to nor connected with each other. The cults, too, show many points of resemblance, though with the southern tribe the plant plays a far more important part in the tribal life, and its worship is much more elaborate. On the other hand, the Huichols use only the species and variety shown in the illustration, while the Tarahumares have several. Major J. B. Pond, of New York, informs me that in Texas, during the Civil War, the so-called Texas Rangers, when taken prisoners and deprived of all other stimulating drinks, used mescal buttons, or "white mule," as they called them. They soaked the plants in water and became intoxicated with the liquid.

The plant, when taken, exhilarates the human system, and allays all feeling of hunger and thirst. It also produces colour-visions. When fresh, it has a nauseating, slightly sour taste, but it is wonderfully refreshing when one has been exposed to great fatigue. Not only does it do away with all exhaustion, but one feels actually pushed on, as I can testify from personal experience. In this respect it resembles the Peruvian coca; but unlike the latter, it leaves a certain depression, as well as a headache. Although an Indian feels as if drunk after eating a quantity of hikuli, and the trees dance before his eyes, he maintains the balance of his body even better than under normal conditions, and he will walk along the edge of precipices without becoming dizzy. At their nocturnal feasts, when drinking heavily of both tesvino and hikuli, many persons may be seen to weep and laugh alternately. Another marked effect of the plant is to take away temporarily all sexual desire. This fact, no doubt, is the reason why the Indians, by a curious aboriginal mode of reasoning, impose abstinence from sexual intercourse as a necessary part of the hikuli cult.

The effect of the plant is so much enjoyed by the Tarahumares that they attribute to it power to give health and long life and to purify body and soul. The little cacti, either fresh or dried, are ground on the metate, while being mixed with water; and this liquor is the usual form in which hikuli is consumed.

Hikuli is also applied externally for snake-bites, burns, wounds, and rheumatism; for these purposes it is chewed, or merely moistened in the mouth and applies to the afflicted part. Not only does it cure disease, causing it to run off, but it also so strengthens the body that it can resist illness and is therefore much used in warding off sickness. Though not given to the dead, since the dead are no longer in need of remedies, hikuli is always partaken of at the feasts of the dead.

Moreover, hikuli is a powerful protector of its people under all circumstances, and it gives luck. If a man carries some hikuli in his belt, the bear cannot bite him and the deer cannot run away, but become quite tame and can easily be killed. Should he meet Apaches, hikuli would prevent them from firing off their guns at him. It gives luck in foot-races and all kinds of games, in climbing trees, etc. Hikuli is the great safeguard against witchcraft. It sees even better than the shamans, and it watches that nothing bad is put into the food. The Christian Tarahumares, when they partake of hikuli, think that the devil runs out of their stomachs. Hikuli purifies any man who is willing to sacrifice a sheep and to make native beer. There is, however, no remedy for a murderer; not even hikuli can cure him.

The Christian Tarahumares make the sign of the cross when coming into the presence of the plant, and I was told to lift my hat to it. It is always saluted in the same way as a man, and is supposed to make the customary responses to the salutations. Hikuli is not as great as Father Sun, but sits next to him. It is the brother Tata Dios; and the greatest hikuli is his twin brother, and is therefore called uncle.

Sometimes these plants are dressed up in pieces of blankets, and cigarettes are placed before them. Boys must not touch hikuli, and women only when they act as the shaman's assistants and have to grind it. As a matter of fact, only shamans can handle it properly, and even they wash their hands carefully, and sometimes elect not to touch it at all, making use of little sticks instead of their fingers. Certain shamans washed their hands and rinsed their mouths immediately after eating from my vessels, because hikuli would be angry with them for eating strange food cooked by strange people.

Hikuli is not kept in the house, because it is extremely virtuous, and might become offended at the sight of anything immodest. It is placed in a special jar or basket, in a separate store-house, and is never taken out until tesvino and meat have been offered to it. If this were neglected, it would eat the Indian's soul. If anything happens to hikuli—for instance, if irreverent mice eat it—the owner fears that he may be made crazy as a punishment for his failure to guard it. If anyone should steal hikuli, he would be sure to go crazy, unless he returned the plant to its original owner. He must also kill an ox and make a big feast, in order to set himself right again with the mighty god and with the people.

After four years, hikuli grows old and mouldy, and loses its virtues. It is then buried in a corner of the cave or the house, or taken to the place where it came from, and fresh plants are obtained instead. According to tradition, when Tata Dios went to heaven in the beginning of the world, he left hikuli behind as the great remedy of the people. Hikuli has four faces and sees everything. Its power is well shown in the following myth:

The Bear in a cave said to Hikuli, "Let us fight and let us first smoke over there." They smoked and they fought, and Hikuli was stronger than the Bear. When Hikuli threw down the Bear, all the wind went out of the Bear; but the Bear said again, "Let us smoke and let us fight a few times more." And they did so, and Hikuli again threw the Bear down, and the Bear seated himself on a stone and wept, and went away, and never returned.

Hikuli is not indigenous to the Tarahumare country of today. To obtain it long and until recently perilous journeys have to be undertaken every year to the plateaus of eastern Chihuahua, in the Sierra del Almoloy, near the railroad station of Ximenez, and to the Sierra de Margoso, beyond Santa Rosalia de Camarga, crossing the tracks of the Mexican Central Railroad. From two or three to a dozen men start out to get the plants, first purifying themselves with copal incense. It takes a week or ten days to get to the Sierra de Margoso, where the plants are chiefly found, and about a month is consumed on the entire journey. Until they reach the hikuli country, the Tarahumares may eat anything; but once there, they must abstain from everything except pinole. Upon arriving at the spot, the pilgrims erect a cross, and near it they place the first plants taken up, that these may tell where others may be found in plenty. The second batch of plants gathered is eaten raw, and makes the men drunk. As speech is forbidden, they lie down in silence and sleep. The following day, when perfectly sober again, they begin early in the morning to collect the plants, taking them up with the utmost care, by means of sticks, so as not to touch or injure them, because hikuli would get angry and punish the offender. Two days are spent in gathering the plants, each kind being placed in a separate bag, because, if they were mixed together, they would fight. The bags are carefully carried on the backs of the men, as the Tarahumares generally have no horses.

In the field in which it grows, it sings beautifully, that the Tarahumare may find it. It says, "I want to go to your country, that you may sing your songs to me." It also sings in the bag while it is being carried home. One man, who wanted to use his bag as a pillow, could not sleep, he said, because the plants made so much noise.

When the hikuli-seekers arrive at their homes, the people turn out to welcome the plants with music, and a festival at which a sheep or a goat is sacrificed is held in their honor. On this occasion the shaman wears necklaces made of the seeds of *Coix Lachryma-Jobi.* In due time he takes them off, and places them in a bowl containing water in which the heart of the maguey has been soaked, and after a while everyone present gets a spoonful of this water. The shaman, too, takes some, and afterward wears the necklaces again. Both plants, the *Coix Lachryma-Jobi* as well as the maguey, are highly esteemed for their curative properties; and in his songs the shaman describes hikuli as standing on top of a gigantic seed of the *Coix Lachryma-Jobi,* as big as a mountain.

The night is passed in dancing hikuli and yumari. The pile of fresh plants, perhaps two bushels or more, is placed under the cross, and sprinkled with tesvino, for hikuli wants to drink beer, and if the people should not give it, it would go back to its own country. Food is also offered to the plants, and even money is placed before them, perhaps three silver dollars, which the owner, after the feast, takes back again.

During the year, feasts may be held especially in honor of hikuli, but generally the hikuli dance is performed simultaneously with, though apart from, rutuburi or other dances. On such occasions some shamans devote themselves exclusively to the hikuli cult, in order that the health of the dancers may be preserved, and that they may have vigor for their work.

The hikuli feast consists mainly in dancing, which, of course, is followed by eating and drinking, after the customary offerings of food and tesvino have been made to the gods. It is not held on the general dancing-place, in front of the Tarahumare dwelling, but on a special patio. For the occasion a level piece of ground may be cleared of all stones and rubbish, and carefully swept with the Indian broom, which is made of a sheaf of straw tied in the middle.

Meanwhile some people go into the woods to gather fuel for the large fire which will be needed. The fire is an important feature of the hikuli-feast, a fact indicated by the name, which is napítshi nawlíruga, literally, "moving (*i.e.,* dancing) around (nawlíruga) the fire (napítshi)." There seems to be a preference for fallen trees, pines or oaks, but this may be because they are found in plenty everywhere, are drier and burn better, and finally save the men the labour and time of cutting them down. Quite a number of such trunks are brought together, and placed parallel to each other in an easterly and westerly direction; but not until after sunset is the fire lighted.

The master of the house in which the feast is to be held gives some plants to two or three women appointed to the office of shaman's assistants. At an ordinary gathering, a dozen or two of the plants suffice. The women are called rokoró, which means the stamen of the flower, while the shaman is the pistil. The women grind the plants with water on the metate, and then take part in the dance. They must wash their hands most carefully before touching them; and while they are grinding them a man stands by with a gourd, to catch any stray drop of liquor that may drip from the metate, and to watch that nothing of the precious fluid is lost. Not one drop must be spilled, and even the water with which the metate is afterward washed, is added to the liquid. The drink thus produced is slightly thick and of a dirty brown colour.

The shaman (sometimes there are two) takes his seat on the ground to the west of the fire, about two yards off. On the opposite side of the dancing-place, toward the east, the cross is placed. The shaman's male assistants, at least two in number, seat themselves on either side of their principal, while the women helpers take a position to the north of the fire. On one occasion I observed that the men grouped themselves on one side of the shaman, the women on the other. Close by the shaman's seat a hole is dug, in which he or his assistants may spit, after having drunk or eaten hikuli, so that nothing may be lost. After this impoverished cuspidor has been used, it is always carefully covered with a leaf.

As soon as the shaman has seated himself, he takes a round drinking-gourd, and by pressing its rim firmly into the soil and turning the vessel round, makes a circular mark. Lifting up the bowl again, he draws two diametrical lines at right angles in the circle, and thus produces a symbol of the world.

In the center he puts hikuli, right side up; or he may dig a hole in the centre, to the depth of five or six inches, and place the hikuli in this. He then covers it up with the gourd, bottom up, so that the plant stands within a hollow sphere. The gourd may be replaced by a wooden vessel of similar shape; but in any case it is firmly planted in the ground to serve as a resonator for the musical instrument,—the notched stick, which the shaman leans against the vessel, and on which with another stick he rasps an accompaniment to his songs. If he does not plant the gourd carefully in the ground, it will make a discordant sound, which will vex the demi-god, and he will cause someone in the house to die. The noise produced by the rasping is enjoyed by Hikuli; that is why he is placed beneath the bowl. He is powerful, and manifests his strength by the noise produced.

The notched stick, as well as the rasping-stick, is made from the heavy, hard Brazil-wood, brought from the vicinity of San Ignacio, the hikuli country. The shaman holds the notched stick in his left hand, a little away from himself, so that it touches the vessel at a point below the middle of its length, the part between the shaman's hand and the point of contact being a little longer than the portion from that point to the end of the stick.

The notched sticks from a Tarahumare burial-cave, are apparently of considerable age. The Indians to whom I showed them did not know them, but they all affirmed that they were rasping-sticks. On two sides of one of them are slanting lines, which symbolize the road of Tata Dios; on the intervening sides are transverse lines which represent falling rain. As the implements were found near Baborigame, they may possibly have belonged to the Tepehuanes, the northern members of whom also have the hikuli cult.

When the shaman begins to rasp, he starts from the farther end of the notched stick, though not quite at the point, and runs his rasping-stick quickly and evenly, about twenty-six times, toward himself, and away again; then he makes three long strokes down and outward, each time throwing out his arm at full length, and holding the stick for a second high up toward the east. This is repeated three times, and is the prelude to the ceremony. Now he begins to sing, accompanying himself with even strokes on the notched stick, playing regularly, one stroke as long and as fast as the other, always first toward himself, then down again. His songs are short, lasting only about five minutes.

Presently the shaman's assistants, men and women, rise. They carry censers filled with burning charcoals and copal, and emitting a heavy smoke, and proceed toward the cross, to which they offer the smoking incense, kneeling down, facing east, and crossing themselves. This feature, if not wholly due to Catholic influences, is at least strongly affected by it.

Having offered incense to the cross, they return to the shaman. The women now sit down again in their previous places. The men receive from the shaman rattles *(sonajas)* consisting of deer-hoofs tied with bits of reed to a strap of leather. They are either held in the right hand or slung over the shoulder. When there are not enough rattles for all assistants, a bell may be substituted.

Finally everything is ready for the dance to commence. The men wear white blankets, in which they keep themselves wrapped up to the chin throughout the night; but they have no sandals. The dance is performed by the shaman's assistants, and consists of a peculiar, quick, jumping march, with short steps, the dancers moving forward one after another, on their toes, and making sharp, jerky movements, without, however, turning around. They dance in the space between the fire and the cross, and move in a direction opposite to the sun's apparent movement. Nobody present is allowed to walk in contra-direction to the dancers. After six or eight rounds, they enlarge the circuit so as to include the fire; and whenever a dancer finds himself just between the shaman and the fire, he quickly turns around once, then, dancing as before, moves on to the dancing-place proper. Now and then the dancers give vent to what is supposed to be an imitation of the hikuli's talk, which reminded me of the crowing of a cock. Beating their mouths quickly three times with the hollow of their hands, they shout in a shrill, falsetto voice, "Hikuli vava!" which means, "Hikuli over yonder!"

The women take their turns separate from the men, though sometimes they dance simultaneously with them. They move around in silence, and their dance is slightly different from that of the other sex. Sometimes two and two may be seen dancing toward each other. They all wear freshly washed, clean white skirts and tunics, and the entire scene around the big fire is marvellously picturesque.

The dancing may sometimes lag, but the singing and the rhythmical rasping of the shaman are kept up through the night, interrupted only once or twice, when he sees fit. He politely excuses himself to Hikuli, and formal salutations are exchanged with the plant under the bowl both when he goes and when he returns. On such occasions he stops his singing and rasping, and notifies Hikuli by striking the notched stick several times quickly with the rasping-stick, and finishing off with three slow beats.

His songs describe how Hikuli walks with his rattles and with his staff of authority; he comes to cure and to guard the people and to grant a "beautiful" intoxication. To bring about the latter result, the brownish liquor is dispensed from a jar standing under the cross. A man serves it in small quantities from a gourd, which he first carries around the fire on a rapid run, making three circuits for the shaman, and one for the rest of the assemblage. The spirits of the feasters rise in proportion to their potations. Sometimes only the shaman and his assistants indulge in the drinking; on other occasions all the people partake of the liquor.

The secondary effect of the plant, depression and drowsiness, shows itself more plainly on the company when they sit down between the dancing, than on the well-trained shaman, who, besides, is kept awake by his occupation. As one or the other of his assistants succumbs to sleepiness, he has to ask permission of Hikuli, through the shaman, to go off and rest for a while, and must properly notify Hikuli of his leaving and returning to duty. Toward morning all the assistants are struggling hard to overcome somnolence, while the shaman sings and rasps as conscientiously and enthusiastically as ever.

But all rouse themselves for the important acts of curing the people by rasping and of despatching Hikuli. Just at daybreak, as the fire is dying out, the shaman gives the welcome signal that the dance is over, by the three final rasps on his notched stick. Then the people gather at the eastern end of the dancing-place, near the cross. The shaman rises from his seat, carrying in his hands his rasping implements, and, followed by a boy who carries a gourd with water, he proceeds to confer upon everybody present the benediction. Stopping in front of each one, he solemnly dips the point of the rasping-stick into the water, and after touching the notched stick lightly with the wetted end, first in the middle, then on the lower end, and finally on the top, he daubs the head of the person three times with it. Then he rests the end of the notched stick against the man's head and rasps three long strokes from end to end, throwing out his hand far into the air after each stroke. The dust produced by the rasping, infinitesimal though it be, is powerful in giving health and life. Now he turns toward the rising Sun, holding out his implements to him; and, quickly rubbing up and down a few times at the lower end of the notched stick, he makes a long stroke from end to end, passing the hand far out from the stick toward the Sun. By this act, three times performed, he waves Hikuli home. In the early morning, Hikuli had come from San Ignacio and from Satapolio, riding on beautiful green doves, to feast with the Tarahumares at the end of the dance, when the people sacrifice food, and eat and drink. The greatest Hikuli eats with the shaman, who alone is able to see him and his companions. If Hikuli should not come to the feasts, there would always be on the Tarahumares the breath or stain of sorcery.

Having bestowed his blessings, Hikuli forms himself into a ball, and flies home to his country, accompanied by the owl, who also flies to its shelter at that hour.

The dust produced by the rasping of the shaman in the course of the night is carefully gathered up and kept in a buckskin bag as a powerful remedy for future use.

After the feast everybody has to wash his face and hands, a duty esteemed most important.

Besides hikuli wanamé ordinarily used, the Tarahumares know and worship the following varieties:

1. Mulato *(Mammillaria micromeris)*.—This is believed to make the eyes large and clear to see sorcerers, to prolong life and to give speed to the runners.

2. Rosapara.—This is only a more advanced vegetative stage of the preceding species—though it looks quite different, being white and spiny. This, too, must only be touched with very clean hands, in the moral sense, it would seem, as much as in the physical, for only people who are well baptised are allowed to handle it. It is a good Christian and keeps a sharp eye on the people around it; and when it sees anyone doing some wrong, it gets very angry, and either drives the offender mad or throws him down precipices. It is therefore very effective in frightening off bad people, especially robbers and Apaches.

3. Sunami *(Mammillaria fissurata)*.—It is rare, but it is believed to be even more powerful than wanamé and is used in the same way as the latter; the drink produced from it is also strongly intoxicating. Robbers are powerless to steal anything where Sunami calls soldiers to its aid.

4. Hikuli walúla saelíami.—This is the greatest of all, and the name means "hikuli great authority." It is extremely rare among the Tarahumares, and I have not seen any specimen of it, but it was described to me as growing in clusters of from eight to twelve inches in diameter, resembling wanamé with many young ones around it. All the other hikuli are his servants. The reason why so few of these plants are brought to the Tarahumare country is that he is very greedy, requiring oxen for food, not being satisfied with sheep, goats, or anything else. Therefore but few Tarahumares can afford to entertain him in their country. If an ox is not killed for him, he will eat the Indian. He always holds his head down, because he is listening to all the ceremonies that are being held in the Tarahumare land, and he is always full of thoughts of how he may cure his sons, the Tarahumares. He never dies. When a person is very ill, and there is no such hikuli in the country, the shaman in his thoughts flies to the hikuli country, where "the great authority" stands looking at his children, the people, and offers him the soul of an ox that has been sacrificed. Hikuli accepts the offering, and sends back his blessings by his servants, who are always well dressed and wear straw hats, "like regular Americans," as my shaman friend Rubio expressed it. Only the shamans, however, can see them come, to cure the hearts of the people and to clean their souls.

All these various species are considered good, as coming from Tata Dios, and well-disposed toward the people. But there are some kinds of hikuli believed to come from the Devil. One of these, with long white spines, is called ocoyome. It is very rarely used, and only for evil purposes. If anyone should happen to touch it with the foot, it would cause the offending leg to break. Once when I pushed one of these globular spiny cacti out of my way with a cane, my Indian attendant immediately warned me, "Leave it alone, or it will make you fall down precipices."

At one of the feasts which I witnessed I wished to taste hikuli, as it was new to me. A lively discussion arose between the shamans, and I was finally told that I might sit with them, as it was known that I had some of the sacred plants in my possession. The condition was made, however, that I should take off my sombrero. It happened to be a cold and windy December night, but I obeyed and put my handkerchief over my head, to which no objection was raised. The man who carried the gourd, first danced in front of the shaman, then around the fire, and finally brought it to me. The liquid tasted somewhat bitter, but not exactly disagreeable; and while I drank, the man looked at me with astonishment, as if he had expected that hikuli would refuse to be taken by me.

I drank only a small cupful, but felt the effect in a few minutes. First it made me wide awake, and acted as an excitant to the nerves, similar to coffee, but much more powerful. This sensation lasted for about ten minutes, when it was followed by a depression and a chill such as I have never experienced before. To get warm I almost threw myself into the fire, but not until morning was the feeling of cold conquered. Some Tarahumares told me that they are similarly affected, and for this reason they do not take it. When I told the shaman about the effect hikuli had on me, he asked whether I had rasped on the notched stick, because, he said, hikuli does not give chills to people who rasp. In other words, according to him, the effect might be warded off by physical exercise.

A shaman who agreed to sell me some hikuli took me with him to his house. Then he walked over to a storehouse of pine boards, and with a long stick undid the lock from within, taking off a few boards from the roof to get at it. After some searching, he produced a small closed basket. Holding this in his hand, he rapidly ran around me in one ceremonious circuit, and said in a scarcely audible voice: "Thank you for the time you have been with me; now go with him; I will give you food before you go." The smoke of copal was blown over the plants in the basket, that they might eat; and I had to smell of the incense, so that hikuli might find pleasure in being with me. The shaman then opened the basket and asked me to select what I wanted. I picked out twelve plants, but, as he asked $10 for them, I contented myself with three.

On my way back to civilisation, I spent some time at Guajochic, near which place the great hikuli expert, Shaman Rubio, lives. He is a truly pious man, well-meaning and kind-hearted, living up to his principles, in which Christianity and Paganism are harmoniously blended. He is highly esteemed by all his countrymen, who consider him the greatest hikuli shaman in that part of the Tarahumare country. His profession brings him a very comfortable living, as his services are constantly in demand, and are paid for by fine pieces of the animals sacrificed. For curing the people he even gets money; and what with praying and singing, drinking tesvino and hikuli, fasting and curing the sick, he passes his days in the happy conviction that he keeps the world going. From him I obtained specimens of the various kinds of cacti which the Tarahumares worship,—a betrayal of the secrets of the tribe, for which the other shamans punished him by forbidding him ever to go again on a hikuli journey. Though in the first year he obeyed the sentence, he did not take it much to heart, feeling himself far superior to his judges, who, he knew, could not get along without him, and in the end would have to come to him; for he is the most virtuous of them all, and therefore knows the commands of Tata Dios better than anyone else.

It is to him that I owe a good deal of what I know about this plant-worship, as well as several songs used in the cult. He came often to see me, and one day told me in confidence that the hikuli in my possession would have to be fed before they started on their long journey to the United States; for it was a long time since they had had food, and they were getting angry. The next time he came he brought some copal tied up in a cotton cloth, and after heating the incense on a piece of crockery he waved the smoke over the plants, which he had placed in front of him. This, he said, would satisfy them; they would now go content with me, and no harm would come to me from sorcerers, robbers, or Apaches. This was a comfort, for to reach Chihuahua I had to pass through some disturbed country, and there were rumours of a revolution.

It seems that at present only the districts around Nararachic and Baqueachic get hikuli from its native country, and that all the others procure it from these two. Until recently the people of Guachochic also went to fetch plants, and a few may yet undertake the journey. One old man showed me some hikuli which he had gathered thirty-five years ago. At Nararachic they use hikuli all the year round, that is, as long as they have corn, because "hikuli wants tesvino." The people in the barrancas are too timid to go on the expeditions, and they buy the plants at the price of a sheep apiece. The purchaser holds a feast, not only when he brings the demi-god to his home, but also a year after the event. In the eastern section of the country, and in the foot-hills around Rio Fuerte, hikuli is not used at all. It is very rarely planted by the Tarahumares; the only instance I saw of it was in Tierras Verdes.

A significant light is thrown on the antiquity of the cult, as well as on the age of the tribe itself, by a certain variation in the ceremonial which I observed in the southwestern part of the Tarahumare country. There it is the custom of the shaman to draw underneath his resonator-gourd a mystical human figure in the sand, and to place the hikuli in its centre. Regarding this mystical figure, my lamented friend, Frank Hamilton Cushing, informed me that similar or almost identical drawings are found depicted on the lava rocks of Arizona. In a letter dated October 30, 1893, he said:

> The figure you sketch for me is closely allied, for example, to very ancient ritualistic petrographs in the lava regions of Arizona. You will see this at a glance by the figure of one of those petrographs, which I reproduce in juxtaposition with yours;

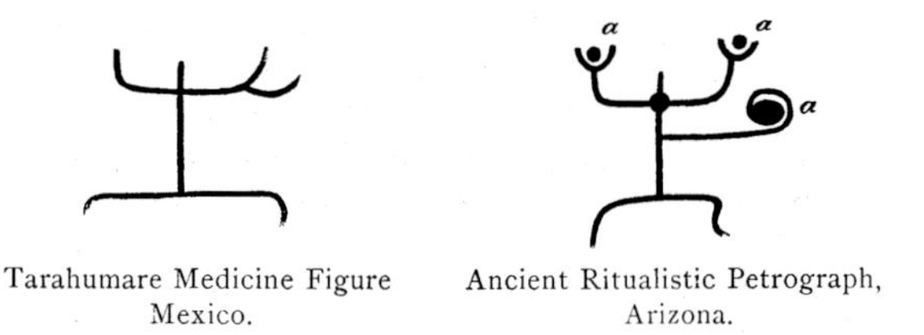

Tarahumare Medicine Figure Mexico. | Ancient Ritualistic Petrograph, Arizona.

> Others which I have recorded are even more strikingly similar. I have always supposed that these figures were designed for "medicine" ceremonials, but thought of them rather as pertaining to the medicines of the elements, wind, rain, water, etc., used in connection with sacrifices (with which ceremonial rites were terminated) than as connected with actual medicinal ceremonials. I was led to this belief by finding in connection with some of them little cup-shaped concavities pecked into the angles of the figures. You will observe that a line is drawn from the middle and straight portion of my figure and coiled around the concavity at the right side, and that the terminations of the upper cross lines are bifurcated around similar though smaller concavities. This entire figure represents a water-animal god, one only of a number of semi-human mystic monsters. For convenience his heart

is drawn out to one side, and within it is placed the cup of the "chief" medicine; while in his left hand is the cup of the "good" medicine, and in his right the cup of "bad" (*i.e.,* strong) medicine. If in the light of this you re-examine your figure, you will see with me that it represents a man-god sitting, his legs doubled under him and his medicines distributed around and upon him according to his parts, and in accordance also, probably, to their importance and the case in hand. He must always have the chief of all medicines placed on his heart, as the renewer of life. Then, strictly with reference to the ailment to be treated, and its location in the body or limbs of the patient (I should say), the other medicines. I throw this out as a suggestion, yet with much confidence in its at least approximate correctness as indicated by my comparative studies. Probably a consultation of your notes and the remembrance of variations of the ceremony you have seen, will signify to you whether I am right or not. Remember that if these people have this ceremonial in connection with the treatment of disease, they will also have it in the treatment of the weather, etc., when "diseased," so to say. You have opened up a new significance of many outlines among the older lava-remains, and if my record of these in turn has helped to explain your diagram, etc., you can judge of my pleasure and appreciation.

Chapter 20

The Tarahumare's Firm Belief in a Future Life—Causes of Death—The Dead Are Mischievous and Want Their Families to Join Them—Therefore the Dead Have to Be Kept Away by Fair Means or Foul—Three Feasts and a Chase—Burial Customs—A Funeral Sermon.

The idea of immortality is so strong with the Tarahumares that death means to them only a change of form. They certainly believe in a future life, but they are afraid of the dead, and think that they want to harm the survivors. This fear is caused by the supposition that the dead are lonely, and long for the company of their relatives. The dead also make people ill, that they too may die and join the departed. When a man dies in spite of all efforts of the shamans to save his life, the people say that those who have gone before have called him or carried him off. The deceased are also supposed to retain their love for the good things they left behind in this world, and to be trying every way to get at them. So strong is the feeling that the departed still owns whatever property he once possessed, that he is thought to be jealous of his heirs who now enjoy its possession. He may not let them sleep at night, but makes them sit up by the fire and talk. To soothe his discontent, tesvino and all kinds of food are given him, because he needs the same things he needed here. In the course of the year several ceremonies are performed, by which he is actually chased off, and the survivors constantly take precautions against his return to bother them.

Sometimes the dead are sent by sorcerers to harm people and make them ill, but generally they come of their own accord. They enter the house at night and drink the tesvino and eat the food prepared for a feast, and what they cannot eat they spoil. To protect the beer against such mischief the people place bows and arrows next to the jars, and cover the vessels with sprigs of the odorous artemisia. The dead will also kill cattle and sheep, and spit and blow in the faces of the people, to make them ill, and possibly cause their death. Sometimes the dead are viewed as spirits, and the shaman sees them flying through the air, like birds. If the spirit of a dead person takes up his abode in a house, the owner of the dwelling will feel a choking sensation, dry up, and die, unless the shaman gives to the dead plenty of tesvino, and drives him away with incantations.

The dead are supposed to be about at night; therefore the Tarahumares do not like to travel after dark, for fear of meeting the dead, who whistle when they pass the living. Only shamans can travel at night, although sometimes even they have to fight with the dead, who come running out of the caves on all fours. In the daytime the Tarahumares are not afraid of the dead, though even they do not dare to visit burial-places, modern or ancient. I found it difficult to get Indians to carry bones of skeletons excavated from ancient burial-caves, and even the Mexicans would not allow their animals to carry burdens of that kind, for fear that the mules would get tired, that is to say, play out and die.

When a person dies, his eyes are closed, his hands crossed over his breast, and the relatives talk to him one by one, and bid him good-bye. The weeping widow tells her husband that, now that he has gone and does not want to stay with her any longer, he must not come back to frighten her or his sons or daughters or anyone else. She implores him not to carry any of them off, or do any mischief, but to leave them all alone.

A mother says to her dead infant: "Now go away! Don't come back any more, now that you are dead. Don't come at night to nurse at my breast. Go away, and do not come back!" And the father says to the child: "Don't come back to ask me to hold your hand, or to do things for you. I shall not know you any more. Don't come walking around here, but stay away."

The body is wrapped in a blanket almost before it is cold, to be buried later, but food is at once placed around it, and ashes are liberally strewn over and around the corpse, to enable the relatives to discover, by the tracks, into what kind of animal the dead has changed. At night some fox or coyote, polecat or rat, is sure to be attracted by the smell of the food; but the people believe that it was the departed who returned in the form of the animal to get his food. A shaman, without even looking at the tracks, may be able to tell what animal shape the dead assumes.

Within twenty-four hours the corpse is taken away to be buried. It is tied in three or four places to one or two poles and carried by two men. Women never go with them to the funeral. As soon as the undertakers have accomplished their task, they immediately wash their persons well. Upon their return, branches of the mountain cedar are burned inside of the house, to "cure" it.

The body is laid at rest in a shallow grave inside of a cave or just outside of it, with the head to the east and the feet to the west. In some caves, however, this rule is not adhered to, for I found corpses placed in accordance with the formation of the floor of the cave. The body is covered with an inch of earth, then with a row of pine or palm sticks put on lengthwise, and over this a layer of earth is spread five or six inches deep. On top of all, stones are thrown. The bodies of grown persons are stretched out to their full length, but with children the knees are generally drawn up.

This is one way in which the pagan Tarahumares bury their dead. Another mode, equally common, is to place the body lying on its back, on the surface, without any earth to cover it; in this case the mouth of the cave is walled up with stones, or stones and mud, and several bodies may be found inside.

When exhuming skeletons I have frequently found bits of charcoal, which was explained by the fact that during the first night the mourners keep a fire near the grave, which to-day serves the same purpose as candles. This also accounts for the smokiness of the interior of the burial-caves, even of the ancient ones.

The dead keeps his buckskin pouch and three small gourds with beans. Three ears of corn are placed to the left of his head, as well as a small jar of tesvino. Another small jar of tesvino is placed near his feet, as well as his bow and arrows, the stone with which the arrows are stretched, reeds and sinews, his steel for striking a fire, the small stick with which paint is put on the arrows, his sucking-tubes when the deceased has been a shaman, in fact all his light-weight belongings, besides balls of gum from the pine-tree, necklaces *of Coix Lachryma-Jobi,* and a hikuli plant. Everything heavy, such as his axe, machete, beads, and money, he leaves, as it is thought that the weight would hinder him from rising to heaven. This is the practical view the Indians have taken since their contact with the whites, as valuables frequently attract marauders. The dead man's sandals, his violin, and the vessels from which he used to take his food, are kept in a separate place for a year, that is, until after the last function for the dead is over; then at night the shaman and other men take them away and bury them somewhere, but not with the dead. The skins on which he died are treated in the same way, and are never used again, lest a very ugly dog might be born of them. The house is always destroyed, and the metate and many jars and baskets are broken.

On the third day after the death, the relatives begin to prepare the first feast for the dead, which is held within a fortnight. One or two sheep or goats are killed, and the lungs, the heart, the windpipe are hung from a stick outside the burial-cave.

As soon as the tesvino is ready the feast comes off, although comparatively little of the liquor is used at this first function. The relatives, men and women, visit the grave and leave a jar with pinole, a small jar with tesvino, three tortillas, and three cigarettes with the dead, if he was a man; with a woman, four tortillas, etc., are required. The size of the tortillas varies with the age of the person. For adults the ordinary tortilla is used; to young people over six years old, medium-sized ones are given; and children get small ones, about an inch and a half in diameter. I have seen medium-sized ones made into the shape of a cross.

All the mourners talk to the departed, the shaman first. He tells him that he had better take away everything they have given him, and not come and disturb the people he has left behind. He should leave them alone, and some day they, too, will have to go where he is. He should not kill any of the animals belonging to the family, as they have killed a sheep for him and given him the best part, the lungs, that he may eat and be satisfied and not take what now is theirs.

At the first feast I have seen worn in the hair by both men and women a peculiar kind of artificial flower. It is made from a short bit of reed in one end of which four incisions are made, with the parts turned outward to stand out like the corolla of a flower. It is stuck under the hair-ribbon at one side of the head. The mourners also make crosses on their foreheads with charcoal.

The second feast is given half a year later, and again animals are killed and a large quantity of tesvino is made. Three men and three women carry food and tesvino to the grave, the relatives remaining at home. On their return they stop at a distance from the house and throw ashes over each other's heads before entering.

For the third function, which is the largest, an animal is selected from among those last acquired by the deceased, and quantities of food and beer are prepared. This feast is the final effort to despatch the dead. A large earthen bowl is made especially for the purpose. It is about two feet in diameter and six inches deep. It is filled with water, and a drinking-gourd placed inside of it, upside down. The shaman beats this gourd with a corn-cob fastened to the end of a little stick. His assistants help him, one by swinging the rattle, the other by singing. After a while the shaman lifts the bowl up and after carrying it about in three ceremonial circuits throws it into the air. It falls to the ground and breaks into many pieces, and the people dance and trample on the sherds and on the drinking-gourd.

The young people conclude the function by running a race of some hundred yards. The men have their ball, and as they run they scatter ashes to the four cardinal points to cover the tracks of the dead. They return rejoicing, manifesting their delight by throwing up their blankets, tunics, and hats, because now the dead is at last chased off. If the deceased be a woman, the women run a race with rings and sticks.

A very elaborate third function, given by a widow, was described to me as follows: There were five patios. On one, for the dead, was erected one large cross and two small ones, and three gourds with tesvino and a basket with uncooked meat were placed near by. A fire was lighted, and one man had to watch here. On another patio one cross was raised, and a branch from a pine-tree placed next to it. Here, too, a jar with tesvino and a basket with uncooked meat were deposited, and one man and two women kept watch, but no ceremonies were performed. A third patio was for the hikuli cult, where the shaman rasped and sang. On the fourth patio, yumari was danced, and one large cross and two smaller ones had been erected. Finally, on the fifth patio four torches of resinous pinewood, each a yard high, were placed at the four cardinal points. A peculiar feature was that one man alone danced here between these four torches, cutting with his knife three times through each flame as he danced. This he did in reprises.

According to the names which the Tarahumares apply to the three functions for the dead, the main idea of the first is to give food; of the second, to replenish the first supply; and of the third to give drink. The three feasts are on an increasing scale of elaborateness, the first being comparatively insignificant. Each generally lasts one day and one night, and begins at the hour at which the dead breathed his last. There is always a special patio prepared for the dead, and another one for the hikuli cult, besides the ordinary dancing-place, and much howling and singing goes on, especially at the last.

At the feasts, the shaman steeps herbs in water and sprinkles this medicine over the people. Hikuli dancing and singing always play a prominent part at all the festivities, for the plant is thought to be very powerful in running off the dead, chasing them to the end of the world, where they join the other dead. Yumari is danced at intervals and much tesvino is used, and at all feasts the survivors drink with the dead.

There are three feasts for a man, and four for a woman. She cannot run so fast, and it is therefore harder to chase her off. Not until the last function has been made will a widower or a widow marry again, being more afraid of the dead than are other relatives.

After the death of a person, anyone who rendered him any service, as, for instance, watching his cattle for a week, claims something of what the dead left. He is satisfied, however, with a girdle or the like.

Once I was present at the burial-feast for a man who had hanged himself a fortnight before, while under the influence of liquor and angry over some property out of which he considered himself cheated. He had changed into a lion. Two men and two women carried food and tesvino; the wife did not go with them, as the deceased had died alone, and she was afraid of being carried off by him. His father-in-law led the procession, carrying a goat-skin with its four feet remaining. The animal had belonged to the deceased and had been sacrificed for him, and the skin was to be given to him that in his new life he might rest on it. The suicide had been buried in a little cave with his feet toward the entrance. Having deposited the food near the dead man's head, the women sat down on a stone inside, while the men stood up near the mouth of the cave, all faces turned toward the grave. The father-in-law seated himself on a stone near the feet of the dead. It was a dreary winter evening in the Sierra and the scene was singularly impressive. The old man was a strong personality, powerfully built, and a shaman of great reputation, who in his entire bearing showed his determination to keep the dead at bay. He seemed to exercise a reassuring influence over the whole assembly.

I shall not easily forget the solemn and convincing way in which he upbraided the dead for his rash act. Taking the reed flower from his hair and holding it in his right hand, he waved it down and up, as if swayed by the force of his own thoughts, in accentuating his points, and he talked and argued with the dead for a quarter of an hour. The man was a great orator, and spoke so earnestly that my interpreter Nabor was affected almost to tears. The speech was a kind of dialogue with the dead, the speaker supplying the responses himself, and this is the gist of it:

Why are you there? — Because I am dead. — Why are you dead? — Because I died. — Why did you die? — Because I chose to. — That is not right. You have no shame. Did your mother, who gave you birth, tell you to do this? You are bad. Tell me, why did you kill yourself? — Because I chose to do it. — Now what did you get for it, lying there, as you are, with stones on top of you? Were you not just playing the violin in the house with us? Why did you hang yourself in the tree?

Here I leave this tesvino and food for you, the meat and tortillas, that you may eat and not come back. We do not want you any more. You are a fool. Now I am going to leave you here. You are not going to drink tesvino in the house with us any more. Remain here! Do not come to the house, for it would do you no good; we would burn you. Good-bye, go now; we do not want you any more!

All present then said good-bye to him, and all the women added, "Fool!" and then they all ran quickly into a deep water-hole, splashing into it clothes and all, that nothing from the dead might attach itself to them. They changed their wet attire after their arrival at the house. Later in the evening a magnificent hikuli feast was held. The Indians sat around the big fire, which cast a magical light over the tall old pine-trees around the patio, while the dancers moved about in their fantastic way through the red glow. Such a scene makes a deeper impression than any that could be produced on the stage.

The Christian Tarahumares believe that the shaman has to watch the dead throughout the year, or the deceased would be carried away by the Devil. If the feasts were not given, the departed would continue to wander about in animal shape. This is the direful fate meted out to people who are too poor to pay the shaman. Sometimes, if the dead person has not complied in life with the customary requirements in regard to feasts and sacrifices, the shamans have a hard time in lifting him to heaven. It may take hours of incantations and much tesvino to get his head up, and as much more to redeem his body. Sometimes the head falls back, and the shamans have to call for more tesvino to gain strength to lift him up again.

The Tarahumares had no great scruples about my removing the bodies of their dead, if the latter had died some years before and were supposed to have been properly despatched from this world. Where a body had been buried, the bones that were not taken away had to be covered up again. One Tarahumare sold me the skeleton of his mother-in-law for one dollar.

Chapter 21

Three Weeks on Foot through the Barranca—Rio Fuerte—I Get My Camera Wet—Ancient Cave-dwellings Ascribed to the Tubar Indians—The Effect of a Compliment—Various Devices for Catching Fish—Poisoning the Water—A Blanket Seine.

On a cold day in the end of October I started from Guachochic bound for the upper part of the great Barranca de San Carlos and the country southward as far as there were Tarahumares. Everything seemed bleak and dreary. The corn was harvested, the grass looked grey, and there was a wintry feeling in the air. The sere and withered leaves rustled like paper, and as I made camp near an Indian ranch I saw loose stubble and dead leaves carried up in a whirlwind, two or three hundred feet up toward a sky as grey and sober as that of northern latitudes at that time of the year. We travelled to the southeast from Guachochic over pine-clad hills, coming now and then to a lonely ranch.

About seven miles before reaching the barranca I arrived at a point 8,600 feet high, from which I could look over this vast expanse of woodland, extending all the way up to the deep gorge and diminishing in breadth toward the northwest. At San Carlos, a ranch but recently established in this wilderness, I left my animals, and immediately prepared for an extended excursion on foot into the barranca and its neighbourhood.

Nearly the whole country of the Tarahumares is drained by the river Fuerte, which, with its many tributaries, waters as many barrancas. The main one, namely Barranca de San Carlos, is from 4,000 to 4,500 feet deep, and sinuous in its course. If there were a passable road along its bottom, the distance from the source of the river to a point a little below the village of Santa Ana, where Rio Fuerte emerges from the Sierra, could be easily covered in two days; but as it is, a man requires at least a week to travel this distance, so much is he impeded by the roughness of the country.

Having descended into the barranca, which now felt almost uncomfortably warm, after the piercing winds of the highlands, I first visited the plateaus on the southern side, where the Indians have still kept themselves tolerably free from the white man's evil influence and are very jealous of their land. One night, while camping in a deep arroyo with very steep sides frowning down on us, one of the Indian carriers woke us with the startling news: "Get up! A stone is falling and will strike us!" I heard a noise, and instantly a stone, half the size of a child's head, hit the informant himself, as he sleepily rose. He lost his breath, but soon recovered, and no further damage was done.

I secured the necessary carriers and went down again to the river, which I now followed westward from Nogal for about twenty-five miles. The elevation at Nogal is 4,450 feet, about 800 feet higher than the place at which we left the river again. At the outset we came upon two very hot springs, the water of which had a yellow sediment. The gorge was narrow throughout. Sometimes its two sides rose almost perpendicularly, leaving but a narrow passage for the river. We then had either to wade in the water or to ascend some thousand feet, in order to continue on our way. But generally there was a bank on one side or the other, and now and then the valley widened, yielding sufficient space for some bushes, or even a tree to grow, though it soon narrowed again. In some such spots we found a shrub called baynoro, with long, flexible branches and light-green leaves. Its small, yellow berries were as sweet as honey, but they did not agree with the Mexicans, who had stomach-aches and lost their appetites after eating them. The Indians made the same complaints, but I felt no ill effects from them.

Along the river we saw the tracks of many raccoons and otters, and there were also ducks and blue herons.

The colour of the water in the deep places was greyish green, and as the river rises in the high sierra, it felt icy cold to wade through. One day we had to cross it eight times. On one such occasion, while wading waist-deep, the Indian who carried the photographic outfit in a bag on his back, forgot for a moment, on account of the stinging cold, how far his burden hung down, and let it dip into the water. The prospect of being prevented, perhaps for a long time to come, from photographing, was very annoying. Six plate-holders were so wet that I could not even draw the shutters out, but luckily I had more elsewhere.

We came upon several ancient cave-dwellings, all of which were rather small, and attributed by the Tarahumares to the Tubar Indians. One of them was situated about 250 feet above the bottom of the barranca. A two-storied, rather irregularly shaped building occupied the entire width of the cave, without reaching to the roof. The floor of the house was scarcely two yards broad, but the building widened out very much, following the shape of the cave. The materials used in the construction were stone and mud or, rather, reddish grit; and smaller stones had been put between larger ones in an irregular way. The walls were only five or six inches thick and were plastered with mud. An upright pole supported the ceiling, which was rather pretty, consisting of reeds resting on the rafters, and covered on top with mud. The ceiling of the second story had been made in the same way, but had fallen in. A piece of thick board half covered the entrance. In the first story I found an additional chamber, and in it a skeleton, of which I secured the skull and some typical bones.

Not far from this, and situated in very rough country, was another cave, that contained ten one-storied chambers of the same material and construction. The cave was fifty feet long and at the mouth seven feet high. The apertures of the chambers were fairly squared, and not of the shape of the conventional ear of corn. One door was a foot and a half broad, and two feet and a half high. I crawled through the chambers, which were miserably small. The floor was plastered, and in some rooms I noticed circular holes sunk into the ground in the way that I had already observed in Zapuri. There were also small square holes, the sides being six inches long in the front wall.

Twenty miles from here, and just south of the pueblo of Cavorachic, was a third cave which contained thirteen houses in ruins. The material here, too, was the same as before, but the houses were built to the roof of the cave, and were rounded at the corners. Peculiar round loop-holes were seen here, too. Eight of them formed a horizontal line, and one extra hole was a little higher up.

A track could be made out at certain places along the river, but the country was very lonely. In the course of several days only six Indian families were encountered, and two of those lived here only temporarily. We also met five stray Indians that had come down from the highlands to fetch bamboo reeds for arrows, etc. It was quite pleasant to meet somebody now and then, although, unfortunately, no one had anything to sell, except a few small fish, the people being themselves as hard up for food as we were. We carried our little metate on which we ground corn for our meals, but we found it very difficult on this trip of four weeks' duration to secure from day to day corn enough to satisfy our wants. One item in our menu, new to me, but common throughout northern Mexico, was really excellent when we could procure the very simple material from which it was made, namely squash-seeds. These were ground very fine and boiled in a saucepan. This dish, which is of Tarahumare origin, is called *pipian,* and looks like curds. Mixed with a little chile it is very palatable, and in this period of considerable privation it was the only food I really enjoyed.

But such luxuries were not served every day. Far from it. For several days in succession we had nothing but corncakes and water. Therefore our joy was great when at last we espied some sheep on the other side of the river. They belonged to a woman who watched them herself, while wintering among the rocks with her herd of about a dozen sheep and goats. I sent my interpreter over to make a bargain for one of the animals, and as he did not return after a reasonable lapse of time, and as we were all hungry, I went across the river myself to see the dashing widow. I found my man still bargaining, lying on the ground stretched out on his stomach and resting his head on his hands. She was grinding corn on the metate and seemed to pay little attention to either of us, but her personal attractiveness at once impressed me. She was still in her best years and had fine bright eyes. A ribbon dyed with the native yellow dye from lichens ran through the braids of her hair, and was marvellously becoming to her almost olive complexion. I could not help saying, "How pretty she is!" to which the interpreter, in a dejected mood, replied: "Yes, but she will not sell anything, and I have been struggling hard." "Of course, she will sell," I said, "handsome as she is!" at which remark of mine I noticed she smiled. Though I judged from the way in which she wore her hair, in two braids, hanging in a loop in the neck, that she had been in association with the Mexicans, I did not expect that she could understand Spanish so well. I immediately returned to my camp to fetch some beads and a red handkerchief to make an impression on my obdurate belle. But on my way back to her I met my interpreter, who brought the glad tidings that she had made up her mind to sell, and that I might send for the animal whenever I wanted it. The price was one Mexican silver dollar. So I sent my "extras" along with the money, and in return received a fine sheep with long white wool, when all we had hoped for was only a goat. There is not the slightest doubt in my mind that my felicitous compliment brought about this happy result.

During our travels along the river, every day we came upon traps for catching fish. The Tarahumares have various modes of fishing. Sometimes they manage to catch fish with their hands in crevices between stones, even diving for them. In the shallow parts of the rivers and in the brooks, following the course of the stream, two stone walls a foot or two high are built. These walls converge at the lower end and form a channel, in which is placed horizontally a mat of stalks of the eagle fern *(Pteris aquilina).* When the fish attempt to cross this mat, through which the water passes freely, they are intercepted. Often the fish caught in this way are only an inch long, but none is too small for a Tarahumare to reject.

Other similar walls form square or oblong corrals, where the fish can easily enter, but not so readily find a way out. After dark the owners come with lighted torches and carefully examine the corrals, turning up every stone. The fish are blinded by the glare of the light and can be caught and thrown into baskets. Frogs, tadpoles, larvae, and water-beetles are also welcome.

In the central part of the country they use a spear made of a thin reed and tipped with thorns of the nopal. Sometimes it is shot from a diminutive bow, like an arrow. But a more interesting way is to hurl it by means of a primitive throwing-stick, which is nothing but a freshly cut twig from a willow *(jaria)* about six inches long, left in its natural state except for the flattening of one end on one side. The spear is held in the left hand, the stick in the right. The flat part of the latter is placed against the end of the spear, which is slightly flattened on two sides, while the end is squarely cut off. By pressing one against the other, the throwing-stick is bent, and sufficient force is produced by its rebound to make the spear pierce small fish. Many a Tarahumare may be seen standing immovable on the bank of a streamlet, waiting patiently for a fish to come, and as soon as he has hit it throwing himself into the water to grab it.

But a more profitable way of catching fish is by poisoning the water. In the highlands a kind of polygonum is used for this purpose. It is pounded with stones and thrown into the small corrals. When the fishing is to be done on a somewhat extensive scale, two species of agave—the amole (the soap-plant) and the soke—are used, and many households join in the sport. First of all maguey plants have to be collected, and wine made, as this is indispensable to the success of the undertaking. At the place selected for the fishing the people assemble, and two managers are appointed, one for each side of the river. It is their duty to see that everything is done in the right and proper way and all the requisite ceremonies are observed. The women are a couple of hundred yards back cooking herbs and making pinole for the men to eat. No pregnant women are allowed to be present, as then the fish would not die.

Half-circular corrals of stone are built to intercept the fish that drift along, irrespective of any private traps that may be found on the place. Fish caught in the latter belong to those who put up the traps. While constructing these corrals, the men catch a few fish with their hands, between the rocks, open them in the back and give them to the women to broil. When they are done, the men pound the fish to a pulp, mix it with pinole, and roll the mass into a ball two or three inches in diameter. One of the managers then goes down stream, below the corrals, and places the ball in a water pool. It is a sacrifice to the master of the river, a large serpent (Walúla), which makes an ugly noise. Every river, water-hole, and spring has its serpent that causes the water to come up out of the earth. They are all easily offended; and therefore the Tarahumares place their houses some little distance from the water, and when they travel avoid sleeping near it. Whenever the Tarahumares make pinole while away from home, they sacrifice the first part to the water-serpents, dropping it with the little stick with which the pinole is stirred. They sprinkle it first forward, then to the left, then to the right, and then upward, three times in each direction. If they did not do this, the water-serpents would try to catch them and chase them back to their own land. Besides the sacrifice of the fish ball, they offer axes, hats, blankets, girdles, pouches, etc., and especially knives and strings of beads, to the master of the fish, who is considered to be the oldest fish. This is in payment for what they are going to catch, and the donations are either hung to a cross or a horizontal bar specially erected in the middle of the river, and remain hanging there until daybreak, when their respective owners take them back.

In the meantime eight or ten men have gathered the amole and soke. They wrap the plants in their blankets and bring them direct to the river, where they are to be used. The leaves are pounded with stones and spread out for a while before sunset. As soon as it is dark the men throw them into the water, and trample on them to make the juice come out. Three or four men take turns, standing waist-deep in the water, treading with all their might and howling. The effect of the poison in the course of the night is said to reach down some 300 yards. It stupefies the fish, and although many of them revive, a few are killed and may be eaten, as the poison does not affect the meat.

The managers see to it that everybody does his duty and that no one falls asleep during the night, while the women help by watching the mats, that the otters may not eat the fish caught in them.

A curious detail is that one man on each side of the river is deputed to heat stones and throw them into the river three or four at a time, every half-hour, possibly to frighten off the serpent. During the night not one fish is taken up, but at daybreak the managers go down the river to investigate the effect of the poison, and upon their return the fish are gathered in, the men often diving into deep water for them. The work is done with great earnestness and almost in silence, the women helping the men in catching the fish. While the fishing is going on they do not eat any of the fish, for fear of not getting more, but during the day quantities are broiled and eaten, without salt or chile, however, and the bones are invariably thrown into the fire. Most of the fish are cut open in the back and placed on rocks or on trees to dry for future use. Such fishing may last for two days and nights, and is finished by dancing yumari and drinking maguey wine. On one occasion as much was caught as ten men could carry. Expeditions of this kind may be repeated two or three times a year; but when food is plentiful a whole year may pass without one being undertaken.

Palo de la flecha, too, is used as poisoning material, and seems to be even more powerful than the two plants mentioned. There is a milky juice under the bark of this tree which, when it comes in contact with the human skin, makes it smart like a burn. The water is poisoned by cutting the bark from the trunk and boughs directly into the water, the people taking care to stand to the windward. One man who neglected this precaution got some juice in his eyes and was blinded for three days, though an application of salt water finally cured him.

Although a single man may poison fish in a small way even in winter, he is hardly likely to do so except in summer-time, when provisions are low. The Indians dislike going into cold water; besides, they say that the cold impairs the effect of the poison.

In summer-time the Indians may also improvise a net with the help of their blankets, and drag the river at suitable places. Farther down on the Rio Fuerte, I once saw them make a large and serviceable net by fastening sixteen blankets together lengthwise with a double row of wooden pins. Along the upper edge of this net they made a hem three inches deep, and through this they passed vines securely joined together by means of the fibres of the maguey to do duty as ropes. The opposite edge of the net had a hem four inches deep and this was filled with sand to sink it as it was dragged in. The boys and girls were told to go ahead and splash all they could in the water to prevent the fish in the net from swimming out, and it was funny to see them dive heels over head into the water over and over like porpoises, the girls as well as the boys, with their skirts on. The fishermen advanced slowly, as the net was heavy. When it was brought in toward the shore, the women, even those with babies on their backs, helped to drag it. As the two ends of the net reached the bank, the big fish were picked out and thrown landward, while the remainder were brought up with a dip-net made of three blankets. Eighty good-sized suckers were secured, besides a large quantity of "small-fry."

Chapter 22

RESUMPTION OF THE JOURNEY SOUTHWARD—PINUS LUMHOLTZII—COOKING WITH SNOW—TERROR-STRICKEN INDIANS—A GENTLEMANLY HIGHWAYMAN AND HIS "SHOOTING-BOX"—THE PERNICIOUS EFFECT OF CIVILISATION UPON THE TARAHUMARES—A FINE SPECIMEN OF THE TRIBE—THE LAST OF THE TARAHUMARES.

From this trip I returned to San Carlos, mainly over the highlands south of the barranca, and shortly afterward was able to continue my journey toward the southwest. The cordons here, generally speaking, have a southerly direction, running parallel to each other.

Reaching at one place an elevation of 8,800 feet, I had a fine view of the entire central part of the Tarahumare country, seeing as far as Cerro Grande, at the northern end of the llano of Guachochic, in which direction the country, as a matter of course, looked quite flat. Nearest to us were wild-looking arroyos and cordons, covered in the lower portions with oak-trees, and higher up with pines. We were in the midst of vast pine forests, and even the country north of us looked like one uninterrupted forest of pines.

The Tarahumares have names for six kinds of pines. One species, first met with near Tutuhuaca, was new to science. Though not a large tree, it is very ornate, owing to its slender, whip-like branches, and its hanging needles, from eight to ten inches long. It grows here and there in groups, at high altitudes, on decomposed volcanic tuff. The needles are boiled by the Indians and the Mexicans, and the decoction used as a remedy for stomach troubles. It is not disagreeable to take, the taste resembling that of aniseseed. The Tarahumares prefer the wood of this variety of pines for the making of their violins. I found this species as far south as the sierra above Pueblo Nuevo, in the State of Durango.

The vegetation of the Sierra Madre is incomparably stronger and more luxurious than that of the cold North. The pine-trees in higher altitudes, for instance in Norway, appear miserably puny and almost stunted when compared with the giants of the South. Trees of 100 to 150 feet high and 10 to 15 feet in girth are frequent. We noticed some species of pines the needles of which were over a foot long.

The region through which we were passing seemed uninhabited, and there were really but few Indians living here. The cordon nearest to the one on which we were standing was covered with snow, and we climbed without difficulty to a point 9,300 feet high. There was no water, but snow three inches deep in some places, yielding all the water we required, though it had a slight flavour of the pines. The Mexicans did not like it, and said they would not eat food cooked with snow; but after I had shown them that the water obtained in this way was very good, they also took to it.

On our arrival at some Indian ranches, the people screamed with terror, ran away and hid themselves. There was something so unusual about their fright, that the interpreter and I went out of our way to investigate the matter. I saw two children making their escape among the bushes as best they could, a boy leading a three-year-old girl all the time, never deserting her. We found the children and a young woman on top of a rock. After we had succeeded in allaying their fears, they answered our questions readily. It appeared that two men from this place had recently been hanged by some people from Cienega Prieta, the ranch for which we were making. One of the victims had been revived, but the other had died. My Indian boy Patricio knew about the outrage, too.

I had at the outset been warned against robbers south of Guachochic, and advised never to sleep in houses—a thing I rarely did, anyway, for other reasons. One man especially, Teodoro Palma, had an unsavoury reputation as a "gentlemanly highwayman." In the desolate region where his residence lies, his father had maintained a band of valiant men, who made regular plundering expeditions, driving cattle away, etc. It was a common tale that travellers who had to pass his place were invited to come in, but never came out again. The bodies of the victims, it was said, were buried at night in the cemetery of the Indian village of Chinatu, a few miles distant. Times had changed since then, and the son was more guarded in his operations, but still sufficiently active.

In order to avoid a long detour to the east, I had chosen to follow the track which passes this place, though travellers generally give it a wide berth; besides, I thought it best to take the bull by the horns. When I reached the robber's stronghold, I did not find Don Teodoro at home, though he was expected to return the next day. In the mean time the superintendent showed me around the house and sold me some necessary provisions.

The house looked forbidding enough. A wall of adobe, eighteen feet high, ran all around the establishment, shutting it in securely. It was provided with two small towers, which had loop-holes for rifles.

In the house was a small chapel, in which Don Teodoro and his father before him had frequently knelt to pray. The altar was decorated with the pictures of many saints, and in the centre was a painting of the Christ-child, a crucifix, and an artificial apple.

When the lord of the manor arrived the following day, I immediately went to see him. As I passed through the enclosure he was scolding the superintendent, but on perceiving me he stepped forward to receive me. This modern Fra Diavolo was about thirty years old, rather short of stature, but unusually well built. He wore an embroidered brown jacket and a blue waistcoat, and around his neck was thrown a many-coloured scarf. On one side of his sombrero was a scarlet rosette. Under it gleamed brown, piercing eyes. His hair was cut short. Altogether he was quite good-looking, except for a cruel, sensual expression of the features. His entire manner, erect carriage, and quick, decisive movements told me he was a man of violent temper and extreme determination.

He led the way into a room, and I handed him my letter of recommendation from the Mexican Government, and explained what I was doing in the sierra. After he had read the letter, he said that he was my friend. I told him that I had heard there were robbers in the vicinity, and in case I was molested I should apply to him for assistance, since he was a very influential man. Of course I knew as long as he did not rob us we were quite safe. I then photographed him and his house, and he evidently felt quite flattered. He accompanied me for a mile down the road, and then, taking me aside, handed me back the paltry sum I had paid for the provisions, saying he did not accept payment from his guests. This was rather embarrassing, but there was no way out of it, and I had to accept it. I afterward sent him a copy of his photograph to even up matters.

The guide with whom Don Teodoro had provided me pointed out to us a place where his master last year killed and robbed a man. "He is a poor shot," he added, "except at close range, and he generally travels at night." In 1895 Don Teodoro Palma himself was killed by the Indians. If half the rumours about him are true, he certainly deserved his fate. He never dared to go down to the lowlands, because "he owed so many dead," as the saying goes. A few years before my visit, an American had been killed and robbed in the vicinity, and his countrymen in Chihuahua offered a reward for the apprehension of the murderer, dead or alive. Don Teodoro know that a certain friend of his had perpetrated the crime, and in order to secure the reward he invited him to his house and shot him down in cold blood.

I arrived safely in Guadalpe y Calvo, a once flourishing place, but now quite dead, since the mines have ceased to be worked. There are large Mexican ranches southeast of the town, and whatever Tarahumares live hereabout are servants of the Mexicans and frequently intermarry with the Tepehuanes.

I thus traversed from north to south the country over which the Tarahumares once held sway. To-day we find this tribe, approximately, between Guadalupe y Calvo and Temosachic; roughly speaking, between the twenty-sixth and twenty-ninth degrees northern latitude.

Civilisation, as brought to the Tarahumare, is not fraught with benefits for him. It rudely shakes the columns of the temple of his religion. The Mexican Central Railroad crushes his sacred plants without thought of its anger, which is vented on the poor Tarahumare by sending him bad years and ill-luck. While the Indians deny themselves the pleasure of smoking tobacco in the daytime for fear of offending the sun with the smoke, the white men's furnaces and engines belch forth black clouds of smoke day after day, keeping the people out of the sight of Tata Dios, and thus preventing him from guarding them. In the engine itself they see the Devil with a long tongue and a big beard.

Worse than that, the foot of civilisation destroys his home; for the whites draw the boundary line of his country closer and closer. The better class of Mexicans keep to themselves, and seldom, if ever, bother about the Indians at their doors, whose mode of living and way of thinking are so different from their own. The class of whites on the borderland of such civilisation as the Tarahumare comes in contact with is not the kind that will or can improve him, being ignorant and unscrupulous. The Indian civilised by them is a very unpleasant person to deal with. He has learned to cheat and to steal, and he no longer carries out his contracts and agreements. Having learned the value of money, his greed is awakened, and he begins to look out only for his own profit.

The first white men with whom the Indian gets acquainted are the traders who speak his language, and whose sole aim is to enrich themselves at his expense and compel him to deal with them. If the Indian does not want to sell, the lenguaraz loses his patience, throws a few dollars toward him, takes the ox, and goes off. Many will go still further. They force the native to borrow from them, whether he wants the money, the cloth, the mescal, or the use of the horse, or not. Many Indians would refuse mescal, satisfied with their native stimulants, but see no other way of getting rid of the unwelcome and obtrusive white than by yielding to his demand. The agreement is made that he must return the so-called loan on a certain date, two or three months hence; the Indian, of course, having no almanac, easily makes a mistake in his calculation, and the date passes. The dealer has gained his point. He saddles his horse, looks up the Indian, and makes a great to-do about all the trouble he is put to in collecting the debt, charging not only enormous interest for overtime, but adding exorbitant travelling expenses and fees. He succeeds by threats and intimidation in getting his damages adjusted in such a way that, in return for the paltry sum he lent the Indian, he now drives off two or three oxen.

The Indians, being honourable in their dealings, do not at first contact with the whites suspect rascality, and many stories are told illustrating the ease with which they have been cheated.

Once a Mexican bought a sheep from a native on credit, and, after killing it, paid for it with the head, the skin, and the entrails. Another man did still better. He paid for his sheep with the same valuables, and "spoke so well" that the Indian was content to remain in his debt as the final result of the transaction. On another occasion a native was induced to sell eleven oxen, almost his entire stock, to a Mexican. It was agreed that the latter should pay two cows for each ox, but not having any cows with him he left his horse and saddle as security. The Indian is still waiting for the cows. When I expressed my surprise at the ease with which he allowed himself to be swindled, he replied that the Mexican "spoke so well." They are so delighted at hearing their language spoken by a white man, that they lose all precaution and are completely at the mercy of the wily whites, who profit by their weakness.

Some tough lenguaraz is not ashamed to cheat at games until the Indian has lost everything he has. One poor wretch lost several oxen in one game of quinze. Other sharpers borrow money from the natives and never pay back the loan, or else impose fines on the Indians under the pretext of being authorities. Some foist themselves upon the Tarahumares at their feasts, which they disturb by getting drunk and violating women. Where the Indians are still masters of the situation they catch such an offender and take him before the Mexican authorities, insisting upon his paying for all the requirements for another feast, as he has spoiled the value of the one on which he intruded. In the central part of the country, near Norogachic, they may even kill such a transgressor.

It is generally through mescal that the Indians become peons. When the Indian has once developed a taste for mescal, he will pay anything to get it, first his animals, then his land. When he has nothing more to sell, the whites still give him this brandy and make him work. And there he is. To work himself free is next to impossible, because his wages are not paid in money, but in provisions, which barely suffice to keep him and his family alive. Indians are sometimes locked up over night to force them to work.

The children of such parents grow up as peons of the Mexicans, who deal out miserable wages to the descendants of the owners of the land on which the usurpers grow rich. Before the occupancy of the country by the new masters, the Tarahumares never knew what poverty was. No wonder that the Christian Tarahumares believe that hell is peopled so thickly with Mexicans that there is not room for all. Some have been crowded out, and have come to the Tarahumares to trouble them. The Indians in some districts have been cheated so much that they no longer believe anything the white men tell them, and they do not offer food any more to a white stranger if he is what they call "deaf," in other words, unable to speak and understand their language and explain what he is about.

They make very good servants when treated right, although they often want a change; but they will return to a good master. I once had a Tarahumare woman in my employ as cook. She was very industrious and in every way superior to any Mexican servant I ever had. When not busy with her kitchen work, she was mending her own or her two children's clothes. While very distrustful, she was good-tempered and honourable, and spoke Spanish fairly well, and her eyes indicated unusual intelligence. A white man had deserted her to marry a Mexican woman, and she grieved much, but in time she became reconciled to her fate, though she declared she would never marry again, as all men were bad.

The Tarahumares have made excellent soldiers in fighting for the Government. In one of the civil wars, their leader, Jesus Larrea, from Nonoava, a pure-bred Tarahumare, distinguished himself, not only by bravery and determination, but also as a commander. In private life he was civil and popular.

The majority speak their own language, and in the central and most mountainous part, the heart of the Tarahumare country, they are of pure breed. Here the women object to unions with outsiders, and until very recently light-coloured children were not liked. Mothers may even yet anoint their little ones and leave them in the sun, that they may get dark. The consensus of opinion among the tribe is that half-castes turn out to be bad people and "some day will be fighting at the drinking-feasts." A few instances are known in which women have left their half-caste babies in the woods to perish, and such children are often given away to be adopted by the Mexicans. In the border districts, however, the Indians have become much Mexicanised and intermarry freely with the whites.

Be it said to the credit of those high in authority in Mexico, they do all in their power to protect the Indians. But the Government is practically powerless to control the scattered population in the remote districts. Besides, the Indians most preyed upon by the sharpers cannot make themselves understood in the official language, and therefore consider it hopeless to approach the authorities. In accordance with the liberal constitution of Mexico, all natives are citizens, but the Indians do not know how to take advantage of their rights, although sometimes large bodies have banded together and travelled down to Chihuahua to make their complaints, and have always been helped out—for the time being. The efforts of the Government to enlighten the Indians by establishing schools are baffled by the difficulty in finding honest and intelligent teachers with a knowledge of the Indian language.

Where the Indians have had little or nothing to do with the whites, they are obliging, law-abiding, and trustworthy. Profit is no inducement to them, as they believe that their gods would be angry with them for charging an undue price. As a matter of fact, they sell corn all the year round, whether it be scarce or plentiful, at the same price, though the Mexicans charge them very different prices. The almighty dollar has no devotees among these Indians. They have no need of aught that money can buy, and are swayed by persuasion and kind and just treatment more than by gold. If they have a few coins, they place them in a jar and bury them in some remote cave, taking from the horde only a little when they have to buy some necessity of life.

Among the pagans in Pino Gordo I met the finest specimen of the Tarahumare tribe, a shaman, called Juan Ignacio. Although he had never been as far as Guadalupe y Calvo, and only twice in his life to Baborigame, and had thus spent his life in the mountains among his own people, he showed a courtesy and tact that would have graced a gentleman. He took splendid care, not only of myself, but of my men and animals as well, giving us plenty to eat, sending his man to chop wood for us, etc. He was possessed of the nicest temper, and was truthful, a rare quality among Tarahumares, as well as square in his dealings. His uprightness and urbanity commanded respect even from the lenguarazes, and they did not rob him as much as the other Indians of the district; consequently he was quite well-to-do.

While living among the heathen, of whom there are yet some three thousand left, I had no fear of being robbed of any part of my outfit. The Indians themselves would not touch anything, and there were no strange Mexicans about. If they had come, the Tarahumares would have immediately warned me. Everything was perfectly safe as long as I had an honest interpreter. The Tarahumare in his native condition is many times better off, morally, mentally, and economically, than his civilised brother; but the white man will not let him along as long as he has anything worth taking away. Only those who by dear experience have learned to be cautious are able to maintain themselves independently; but such cases are becoming more and more rare.

It is the same old story over again, in America, as in Africa, and Asia, and everywhere. The simple-minded native is made the victim of the progressive white, who, by fair means or foul, deprives him of his country. Luckily, withal, the Tarahumare has not yet been wiped out of existence. His blood is fused into the working classes of Mexico, and he grows a Mexican. But it may take a century yet before they will all be made the servants of the whites and disappear like the Opatas. Their assimilation may benefit Mexico, but one may well ask: Is it just? Must the weaker always be first crushed, before he can be assimilated by the new condition of things?

Future generations will not find any other record of the Tarahumares than what scientists of the present age can elicit from the lips of the people and from the study of their implements and customs. They stand out to-day as an interesting relic of a time long gone by; as a representative of one of the most important stages in the development of the human race; as one of those wonderful primitive tribes that were the founders and makers of the history of mankind.

Rattle for Ankle, made from Empty Pods of a Palm.

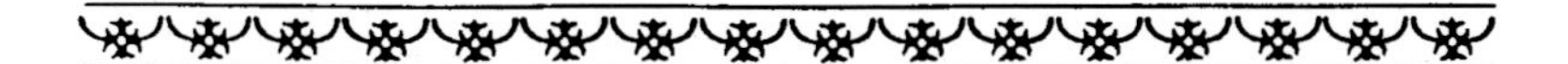

Silver Magnet

Grant Shepherd

Chapter 1

Departure

In the year of our Lord 1880, my father, Alexander Robey Shepherd, erstwhile Governor of the District of Columbia, and his lovely, brave and devoted wife, with their children, servants, dogs, employees and friends, packed up bag and baggage in Washington, D.C., and set out for the ancient village of Batopilas in the state of Chihuahua in the country of Mexico.

To this modern generation such a journey presents no features of especial discomfort. But fifty-seven years ago it took forty days . . . this trip into that little known and as little traveled country. It was made feasible by a letter to the Commanders of the Army Posts throughout the State of Texas from General Sherman, who was my father's very good friend; the Baltimore & Ohio Railroad and others; ambulances, wagons, horses, mules—human and otherwise.

The first Army Post in Texas where we rested for a few days during this adventurous period of travel was Fort Concho. There I experienced the first great fright of my life. I was perfectly terrified despite the fact that I fought, like all small boys do, with my young brother, and only within the last half hour had been pulled from off him by my long-suffering nurse. But it seemed to me at the age of five years that he was in imminent danger of being trampled to death beneath the feet of marching troops, and it threw a scare into me that makes this particular incident of those long-past days vividly clear. It is really much clearer than many other and far more important occurrences of that memorable trip.

Of course, he was not trampled to death. Those whom I had regarded as ferocious soldiers opened their ranks very slightly, and the Kid passed through them unharmed, marching in time to the drum with his little stick on his little shoulder entirely oblivious of the fact that he had caused considerable consternation to his family who were admiring the parading troops on the parade ground. Oblivious, yes. Until his nurse, a red-cheeked, buxom Irish girl landed on him and ignominiously swung this venturesome three-year-old into her arms with voluble and heavy-brogue remonstrances.

Mary Jones she was, and far from the shores of the Emerald Isle. There were many, many new things she had to learn, along with her employers, in this recent service, an early and very painful one being that the prickly pear is not, as she had fondly believed "sure the gr-r-andest, foinest Shamrock I ever-r-r saw!" Poor Mary Jones! And poor mistress who later had to pick out the thorns from the too eagerly grasping fingers.

There must have been considerable rivalry between the gallant Infantry at the various Army Posts through which we passed and the long-moustachioed teamsters over Mary's charms. But stops at Army Posts were brief at best. Mary as history records arrived unscathed with all the rest of us at her final destination, a then small ancient silver-mining camp in the Sierra Madre Mountains of Mexico. For many long years, with only an occasional ruction with my own much beloved German nurse, Dora, she helped to get that big family shaken down into the routine of a novel and entirely extraordinary environment.

Dora was a dear, faithful creature, devoted and loyal to the heads of the family, as well as to the seven less important members, during that long term of years. She saw them grow up, marry, bring forth other generations in their own good time. These others like their parents spoke Spanish, played and fought with the little Mexican children; rode burros when they were quite small and were promoted first to ponies and then to true saddle animals. Dora forgave me mch and forgave it often for I was, in truth, a vexatious small boy.

But I have traveled a thousand miles or more in six or seven paragraphs.

Let us attempt to visualize the Baltimore & Ohio Railroad Station in Washington on the evening of May 1, 1880, at the hour of ten. It will be difficult to do this, for while the Baltimore & Ohio Station was located more or less on part of the same ground now occupied by the Union Station, there is a vast difference now between those two places.

The family consisted of seven children . . . May, about nineteen; Isabella who was eleven, with Susan and Grace at appropriate ages between those two; there were three young male animals, Alexander II aged eight; Grant, five; and John Conness aged three; their parents, their four dogs, their two nurses; and Uncle Jack. Uncle Jack was beloved by all of us; in his early twenties, fine-looking, and a good horseman. These made up the members of the family, a total of twelve. Aside from this family group the following gentlemen were in the party, who were going down to Batopilas as the American nucleus for the organization at the mines: Dr. Ross, surgeon; Colonel Morgan; L. M. Hoffman; Lyman Lamed; and Mr. Lindsay, engineer. We were seventeen souls and it is readily understood that a special Pullman was needed and used for the railway part of the journey.

The general outline for this route was from Washington, D.C., to St. Louis, Missouri; and from that place to San Antonio, Texas, by rail. From San Antonio by wheeled vehicles and "hay burners" to Forts Concho, Stockton, Leon Holes, Davis; on to the last place in the United States of America, which was Presidio del Norte, then across the Rio Grande to the city of Chihuahua in Mexico. From this last-named city we were finally to set forth for our objective, Batopilas.

At the hour and date mentioned, many friends and relatives were assembled at the railroad station in Washington. There began the stowing away of innumerable bags, baskets, boxes of fruit, lunches and candy; four dogs . . . of which two were in crates. The other two dogs were too large for any crate, they were magnificent mastiffs. The crated canine sufferers were a Chesapeake Bay pup, a gift to my father from his friend General Babcock; and a setter pup presented by Tom Cropley.

I have been told that the parting was a sorrowful one. It was a big jump into the unknown; not a person in the party except my father had made the trip previously. While the journey made by my father in the year 1879 presented no particular difficulties to a man of determination and physical vigor like himself, that same trip was an undertaking indeed when it was repeated with a household such as I have described.

The lighting in the railroad coaches was furnished by coal-oil lamps of assorted sizes and construction. Therefore, it was easier than it would be now to disguise tears and blushes, although both of those peculiarities were more freely indulged in then than now. Gradually the Pullman filled up, and the tearful good-byes began. The confusion somewhat subsided as the conductor gave his "All aboard!" Too-full throats were cleared, tears were transferred from cheek to handkerchief, and the train started to rock its way toward distant St. Louis. You might have thought that then all would be serene. But other ordeals still had to be gone through with . . . the putting to bed of the children, the locating of different pieces of hand luggage in which were night-shirts, and so forth. The children were tired out and must have been performing as all obstreperous tired children will and do perform on a railroad journey.

I quote from my mother's diary: "There is no time for sad thoughts, for tired and excited babies must be bundled into berths which they occupy for the first time in their short lives; notwithstanding which fact, they lie down without remark upon the novelty, save perhaps a tired _isn't this funny?' and are soon asleep."

Possibly the man who wrote "Rocked in the Cradle of the Deep" received his inspiration from a sea voyage; he could have got just asvivid a picture by taking any railroad journey in those days. The fact that we suffered from car-sickness was more than pardonable, almost justifiable, though nevertheless decidedly unpleasant. My poor mother first, and then everyone, is entitled to our sympathy; in charity let that first night remain with no further description.

As I said before, my father in the year 1879 made the trip into Mexico, lured by the silver magnet, to investigate the possibilities of the ancient property known as Batopilas, which had been first discovered in 1632. He sailed from New York City down the Atlantic Ocean to Panama, and crossed the Isthmus on the railroad. He went up the Pacific Ocean northward in a sailing vessel to the Mexican port of Ajiabampo. From that place the hot coastal plain was crossed on the hurricane deck of a mule, and so into the Sierra Madre Mountains to the silver-mining camp of Batopilas. On the return trip back into the United States, he came out of Mexico northeast across the Sierra Madres, still on the hurricane deck of a mule, to the City of Chihuahua and thence into the United States, exactly the same route you are going to take with me, but in reverse order.

It took us three long, dusty days to reach St. Louis. We children were sick many times as a result of too much candy, the Baltimore & Ohio Railroad bed, and so on. We made even more than the usual nuisances of ourselves. At St. Louis we transferred to another railroad and to yet another special Pullman and had opportunity to observe many unfortunate emigrants with their unwashed faces, their dirty bundles, their strong smells, who were on their way to settle that great Western country of ours.

The major portion of our movements from day to day is extremely hazy to me. I do recall very vaguely that upon arrival in Houston, Texas, the train onto which our Pullman was to have attached as tail-end had already left. There was no small verbal warfare, for my father was a forceful man. A special Pullman with a dozen or more passengers was something which ought to have been waited for, unless the train which was pulling it was so very late that it could go as well on tomorrow's schedule as on today's. . . .

After Houston, what? The Hotel Menger in San Antonio is the answer. In 1880 that hostelry was an unanswerable argument.

We bade good-bye to the hospitable people in San Antonio with reluctance, but not so with the Hotel Menger. There we also said good-bye to the "iron horse" and outfitted for the over-land-and-sand journey to the last halt in the United States, Presidio del Norte on the Rio Grande. To be a true 1880 Texan, you pronounced that river Rio Gran, with the emphasis on the "I" as in "eye."

Outfitting, that was some job of work!

Having grown up in an atmosphere of miners, teamsters, arrieros, in later years I could begin to appreciate what a task it really was. What a sweet time the natives of San Antonio, experts in the ancient and honorable profession of home and mule barter, must have enjoyed with my father and my uncle and the other male tenderfeet in the party. Both my father and my uncle knew a good deal about blooded horses, but about a quantity of wagons with their six- and eight-mule teams making up a wagon-train, they were so very ignorant that they flinched in both front and hind feet.

There were several ambulances in the cavalcade. The family, the accompanying physician, and the other gentlemen in the party rode in this luxurious mode of conveyance. An ambulance is a heavy Dayton wagon, only more so. You who drive your five hundred miles a day over roads as smooth as a billard table in an automobile can have no conception of how your back feels after, say, fifty miles "cross country" in one of those vehicles. I expect that is one of the many reasons which gave those oldsters a stiff backbone and a small diameter at the equator.

The wagons with the supplies were given a ten-hour start of the ambulances from the town of San Antonio. But we overtook them before Leon Springs was reached. The first night in camp was passed in grave anxiety at that plae, and two or three days besides, while the doctor labored to save the life of my mother, who had succumbed to the effects of the food at the Hotel Menger.

I am not describing any "covered wagon" episodes. Our travels for that time were trekking de luxe. In fact, I clearly remember one morning my father was tremendously incensed and more than probably decidedly profane because some of the teamsters had stolen an entire case of his best Port wine, and were, therefore, in no condition to start out. His ire, as was the case in Houston when we missed our connection there, was not on this occasion so much at the loss of time entailed in contending with heavy-lidded drivers—who were absolutely poisoned by good Port—but because he had progressed far enough out "at sea" to appreciate the fact that the purveyor of all good things to eat and drink was a mighty long way to the north of him.

It was on that same morning while I was riding proudly on the driver's seat beside "Dolf," with his long-horn moustache, that I had the thrill of seeing him offhandedly shoot a great rattlesnake which was coiled near the roadside. Those roads consisted of a very occasional wagon track in the sand and mesquite filled with rocks of assorted sizes. One day my father was almost disjointed after miles of such travel, and he promised the driver a bottle of beer for every rock he would miss. I fear that the debt was never paid in beer. Those old Texans liked their liquor with "the thorns still in it" and at the rate of ten drinks to the full quart. Maybe he found, in some of those little towns and Army Posts through which we passed, enough whiskey to pay the debt. Any driver would have to miss a few of those rocks no matter how carelessly he drove.

The boys who have longed to be street-car drivers, or motor-men, racers of automobiles, fliers, and so forth can imagine the yearning to become a "Dolf," with a long yellow moustache shaped exactly like the horns of a water buffalo and nearly as long. A "Dolf" with a lean, sun-tanned face, sitting up there having a six-shooter strapped to you, your hand full of the six lines attached to those ornery, jackrabbit-eared mules, and a hickory-stock whip with which to pop a horsefly from a mule at any time in the most nonchalant and fetching manner.

It will always be a mystery to me how buxom Mary Jones ever resisted him or the many others, in fact. I'm sure had I been a Mary Jones there would have been a different tale to tell. After the passage of all these years, I fail to recall whom it was that Mary selected as a mate, but I do remember that it was a successful marriage, and that the couple lived not far from El Paso, Texas.

A child in later years may recollect certain incidents, a few at any rate, of such a journey. It must be remembered that the lucky child when weariness overtakes him goes to sleep in some grown-up's lap or other comfortable place, the making available of which has necessitated the still greater discomfort and crowding of the grown-ups. They must for hours endure true aches and pains sitting long in cramped positions, while the patient, weary mules drag the heavy vehicles over miles and miles of bad roads, across a hot, dry, dusty country to a temporary camp at night; or to an occasional by comparison gloriously commodious Army Post, where every kindness and consideration possible is shown to the almost exhausted travelers.

Those camps must have been a tedious ordeal to the grown people, particularly as the colored man-cook, picked up in San Antonio, turned out to be an incompetent and useless fellow. It was here that Dora's devotion to my mother and her seven children demonstrated that she was a true and godly Christian. I have, since those days, met many men and women called godly, and some of them were; but it is my firm conviction that when dear old Dora arrived at the pearly gates there was no delay in the opening of them, nor in her being escorted to her well-earned place of the greatly deserving.

Of the kindness and affectionate welcome accorded to us by the officers and their wives at these isolted Army Posts, I personally, of course, recall but little. Such things a small boy takes in his stride, blessed as I was, and undoubtedly with both of my brothers greatly spoiled; there is left no indelible brand upon his brain or whatever is the recording instrument where such things are noted down. But many, many times have I heard my parents speak of this unselfish happily offered succor to their jaded selves. The much greater security we enjoyed across the State of Texas we owed to our departure from the first Army Post, Fort Concho, being made to coincide with that of Major Wasson, the Army Paymaster. He was about to make his monthly trip when we got there, so that "the ghost might walk" for the doughboy and the cavalry. The Paymaster's escort, which accompanied us in consequence, was a safeguard against the Apache and other Indians, who at that time had not yet yielded to the blessings of civilization—or was it the Henry rifle?

I have a dim picture of some dashing officers riding alongside the ambulances to attend us for the first few miles beyond some of the Posts. In after years, I have realized that the true reason for this attention was not an interest in myself that I might revel in their handsome mounts, as I had then supposed; but that four very attractive sisters between the ages of thirteen and twenty years had more than a little bit to do with the consideration shown to three messy, normal, hence annoying small boys of the ages of eight, five, and three years.

As the journeying progressed the wretched pups had outgrown their crates, so these wriggling, squirming pests were then added to the discomfort of the grown-ups. One especially gallant young officer had given us constant and visible proof of his devotion to my third sister by insisting that we should take with us yet another puppy. This one was a strange animal of the Texi-cactu-mongrelous breed, whose life came to an untimely end in Chihuahua shortly after our arrival in that city. At this place of rest and enjoyment when the family might better have taken pleasure in his cute ways, this pup's life terminated.

The incident of his demise was the first demonstration of any homicidal tendencies in the Kid, his attempts heretofore upon my own life and that of his oldest brother being accepted as the regular tendencies of a boy of three responding to the life-giving rays of a Texas sun. We, therefore, were more than a little shocked when he dropped this poor unfortunate pup from a second-story window to see if he would land on his feet as the cat had always managed to do under like conditions.

It occurs to me here that this desire for scientific accuracy of knowledge on the part of Conness was the cause in after years of his likewise dropping a man who annoyed him out of a convenient window. . . .

General View of Hacienda San Miguel

1. Refectory
2. Office Buildings
3. Corral and Stables
4. General Manager's Residence
5. Machine Shop
6. Foundry (Iron)
7. 25 Stamp Mill
8. Amalgamation Sheds
9. Refinery
10. Cyanide Works
11. Store
12. Assay Office
13. Lixiviation Works

Chapter 2

Arrival

We must backtrack . . . we have arrived in Chihuahua with far too little travel and trouble.

The last days before we reached Presidio del Norte seemed to be the most trying and tiresome of all the pilgrimage. This was a small place on the banks of the Rio Grande. There was an adobe building or two, an American Consul, Mr. Russell, and some other kind people, among whom was Mr. Moses Kelley, who was extremely thoughtful and attentive. He did his very best for us on the United States side of the river where he had an adobe warehouse. Among his attentions was an immense tin bathtub, which was filled and emptied many times for our numerous baths in the muddy waters taken from that river which separates the sovereign State of Texas from the Republic of Mexico. At that period this river was a reminder more vivid than now of the amounts of powder exploded and the quantities of blood shed in the establishment of this boundary, where upon the day of our arrival the mercury stood at 115 degrees in the shade!

The next morning to us was comparable in importance to the Fourth of July, or any other great event in the history of the world. It was on this morning that we forded the Rio Grande, which was very wet.

The teams of six or eight mules to each wagon and to each ambulance were doubled in order to insure us against sticking in the mud and sand. Mr. Kelley led each division, driving in his especially made high-wheeled buggy drawn by two powerful mules, and the feat was accomplished. This eventful incident in the lives of my tribe brought to a successful conclusion, we reached the land of Mexico in which country more than one of the three generations of our family were to spend a good part of their lives in work and comfortable living. There we made friendships, some of which are still strong, but, unfortunately far too few, because many of those friends of childhood and manhood have passed to where beyond these voices there is peace.

When the requirements of the customs had been fulfilled, we resumed our trek toward the city of Chihuahua, the capital of the state of the same name whose plains and mountains, villages and cities make up the land which I know better than I know the land of my birth. While we are yet near the customs house and the town of Presidio del Norte, it is fitting to point out that the innate and active courtesy of the Mexican race, its government, and its customs officials, was then, as has always been my experience, something that could advantageously be imitated by those of the older Republic to the north.

As the crow flies, it is about a hundred and fifty miles from Presidio del Norte to Chihuahua, but we, alas, were not crows! Of necessity this latter portion of the trip was as slow and tortuous as the part which had gone before. But miles are only miles after all, and they can be worn off. One eventually reaches the point aimed at, or, if careless of the road signs, somewhere near the aiming point. Our bull's-eye for this first stretch of our Mexican journey was the city of Chihuahua, but before we gained that destination we came to another place which was but a short distance from there—Bachimba.

Ah, Bachimba! Bachimba!

What a paradise of irrigation, *caramba!* A garden...a dream of loveliness! It was a typical Hacienda, the first we had seen. It belonged then to the MacManus family. One of the MacManus girls had married the American Consul in Chihuahua, Mr. Scott. This gentleman had ridden his horse quite a way beyond Bachimba to meet us. Assisted by a cousin of Mrs. Scott, Ralph O'Neil, at the ranch proper he had prepared for the worn-out travelers a delightful reception in the cool, shady *patio,* a veritable oasis where fruits, vegetables, cooling drinks, fresh meat, eggs and chickens were in profuse and welcome abundance.

It was at beautiful Bachimba that we could once more delight in large trees for the first time in all these eight hundred miles of laborious travel. They were indeed a grateful sight to us who were accustomed to the gracious forests and parks of the East, to whom the dry, sandy, scrub-covered areas through which we had been passing had seemed not only useless but far from restful or prepossessing.

On the afternoon of June 19, 1880, we drove into Chihuahua. There we were housed in a comfortable large dwelling of two stories on the plaza opposite the stately old Cathedral. In her diary, my mother notes delightedly that there "was glass in the windows, a novelty."

In the city of Chihuahua we were the objects of every consideration and kind attention. After two weeks of settling us, my father and the other gentlemen of the party continued their journey into the southwest to Batopilas, where the silver mines were located. My mother and we children made our home in Chihuahua for a few months until my father could send back for us across the three hundred miles of plain and mountains which was the distance between the city of Chihuahua and the mining camp of Batopilas.

Taking a glance at my mother's diary once more, I see that on a certain day before my father left us in Chihuahua, they received a call from the priest, who came to pay a visit of courtesy, although they were of different religious faiths . . . quite different, for my parents were Presbyterians. It was with no little—though carefully disguised—consternation that my mother witnessed the unrestrained and frank enjoyment and relish by El Padre of Dad's very excellent and choice Madeira. Wine at this time was brought into Chihuahua over miles of desert on pack-mules; it was an expensive luxury and difficult to obtain. There is no regulation in the Roman Catholic Church against wine, therefore it is no wonder that El Padre indulged his taste; but to my mother, accustomed as she was to the more reserved drinking by the good Presbyterian pastors of her former life, it was something of a shock.

At the price of seeming inconsistent here, I state that it was, however, entirely possible to experience a small jag from consuming two slices of mince pie made under my mother's directions from her grandmother's recipe. Never since my mother stopped keeping house have I tasted a mince pie "as is a mince pie," with plenty—and then a little more—of brandy and sherry. I suppose if brandy and sherry are cooked, their injurious and intoxicating qualities are eradicated!

Our wait in Chihuahua, I am informed by elders and betters, was an agreeable experience. Many pleasant persons were delighted to meet newcomers who were from a little known and a strange land. The difference in language naturally cramped conversational efforts, but there were one or two Mexican gentlemen who spoke English, and Mr. Scott of course. When calls were made and returned, these patient men were requisitioned to go along or to come along as the case might be to act as interpreters.

The railroad was yet a long way from Chihuahua; it was not connected up at El Paso, Texas, with the Santa Fe until three years later on, and during those three years the only communication with their family and friends in the East which my mother and sisters could have was through letters which came once, and occasionally twice, a month. My mother records in her diary that during the few months when the men were in Batopilas, letter-writing was her chief diversion.

On the 16th of September, Uncle John arrived unexpectedly from Batopilas about dusk with the glad tidings that we were to pack up and come back to Batopilas with him, three hundred miles from Chihuahua.

I can barely recall that there were Shetland ponies back home in Washington at Bleak House. I was now and then held on the back of one of them, when he, snail-like, ambled about the driveway confining the lawn. The past forty and more days of travel had fully impressed me with the fact that mules for progressing over the face of the earth were a great deal more accomplished critters than ponies if they were attached to an ambulance by a good strong harness, and stimulated by a whip in the hands of a "Dolf" or other skillful operator.

But now I was, with those others who for their great sins had the taking care of me, to appreciate the fact that the mule when ridden, or better, sat upon, was a long-suffering safe means of advancing into the unknown. I differentiate purposely between sitting upon and riding an animal. There does, in truth, exist that dissimilarity: if you do not believe me, ask any Mexican saddle-mule.

On this my first journey into Batopilas upon the back of a mule, I shared the saddle, a small part of it, with a Mexican mozo, who was entrusted with my—to my parents at any rate—valuable carcass. I do not remember the name of this unlucky man. But I do recall that he had a long beard and that he kindly refrained from what must have been a burning desire to hurl me over the edge of one of the many tempting gorges with which that old trail is so bountifully supplied, and along which it often skirts for miles.

If you are inclined to regard it as a pleasant or an easy pastime to carry a husky child in front of you while riding a mule over the Sierra Madre Mountains, only try it. Get someone to lend you a child about four or five years old. Procure a mule and a saddle. Go to the Grand Canyon of the Colorado and ride up and down the trail there for seven or eight hours, or until such time as your speedometer indicates that forty miles of Hell have come to an end. Do this for five consecutive days and then . . . well, I leave to your own best efforts the decision as to your attitude towards the child.

Of course, there is the side of the child to this story. But the child at this age is more or less helpless. He can struggle or cry out, but he has no responsibilities; his arms do not grow so infernally tired. He can lean back against the grown-up sufferer to his rear. . . .

There is not so much bother connected with camp-making, pitching of tents, getting of meals, and all the rest of it on the trail as one would suppose, if things are properly organized.

Into and out of deep gorges on corkscrew trails, along pleasant table lands thickly timbered, mostly with great pines, until the end of the fifth day's travel. On that day we set out before daylight. At the beginning of the third hour you come to the edge of the canyon down whose precipitous slopes you must go, some six thousand feet vertically, along winding trails. It takes you three and a half hours of riding before the level of the bed of the river is reached. Fifteen miles down this stream, the Batopilas River, is the haven you started out to attain at the Baltimore and Ohio Railroad Station in Washington, many eventful months past.

If we look backward and very decidedly upward, we can see the edge of the pine-covered bluff from which we departed some three hours previously. Between that spot and our present location on the banks of the river we have passed through pine timber, then oak, then scrub oak, next small semi-tropical growth, largely inhabited by thorns, and finally onto the region of cactus of varying sizes, shapes, and general pestiferousness.

From this place the trail follows the mountain side and accommodates itself and its level in accordance with the mountain side as it varies from steep to very steep and to extremely precipitous. At last, we reach the junction of El Arroyo de Las Huertas. This is forded. On again for a short distance and at last we are come to the Hacienda San Miguel, which has been the true bull's-eye we have been aiming at all the time.

Chapter 3

First Impressions

The Hacienda San Miguel was a perfect paradise for children. There was room to spare. It was walled in against the high waters of the Batopilas River during the rainy season, for this river could rise twenty feet in a few hours. There was a big outside patio where grew immense old orange trees, oleanders, guayavas, *Noche Buenas*. . . . There was one huge *mata de aguacate* whose fruit we know as alligator pear. The beauty of crimson glory, the *Noche Buena,* is so called "Good Night" because this is the name for Christmas Eve throughout Latin-America. We know it as the poinsettia. Those in the patio of the Hacienda San Miguel were not merely plants, but were true trees with trunks of more than four inches in diameter.

We were all too tired the first late afternoon of our arrival to do anything but pay brief heed to the hearty and affectionate welcomes from my father and the others of the advance party, then to supper and bed. Ah! but the next morning! Then I set out to explore the hacienda with its irresistible mysteries. The noisy stamp mill and the whirring amalgamation plant, the machinery of which was driven from the hidden pit in which were the invisible turbines at the bottom of the waterfall from the aqueduct above. . . .

That small mill as the years passed grew into a big plant, and it was the first of three, but not the largest.

It was many years before the secrets were solved for me, the reason for those two revolving vertical pieces of shafting with their intricate cog-wheels and gears made plain. Childlike and manlike I hated to announce my ignorance by asking questions. They all appeared intensely interesting and correspondingly dangerous.

The last romance of Dora's life was mixed up with those pinions and gears. Three years after I first saw them, the boss of the amalgamation plant, Jack Ogden, carelessly allowed his right hand to be taken in, and it was so cruelly mangled that Dr. Ross was obliged to take it off. A stump was made for Jack and he used to poke me playfully in the ribs with it. He attached a useful hook with a clasp to this stump and at mealtimes he could manipulate his knife with dexterity. I was all of eight years old when I had my first experience with assisting the doctor to dress wounds. I can clearly see that old stump of Jack Ogden's now before it had entirely healed.

Naturally, Jack became a great hero and was made much of by Dora who added many a good thing to eat to what Jack was supplied by the regular mechanics' mess. Very shortly after our arrival in Batopilas, Jack and the head carpenter began to pay assiduous attention to Dora. But the latter was only a runner-up. Dora married Jack and they moved eventually to Chihuahua where they took over the management of a hotel. It became the most prominent and the most popular one for many years in that city.

I suppose there would have appeared to be many things perilous to children at the Hacienda San Miguel. But evidently those of our family must have adhered to the instructions they received from those whose duty it was to look out for them and to guide them, for none of us was ever seriously injured.

In a very short time, Conness and I were turned over to a young Mexican boy whose function it was to "ride herd" on us. Alex was a bit too mature to need this attention. Dora supervised the kitchen, and Mary did the general housework with Mexican women to help her. Old Domingo Dominguez did the heavy work.

There is an expression in Latin-America, brought with them by the Spaniards from Spain, which I feel applies particularly to my two brothers and me: *"Dios es grande,"* God is great. This expression is constantly employed in a place where the daily life of the individual brings him into more or less dangerous situations. They say that you are not killed nor hurt because *"Dios es grande."* Not only does this saying apply to our early life and the avoidance of serious accidents to ourselves, but to what we might have done to others.

Almost as soon as I was able to understand anything, the utter foolishness of pointing a gun at anyone was impressed upon me. Only one time did I violate this rule and then I got such a scare that never since have I been guilty of aiming a firearm at a person unless the need was real and I intended to fire it.

Old Domingo Dominguez' duties were many, but the one coming first in the day's activities was the bringing of fresh water for the *ollas,* which were kept in a window where whatever movement of the air was circulating would play upon its sides and hasten evaporation, thus cooling the water, for there was no ice. On a certain morning I was in my father's room looking longingly at the forbidden rack of other implements of offense and defense. I was about nine years old and it had been drilled into me that it was a wicked deed, and the action of a tenderfoot to point a firearm at a person unless it was in actual self-defense. Domingo came into the room carrying the five-gallon *olla* filled with fresh water. He put it down in the deep window and straightened up. The temptation proved too much for my youthful self-control. I succumbed to the sinful desire. I grasped and took down from its rack what appeared to be a muzzle-loader, double-barreled shotgun. I saw there were no caps on what I took to be the nipples of the barrels, but which were unfortunately firing pins. I raised the gun and aimed it at the slowly straightening figure of Domingo. When I pulled the trigger I tumbled over backwards, almost stunned with fright as well as physical pain. I could scarcely bring myself to look at the spot which I was sure could only be designated as that formerly occupied by the late Domingo Dominguez.

How astonished and how thankful I was when the old fellow seized me, stood me on my feet and rushed out of the room to return almost immediately with a broom and a handful of mopping cloths! *Dios es grande,* and Domingo had jumped backward when I fired, through the door into Dad's dressing-room: the load of buckshot had taken great effect on the *olla* and its contents.

This affair could not remain a complete secret, but the heads of the family were away from the hacienda for some reason or other. I suppose it was because of this absence that I had got up my courage to take down that damned shotgun. I never have felt the same about one since. As a matter of fact, I have fired one only a few times in my life. It cost me many of my father's cigars to keep Cook quiet. He had dashed across the *patio* from the kitchen, hearing the noise from the gun and Domingo's yell. I squared old Domingo and stood by him some fifteen years later, when he got into trouble and lost his job. No one ever knew it, but for months during those days I used to slip the old fellow ten or fifteen dollars every now and then, not because he was blackmailing me at that late date, but because of the common feeling that exists between two delinquents.

The only guard needed to keep us out of Dad's private office was Turk. He was a beautiful mastiff, quite gentle with us, but at the same time very positive in carrying out his master's orders. He would stay in the doorway himself to keep out any intruders. He did this effectually: in a mild but perfectly firm way he would punch his big old muzzle in our stomachs and push us back from the door. Turk had lost his handsome mate. She had to be shot when a drunken mechanic fatally injured her one night by giving her a brutal kick. The mechanic had never before been in such danger of his life. My father, the *Patron Grande,* was very kind to dumb animals: Turk and Countess had come all the way from Washington with us and they were his joy and delight. I have been creditably informed that what happened the night word was brought to him about Countess had the makings of a real tragedy. That is the correct expression, I believe, when it is applied to taking the life of a so-called fellow human being, which my father almost did.

It was necessary to keep us children out of my father's private office during his absence at the mines or elsewhere, because at the age of seven to ten we used to steal his best cigars to present them to some favorite of ours among the arrieros or even at times to smoke ourselves. Our special spot for these manly diversions was the roof. The flat roofs, the chimneys, and the accessibility of Dad's big, very good cigars were a challenge that must be accepted by young men like my kid brother and myself. When he was of the mature age of six and I eight, having sneaked a couple of these cigars into our pockets, we would upon occasions retire to the flat roof and selecting a place behind one of the chimneys where the thick foliage of the orange trees made it impossible for us to be seen from that side, we would light up. Then we could luxuriate in a delightful aura of dizziness, not enough to make the experience unpleasant, but just a mild drunk, enough to revel not only in the delicious fragrance of the first inch or so of a good cigar, but in that slight giddiness that went with it.

This all came to an end because we were seen by someone passing along the upper *patio,* who looking down upon us told it to someone else as a joke. Of course, this joke was passed on and on until it reached the ears of those that had the power and inclination to see that this pastime lost its charms. Despite this precocious start all three of my father's sons never became smokers until they were over six feet tall and the youngest one seventeen years of age.

The things we did to make the lives of those miserable informers unhappy kept us busy for quite a while. Thorns from any sort of cactus discreetly distributed between the sheets of an enemy's bed are no mean revenge. Poisonous insects such as *alacrans,* or better still a hideous tarantula, make any man regret his misdeeds if he realizes that they are a penalty he is paying for these transgressions. If he cannot possibly prove it on the culprits his exasperation is something greatly to be relished by the promoters.

Our diversions for the next few years were primarily an unflagging interest in goats, burros, stray dogs, most of them very hungry; whittling mules from cigar boxes, and arranging pack-trains with them. We made long spears with which we chased cats, assisted by the dogs and some young Mexican playmates as savage as ourselves. We caught mice in the orthodox local manner. This was done by using an empty spool and an empty tin cup. Into the center hole of the spool we stuffed a small piece of cheese; the cup we carefully balanced on the outer edge, the body of the spool extending back into and under the cup. When the mouse would creep under the cup to taste the cheese, he would jiggle the spool sufficiently backwards so that the cup would fall and thus make him a prisoner.

We were constantly seeing large numbers of raw hides being brought in for many uses about the business. 'What was more natural than that, in our efforts to reproduce in miniature the life and work of the adults around us, we should skin these captured mice (after killing them, I will say that), stake out the hides—we insisted on using that word, and salt them down to wait until they were in the proper condition to fold and pack in the same manner that we saw prepared the cow hides that came into the storehouse. This business of ours was done on the quiet and kept secret.

Of course, we had a grand time when the oranges and the guayavas were ripe. The orange trees were very old ones, their limbs were high above our heads. We would procure long fishing poles, tie a short stick near the small end in such a way that it would form a sort of hook. While one of us reached up with the pole and hooked the orange exactly where it joined the twig and, by a sudden jerk detached it, the others stood about to catch the golden fruit as it fell. If these perfectly ripe oranges were allowed to strike the ground from those tall trees they would burst open.

Another thing which was attractive for us was out of bounds, and, therefore, prohibited. This was to sit on the edge of the ore cars while they were driven at a trot to and from San Miguel Mine a mile away from the Hacienda San Miguel. Since stones were sometimes rolled down the mountain side by goats or other forces of nature, very often the cars would hit a stone which had lodged on the track, jump the track and upset. The contents of the cars would be precipitated over side of the road, from which place there was a nearly vertical fall to the river, a distance of over seventy feet. This, therefore, was considered dangerous by our parents and it was also damned hard on the seats of our knee pants. . . .

The dwelling part of the Hacienda San Miguel was in the shape of an L. The bottom arm made the upstream or northern end and the vertical arm formed the side which would have been against the retaining wall of the mountain side were it not that, for the sake of light, ventilation and drainage, there was a ten-foot alley way at the back between the building and the retaining wall. This retaining wall extended up about thirty feet to another narrow bench, from which still another wall carried up to the last level or Upper Patio. On the last level was the narrow-gauge track over which the ore from San Miguel Mine was transported in small ore-cars drawn by mules from the mine to the bins of the fifty stamp mill. Over beyond these bins was another area upon which the thousands and thousands of mule-and burro loads of wood were received and measured. When the wood was measured and

the receipt for it given to the woodmen, it was thrown down a distance of seventy feet to the level of that part of the hacienda, the down river side, where were located the boilers, sawmill, lixiviation plant and roasting furnaces, as well as the terminus of the aqueduct which emptied into the turbine pits.

The dwelling houses of the hacienda were of one story, of solid rubble masonry, with flat roofs covered with mortar and brick. There was a wide portal in front and between the portal and the river wall there was a garden. It was a lovely, spacious place at least two hundred and fifty feet long and about seventy-five feet wide. A double row of orange trees and guayavas grew in the garden just beyond the edge of the portal.

Chapter 4

Murder

As I look back through the years there come crowding forward so very many recollections, so very many incidents that it is with perplexity a selection can be made best to illustrate the life of a young North American boy growing up in that entirely new environment. Yet that is not really true as we analyze it. What we now call new is not that to a little child; his customs and habits are not crystallized enough to be dignified by the definite remembrance of any one thing which would make the new particularly strange. The difference in language means nothing; the point where he begins to speak the foreign tongue is reached early and easily and so is not apparent to him. The acquisition of local habits and customs is about the same as was the learning of those that went before in the two or three conscious years antedating the change.

Until the time in 1883 when General Porfirio Diaz took command of the Government of Mexico, the so-called established government was a disorganized affair. Distances were very great between the capitals of the states; means of transportation were limited and very slow. Each small city or town maintained order as best it could with the restricted means at hand. There was no central power which had the capability to enforce the law in this isolated region when a band of *pronunciados,* of sufficient size to overawe the few local police or soldiers, appeared. During the first few years of our lives in Batopilas, every once in a while there would be an alarm of *"Los Pronunciados!"* Then all the men within the hacienda, American and Mexican employees, would go to the main office to receive arms and ammunition. There would be extra night watchmen placed at the proper places. The *Jefe Politico,* Don Jesus Hernandez, would ride up on his fine bay horse from the town. He and my father would agree on the methods of repulsing any attack that might be made, whether it be made from up river or down; in the former case our hacienda would be the first to feel it, if from down river then the town would feel it first.

Arrangements would be made for sending immediate messengers between the town of Batopilas and the Hacienda San Miguel, a mile apart. The canyon was an extremely narrow one, space was very scarce, and the road leading from the hacienda to the town was actually one long street. Wherever it was wide enough to permit of it, there was a dwelling or a store of the simplest character on either side of the road. It was generally above highwater mark unless there should happen to be an unusually heavy rainy season with a cloud burst up the river. As I said before, this was the only long street benched or cut into the mountain side.

Those *pronunciados,* as the name implies, were a group of men who were pronouncing against or rising against the constituted authority. They carried a flag of some color, often red or blue. The color meant nothing in particular, it was simply a symbol; and in this case red hadn't its present-day significance. They designated themselves as the "reds" or the "blues" or any other color that they had selected or found conveniently available in a piece of material large enough to serve as a banner under which, or better, behind which, to march.

However, I very much fear that the object behind the *pronunciados* was of no political significance, but was simply the desire to take away money or silver or supplies. They seldom were determined enough to put up much of a fight if the resistance amounted to anything; or if they received word that the town was armed and that we were prepared to give them a warm welcome, the threatened attack never materialized.

This was very exciting to kids from ten to five years old. It was the sure reason for the strapping on of wooden pistols, knives, the shouldering of wooden guns, which had the *pronunciados* only known it would probably have been quite as effective as the true weapons in the hands of some of the tenderfoot mechanics. But concerning this, as well as many other important and much-debated historical facts, the truth will never be known. Since General Diaz was now in full possession and Don Jesus Hernandez was resolved to fight to the last ditch, the *pronunciados* saw that an inflexible defense was certain and they gave it up as a bad job, returning to their homes in the mountains or in the Hot Country to the south and west of us.

We were about six, eight, and ten years old when the first tragedy came into our lives at Batopilas. Young Charles Mayhew, an exceptionally fine young American, was killed, shot in the back by a renegade Yaqui Indian who had been working at La Descubridora Mine where Charlie was timekeeper and assistant superintendent.

Mayhew was on his way to La Descubridora from the Hacienda San Miguel with several hundred dollars in his saddle-bags for the weekly payroll. La Descubridora was fifteen miles from the hacienda. You rode down river through the town, turned up an *arroyo* to the right, continued along this, climbing steadily for some miles until an altitude of some forty-five hundred feet was reached. Here the trail left the *arroyo* and made a laborious ascent to a small *mesa,* where the houses of the workmen were located with the mill. Across this another steep hillside climb brought you to the mouth of the mine close up under the bluff at an altitude of some five thousand feet.

Apparently when Charlie had been within two or three miles of the mine, just before he left the old trail to the Hot Country, the Camino Real, which he had been traveling, he was accosted by one of the workmen and detained in conversation by him. When this took place, a big Indian named Alejandro, a one-eyed devil who had a reputation for violence and was wanted in Sonora (this developed later) for murder, stepped out from the bushes behind Charlie and shot him in the back without a word. As he fell from his horse, Charlie drew his gun and fired at the man facing him with whom he had been talking, realizing evidently that it was a hold-up. Charlie did his best as he dropped fatally wounded to retaliate upon the bandits.

This unexpected resistance so disrupted their plans that they fled, leaving the money untouched in Charlie's saddle-bags.

A woodman with his loaded burros on the way to town came upon the still warm body. He left his burros to the care of his small son and trotted on foot the ten or twelve miles to town to notify the authorities.

Immediately Don Jesus Hernandez sent word to my father, and himself followed closely on the messenger with several other mounted men. Quickly the posse formed and started out by two different trails in the attempt to cut off Alejandro and his companion. The number of these was not exactly known at the time. Only one person was believed to be with Alejandro, however, since all of the workmen except himself and one other were at the mine awaiting the arrival of the payroll.

A group of soldiers had been dispatched from the Jefatura as soon as word of the murder was received, with orders to follow the trail to the Hot Country. Next morning, the posses returned with jaded mounts after eighteen hours in the saddle. There was nothing to report but that the culprits had evidently departed from the trail to take to the ridges in a northerly direction.

It is impossible on horse or mule back, to follow an individual who knows the country and who takes to the mountains, only a human being on foot—or a goat—can do this.

The excitement and interest aroused in our minds, the speculations as to how and when the pursuers would bring in the murderers in a few hours, as is the case with most children, dimmed the sorrow for the untimely death of the young gentleman who had always been kind to us and for whom we felt nothing but respect. This sorrow, however, was freshened whenever we were in the presence of my father and mother. We knew instinctively that they were suffering, and that their feelings of responsibility to the parents of young Charles Mayhew and his family, and the letters they had to prepare for the next mail advising them of this casualty, were heavy on their minds and souls.

There was a lengthy consultation between Don Jesus Hernandez and *El Patron Grande*. A messenger was seen hurrying away from the main office, and shortly afterwards two individuals mounted on mules appeared with their blankets rolled and tied at the backs of the saddles. They were armed with .44 Winchester carbines in boots, and six-shooters. The names of these two riders were Andrez and Martin, both with reputations for being men of valor, *"muy hombres";* they were about twenty-five years old at the time.

After a deliberation with Don Jesus and *El Patron Grande* in the main office, they emerged and, mounting, took the road through the main gate of the hacienda down the cobble-stoned ramp to the river. This they forded, and followed the main road leading up the canyon. My father offered a big reward for the assassins dead or alive. He and the *Jefe* believed that the two men sent after them would be successful in capturing them, particularly since the reward was considerably more than the amount of money a good miner would earn in a year—not less than a thousand dollars.

In discussing the matter that Saturday night on the plaza and in the cantinas, Andrez and Martin concluded that Alejandro was the instigator of the crime, and that his companion was El Mocho, so called because he lacked two fingers to his left hand. The two men had not shown up to draw their pay, they were not to be found at their homes, their women had not heard from them since they left on Friday night, when they had gone to work on the night shift. On Saturday when the miners came off shift, they would remain at the mines until the afternoon when the payoff was made.

Alejandro was called El Tuerto because he had but one eye. He was without money, so Andrez and Martin believed that being a Yaqui Indian he would want to go to a section of the country where he was known. This meant that they would travel north. When the murderers had covered what they considered to be a safe distance, they would return to the Camino Real, since on the trail alone was there opportunity to secure food.

Blood had been discovered on the trail a few feet beyond the place where Charlie had fallen and died, and this would indicate clearly that one of the murderers had been wounded.

The deputies rode hard and fast. By three o'clock in the morning on Monday they reached Teboreachic, where inquiry of the station keeper brought to light the information that he had *seen* no one, it had been a very dark night, but his dogs had awakened him. They were excited so very greatly that he had come out from his house to investigate. Two of the beasts stayed with him in the yard, the other one did not and he could hear this animal's bark, furiously violent, farther up the trail.

"And," continued the station keeper, "you know there is a short cut which the Tarahumare Indians use which leaves this *arroyo* ten miles above this place. This short cut leads to Eurique, from there it is not so far to the other *barranca* and the Yaqui Country."

Andrez listened to this reasoning and agreed.

"Have some breakfast with us and rest yourselves. When daylight comes I myself will show you the spot where this trail departs from the *arroyo.* You could not find it for yourselves, even I could scarce do so in the darkness. You need food, also it will not hurt your mules to eat something. Let us delay *un rato* by which time we will be able to see clearly."

The station keeper was an elderly man, very intelligent. While they were sipping their coffee, he resumed:

"I know every trail and short cut in this part of the country. Now, if I had occasion to come cross country from where these assassins found themselves, if I desired to go where you believe they are going, I would have come straight up the *arroyo* exactly as did those unseen men last night. It is the most direct line. If you keep down this *arroyo* for seven leagues you come out into the Arroyo del Cerro Colorado above the big bluff."

"But do you believe . . ." began Martin.

"Wait a bit. If they came along the ridge of the Algarin which they must have done—there is no other way they could have made it—they would have come into the Arroyo del Cerro Colorado at that very point and at no other. The bluffs make it impossible to get off the ridge at any other place."

Came dawn. The three men reached the place in the *arroyo* where it branched from the Camino Real. They abandoned the road to climb to the *mesa* above, keeping up the creek for about two miles. Presently they turned into a nearly impassable tributary of the *arroyo.* Here their guide left them and returned to the station. Cautiously, Andrez and Martin dismounted, seeking the few spots where tracks could have been made. They came upon marks of what was apparently the passage of two men. They followed these nearly invisible traces for two miles when they disappeared. The deputies continued seeking, seeking, and were finally rewarded by finding tracks indicative that one man only had gone on from there. These marks were very fresh indeed.

The lay of the land permitted their remounting, which they did, and hurried their weary animals as fast as possible. Within a few miles they were halted by the sharp report of a pistol and the hum of a bullet close to Martin's head.

"Por Dios y la Santa Virgen!" exclaimed this one as they did a disappearance act. Each man slid from his mule and drew from the boot of the saddle his Winchester carbine. Quicker than it takes to tell it, the place from which the shot had been fired, where signs of the black powder smoke still showed in the air, was covered by a series of rapid shots. Some of them spattered against the boulder from behind which ambush Alejandro had fired one of his few remaining rounds. El Tuerto fired once more from this vantage point at the motion in the bushes to right and left, showing him that Andrez and Martin were crawling around to either side of him. Within a few minutes, they fired with sufficiently accurate aim to manifest to Alejandro that the game was up, and that they were indifferent as to whether they took him alive or dead.

The love of life was strong in this renegade Yaqui. He knew that there is always a chance for escape from human captors; he also knew that there is never any escape or even a chance for escape when one is dead. Firing his last two rounds into the air, he called out:

"Me rindo! no tiran mas! I surrender, do not fire again."

"Throw your gun over this way and throw it as far as you can so I can see it," was Andrez' reply. As the gun fell into the bushes all three men stood up, Alejandro's hands were tied behind his back and the noose of one of the *reatas* was slipped over his head.

Led thus by Martin and followed by Andrez they returned by the way they had come to the station of Teboreachic. There El Tuerto was fed. He wolfed his food ravenously, having had nothing, he explained, since leaving the Arroyo del Cerro Colorado the morning before. At that place he and El Mocho had taken the food *"bien poco por lo cierto,* a very little sure enough," from a couple of young goat herds.

"Where is El Mocho now?"

"Que sepa Dios, God knows!" answered El Tuerto.

"You left him where? We know that he was wounded and that is why he is not with you. Now, just where did you leave him?"

"Near the Arroyo del Cerro Colorado," replied El Tuerto with no hesitation. "He could no longer travel. He told me that a charcoal burner who lived nearby was a friend of his and would take care of him until his leg was well enough for him to go away."

Andrez looked at the sun and remarked:

"When the sun is there," pointing to a spot in the heavens where if you had observed the hands of your watch they would have been at two o'clock, "we will leave for *El Real*. With the moonlight to aid us during the first hours of the night, we can reach there before ten o'clock. Sleep, Indian, you will have to move fast on the way back."

"Loosen my hands so that I can sleep."

"Bien. But we will tie them in front of you. We will also tie your feet," was Martin's response. This was done. The son of the station keeper was delegated to act as guard while they, the pursued and the pursuers, slept.

While these were sleeping, the station keeper went to the corral, saddled his sturdy pony and took the trail up the arroyo. He had learned of the easy capture from Andrez. When Andrez told him they first had thought there were the tracks of two persons, the old station keeper had nodded his head and said:

"There is a cave not far from the place where you tell me this happened. While you sleep I will ride up there to see what I can see."

This wise old man with a lifetime of experience in finding strayed animals, and in living in the Sierras, soon was off his pony and examining with the care of a veteran the footprints described to him. He presently tied his pony and disappeared into the bushes, alongside the trail, which covered the hillside. He rapidly climbed to the place where an overhanging shelf of rock, not visible from the trail, made a natural cave extending back in the hillside some twenty-five feet, there it widened out leaving two shoulders on either side forming two niches.

Inside there was insufficient light to allow him an examination. Before he had left his station, old Julian had thrust through his *faja* a piece of fat pine. This he withdrew and split its end in several directions with his knife which he kept also thrust through his *faja.* From the pocket of his trousers he produced a flint and steel with a bit of punk. He lighted the fat pine, held it upside down until it was blazing well, then moved into the darkness of the right-hand niche. There could have been heard a sudden grunt: "Ugh, *asi lo creia,* as I thought!"

Julian spoke gently to the still body lying on the ground in the cave. There was no reply; he observed it closely by the flickering red light; with a shrug of his shoulders, he muttered:

"Indio, esto es demasiado sangre fria, Indian, this is too much cold blood."

For an instant he held the hand of the dead man in his own, it was quite cold, this mutilated hand. He peered yet more closely and turned the body over; this movement exposed the side fully . . . protruding from the ribs was a knife handle. He examined the legs of the corpse and discovered that one leg and foot were swollen and inflamed, which demonstrated that El Mocho had traveled miles on a terrifically painful foot and leg. It proved that Alejandro's companion had at last reached a point where it was utterly impossible to go any farther. They had found this shelter and had hidden there. El Tuerto had made up his mind to get rid of his friend who was now only an encumbrance. The simplest and best way to accomplish this was to stick a knife into his friend and thus to let the life out of him.

Julian took his neckerchief from about his own neck, unwound its folds and extracted his tobacco and *hoja.* These he placed in the crown of his hat. He shook out the neckerchief and put it quietly over the face of the dead man; he made the sign of the cross, left the cave, returned to his pony, mounted and started back to his station. Along the way he rolled a cigarette from his *macouchic* in a cornhusk *hoja.* Getting out his flint and steel as the pony ambled down the trail, he struck a spark which fell on the charred end of his bit of punk. This he applied to the bent end of his cornhusk cigarette, and when the tobacco was burning satisfactorily he obtained great comfort from its fumes . . . for fumes they are indeed. *Macouchic* gives off fumes, you do not have to smoke it in order to prove this, only ride behind a man who is smoking it! When Julian reached Teboreachic he went about his own affairs, not waking the tired deputies.

"Why should I waken them? There is no doubt of the identity of the man who lies dead in the cave. His left hand is mutilated as they described."

There was no need to waken them. The young guard was anxiously debating within himself as to whether or not the sun was in the exact spot in the sky indicated by Andrez, when this one came alive. He rose, wakened Martin with a touch of his foot. The other came to his feet with a startled murmur.

"Vamos a comer y largarnos de aqui, come let us eat and leave this place."

Speedily the meal was in readiness. Julian's wife called her son to take it from the kitchen; it was forthwith dispatched with gusto since it evidently was as savory to the palate as it was to the nose.

While Andrez and Martin were saddling in the corral, Julian made them acquainted with his finding of the murdered body of El Mocho with the knife projecting from the side.

"Well, he is better off dead now than to be shot later commented Andrez. "I will notify the judge. He can come out here to see the body for himself. I will not attempt to take it with us. I do not like that fat judge anyway, and this ride will make him thinner." They rejoined the Yaqui and his youthful guard.

"You, Yaqui *condenado,* be on your good behavior. On that alone depends your safe arrival alive at the *jefatura.*" he further elucidated with a shrug, "we will get the *mil pesos* of *El Patron Grande* whether you reach there alive or dead."

These comforting words were being addressed to El Tuerto while his feet were being untied.

"And," added Martin, "for the good of your soul you will travel these forty miles *pie a tierra,* foot to the ground. The *reata* around your neck will have its end on my saddle horn. Andrez will be behind with his *pistola* and his *carabina.* All of these things will induce you doubtless to have the proper care of your actions."

They made their good-byes and started off. El Tuerto was rested and strengthened for the trip by his two ample meals and four hours of sleep. He seemed to be perfectly willing to proceed, realizing that his chance for escape from his two captors was slim indeed.

Contrary to first instructions, they traveled slowly and rested before they reached the place in the canyon opposite to the dump at the San Miguel Mine. Neither Andrez nor Martin wished to miss the opportunity to demonstrate that "they had their man," by conducting him down that long street of the town at the hour when men were on the move to their work and the women were sweeping the trash from their houses into the street, to be collected and burned later in the day, when the *chimilcos* were open or just about to open—in other words about six o'clock in the morning. Then the night-watchman at San Miguel Mine would see them as they came down the trail across the river; the occupants of the scattered houses on the roadside would have the pleasure of seeing both culprit and captors. *Las viejas* and *las muchachas* would get their eyes full. This did not fail of its appeal to them both, particularly to Andrez who was as adept in making attacks on the hearts of *las muchachas* as he was in swinging a sledge, and in *knowing las pintas* . . . colors of the different veins of ore when certain signs appeared which were a sure indication that a *bonanza* was near at hand. It did not hurt his standing nor strengthen the possible resistance in the fair sex to have this additional demonstration of his courage and capabilities.

The tragedy of Charlie Mayhew's murder, the sudden taking off of a young gentleman who was loved by many and respected by all, threw a heavy cloud over the family. We children reacted to it according to our natures and ages . . . the bringing of Charlie's body to the hacienda, the lying in state for the necessary hours before it was carried to the Campo Santo located on a small, less sloping spot on the mountain side directly opposite to the hacienda, where a spur of the mountain lost its angle of sixty degrees from the horizontal. A tomb was built there overnight by our expert masons, and there rest the remains of this fine young American.

This part of the chapter that deals with the death of Charlie Mayhew came to an end with the incarceration and later with the execution of this degenerate representative of a splendid tribe of Indians.

The Yaquis of Sonora and the Mayos of Sinaloa made up a large portion of those loyal workmen to which the successful development of that camp at Batopilas may be chiefly credited. They were splendid in physique, they possessed unlimited endurance and were perfect Spartans in courage. These men were all fatalists, believing that until your time comes you cannot die, and that when it does come nothing that you can do will prevent it. They made the character of men most needed when there was dangerous work to do.

Chapter 5

Buried Treasure

In Mexico formerly the big holiday of the entire year was Holy Week, *Semana Santa.* Three days' holiday for all, and a whole week for those who were more pious and also financially able to go without work for that length of time. It was a popular time for picnics, and the favorite place for these was Satevo.

Satevo was a charming location where the gorge widened out, giving a broader space in the canyon between the river and the red and yellow porphyry bluffs that towered above Satevo for many hundred feet and practically enclosed this small spot on two sides. Here was the very old and very beautiful church built by the Roman Catholic Fathers more than two hundred years before. This church offers an excellent example of the ability and determination of these great explorers, pioneers, and settlement-makers in the most inaccessible places.

Those of us who have lived and carried out constructive work in the Sierra Madres under the greatly improved conditions of later days, can really appreciate the achievements of those deeply consecrated pioneers. The church stands at Satevo today as a monument to those men whose knowledge of so vast a number of things made it possible, despite handicaps that would appal ninety per cent of the persons today who have the task of establishing a place of worship. It stands there in its majesty and dignity of architectural purity, stability, and beauty, as a memorial to those men and to the Christian Faith and belief in Jesus Christ. A belief so deep-rooted, so profound that the symbol which such a conviction inspired necessitated an erection of a building for all time, even without the ordinary care that the very best of brick construction requires, which is almost too little to mention.

The Fathers put up this church with the aid of one of the most ignorant, one of the shyest of all the Indian tribes in the Sierras, the Tarahumare. They are not rugged as far as manual labor is concerned, but they have tremendous endurance for traveling incredible distances.

They selected the clay, molded the bricks and burned them to a perfect hardness. They broke down the calspar from the true fissure silver-bearing veins in that vicinity, burned this and with the sand from the bed of the river they made a lime-and-sand mortar which is absolutely binding and durable. Wherever it is encountered now it is standing firmer and surer than it did ten years after it was built. There exist in the Dominican Republic among other ancient buildings the beautiful cathedral, the palace of Diego Colon, son of the great discoverer, Columbus, and the remains of his great fortress built not later than 1515, which prove how practically indestructible is this type of lime-and-sand mortar.

This gem of a church at Satevo with its arched dome, its two-bell tower—one of them is marked with dates proving them to have been cast in Spain before Columbus discovered Espanola—always inspired me, even as a young boy, with a feeling that never could be put into words, intangible, abstruse, intense.

My first picnic at Satevo was in 1883. Even then the crypt beneath the High Altar had been broken into and the niches on either side, where the bodies of holy men had been entombed, were torn down and their remains strewn about the floor. This piece of desecration had been perpetrated by vandals who hoped to uncover gold or silver hidden there. The only treasure was the spring sunshine splintering its long arrows of gold on the arched dome.

You will doubtless recall that when it was decided to expel certain orders for real or fancied wrongs, the plans for the expulsion were laid with greatest secrecy. There was to have been a concerted action on a stipulated day in all parts of Mexico, in order that the confiscation might be a thorough one, that they might secure all the treasure amassed by the orders for the benefit of the Federal Government.

The leader of this movement was unduly optimistic in his belief that such a vital thrust could be kept a secret. The Fathers were forewarned and they succeeded in gathering together a large quantity of their treasure and conveying it out of the country. Nevertheless, they were forced to bury huge amounts of gold and silver in various forms. This was done because although the men who were leading the confiscation failed in complete surprise, the information came to the Fathers not very long before the zero hour. That which was sent away had to go shipped through channels unknown to all but a trusted few, and it had to be carefully disguised. All this took time, and when the fatal day arrived there was still some treasure in Mexico belonging to the orders, some unmoved and some in transit on the trails. This had to be hastily buried or otherwise disposed of, and for many, many years it was the cause of interminable search and excavations.

There is no doubt that many hiding places were found and rifled of their contents; but most of these discoveries were never publicly acknowledged, because the law of the country gives title to the Mexican Government of a part of all buried treasure discovered under penalty of complete confiscation if attempt should be made to avoid division in accordance with the law.

When I was a little boy I used to love to look at the shelves in the room on the right-hand side of the High Altar. This room had served as a library, upon them were still a few ancient tomes, one or two adorned by exquisitely executed illuminated work. The parchment of which they were made had been manufactured by the

Fathers themselves. When I returned there a few years later, all these parchment books had disappeared. Whether they had been taken away and shipped to the Capitol in the City of Mexico I do not know. I do remember that my father had offered to bear the expenses for this transfer. They were of great historic interest, were written by hand in Latin, and contained records of the church at Satevo and its monastery.

The buildings which constituted the monastery had their connecting door with the church proper through the library, and it must have been a well-ordered and extensive edifice. Unfortunately the monastery was built of adobe. It was made with tough hay for a binder and was perfectly dried in the hot sun, and the buildings were thoroughly plastered with lime-and-sand mortar, but they were partially destroyed at the time of the expulsion, and the rains during the decades that followed did the rest. Thus that portion of the settlement where the Fathers lived and worked is mined and the non-existent walls of a non-existent garden, where grew fruit trees and flowers, are only barely discernible. One must use his imagination to recreate this one of the many symbols of superhuman efforts on the part of consecrated, religious men who constructed in these wildernesses such monuments to their belief in God Almighty and His Son, Jesus Christ.

On one or two places along the trail where you have in your fancy accompanied me, and at several Tarahumare Indian villages at greater or less distance from the trail, we could trace remains of churches and small establishments where missions had been situated. The priest of these missions taught the Tarahumare how better to raise his corn. With seeds brought by himself from faraway Spain the priest planted the first apple and peach trees in the New World. Although I believe other fruits were planted which would thrive in that altitude and temperature, the apples and peaches were the only ones that remained. And these were very old trees and young seedlings.

Often in the lonely *arroyos,* where now there are no signs of former habitations, these trees give to the Tarahumare Indian two articles of trade purchasable at the mining camps. When the fruit was ripe, he would load his own back or his burro or his pony with apples and peaches to sell. The peaches were quite small and certainly not prize fruit, and so with the apples, but they were eagerly seized upon by both native and foreign inhabitant.

From time to time I have tried to recall the name of the old gentleman who had the self-appointed task of caring for and showing visitors about the church at Satevo. He was a courteous little man, about sixty years old, I should say, in 1883. He was short, very lean, wore a moustache turning gray and he had thinning grizzled hair. He lived in a tiny house up the slope towards the bluff where there was a spring, which was his pride and comfort, because without it water would have to be brought from the river half a mile away. Like its owner, the house was neat and pleasing. Here with his plump little wife and an Indian woman and her son lived my old gentleman. His livelihood was provided by a herd of goats, some chickens, a few pigeons; a little garden was watered from the spring during the dry season, water which was carried by the son of the Indian woman in two five-gallon petroleum cans on the respective ends of a pole balanced on his shoulder.

The few sales were made to the inhabitants up and down the river, and few, in truth, they were. These people made occasional trips to Batopilas some twelve or fourteen miles up stream, which place afforded their only source of supplies.

His interest and care for the church were touching: its keys were his dearest treasure, and he received no remuneration for his services. When visitors came to see the church, which God knows was seldom enough, his satisfaction and zeal in officiating were pleasurable to witness. The story of his coming to this place is interesting. It was told me in later years by that other fine, loyal gentleman, Don Romulo Rocha, the last of a noble descent. Don Romulo was a trusted employee of the former owners of Batopilas from whom our company had purchased it, and he continued on with my father, contented with his lot, giving these two organizations not less than forty years of devoted service.

According to Don Romulo, my old gentleman at Satevo lived in his youth in the city of Mazatlan, a port on the Pacific coast, a pleasant place with which it was my good fortune to be familiar during my life in Mexico.

The family of Senor de Satevo was a wealthy one, and prominent, before and during the reign of the Emperor Maximilian, 1864-1867. His father was an Hidalgo of the old school. Shortly before the battles for independence began to rage, there had appeared in Mazatlan a certain Colonel B. in command of that Department of Mazatlan under the Imperial government. He was a dashing individual not without courage, contented with his personal attractions and the consequence of his position. This Colonel B. was a Frenchman, very intelligent and a clever politician. He felt convinced that there would soon be serious trouble. He liked Mexico, and enjoyed a small income aside from his pay and its not inconsiderable perquisites. He was positive that if the Mexicans made a resolute effort to throw off the yoke of Maximilian there would be a radical change in the form of government. He was determined to be on the winning side of any conflict if there could be any such possibility. If the forces for independence from the French were successful he could easily go over to those victorious forces, thus becoming a patriot of the country where he intended to make his home and one of whose fascinating native daughters he intended to make his wife.

Unfortunately the young lady whose charms had captured the fancy of the colonel was the sweetheart of our Senor de Satevo and had been so all of her short life.

The father of this lady was an Imperialist. He liked his cognac and far too frequently expressed himself forcibly about the "upstart opposition" when he was in his cups. The colonel cautioned him about these opinions being too vigorously uttered, and made himself so very agreeable during those interviews, that when he made a formal request for the hand of the fair young daughter, his suit was favorably looked upon.

Among the aristocratic families the hand of a daughter was disposed of entirely at the discretion of the father, the young lady had no choice whatsoever in the matter. Senor de Satevo remained a tormented onlooker until his sweetheart grew alarmed lest she be forced into a hasty marriage with the colonel. She conveyed her fears to our Senor de Satevo. He felt impelled to take a hand, and this he did promptly and effectively. Relays of good mounts were arranged for along the Camino Real. He took into his confidence some two or three of his intimate friends, whose *haciendas* extended a hundred or more miles in the interior of the country towards the north.

He eloped with his young sweetheart; some of his servants accompanied them, and the maid of his future wife. In the darkness of the night they rode at a gallop away from Mazatlan, and their disappearance was not discovered until the next morning, thus those hours had been wasted for the pursuers. When the chase began, the two lovers were seventy miles inland being married by a priest on one of the *haciendas* belonging to a friend. There was nothing now to do but to send word to his parents and his wife's father. Fast-riding men set forth to do these errands and met the pursuers as these hastened forward on their fruitless mission. They took over the task of notifying the respective fathers, pocketed the letters sent by de Satevo, and returned to Mazatlan.

The married lovers were now fugitives, they could never go back to Mazatlan. Colonel B. was the power there now. It was within his jurisdiction to do things which would have made it unpleasant and more than merely unpleasant for Senor de Satevo. Then, as now, a wealthy widow was a desirable acquisition. The father of de Satevo came under the eye of the colonel, and the old *Hidalgo* was persecuted to such an extent that he saw it would be unsafe for his son to remain within striking distance of Mazatlan. He sent word straightaway to his son by a trusted messenger, conveying a fat purse, to leave for the north. The young couple journeyed to the foot of the mountains at Choix in the State of Sinaloa. There they became enthusiastic to visit "that great and very rich mining settlement at Batopilas from which the Marquis de Bustamente had taken such fabulous wealth." This place was across the border in the State of Chihuahua, a distance of seven hundred miles from Mazatlan.

They made a leisurely trip of fifteen days from the town of Choix to Batopilas. They lived there for a while, where de Satevo lost some of his fast-dwindling money attempting to mine silver. Word was received there, too, of the death of their respective parents. His own property and that of his wife had long ago been confiscated by the new government, the ill-fated Maximilian had been shot, poor Carlotta had gone back to Belgium, and the independents were in full swing.

De Satevo did not care for the resident priest at Batopilas, and he did care very much for the fathers of the order formerly supreme at Satevo. There he moved with his wife and there he rusted out.

Ah, but did he rust out? I used to think that he did when I used to watch him showing visitors about the church, finding it hard indeed to reconcile a dashing elopement with my thin little old man. But now, when experience of many years has had its way, I acknowledge that I am assailed somewhat heavily by doubts with a capital "D." I have worked a great deal harder than he ever did; likewise so have those with whom I have been associated. We produced a lot of so-called treasure from Mother Earth. At present I am nearing the years whose load he was carrying when I first saw him, and what am I doing now, but rusting out with barely enough to live on and nothing to leave behind me?

The sun has reached the edge of the bluff behind the church. We must saddle up and ride home. So, *adios* until another day, Satevo, when we hope once more to talk with your faithful old guardian and to refresh ourselves with thoughts of the days when the good Fathers were here; when this spot was a contented community, filled with growing things, fruits, flowers, people going to Mass, kneeling before your High Altar in prayers. . . .

I wonder if those of you living in this neighborhood are as free now as those who lived here then? Where do your women go to pray, where get consolation from the confessions of their sins? Was not the influence of the padre then as strong to prevent transgressions of the law as that of the local magistrate miles away? Somehow, although you have held on to your faith to a remarkable degree, I cannot but feel that you have lost a great deal that those who were in Satevo under the good Fathers rejoiced in, perhaps unconsciously.

In truth, there is something deeply esoteric in the symbol of the cross, or else the cross would mean nothing in these late days. In those Tarahumare villages remote from civilization, you frequently come across, on the very highest peak within vision, the silhouette of a wooden cross hewn from great pine trees, standing stately, aloof, held in place by veritable tons of rocks laboriously taken there by the Indians themselves on their bended backs and piled about its base to hold the symbol steady.

Only at rare intervals following the expulsion did the people see a priest. A very few times he could get there to perform baptisms, solemnize marriages, and collect his *peso fuerte* or his *fanega* of corn for each of these functions. The Indians could have fled to the farther hills during the coming visit of the priest to avoid their meager contributions. Do not think that they were ignorant of his advent. They knew about his making his toilsome way from settlement to settlement several days in advance. But with no trouble at all the priest could collect his dues for performance of the rites. There are few cases, if indeed there are any, where an Indian has told of a worth-while mineral deposit whose location has been confided to him in secret; or has divulged the whereabouts of anything hidden during the exodus, information about which he had been forbidden to disclose. This knowledge, which they undoubtedly possess, has been handed down from generation to generation, and some mighty smart hombres have tried in the past by bribes, by presents, by argument, by threats, to get some of it, and they have failed miserably.

Chapter 6

El Patron Grande and Batopilas

When a man in the year 1880 took over a mining business in a locality such as Batopilas, the difficulties were many. There was no rail connection for approximately six hundred miles until 1883, when the Mexican Central got as far as El Paso, Texas. Then the distance between the mines and the railroad was reduced to three hundred or more miles. But those three hundred miles had to be traveled and freight had to be transported across them, for the first hundred and eighty-five miles on the backs of mules, and the last hundred and fifty miles in wagons or ox-carts.

After a few years' residence in Batopilas, we accepted the unavoidable mountain trip to Chihuahua as a necessary evil, a part of the essential game of getting the silver bullion from the mines to the market, and, in turn, securing the safe arrival into Batopilas of supplies.

Proper houses and corrals were established, with a resident station keeper, at the end of each day's march. Therefore, feed was available for the pack and saddle animals; chickens, eggs, turkeys, sometimes even milk, for the two-footed traveler. This journey was made with exact regularity and on perfect schedule every thirty days accompanied by the natural fatigue that comes of five days in the saddle, but no more. Conditions for making these monthly trips as comfortable as possible were taken care of by the company. A two-room house built of stone was constructed for the *conducta,* with a kitchen always ready for use by our competent cooks who accompanied the bullion trains. There was a portal all the way along the front of the house. In one room were two big chests or bins in which were kept the cooking utensils, cups and saucers, plates, knives and forks, spoons. . . . In each room there were folding canvas cots for the comfort of the employees who traveled for the company, and for any guests who were to visit us, to save the trouble and expense of the extra mules which would otherwise be needed to transport all such needed equipage. So much for the ease of the two-legged traveler. Let us look for the comfort of the patient, steady mule who carries this traveler.

If he is to make forty miles each day for five consecutive days and to remain in good condition, he must not be turned loose to graze and to search for and find his own food, thus to spend a greater part of the night in satisfying his justifiably big appetite acquired by seven hours of climbing up and down mountain trails with a mighty heavy load on his back. Besides, if he is allowed to be loose to graze there is always the chance that he might stray for many miles and be lost. The herder would be compelled to lose valuable hours in trying to find him, this would mean a late start, or a day lost on the trail. Some wary old mules are experts in hiding out so as to escape a hard job. It was, therefore, apparent early in the life of the company that regular stations with accommodations for both man and beast were an absolutely indispensable adjunct for the orderly running of the monthly bullion trains. They always took not less than fifty bars of silver bullion worth about sixty thousand dollars; more often they conveyed a hundred bars; on especial and unusual occasions they had as high as two hundred bars or even more.

Since each mule carries two bars of silver, you will readily understand that these trains are made up of from thirty to a hundred or more mules. Now, that is a lot of mules. The corrals and the barns for the storing of hay and corn and the housing of the mules made no small plant at the end of each day's march. It was highly important to have a resident station keeper. He supplied the corn and hay purchased by him from the Tarahumare Indians within a radius of fifty miles or so. The hay was native hay and a price was fixed. In bad years it had to be brought in from a greater distance. The station keeper maintained his home here, he had his family, chickens, every now and then there would be a cow even, his turkeys, which all afforded a variety in the menu for the travelers. The arrival of the *conducta,* which was the bullion train, was a welcome event in the lives of the station keeper and his family.

The town of Batopilas itself presents an interesting picture of the early explorations made by the Spanish priests and *conquistadores*. In truth, they were tireless and intrepid men. History has no greater example of determination and courage to endure danger and hardships than that exhibited by them. They arrived in this mountain gorge eight hundred miles northwest of the City of Mexico more than two hundred and fifty years ago. They had no maps, it was an unknown wilderness of the most rugged mountainous country . . . a series of huge canyons between mountain crags from seven thousand to ten thousand feet in altitude. In the gorge two thousand feet above sea level, they established this town whose old masonry buildings were enduring and in a good state of preservation in 1914. Some of them in the center of the place were of two stories. Five thousand inhabitants, and a few more, lived there during our era.

My father's job as vice-president and general manager of the mines was not so much of a sinecure. There were five major mines—The San Miguel, Roncesvalles, Camuchin, Todos Santos, and La Descubridora. The needed hundreds of tons of freight, including foodstuffs and clothing, made a big problem to be solved. He had to maintain a close and careful supervision of the work at the mines, the transportation of ores to the Hacienda San Miguel, the treatment of these ores, the extraction of silver values, the melting and refining of the silver into bars of bullion, and their shipment each month. When you get your silver extracted from the ores and in shape to melt into bars, you might imagine that the work was about concluded, but here is what happened from that point:

The silver came from the ores of five different mines. Each had to be treated separately and exact account kept of each lot of ore and the silver returns from it. Each mine was credited with the silver it produced. Later when the silver was converted into dollars, the dollars were credited against the total expense of operating that particular mine.

Let us say that it is near the end of the month and the silver must be melted down and poured into bars of seventy-five pounds in weight. It must be accurately weighed, numbered and assayed; the number is stamped upon it, also the exact weight in kilos and decimals; two check assays must be made from chip or dip samples of each bar. Your shipping list often was for two hundred bars or better, this was in columns.

No. of Bar . . . Weight of Bar . . . Assay of fineness of Bar . . . Value in dollars of Bar.

Added to my father's duties in supervising these constant jobs was the overseeing of the big building program which was going on. We were building a dam three miles up the river; an aqueduct three miles long; putting in a low-grade mill of a hundred stamps, of a thousand pounds each: Pelton wheels to drive the mill; compressors, an electric light plant, and the Lord only knows what else, including a hospital.

In a stamp mill of fifty stamps, if you use Fru Vanners for concentration you have two Fru Vanners for each battery of five stamps. In the early days, a Fru Vanner was the accepted concentrating table. There was a great deal of shafting and counter-shafting which carried pulleys of various sizes and drive belts. One of our early jobs was cleaning these many feet of different-sized shafting, all revolving at one speed or another, keeping them free from grease, slime and rust; filling grease and oil cups. We were paid for this work, but it was given us first to keep our minds occupied, and our young hands out of mischief, and second, to train us to run any part of the business in the future.

The ores of Batopilas, first discovered as I have said in 1632, are specifically native silver ores. Seventy-five to eighty per cent of all silver values contained are pure native silver, occurring in irregular masses, plates, and crystals imbedded in the vein matter. This is largely lime. When the rich pockets or *bonanzas* are encountered there is always a great amount of calspar. The native silver crystals, which in their turn have been covered by this crystallization which is quite transparent, are entirely imbedded in it. It is very beautiful.

The veins of the Batopilas native silver district are true fissure veins. That is, they are the result of some excessive pressure of the hard rock in geological ages past, leaving big cracks in the rock from three feet wide to say twelve feet. These cracks have been filled in by minerals carried in solution from the lower levels in the rock up through these cracks. The deposition of minerals contained in solution upon either side or wall of the cracks continued until these were filled in entirely with solid matter. That is what is known as a true fissure vein.

The solution in that district contained lime, silver, sulphur, lead, zinc, iron, and small amounts of antimony and arsenic. All of these elements are, therefore, found in the ores generally in a crystallized state. A mineral solution, when it encounters the condition appropriate for it to become a solid, is formed into crystals which are deposited upon the first available solid matter present.

The outcrops of vein matter on the mountain side when discovered more than three hundred years ago by the Spaniards often showed the native silver quite visible to the naked eye. It was, therefore, a simple matter to extract and commercialize it. When my father took hold in 1880, the properties had been worked as deep as they then could be worked by the primitive methods employed. On the backs of men it is possible only to carry ores up ladders for five hundred feet, more or less. The best peon, a laboring man, will carry one hundred to one hundred and fifty pounds in a *zurron* up a distance of five hundred to a thousand feet of ladders . . . but he cannot make many such trips in a day. Hence, the cost becomes prohibitive. There is always a greater amount of valueless material produced in mining pay dirt at Batopilas than there is valuable ore.

We used horse whims, then steam hoists; afterwards came gasoline hoists, and compressed air drills, and for many years the longest mining tunnel in Mexico, the Porfirio Diaz Tunnel, with shorter tunnels at lower levels on the mountain side, were the methods which were employed for over thirty-five consecutive years of activity in our camp. Our total mileage of underground workings was over seventy miles.

Low grade ores cannot be worked profitably unless the cost of production is reduced to its lowest point. The cost of working a mine increases as its depth increases, and the ores and waste must be hauled to the surface from great depths. The means to obtain economical power for treating low grade ores, the building of the hundred-stamp mill (each stamp of a thousand pounds), and the way to convey the ores to the mill were another demonstrated picture of my father's always looking ahead years farther than does the average man. The result was the Porfirio Diaz Tunnel. Within a hundred yards of its mouth was the mill and also was located the end of the aqueduct, whose waters after a fall through flumes for a distance of sixty-five feet and by the assistance of Pelton wheels, delivered some eight hundred horse power. The Porfirio Diaz Tunnel required several years to drive. It cut all that group of veins found on the western side of the river. From the Portal to the point where it tapped the Roncesvalles vein is seven thousand and fifty feet. It is continued on this vein and the Todos Santos vein for two thousand feet more. The old shafts and workings from above are connected with the tunnel; therefore, instead of being compelled to hoist them, the ores roll down to tunnel level, making a much more economical proceeding altogether From this place they went direct to the bins of the mill.

The rock of this country is a diabase and very hard, far from easy to drill but it breaks fairly well.

A visitor from the north described the life at Batopilas as a perfect type of the old feudal days. I know that there was a perfect discipline founded upon respect and affection for those in command; an intelligent set of rules impartially enforced; good pay and a personal interest taken by *El Patron Grande* and the *Patroncitos* in the lives and welfare of all the employees.

My father perceived almost from the beginning that it would be necessary to found a hospital and dispensary, not only for the American and other foreign employees but for the natives as well, It was, however, with difficulty that they could be persuaded to attend; this complication of affairs lasted for some months after things were established. We made no effort to force them, and gradually they began coming of their own accord to be helped in minor illnesses and to be carefully nursed in major ones. Any man badly injured in a mine accident (such cases were comparatively few) was taken at once to the hospital, willy-nilly, and kept there until he was completely cured.

Dr. Ross came down with us from Washington, and was our first medico, a good man. There came next Dr. Lee, followed by Dr. Frank Merchant, our first cousin, who married my sister Grace. Dr. Charles Morrow came next who after-wards became a surgeon in the United States Army. I ran into him at Robert de Espagne in France in 1918, he was Divisional Surgeon. Dr. Robert Wagner came after him, and he married my sister Isabel. Phil Riley was the last of our medicos, and he now wears the Army uniform of Uncle Sam.

The complete hospital was built about the time Dr. Robert Wagner came to Batopilas; two able professional nurses came from the States to take charge. A clinic was instituted and both employees and non-employees received skilled medical care and attention free of charge. This, combined with plenty of good food and other care, brought the health standard of the camp to a very desirable state. The men who functioned during those thirty or more years gave an unexcelled proof of what a competent and conscientious M.D. can do to benefit humanity.

El Señor Doctor was a person of great and deserved importance in the community, a strong influence for the general good. All of these men reached enviable positions of prominence during their lives and medical service to humanity in other places when we shut down in Batopilas. All of them with the exception of Phil Riley have passed on. They were comparatively young men when death overtook them, it is quite probable that the hard work, the confining duties of their constant jobs helped to wear out the machines that otherwise would still be running.

Governor Alexander Robey Shepherd on "Sutton" in front of main office. Main gate in background. (above)

Town of Batopilas, Chihuahua, Mexico looking up Batopilas River Valley, toward Hacienda San Miguel, on right, 1885 (about). (right)

Chapter 7

Everyday Matters

If boys grow up in a country where it is customary to buckle on one's six-shooter as a matter of course, whenever one leaves the house, it is only to be expected that their greatest longing in life is to do likewise. Carrying your gun in a proper holster makes pulling it out smooth and easy with no risk of loss of time in the draw. It insures the gun's remaining at your side and not thumping the Hell out of you, or flying out from an inadequate holster when you are riding your horse or mule at a dead run over a rough country where the animal, frequently in full stride, must make a cat-like spring up or down, or to one side or the other.

Those persons whose not-to-be-envied obligation it is to direct and control your actions during this adolescent period have a bad time of it explaining that a boy of six or eight years of age is entirely too young to "tote a gun," particularly a Colt .44 or .45. The yearning, however, is just as strong in the boy after he has listened to the argument against it as it was before he listened, in concealed boredom, to what the oldster considered a reasonable and able effort in debate.

A gun at your hip in a holster is an absolute necessity. You put in many hours whittling from a piece of board the outline of a grand old Colt .44 or .45, with a six-inch barrel, that has been obtained as a model by stealth while some lucky grown-up—one of the young uncles probably—was absent from his room and the cherished gun hanging in its holster on the bedpost.

But there is a substitute for a six-gun when the real article is beyond your attainment. This was very much to be coveted because its possession was secured by exercising acuteness in scouting and caused immense wrath among the carpenters . . . this substitute was a claw hammer. The habit of making use of claw hammers in lieu of six-guns was put down by my father after we had made a successful raid on a certain tool-chest in the storeroom during the owner's absence on his annual vacation.

Mr. Kemper was very tall, very angular as to physique, disposition and temper. He valued his tools to the point of an obsession; they were as fine and complete a set as any master carpenter could possess and they justified his pride in them.

We filed away two massive padlocks. We lifted the lid, removed the well-filled drawers from his tool-chest, and uncovered a veritable treasure trove that caused the three of us to swell with joy. This was all the more intense because we knew that Hell would pop as seldom it had popped before in our lives when the old boy came back from his vacation and realized that his precious chest had been violated. This return happened sooner than we expected and before we had rejoiced in even a short two weeks of toting two old and one beautifully new, nickel-plated claw hammers.

We will not delve too deeply into particulars. We succeeded in getting the hammers back into the tool-chest and kept mum. But when old Kemper, or Temper as we called him, saw his tool-chest, beheld the two massive padlocks filed off, witnessed the further defilement, he got red hot from his feet to the top of his head. In this state he arrived in the main office shivering with ire.

He really did forget himself and that my father was six feet two inches tall and weighed two hundred and thirty pounds of the most forceful and emphatic material he ever saw. Needless to say what took place between them was not seen by us, but we got a detailed statement from the bookkeeper, who hated Kemper, as did nearly every one of the other employees.

By the process of deduction we appreciated the enormity of our crime when we were finally discovered by old Domingo. He was general errand boy and chambermaid for the rooms of the American employees. Domingo was fond of us boys and he gave us an outline of battle conditions. There was to be no escape for us. We tried to bribe Domingo to report that he had been unable to locate our hiding place, but his respect for *El Patron Grande* was such that this could not be accomplished.

Should we deny any knowledge of the facts?

"Impossible," stated Domingo. "The storekeeper in order to protect himself against suspicion of allowing you to take the hammers was obliged to tell your father that he had seen you boys with them. And," continued Domingo, "he is very angry with you still for taking his cats for your dogs to chase."

We went to the tribunal. Let us draw the curtain of charity over the rest of the episode except to state that we were the recipients a short time afterwards of three of the very nicest and most realistic, life-sized wooden six-shooters that could be found anywhere. They were presented to us by one of the under carpenters whose detestation of Kemper was so great he felt it must be manifested to his own inner satisfaction by working overtime to make these quite wonderful wooden guns for us. Poor Kemper was employed by the company for many years, but I honestly believe he always hated us with a deep and fervid hate, even when we were almost grown. He was, however, a very fine carpenter.

Several years after this a young American came down from the States to work for my father. Louis M. became enamoured of Kemper's daughter, a young girl unhappily endowed with a large nose, but with a figure that might almost be taken as a miracle when you considered the physical architecture of her father and mother. Louis' suit did not prosper, and the disgruntled suitor composed some verses for "Ta-ra-ra boom de aye," which jingle having made a hit in the United States came to Batopilas by way of Louis M. During the interlude between the claw hammer incident and growing older, I had been unable to conceive of any way to revenge myself on old Kemper. Therefore, it was with a feeling of complacency I used to sing one verse that went like this:

"I got a girl in Mexico,
Insect bit her on the big toe,
Now she's where the cactus grow.
The name of that insect you all know . . .
Ta-ra-ra-rantula!"

Louis M. was a talented young man some years older than ourselves, but he was very companionable and exceedingly entertaining.

About this time the Governor of the State was coming to make an official visit to this ancient settlement of Batopilas, of such great importance to the State financially and otherwise. Naturally it was to be a very particular event and everyone wanted to make the most of it. The records showed that never prior to this time had a governor made that arduous ride across the mountains to this place which had been famous for many years as a producer of silver. Great preparations were set on foot by the townspeople collectively and individually. Arches were erected bearing *"Bienvenida"* in big letters, others with *"Viva, Señor Gubernador."* There were to be a series of *bailes, serenatas* with all manner of other entertainments; also speeches early, often and many.

The Governor arrived with a large staff of secretaries, a detachment of cavalry, one of infantry, his military staff and his servants. For nearly two weeks official calls, inspections, dances, *serenatas,* banquets, kept everybody busy. I was at the Prep school age and it is all as clear as yesterday. One special happening stands out in which Louis shone with his customary amusing light.

My father gave an official dinner for His Excellency. It was quite an affair. As usual there was the customary ample supply of all kinds of wines and liquors. The band was engaged to play, the moon shone softly bright, the orange blossoms perfumed the atmosphere with their fragrance . . . the setting was one that inclines the spirit towards liberality of thought in relation to liquid refreshment. The time came for the guests to take their departure. Elaborate farewells were being spoken and replied to by the host, my father. Louis M. was dispatched to the room set aside for the gentlemen's dressing-room, some distance down the long portal, to bring the Governor's hat and cloak to him. The party congregated at the steps where the mounts were assembled, held by *mozos* arrayed in their resplendent best. Louis did not appear, neither did the hat and cloak. Everyone waited. The Governor and my father turned to stroll towards the dressing-room engaged in close confidential conversation. They arrived opposite to the door, and Louis waveringly arose from the chair upon which he had surrendered to the effects of orange blossom perfume and other fumes. With the high silk hat of the Governor reposing on his own head he exclaimed:

"I am very sorry, sir. I do not think that His Excellency the Governor wore a hat, or else someone has taken it I have searched for it everywhere."

In deep mortification my father seized the hat from Louis' head, apologizing profusely to the Governor. But this one was a good sport, and although he understood no English, he was entirely conversant with many other things . . . and their potent effects.

When I was still at Prep school age I used to ride, as did my brothers, to the different mines on Saturdays and sometimes on other days, to come down as guard with the pack trains of first-class ores. Then I was permitted to strap on a very small .22 revolver handed me by my brother Alex, who by that time was fourteen years of age and sufficiently responsible to be allowed to tote a .38 or even a .41.

On a certain morning I reported at the main office for the payroll money. The expression of my father's face, quizzical, kindly, amused, touched, will long remain in my memory as he looked at the old .44 frontier Colt I had strapped on me. Although I was a very well-grown boy it nearly reached to my knee. I had inveigled the cashier in the front office to let me slip it from the arms closets which were under his care. After many hours of rubbing it and soaking it in oil, it was in a condition to kill anyone or anything as effectively as any newer and flashier gun. A big part of my savings for months had been invested in the box of fifty cartridges . . . they cost five dollars for fifty. When I got that old loop belt cut down to fit my waist, had filled it with .44 cartridges, and was seated on my pony or mule, my pride was such that I would have taken, I actually believe, a chance at firing that gun even if attacked by Billy the Kid.

We used to love to play *palio,* it was a favorite game with us. *Palio* is a vigorous form of the game of hockey as it is played in Ireland. The ball is a solid wooden one or it may even be a round rock procured from the conveniently close river bed. The stick is a shorter one than is the regular hockey stick, heavier, and it is wider too; instead of a hook, the end is slightly bent with a spoon-like effect. It is thick and weighty enough to scoop the ball into the air, and before it hits the earth you can drive it farther still by belting it lustily. It sometimes happens that the ball may be sent back by an opponent before it hits the ground. Quite a large number play on each side, the grounds are usually alongside the river and are covered with all sorts of stones and gravel and coarse sand. It is rough going since you generally play in a shirt and pants, wearing an ordinary cap or hat, or maybe you are bareheaded, with no guards. It is decidedly not a game for a mother's darling or for boys or men who allow themselves to feel pain unduly. It is not uncommon to be knocked flat and stunned by a blow on the head. The young North American soon learns to be as Spartan as are the young Mexican and Indian.

To be made to groan or to cry out is to be branded by a certain name that is regarded the very last thing in the way of high-class insult. I have often seen a fallen warrior, thus offended, rise from the ground in a fury of rage only to beat and bang the offender into a recumbent position in his own turn. The first individual is thus reinstated to good standing. It is harsh, boisterous; but it is very good training. Some of the cracks on the head may be the cause of certain eccentric actions you may be guilty of performing in after life, but I do not really believe that such is the case . . . those delinquencies would better be laid to normal general cussedness.

When your early youth is surrounded by swearing in two or more languages—there were Italian stone masons, German mechanics, and others on the payrolls during those first years—you acquire a vocabulary filled with terms unprintable although appropriate to the many lines of endeavor with which you come into contact.

For instance, the *arrieros* have a poetic and charmingly vulgar line, but never do they take the name of the Lord in vain. The miner is almost as accomplished as the *arriero.* Then, of course, the stone mason of Spanish or Italian lineage has his specialties. The inartistic mechanic, German or American, whose "cussing" efforts are not in the same class, has a much less esthetic effect. Estheticism played but a minor part in our lives.

My mother and older sisters tried to teach us three youngsters, and they did their best to make the lessons interesting to us, but we found the outdoor activities much more exciting. We watched the building of stone masonry walls or adobe plastering, the mixing of sand and lime for mortar, the blending of the mud-clay and straw for adobe. You could not drag us away when the workmen were riveting boiler plates or placing and expanding tubes in the boilers, or keying cams on cam shafts for the batteries in the stamp mills, or keying bossheads to battery stems, or wedging the shoes of the bossheads. By the time most boys are considered old enough to play ball on a vacant lot we had acquired a general knowledge of material things and it was a very simple matter for us to take our places in the picture and assume the at first small jobs that *El Patron Grande* allotted to us.

Chapter 8

All Kinds of Education

About the year 1885, the very nice, kind, long-suffering Miss Griswold came to Batopilas from the States as a governess for my two youngest sisters and for us three boys. Due to her efforts and those of my sisters who read aloud to me a great deal, I developed a fondness for reading at rather an early age. *St. Nicholas,* of course, came regularly to the Camp and we had bound editions of it for the years preceding those when I first learned to read haltingly for myself. Then I had boys' books, *Frank on the Prairie,* and *Frank on the Mississippi,* until my wise mother decided that such fiction might be supplemented to advantage by more instructive reading which would also inspire patriotism. One Christmas when the steamer trunks of Christmas presents arrived from New York, there appeared *The Boys of '76, The Sea Stories of 1812,* and many other thrilling accounts of historical incidents. There were *Young People's Encyclopedia,* one volume of *Persons and Places,* and one of *Common Things.*

Miss Griswold exhibited great determination and courage in standing the strain of teaching us for some time, and we were forced to waste on the acquiring of preliminary book-learning many hours which could have been devoted to *palio,* mules, horses and other exciting things. But after two years of us, poor Miss Griswold gave us up for lost and returned to the States. Our education then continued at home for a while.

All the family, except my father, returned to Washington in 1886 for the double wedding of my two oldest sisters, which took place at St. Paul's Church, Rock Creek Parish. May married E. A. Quintard, the son of the Bishop, and Sue married W. M. Brodie, a Scotch engineer. It seemed to me a very large affair, I was duly impressed by the Bishop, and Bleak House was crowded. I remember as though it took place only last month the three-mile drive from Bleak House to the church; down the driveway, through the gate into Seventh Street Pike, the turn to the right past the Lay Place, where is now located Walter Reed Hospital, past Fort Stevens to Brightwood. In those far-off days there were an inn and a race track at Brightwood. We made a left turn into the country road known as Shepherd's Road, on past the farm that once was owned by the grandfather of the brides, and finally into the beautiful wide churchyard.

I recollect nothing of the drive back to Bleak House after the wedding, there I was completely submerged by the ocean of good things to eat awaiting us. We ate in the front of the house with the rest of the guests, and then we wheedled rich and indigestible foods from the servants in the kitchen and pantry. That splendid debauch we regretted some hours afterwards with all of our digestive apparatuses.

About a year later on, when I was twelve years old, another return was made to the States. We did not stay at Bleak House then, because it was winter time, but rented a small house. My mother made up her mind that the Kid and I ought to go to school and she selected the Friends' School. I hated it. For some reason I was a victim of shyness, and fear of the ridicule that might come to me if I failed when called on in class made every day a nightmare. The worst ordeal was spelling class. We were lined up, standing, and if you failed to spell a word you were sent to the bottom of the line. Such was the agony of this torture that I pretended to be sick morning after morning. Some mornings, I went to the School a moment too late, then I would come on back home telling my mother that the doors were closed and locked. Several times, my amiable sister enticed me into the pony-cart and drove me to the School where she left me, hoping that I would not run away. But usually I would arrive home before she did. I ran away one morning, determined never to return either to the School or home. I wandered east as far as Fourteenth Street, turned north and went up Fourteenth for many blocks. I came to a store window in which were displayed some bantam chickens. I gazed and gazed until I grew so fascinated by the idea of possessing a pair of bantams that I made up my mind to strike a bargain with my mother. I would overcome the horror of the Friends' School if she would give me a pair of bantams. I do not recall what excuse I gave her for skipping school or what lies I told, but I did not get the bantams.

Needless to say, the Kid and I were delighted to get back to Mexico.

I think it was in 1887 that my father made one of the two trips away from Batopilas in the twenty-two years he was in that camp. Some of the family accompanied my parents to the City of Mexico, and the Kid and I went too. They spent two or three weeks at the Hotel Iturbidi, which had been converted into a hotel from the old palace of the Emperor Iturbidi, in order to see President Diaz, and to attend personally to a press of affairs in connection with the company's business. This was a memorable trip for the Kid and me. John Worden had changed his run on the railroad, and he was now pulling the passenger train from Chihuahua south for a long run, a full day at least. He had given our company good and faithful service before he was employed as an engine driver on the Mexican Central Railroad, and he was very fond of the Governor and of us boys. Consequently he permitted us to ride on the engine all day. That was a grand sensation, and did we simply fly! "I betcher" we made, in a few of the places where the tracks were good, as much as thirty-five miles an hour.

It was our first visit to the capital and we surely had a full and satisfying experience. It was there I had my introduction to the old-fashioned hat tub. On our first morning a couple of *mozos* came up to our room, the Kid's and mine, bringing a large round tub made in the shape of a wide-brimmed beach hat upside down. On one side of the wide brim were fastened two little legs, and you were supposed to sit on the seat-like arrangement, supported by these legs, place your feet in the crown of the hat, so to speak, and with a sponge proceed to wash yourself. They put the tub in the middle of the floor, poured five gallons of warm water into the crown and took their departure.

"This is a funny-looking bathtub," thought I. "But here goes!" I stepped over the wide brim into the center of the crown and sat down on the brim. But being stupid I had failed to realize that the place to sit was on the spot supported by the two little legs. Of course, I went over backwards accompanied by the tub and the water, and the squeals of delight from the Kid.

The next year when I was thirteen I was sent to the States to Lawrenceville, New Jersey, where Alex was now entering his second year. The masters at this estimable seat of learning, having had many years' experience with youth, had found it expedient to institute a preparatory grade for the first form. This was known as the shell. My stupidity as to lessons insured my joining some fifteen other boys as occupants of the shell. We enjoyed ourselves, had a pretty good football team, and since I was a big, clumsy boy, I made an excellent center rush. We played the second first-form team and often defeated them much to their mortification and to our delight. I was mighty homesick for Mexico for a while, but after that wore off, I had a good time at Lawrenceville.

There are many places I want to see once more before I shove off for the last cruise. I want to go back to Lawrenceville, see the early morning of an early summer day, the morning of the day when Princeton played baseball against Yale at Princeton.

I am anxious to compare the kick I will get from going over to Princeton from Lawrenceville to witness the game at the age of sixty-odd, with the kick I got that morning of the eighth of May in the year of our Lord 1889. Figure it out for yourself. A kid between the ages of thirteen and fourteen, who, had he devoted the same amount of time to his books that he did to football and baseball, would have been in the first form instead of being in the shell. He was to go in a big 'bus drawn by none too fiery steeds from the Hamil House, which was his Hall, to Princeton to be present at a baseball game in which the batteries for Princeton were Snake Ames and Fred Brokaw; for Yale, Alonzo Stagg and Poole. What a day! What a day!

It was a hot day, it was a day when Princeton was victorious fourteen to eleven. My hazy recollection of that game and the players has been clarified by a letter that Asa S. Bushnell, graduate manager (Princeton), was kind enough to write me in reply to an inquiry of mine as to the make-up of the teams. Here it is, probably some of you may also be interested in the archeology of baseball.

	Yale		*Princeton*
p	Stagg	p	Ames
c	Poole	c	Brokaw
1b	McBride	1b	Dana
2b	Calhoun	2b	Osburn
ss	Graves	ss	Knickerbocker
3b	Noyes	3b	Watts
if	N. McClintock	if	Payne
cf	Dalzell	cf	Durrell
rf	G. McClintock and McClung	rf	King

I can see the field, I can renew somewhat the thrill as the game was called and things started. No two more different men than Snake Ames and Stagg ever faced one another as pitchers in any game. They were dissimilar in physique and in temperament; it was a hot game; there were times when Ames grew irascible, after which he would wind up and his intensity of delivery would make you wonder why his arm was not torn from the socket and did not follow the ball to the plate. Stagg, more composed, sweated profusely as he calmly stuck to his knitting. Seems to me I see him in a knitted blue quarter-sleeved jersey with the Y on his chest. . . .

Lawrenceville sent many leading athletes to both Princeton and Yale. When I was there I can recall Pop Warren of football fame, Mitt Lilly, the Jacksons (brothers), Huss, Sam, and others who earned national reputations.

The term ended, and after a summer at Bleak House, my parents resolved to try a tutor for us. In the fall of 1889 it became the misfortune of Mr. Clarence Stoner to labor with the brains of the three Shepherd male children.

It was good to return to Mexico. Fourteen years seemed to me to be a dignified and mature condition of manhood, and our earlier methods of play were too childish for me. I had acquired a strong liking for reading, and spent as much time as I could with *Charles O'Malley, the Irish Dragoon, Tom Burke of Ours,* and all the rest of Lever. It was hard for me to decide whether Charles O'Malley or Tom Burke was the world's greatest hero. I was a strong admirer of Napoleon Bonaparte, but I could never work up an excessive rise in temperature over Wellington.

We had no idle time on our hands, which was undoubtedly fortunate, for the Lord knows we got into mischief enough as it was.

As I said before, on Saturdays and sometimes on other days, we were employed as guards for the pack trains bringing down the rich first-class ores from La Descubridora, Roncesvalles, Camuchin and San Miguel. Often we acted as guards and watchmen at the twenty-five-stamp mill while these rich ores were being broken up by sledge and hammer into fragments sufficiently small to permit their entrance into the batteries. After crushing in the batteries, the heavy silver which would not pass through a forty-mesh screen was cleaned out of the mortar bed. This required careful supervision for there were always heavy chunks of pure native silver and nuggets from a few ounces to many pounds in weight.

Such ores are a tremendous temptation to a certain proportion of those men employed in the mining and treatment of them. A prudent overseeing is necessary to prevent any thieving.

It may appear strange that boys from eleven to fifteen years of age could be entrusted to prevent theft of such material when often it was worth several dollars to the pound. Quite frequently when breaking up the ores, chunks of pure silver were present even in the ore shipments. But we boys had been brought up among the workmen; we spoke Spanish like natives; we understood the mental attitudes and the mental reactions of them. The men had an enormous respect and loyalty for *El Patron Grande* and all the members of his family.

At an early age we boys were entrusted to keep an eye on shipments of ore when they were packed in heavy leather sacks, loaded on mules, and this pack-train made the journey from the mines to the hacienda. There they would be properly weighed once more, this having been done already at the mines. The twenty-five-stamp mill was used for crushing only the high-grade ores. An advanced duty was assigned us not only to act as guard but to assist in breaking up these ores as well as to feed them to the batteries.

Before we had a hospital, when I was fourteen years old, I gave chloroform in a major operation. It was an amputation above the knee, extreme infection had set in and gangrene was working overtime. Alex helped the surgeon, our cousin Dr. Frank Merchant. There was no one else to do it, and it was absolutely imperative if the man's life was to be saved. He was a policeman who had been shot in the leg; the bone was shattered. A native doctor had been treating the man.

He could not or would not be moved from the house where he lived in one of the two rooms. The front one was a small shop where his wife, when he was on duty, dispensed a very insignificant line of groceries such as panocha, which is a little block of unrefined native sugar, beans, corn, salt, a bit of coffee, tallow candles, *cerillos*, which are wax matches, a few bottles of *tequila* or *mescal.* This is a native liquor distilled from the juice of the maguey or *henequen* plant.

The counter of this place was covered with tin from five-gallon petroleum cans, it was very narrow. We spread a sheet over this, the wife boiled water in a shed back of the store, which was her kitchen. The patient was in a bad way, running a dangerously high temperature. We laid him on the prepared counter. I had a cone made from a newspaper with a little sponge in it, and I gave the chloroform. The surgeon and my brother commenced to work. The antiseptic was carbolic acid. It was not easy for me to gauge the anesthetic. When I got to the point where the almost imperceptible pulse began to get fainter still, I would let up on it. The doctor finished sawing the bone, he was getting ready to draw the edges of the flap together after putting in the drainage tube. From some muscular contraction, the head of the patient rolled and his eyes opened, or at any rate his eyelids fluttered. At that instant the policeman was never nearer to death. The fright it gave me made me empty an awesome amount of chloroform on the sponge and give him a dose of it that would surely have killed him if "his time had come." But *Dios es grande* and he survived.

We had comparatively few mine accidents, but over a period of many years of underground work, breaking hard rock with dynamite, there were bound to be some. In those early years, it was often one of my jobs to hurry to the mines on horseback with the surgeon and rush inside. Or I would help at operations outside as soon as the injured person was brought out. But I never did like it much. In after years, the familiarity with badly cut-up or burned men was increased by the necessity of helping to get them out of difficult places. This was when I had returned from college in the States, though, and went to work underground myself, first as Assistant Superintendent and later as Superintendent in charge of a mine.

You can readily understand that our education in all branches was far from being neglected.

Mr. Clarence Stoner, if I mistake not, was from the vicinity of Hagerstown, Maryland. He had completed his college course just before coming to us and was preparing to study medicine. Like many men who are determined to win out in that great profession, nothing was too terrible for him to undertake if it helped him make the money to complete his medical education.

Maybe Dr. Stoner (I call him that, for he has been a very able M.D. for many years, and I hope is still going strong) might not have undertaken the job if he had known as much about it at the beginning as he did at the end of his tour of duty in the front-line trenches with the Shepherd Infantry. He was possessed of one trait or characteristic which stood him in good stead, which was estimable and much to be desired in the piece of work he had taken on—he was of a serene nature, he took things quietly, never became ruffled, and had infinite patience; hence, at the end of his term of duty with us instead of being a nervous and physical wreck, he had put on weight, and was in the very best of health.

Once a member of the force at Batopilas who was a quick-moving, nervous, incessantly busy person, burning himself up and ruining his health, accused Dr. Stoner of being lazy. The reply of the doctor was characteristic and very true: he drawled, "If I am lazy and if you are not, then I am proud of my laziness!"

He went to California years ago, and "doctored" me once out there in the late Nineties. He was a very successful and prominent citizen of that great State. Taking it all in all Clarence Stoner did accomplish something with us. In the early spring of 1891 Alex was able to enter the University of the South, at Sewanee, Tennessee. After one term in the Grammar School by way of preparation, I managed to pass on to the University, and the next year Conness did the same thing.

When I went to Tennessee for Grammar School, I took with me my *Young People's Encyclopedia, Persons and Places,* and *Common Things.* When I read my first essay before Sigma Pi, the Grammar School Literary Society, it was on the American Indian, and it was copied from the encyclopedia practically word for word. Mr. "Mac" was the Grammar School instructor and the presiding officer at Sigma Pi; he was also house master at Ellmore Hall where I lived. He complimented me on the excellence of the essay. Naturally I felt considerably puffed up with pride. Promptly I went to my room, removed the encyclopedia from my shelf of books, and placed it at the very bottom of my steamer trunk. From that time on the key of the locked trunk remained in my pocket. During my stay in Grammar School I was called on for an essay at Sigma Pi on various occasions; by unlocking my trunk I was able, with the assistance of that book, to prepare "my" essays with the greatest of ease.

Alex and 'Conness and I loved Sewanee, therefore during our four years there we did not acquire too bad reputations. The long vacations at that place were in the winter, from the fifteenth of December to the fifteenth of March. We were allowed to leave as soon as we had finished our exams and we did some hard riding in order to get home to Batopilas by Christmas Eve.

At the World's Fair in Chicago in 1893, our ores from Batopilas took the premium in their class. The biggest piece weighed three hundred and eighty pounds. We had three of our very strongest pack-mules to bring it out with the regular pack train and they made the customary forty miles each day. This was done by changing the load every ten miles; and it was a tremendous nuisance. I know, because I helped to bring it out across the trail and I took a week off in football season from Sewanee that fall to see it in place in Chicago.

I think I saw it there. But my feet hurt me so badly during that week of sight-seeing at the World's Fair I cannot really remember anything clearly except the state of my pedal extremities.

When I entered the University I was sixteen, Conness was fourteen, and Alex was in his nineteenth year. We behaved fairly well, did not smoke, and drank only sporadically, because we all three were in training most of the time for football and other sports.

Alex left Sewanee in December 1893, and went back to work in Mexico. Conness and I left in December 1894. We worked in Mexico for two years, then we returned to the States in October 1896, with Alex, who was married that fall to Miss Phoebe Elliott, the charming daughter of Stephen Elliott, the Bishop of Texas.

Conness and I remained in the States and took special courses in the school of mines, he at the University of Pennsylvania and I at Columbia University in New York during the 1896-1897 terms. We returned to live and to work at Batopilas in the summer of 1897.

Chapter 9

Fourteen Mules to a Stage Coach

In Chapter III I spoke of Jack and Dora's hotel in Chihuahua. That city advanced very rapidly with the coming of the railroad and the increased bullion shipments as the various mines in the Sierras developed. When the ones at Santa Eulalia came into production the shipments of ores and bullion ran into values of many millions of dollars through Chihuahua. This necessitated the erection of all kinds of new buildings, machine shops, a brewery. But Chihuahua was an ancient town and the charm of a Spanish city was never submerged by the usual jerry-building boom.

The hotel of Jack and Dora did extremely well. They were beloved by all those who stayed there off and on. The meals were uncommonly good and there was a greater variety of food than customarily is possible for the price paid. Ham and bacon which were very expensive, due to high import duties, was found on the table always. After the railroad was built, Chihuahua was a divisional terminal and many railroad men stopped there at their hotel.

Before John Worden changed his run to pull the passenger train from Chihuahua south, he was the engine driver on the passenger train from El Paso, Texas, to Chihuahua. One time he got a confidential message as he was leaving from El Paso:

"The very first thing after you pull into Chihuahua, your tender tanks are going to be inspected for contraband."

The inspection in Chihuahua duly took place; nothing contraband in the way of ham or bacon was discovered. But they did find a false water-tight tank inside his regular water tank, and it was absolutely empty. It is said on the best of authority, however, that the thick smoke breathed by the passengers for a while on the run down to Chihuahua smelled mighty like ham and bacon. This old friend of mine, when I taxed him with his duplicity said: "The story is a libel. I never did in all my life fire my engines with ham and eggs!"

Nowadays when one talks about mines, the mind of the uninitiated turns instinctively to some nationally known colossal companies so vast and so grand that their places on the list of the Stock Exchange or Curb are exactly known, and the eye turns involuntarily to that line on the very long ladder of names. There was a time, however, when there was more romance about mining and more individuality.

Miners in those days were apt to be men who had been in abject poverty, wearing ragged cotton drawers, whose *guaraches*, sandals, were all but gone into fragments of leather, or even rawhide—and rawhide was the last thing in bad form where *guaraches* were concerned; men who had eaten their last meal many a long hour before, whose gourd or canteen was empty of water; men who had no place to return to where they could get another meal unless it was offered by a friend out of kindness. When ready to quit and drag himself to the nearest water, sometimes one of these men would find his El Dorado, his Bonanza, his Open Sesame to a fine house, rich clothes, bullion-covered *sombrero* with large monograms made with his initials in gold or silver, one on either side of the high crown (maybe it would be further ornamented with a four-inch-wide band of "tigre" around the brim), horses, mules, a ranch, good clothes for his woman who from now on was "Doña So-and-so" instead of simply Juana, Dolares, Manuela, or what will you.

I know of no more romantic case than that of Pedro Alvarado from El Parral. The description given above fits Pedro like a glove. He was a *peon,* an honest man, an untiring prospector with that undying hope that keeps them at it year after year. Pedro struck it. With a large assortment of capital letters you can picture only partially how damned BIG he did strike it. Very soon it was not a question of how many hundreds of thousands of dollars Pedro owned, for it went quite a distance beyond six figures.

The ore was "lousy rich" and there was a Hell of a lot of it, and it was easy to get.

Pedro built himself a really big house, an immense pile with a central patio, quantities of costly furniture. . . .

Then as now the salesmen with that unexplainable but infallible instinct which like the graceful bird soaring smoothly in circles alights upon the carcass, swooped upon Pedro as soon as the money, real and undeniable, came in the bank. Pedro liked music, he intuitively liked good music and nice things, for he was that kind of a person. The result was more than one piano; when phonographs were purchasable several were installed in his domicile. It was suggested that Mr. So-and-so was coming down soon from the States on his regular trip, a representative of one of the large silverware manufacturers. Pedro requested that he should come to his home in El Parral to let him look at some of his stuff. The salesman arrived with many imposing heavy trunks, filled with the samples of all kinds of silverware . . . a certain number of each and every design got out by his firm.

A prodigiously long table was arranged in the huge *sala.* Upon this were set out in due order all the samples in the most enticing window-dressing fashion. When this was completed, in were escorted the worthy Don Pedro Alvarado and his good and simple wife. They examined and politely exclaimed over the beauty of the glittering display . . . waiters, pitchers, coffee sets, tea sets, trays, bowls, vases, candlesticks, knives, forks, spoons of every conceivable description in sparkling array. Then Pedro who, when it came to a deal nowadays talked turkey, and hot turkey, spoke up: *"Quanto para todo?"* How much for all of it just as it stands? The fascinated salesman attempted to explain that the display was only the samples, not a complete set of any one thing, but that he could order with pleasure a complete set of whatever design . . . and so forth and so on for a time. But Pedro wanted only what was actually on that table right then and there, and he wanted it to remain exactly where it was to show it to his friends, also and so forth and so on. The bewildered salesman figured it all up and marked it down with a "three-pronged fork" probably, took his money and wired back to the States for another set of samples.

Maybe he sold Pedro the trunks too: they were of no further use to him.

I made use of an expression which may bear explaining . . ."He marked it down with a three-pronged fork."

That expression came into being a long time ago when some wag of a human went to settle his bill at a store in some primitive Mexican village or other in a remote past. . . .

There were many storekeepers who could neither read nor write, nor had they any ideas as to the usual figures employed by the initiated in that mysterious science known as arithmetic. I have known men who did thousands of dollars worth of business, profitable business, whose accounts were kept as follows:

A straight line was drawn across the page from left to right. You came in and purchased on credit one *peso* of goods . . . a circle was drawn half above and half below the line.

Maybe you then bought fifty cents worth of cigars for your friends who had just come in or maybe it was some other things worth fifty cents, *cuatro reales,* or four bits, take your choice. Your account then had a half circle made above the line.

If you bought twenty-five cents worth of anything, you had two lines vertically drawn from above down through the line.

If one *real* worth of salt, for instance, it was one such line.

If a *medio real*—six and a quarter cents—it was a short line just above the horizontal line.

If three and an eighth cents, a short line just below the horizontal line.

Now, if instead of using an ordinary pencil or pen with an orthodox one-point you used a three-pronged fork the result would not be the same, and it would rather favor the keeper of the account and not the purchaser.

Those were grand old days in Chihuahua in the big times. I remember the famous old Turco who many years before had started his career with a trained bear on a chain. Now he ran a monte game with a table a "block long," a bank of a quarter of a million dollars and a reserve of as much again, should it be required. No steel barons ever bucked that game, but I have seen bets made and lost there that no steel baron's press agent need have added zeros to, in order to get a story in our highly conservative press sheets.

Those mining men, who played as a means of relaxation and amusement, went out of the way to keep the facts of their playing from becoming public property; their own crowd knew how much money they made or lost. But they looked upon publicity as bad form. The sources of their wealth were the earth and hard rock. It was not a market for engraved certificates; and what a man did with his own money was his own affairs.

As a small boy I used to come into Chihuahua sitting on the driver's seat of a Concord Stagecoach filled with silver bullion, with fourteen mules hitched to it and going at a full gallop. The long whip of the *cochero* would be popping while we swung dizzily round the corners of the narrow streets of the town. We would pull up with a flourish in front of the Banco Minero. The coach I would be on would be the leading stage, and it was followed by several more all of them loaded with silver bars.

The cochero with his helper, who was the wielder of the short whip, were of much prominence in their social set. Let us stay on the coach and drive around to the old *meson* with the *conductores.* The old *meson* was a species of inn with stables, corrals, and all the other necessaries. The *conductores* were the men who conducted or drove the bullion trains. Train is certainly not meant to convey the idea of a railroad train.

It needed but a brief time for the admiring crowd to assemble as the stages were driven at a smart trot through the huge *saguan,* that was the gateway at the entrance, while one behind the other they came through to line up in the *patio* of the *meson.* Back of this *patio* was an inner one where the corrals and stables were located. The throng was lively, good-natured, pleased and happy at the laughing jests passed back and forth. The *muchachas* and the *mujeres* would blush and hang their dark heads when complimented and teased about their beauty and attractions by those *"caballeros* of the pack-mule and stagecoach, who came from the far-away mineral out in the Sierras where were the mines of so-fabulous wealth."

These were *"muy hombres."* Armed, well-dressed, with money to spend and more than willing to spend it while they were on twenty-four or thirty-six hours' leave in the capital of the State. Let us make the journey back with them as far as Carichic because from that place to Batopilas we ride a mule . . . back across grass-grown plains where immense ranches spread themselves for miles and miles, where thousands of heads of cattle roam; where fine horses and mules are bred by the hundreds. . . .

The mules were smaller than those you see in the United States, but they were quicker, very hardy and sure-footed. With a load of two hundred pounds they would make their forty miles each day for many days on a stretch. To many people, who do not understand, a pack-mule is just that . . . or even less . . . but to us who were totally dependent upon them for all transportation purposes for a long term of years, a pack-mule was more than "just a pack-mule." The same goes for the saddle-mule and for those in harness.

When unlooked-for emergencies arose you had sometimes to ride long distances over very dangerous trails on dark rainy nights. You could loosen your reins and permit your mule to have its head to select and choose its own way for hour after hour. At the end of your journey when you are brought to daylight safe and sound after traveling forty miles from your starting point, your feeling for the mule will be one of respect and affection.

The pack-mule is unlike his brother who makes up the teams for the stages and wagons, and he rarely ever kicks. This is the result of constant familiarity with being handled, because two men always put on his *aparejo* and his *carga.* The men adjust the *reata* so that the diamond hitch will function properly, and this is quite an art. That *reata* is pulled and tugged at from every angle, all slack is taken up to make sure that the load will go safely all day long, up and down hill and along levels, with only an occasional adjustment to take up any little slack that may have developed from the constant motion.

We will take the journey back with the *conductores,* via the *coches* until we reach Carichic. Let us go to the *meson* very early in the morning. . . .

Day is breaking, the driver with his two helpers, who are also the armed guards for each coach, have had their breakfasts—bread cooked by the regular company cook in his cast-iron portable oven. Or it may be corn *tortillas* procured from a near-by *fonda, frijoles* boiled and then fried in a little hog fat, *manteca.* They may have, too, some stew of pounded-up-and-frizzled *carne seca,* which is meat dried in the hot sun. This stew is highly seasoned and mighty good it is too, particularly when it is washed down with a couple of pints of strong, black coffee.

Before we can take our leave of Chihuahua, we must harness our mules, fourteen of them to each stagecoach.

Each man takes the bridles on his arm for the set of mules it is his duty to bridle, and brings the animals from the corral back into place to be hitched. While we are at this point, let us investigate how these men hitch fourteen fat, sassy mules to a stagecoach and go about it in an orderly well-regulated manner. Two mules are hitched in the wheel as is customary the world over. Every vehicle, as you already know, which is drawn by horses or mules has a tongue or pole projecting outward in the front. The pole is a little longer than the animals.

To hitch the wheel team, one animal is placed on either side of the pole, facing front, of course; his harness is put on him, presuming that he has been bridled first. Next the collar is settled in place, and then you raise the harness, put the harness over the collar, strap them together under the collar; buckle the belly-band. You buckle the breast chain and hitch the traces next to the whiffle-tree; the whiffle-tree is attached to the double-tree; the double-tree is fastened by a bolt to the base of the pole, which is in its turn appropriately and very strongly attached to the front running-gear of the stagecoach.

Now, we have the wheel team hitched, or at least the two animals are harnessed and standing ready to be hitched to the coach. There is a hook at the end of the pole. On the hook is a long piece of good oak timber with a ring-bolt in the exact center, which ring-bolt is now hanging from the hook. You observe two double-trees united to the piece of good oak timber near the end. This means that here we have an arrangement which enables us to hitch four mules abreast, and the four mules are directly in front of the two wheelers. . . .

If we look again at the pole what will we see running through staples or eye-bolts along the bottom fastened to the front running-gear assembly at one end, which extends beyond the end of the pole, and farther yet beyond the heads of your first set of four mules which you have just put in place? If the daylight is strong enough by this time (or if it is not, then by the light of a lantern or from a fat-pine torch), you will perceive a chain at a proper distance from the heads of your first set of four mules. There is secured to the chain by a stout ring another tree with two double-trees joined to it exactly like the one to which your first set of fours are fastened. Farther along the same chain is a breast yoke to this tree and between it and the breast yoke you back up and harness your second set of four mules.

Once more, what do we see made fast to the chain? Another one of those same trees and at its end a breast yoke. We will back in another four mules and harness them. Now we can hitch the whole bunch, buckle the side lines that are clasped to the two drive reins of each set of fours, and we are ready—after many, many years of practice—to climb on the box, to take up the eight lines and to shake out the long whip.

It will, however, take you a much longer time to become a safe driver of a fourteen-mule Concord Stagecoach than it will to learn to drive an automobile. It will require a greater degree of skill and bodily strength to gather up all eight of those heavy leather lines in one hand to allow the other hand to be free in order to pop your long whip, to pop it with such acumen that you will not miss any spot aimed at even though it should be no bigger than a fly which is annoying one of your animals.

But, you may say, we have hitched our mules before we got them out of the corral!

That is easy if you have trained teams such as those owned by the company, and if you know how to handle them. Otherwise if you walked out into the corral in the dim light of breaking day, your arm full of bridles, and started in to circulate among that bunch of eager, milling mules, you would in all probability take two or more days to bridle them . . . if you were lucky and did not land in the hospital or at the undertaker's.

But if you (and the mules) are trained, you do this: You and your two helpers walk into the corral, each with the appropriate number of bridles on your arms—each bridle belongs on the head of a certain mule to which animal it has been especially fitted so that it will be perfectly comfortable—and you call out in a deep and manly voice: *"Forman!"* This you do three or four times. After a brief interval of milling about, of scurrying and seeking companions and proper mates, the intelligent, well-kept heads of many mules will be facing you. They will all be in perfect alignment, their tails towards the walls of the corral. Each four that belong together are together. It is almost never that you will have to change the position of any one mule in the four. That is easy, isn't it?

We now put the bridles on the proper heads, buckle the throat latches, clip the bits together with the short straps which are found joined at the exact spot, and you are ready to lead your four from the corral. Now that we are harnessed and hitched to the stage, we must drive out of the *patio* of the *meson* through the *saguan* and turn into the narrow street. We must do this without "hubbing" the stone wall of the arched *saguan*.

You crowd your leaders out onto the sidewalk across the narrow street. In obedience to the pull of the right-hand lines, they gradually straighten out towards the right, but they will not take up any of the slack nor do any pulling of the load as yet. The next four mules behind them do the same, and the next, finally you let the wheelers do the trick, thus the old Concord is eased through the *saguan* and they all are straightened out. Then YES, they take up the slack! To the driver's call of *"Mula! Mula!"* they trot off to the accompanying crack of the long whip, which may be cracking only in fun, but which can at any moment raise the hair from any mule that doesn't behave itself.

The company never had less than five hundred mules, pack and stage. We owned many teams of fourteen mules, all perfectly matched as to size, color, and so on—blacks, grays, sorrels, bays. . . .

Now we are off on our trip back to Batopilas. About four blocks, I cannot exactly remember how many—I have walked, driven, marched very many blocks since those carefree, happy days of youth and young manhood—you round a corner to the right approaching the old stone-arched bridge, barely wide enough for the hubs of your wheels to miss the parapet of masonry two hundred years old. On into the outskirts of Chihuahua, through dirt-paved streets lined with one-story adobe houses sometimes plastered sometimes not, you drive into the road that winds for a few miles along the side of a mostly dry *arroyo*. From this, you go into a wider semi-plain where for some miles the round, rust-colored stones and rocks make the stage, strong as it is, swung on several layers of sole-leather straps for springs, toss about like a dory on a choppy sea.

For three hours we travel. Then we see what appears to be a squat square box with a big keg at each corner. This is first perceived dark against the skyline, because you are gradually climbing eight hundred feet since you left the city of Chihuahua, which is about three thousand feet above sea level. As you draw nearer to this box-appearing structure, it is simple to see that it is a building erected for defense. As its name implies, El Fortin, it is a fort, a defense position, where for many years the Mexican Government maintained a force of soldiers to protect against, and to retard the raids of, the Apache and the Comanche Indians. To my great delight, when this tale first began there was yet a considerable force of Mexican soldiers at El Fortin. There were a quantity of mounds dotted about on the landscape, which were pointed out as graves of fallen Indian warriors who had been killed as they would ride round and round the fort, firing at the armed guards with disastrous results to themselves. This they frequently did even in the late Seventies.

As the years passed, we would only stop at El Fortin occasionally for the night. By that time, it was nothing but a prosaic headquarters and mail-stage relay. We would spend the night there when we had reached this place too late in the afternoon to get to Chihuahua before the bank closed, which would force us to lie all night at the *meson* with the bullion. If we were on our way back to Batopilas, we would stop there for the night, if we had been unable to leave Chihuahua until afternoon.

Now across the plain from El Fortin. . . . The mules are now in a lively trot since we are no longer climbing, and they will keep it up by the hour. On the stage route we make no noon stop. On and on until the sun is low enough to strike well into your eyes, then downgrade into the little valley of the Carretas River, where the village of the same name is located on the edge of a free-running stream where the monotony of treeless, grass-covered expanse of plain is relieved by big alamo trees. Carretas was a pleasant stopping-place. We could always procure eggs, and milk and chickens there, chickens were a welcome change from the eternal *carne seca.*

Carretas was near Santa Isabela where the revolutionists years later held up a Chihuahua & Pacific Railroad train and shot down a number of harmless passengers. It was a pretty little town in another shallow valley on the Camino Real, on which "Royal Road" we are journeying with the stagecoaches. Like Carretas, Isabela was also sometimes used as a place to spend the night if the waning day caught us nearer to it than to Carretas. . . .

Now, we have left Isabela miles behind. About two o'clock in the afternoon we are going more slowly, we are traveling among the foothills of the Cusi Mountains. These mountains we circle in order to get around them onto the plain that leads to Ojos Azules, called this because of the Blue Ponds or shallow lakes. There we will make night camp. This will be the last one before we drive into Carichic, where we leave the stage as a means of transportation, having driven one hundred and fifty miles. From Carichic we will take to the hurricane deck of the good and faithful pack and saddle mule.

You cannot fail to have noticed that we are always making very early starts. This we do from Ojos Azules, reaching Carichic at noon. We have the entire afternoon to arrange the loads for the pack animals and to prepare for a daylight start in the morning. Tomorrow we must make a long, long ride. That day's mileage will carry us out from the foothills and well into the big mountains of the first divide that lands us for our first night's camp in one of the most picturesque gorges in the world. A rapidly running stream of sparkling water winds and dips for miles a twisting course between perpendicular walls, bluffs of solid rock. These bluffs are from three hundred to six hundred feet high, and there is but one opening at each side where it may be entered. The openings in the rock are actually very steep narrow breaks in the great bluff itself. The place through which we will clamber tomorrow morning, as we continue our journey, is only a crack, at the very narrowest place about thirty feet wide, and through this a trail has been built. This stream, the Gauhochic, from which the station takes its name, in geological ages past eroded a small area, a triangular niche on one bank, an area of about twenty acres. It is above high-water mark and it has accumulated a certain amount of silt during all these years. It is on this spot that the first day's ride comes to an end, a ride of forty miles.

Our next day's going is over a romantic-looking country to the station of Pilares, small pillars these, Nature's pillars. We pick our way through a series of these pillars for three hours, while we are in the Arroyo de Las Iglesias. It is called the Gorge of the Churches because the bluffs all about us for many miles are filled with columns and pillars and what can well be imagined as church steeples and towers. Most of them are more than a hundred feet high, many more lofty still, and they are blended with entrancing colors where the erosion of the ages has taken advantage of the softer parts of the rock.

We are out of this *arroyo* at last and onto a tableland of majestic pine forests. We travel along this until a clearing is reached in which rests the Station of Pilares. The old unwashed station keeper welcomes us and receives our greetings with pleasure. We clamber down from our faithful mules who are as glad to discard their burdens as we are to be discarded.

The stations are all built to pattern. In good time we will have our supper, and then to our gratefully occupied beds. Those have been taken inside the house by our *mozos,* unrolled from their leather or tarpaulin coverings, and spread out to receive us on the high canvas cots. We need blankets here in this altitude of seven thousand feet even in the warm weather. But in the winter when the ground is covered with snow and the wild wind howls and moans through the pines, you will be glad indeed to pull more than one over your shoulders when the fire has died down in the fireplace.

Next day we have a few more stiff climbs. Then down into creeks and little rivers we go, especially the Eurique River, whose bed at the place it is forded is not more than forty-five hundred feet above sea level. We ride on tablelands and ridges, through magnificent pine forests whose plumy tops reach for the sky until you have an ache in the back of your neck if you try to look at too many of them.

The sun gets low in the west . . . we arrive at La Laja. This station is in the very tall timbers on the banks of a small constant stream, it is never a dry *arroyo,* of pure cold water. The buildings are on a bare expanse of rock from which this station takes its name, La Laja.

Moving on from La Laja the next day after the usual forty miles we come to Teboreachic. We find the same arrangements of houses, corrals, and everything here, except that the area in which they are located is yet more constricted because this station lies in a contracted gorge. From this place we must make an unusually early start in order that we may reach before dark the edge of the Big Barranca, or gorge, down which we will find the Hacienda San Miguel, the mills, and the mines.

Main Street of Batopilas, with church at left.

Chapter 10

Christmas at Batopilas

Christmas and New Year's Day were THE big days with us at Batopilas. My father and my sainted mother went to measureless trouble and a great deal of expense to make them so. It was not an easy matter to do this, particularly in the early days. They insisted on a full and orthodox observance of any anniversary, whether it were Christmas, New Year's, or just a birthday, in spite of the fact that our large family celebrations necessitated much greater forethought and preparation for months ahead than would have been required in the United States.

The box canyon of the Batopilas River was devoid of farm products, and everything had to be brought from remote points into the camp, from turkeys down to the ingredients for the mince pies and plum puddings. Turkeys were driven in from the mountains, as many as fifty at a time. They would have to come many weeks before the proper date, because they had to be kept up and fattened to recover from their forty- or fifty-mile hike. Very occasionally some of them would be brought to Batopilas on mules, packed in crates.

My father always insisted on having a suckling pig, and they were hard to get hold of, since little or no stock was raised in that section. The hams, of course, came from the States, as did most of the "goodies" that go into Christmas and New Year's dinners at the family table. It was rare indeed when fewer than twenty persons sat down to table—seven children and my parents, the several gentlemen employed by the company, engineers, chemists, the surgeon—and later on as the in-laws came into the tribe it made quite a gathering.

The other American employees and the foreign and native ones were served at a mess. On Christmas Day the children of the employees, several hundred of them, would come filing in through the big gates down the ramp to the street, which ran in front of the storerooms, which were immense stone buildings. They would step through the iron gates into the garden on that same level, up the ramp to the big patio. There under the orange trees would be laid a long table spread with candy bags, nuts, oranges, cakes . . . these things were to be distributed to each one of those shy little tikes who were too overcome to do anything but whisper *gracias,* and smile.

There was plenty for my mother and sisters to do. Although they had all the native extra help they needed, and fairly good cooks, they were very busy supervising everything. The preparing of cakes and other sweets was a labor of days. The mince-meat, of course, had been attended to long before, as well as the other ingredients that went into these delectable pies. I have already extolled my mother's mince pies. I can hear my father now, going over his wine and liquor stock in anticipation of Christmas preparations and requirements, saying:

"And, oh, yes, one more case of brandy for the mince pies!" If during the days of Prohibition or even now, the Supreme Court had seen the kind of brandy that went into these pies they would have declared it was in violation of the Constitution that such vintage liquor should be employed in culinary arts.

The wines and liquors, with the exception of the Scotch whiskey, were chiefly secured in Mexico. The Scotch came at regular intervals during the year from Scotland sent by Mr. George Crystal of Glasgow. This gentleman was the largest individual owner and director of the affairs of the Trinidad Shipping & Trading Company, whose steamers plied regularly across the Atlantic through the Gulf of Mexico to Mexican ports, and made their way home through the Caribbean to Trinidad. The Scotch came in small barrels just the right size so that two of them, one on either side, made a proper mule load.

Conness and I acted once as escorts over the mountains to Mr. Crystal and Mr. L. H. Stevens. We were coming into Batopilas for vacation from Sewanee, at the same time that these two loyal and devoted friends of my father were en route to the camp to pay us a visit. For a Christmas present they gave each of us a beautiful leather case with a silver name plate engraved with our names and the dates. The cases contained a Star safety razor, six blades, a patent sharpener, shaving soap and a brush. Since we were still novices at the dangerous game of shaving, these gifts proved not only our pride and delight, but removed the peril from the ordeal.

There is not one particle of doubt in my mind that those times were the golden age. They were not the horse and buggy days, but the stage and pack-mule age, and there has been nothing fundamentally as fine since those days vanished, whistled down the wind, and the speed mania came into existence.

The apples in the mouth of the baked suckling pig with all of its juicy fellows were brought to us by the Tarahumare Indians. These shy people loaded the fruit in crates of their own construction, and put them on their beautiful small ponies to barter them for supplies or money. The apples had been gathered from the trees which had grown from the seeds brought from Europe three hundred years before by the fearless and tireless men who wore the cloth of the Franciscan and Jesuit orders.

When we were young lads at college and school, our arrival in Chihuahua for Christmas was timed to meet a returning *conducta* if possible, since at that time the stages came into Chihuahua. Later, when the Chihuahua & Pacific Railroad was completed, we went by train as far as San Antonio, which was a way-station on the line, and not to be confused with San Antonio, Texas. The stages and wagons would meet us there. In the first instance it meant a drive of two and a half or three days according to the conditions of the roads. When the railroad was completed this was cut down to about a day to reach Carichic and the company ranch, El Alamo. There we transferred to the faithful mule, pack-saddle and the efficient *arriero.*

The obtaining of Christmas presents was another problem. While the stores in Batopilas carried quite a good stock most of it was of European manufacture. The majority of us were of sufficient age when we came to Mexico to have acquired American ideas as to what a Christmas present should be. The articles purchasable in the way of toys, for example, were out of the question to an American child. Therefore, for Christmas, there always was a quantity of steamer trunks full of Christmas things; the candies generally were of Huyler's make. This was in an era before other candy makers had realized the possibilities of the profits to be enjoyed in fine candies, so that Huyler's was king. The memories of a Huyler's ice-cream soda caused as much water to form in one's mouth then as did the thought of a real "Scotch and soda" highball in the dry days of Prohibition. The trunks were usually packed at the New York offices of the company and shipped to El Paso; or they were brought down by someone who happened to be making the trip from New York to the camp at that season of the year.

Steamer trunks were used because they made a fair load for a mule when one was put on either side of his pack-saddle. During the four or five years we boys were at college in the States, we generally brought them down with us. By diligent travel we could reach home from Sewanee on Christmas Eve. But very often that forced us to make the ride across the mountains in three days instead of the customary five. This was no comfortable undertaking. It was a long hard ride at best when in perfect trim and hardened to the saddle. But to be compelled to double stations and sit in the saddle for thirteen hours on a stretch when we had not ridden for nine months, and to do this during the cold winters which prevailed at five to nine thousand feet elevation, sometimes accompanied with snow storms and high, frigid winds, was no child's play.

Of course you do climb down from your beast every now and then to walk a mile or two and to stir your blood back into circulation; very often you use your Bowie knife to dig the balled snow from the feet of your patient mule, and to "spell the animal." . . . It's not so bad. But at that altitude I do not recommend it if you are on simple pleasure bent.

Once I left Carichic with Marshall Willis, some extra pack and saddle animals, and a bad chest cold. We had to do the trip in two and half days in order to be in the camp on Christmas Eve. We left Carichic late in the day, made Guahochic well after dark, a distance of forty miles, and rested for four hours there. When we hit the *mesa* about four hours' ride out of Pilares (we had come up out of the Eurique valley), I was running a very high temperature and had suffered two shaking, chattering chills. Marshall was greatly alarmed, for my breathing was fast becoming nothing but a sort of rattle. We made camp out in the open. It was bitterly cold. We had the *mozos* scrape back the snow and they built an immense fire. I crawled under a pile of blankets, swallowed another twenty grains of quinine, drank at least a pint of *mescal* mixed with water. I must have slept all of five hours, and awakened refreshed but sopping wet with perspiration. I put on dry underwear in front of the blazing fire, and we started off once more. I recall but little of the hours that followed. We rode, we changed animals when we reached a station, and rode some more and then some more.

At nine-thirty on Christmas Eve we dragged our weary selves into the hacienda in time for all eight of the trunks to be unpacked and the stockings for the children, grandchildren, nephews, and nieces to be filled.

The Christmas days at Batopilas were grand times . . . we even had a tree! This was brought into the camp by men from up in the mountains at Yerbaniz, seven thousand feet high where the pine timber line began.

The Christmas music was supplied by a piano. When I talk about a piano at Batopilas after you have read of the travel it took to reach this place, naturally you are entitled to know how its possession was possible. There were no balloons, and if there had been, they never could have dropped down into that steep-sided canyon which was five thousand feet deep. There were no airplanes and no place to land even if there had been such means of transportation. From what you have read you will realize that although a pack-mule with his arriero is capable of carrying almost unthinkable loads, you cannot see him coming along the mountain trails with an upright piano draped across his back.

But don't forget that we still have the Indian.

If you have the time to spare and if you have a clever Mexican who understands the Indian and who speaks his language, and if you leave it to them with no suggestions on your part, that cumbersome box will eventually arrive, and arrive right side up. It is really quite simple.

When it is unloaded from the wagon at Carichic you cut two long straight pine poles. It is better to have them already cut and the bark removed so that they will be dry and properly seasoned. They ought to be about four inches in diameter at the big end. Put one on either side of the piano in its wooden box and tie them in such a way that the weight is balanced with no tendency to be top-heavy when lifted from the ground. I suggest that you allow the Mexican to do the tying of the ropes; they make a very good job of such things. You now have a piano in a box with two poles the ends of which stick out far enough to have plenty of room for at least two Indians to get under the end of each pole; this makes four of them at each end of the piano. They get under the poles in a squatting position; at the word "Vamonos!" they straighten up. The piano is off the ground, and the carriers move off with inward satisfaction of knowing that all they have to do now is to carry this great box for a hundred and eighty-five miles in fifteen or twenty days. There will be at least twenty-four carriers—that makes three sets—and they spell each other every twenty or thirty minutes. They are well fed at your expense if you want a maximum of efficiency. Each man is paid at the rate of a dollar a day. At the end of the journey he takes his "easy money" and trots back home a hundred and eighty miles or more in about three days, and he has a happy time for some months on his ill-gotten gains!

It is expensive transportation, very. Yes, but think of the pleasure you will derive from that piano. Keep in mind that probably the man who invented the phonograph was a young fellow when this piano made its journey across country and that the voice of the radio was not yet heard in the land. We sang Christmas carols and hymns, gay songs, sad songs, dance music, but you do not require me to itemize the infinite number of musical delights we had with that piano.

On Christmas Day the stamp mills were silent, as they always were on Sundays as well. When I would awaken on Christmas and on Sunday mornings the first thing I would hear would be the cooing of the doves and the brave song of the cardinals in the *guamuchil* and orange trees.

Invariably there was a big *baile* down in the town of Batopilas on Christmas night. In fact there were three dances . . . first class, second class, and third class, *baile de primera, de segunda, de tercera.* Of course we all would attend because there was only the most friendly relationship between the family and the gentlefolk who made up the social life of the town. The *bailes* were subscription dances, committees made all the arrangements, and the expenses were *pro rata.* The ladies dressed in ball gowns and all the gentlemen wore evening clothes. The guests who lived beyond walking distance, like ourselves, rode to the dances on horseback. It was a common sight to see groups of ladies in elegant ball gowns with their long trains looped over their right arms, accompanied by gentlemen in evening clothes, escorted by *mozos* carrying lanterns if there was no moon, clattering along on spirited prancing mounts.

Although we attended the formal dances in long-tailed coats, we dispensed with top hats. We felt that to ride on horseback to a dance in a long-tailed coat was permissible, even though you did discard your holster and belt and wore your gun—which you left in the dressing-room at the ball—in your waist band; but a top hat was a bit too thick. Besides, our horses had never seen us in top hats. When you are all dressed up in a long-tailed coat you do not want a damned fool horse pitching about and disturbing the peace.

I was a very susceptible young man and many is the time I have sent a *mozo* long distances down river where there were a few irrigated gardens, in order to have him trot in with a bouquet of roses for the young lady who at the time was all-in-all to my heart, eyeballs, or whatever organ it may be that is affected under these strange conditions that overtake the youthful *homo sapiens.*

The suppers at the *bailes* were lavish, ample as to spirits and wines to meet varying tastes . . . everything from champagne to brandy. Decorations were plentiful, prodigal in fact, flowers, greens (and these were hard to get), colored-paper streamers. . . . We danced the waltz, the schottische, the polka, the mazurka. Senorita Petra Ramirez with Don Benito Martinez invariably were called on to give us at least one *jota,* and it was well worth watching. When we learned the two-step and the cotillion during our college years, we brought home those dances to Batopilas, which innovations were received more than kindly by the gay Batopilenses. There was no especial hall for the *bailes.* Many of the residents lived in spacious houses which boasted large *salas.* These rooms always opened through one or more doors onto the inner *patio* which was filled with growing plants and flowers of all kinds.

At break of dawn the dance would end. When Alex, Conness and I had finished college and had regular jobs at the different mines, we would have to hurry back home to change our clothes, remount our horses and ride, each one to the mine of which he was superintendent.

Street between Hacienda San Miguel and Batopilas. Tower in background is the main office of the Batopilas Mining Company.

Chapter 11

Marshall Willis and the Hot Country

Marshall Willis, who was taking care of me on the urgent journey into camp in time for Christmas, was one of the four colored employees who were with us at Batopilas. John Gibson, "Sandy," and Charlie Robinson were the others. John was a sort of handy man, valet, general factotum. When I was a young man on vacation from two years' work as superintendent of San Miguel Mine, my father sent me instructions from Batopilas to procure and to bring down with me a good male cook. I had already hired a young colored man, John Gibson, who had done a hitch in the United States Navy as mess boy. From John I got hold of "Sandy" who had been an officers' mess cook; he was now retired and free to be employed in Mexico. I promptly interviewed Sandy and a deal was arranged.

When the time came for me to return to Batopilas, John, Sandy, and the others of us on this particular trip to camp reached Carretas successfully and spent the night there. As day was breaking we pulled out across the little river to begin the climb out of the valley. Sandy was an excellent authority on all things watery and culinary, but he was unfamiliar with things that roamed the face of mother earth.

He was seated on top of the stage and was carrying a little .32 revolver. When we were about half way up the long hill, we were startled by exclamations from Sandy, more properly they should be called shouts of excitement. Followed loud discharges from his little pop-gun. Between each discharge he vociferated:

"There's a deer! Stop the coach! I see a deer!"

It struck us as decidedly odd that a deer should be so near the constantly traveled road. However, we halted; investigation revealed to us two little burros in the roadside brush who appeared unduly agitated. One of them had two slight abrasions on each side of that end of him to which his fly-swatter is attached. . . .

We had considerable trouble in convincing Sandy that he had been shooting at a burro and not at a deer; we even had to point out that deer had horns and that burros had only ears. We mounted the stage; Marshall Willis, who was driving, kicked off the brakes, popped his long whip, while between periods of his inimitably infectious chuckle, he urged his team forward up the steep climb of the Carretas hill.

Marshall Willis had joined the force at Batopilas many years before this little incident. He had been seen wandering about Chihuahua, to which town he had come it is supposed, for some very good reason of his own. Possibly the sheriff in some district in Texas along the Rio Grande had a connection with that reason. Before the sheriff had become interested, I believe, there had been an altercation in some dance hall or other between a number of cow-punchers (Marshall had been a cow-puncher in Texas), and fatalities had resulted which made a change of scene imperative.

He knew all about mules and horses, six-guns, and he spoke Spanish as it was used by the average puncher who worked cows along the Rio Grande in Texas. He became an invaluable man to us. For years he had charge of the *conducta.* He handled hundreds of thousands of dollars represented by silver bars; and hundreds of thousands of dollars in currency for payrolls. His devotion and respect for *El Patron Grande*, with very few lapses from the straight and narrow, made him a man who deserved much and who was rewarded accordingly.

This man could ride almost anything that had hair on its back; his shooting with a .44 was the envy of everyone. It was never any bother to secure a chicken for supper when we would reach a station at the end of the day en route with the *conducta.* This usually tiresome piece of work was solved by having the wife of the station keeper indicate to Marshall which ones of her fowls were for sale to us, and he would shoot their heads off with his six-shooter. From this to the frying-pan or pot according to the age of the bird and the condition of our appetites was a question of not more than thirty minutes if we were hungry and an hour if we were not.

To us kids whose idea of being real men was to be able to shoot, to ride, and to rope, Marshall was the greatest of them all. We were given into his care on the trail, around the camp and all. He taught us these as well as many other useful things. We all were perfectly devoted to him and he to us. He took inordinate pride in the prowess of any of us boys, and particularly in the capabilities of Conness. It was Marshall who taught us to sit up on a pack-saddle with a strong hold front and aft to ride the young mules who were being broken to the pack-train. This was done by roping them, holding them down, putting on the *aparejo* and then letting them loose to buck until they tired themselves out or got rid of the *aparejo*. just as soon as they did that, it was put on them immediately again, and they would start in to buck some more if they wanted to until they were exhausted by the unequal struggle and gave it up as a bad job.

Some years after the death of my father, Marshall took his savings and his bonuses to purchase a small ranch in the Hot Country, where he said he was going to stay until he died. Came the Madero Revolution and the years of unrest and final prostration of our camp. We were all scattered here, there, and everywhere in quest of a living. Marshall was lost sight of entirely.

About eight years ago, the Kid, now a man well past the half-century mark, was working some lead-silver properties not very far from Carichic. When the ore teams got back to the mine from the railroad station in the afternoon on a special day, there was a very old man on one of them. This old man was "Irish." "Irish" was the nickname Marshall had been known by for ages, how or why the Lord only knows.

"Well, I'll be damned," says the Kid, "if it isn't old Willis!" And after shaking hands, "How would you like a drink to wash the dust out of your throat?"

"All right, Mr. Conn. The Governor always asked me that the first thing when I used to run the bullion train and had just got in. It must have been the right thing or the old Governor never would have done it. Lord, Mr. Conn, I am glad to get back to one, at least, of the old-time *Patroncitos!"*

That night many questions were asked and answered on both sides. Old Marshall had been with us since 1884. He had risen by faithful service from cook on the trail to conductor, the boss of the bullion train. He had seen us grow up from little boys to men getting on in years. Many fortunes and many ill-fortunes had been shared in common. This old man was then in his seventies. He heard that one of us was in Mexico working a mine near the old stage road, and he left his home in the Hot Country, saddled and rode his mule five hundred miles across the Sierra Madres to come to my brother's camp. Here he died a short time later.

Marshall Willis had his faults, and his weaknesses. I have never met a man who was worth a damn who did not. But he surely did have loyalty and affection. Unless you have ridden across the Sierra Madres you cannot truly appreciate just what a real good reason there must be to make you do so under the very best of conditions. When old Marshall made his last ride over them, the conditions were anything but favorable, even for a young man, much less for an old one with a very limited supply of money.

This old stager used to say that he did not have to work for a living. "When my father died, I inherited the whole State of Georgia." When the proper interval had passed he would add: "To work in at a dollar a day." And he would chuckle at his own wit. I must have heard old Marshall tell that story one hundred times every year for twenty years, and the last chuckle was just as full of enjoyment as the first.

Charlie Robinson has his own part in this narrative, which will come after a while.

It may be well to explain here that Hot Country does not mean Hell. The Hot Country, or Tierra Caliente, was that part of the Pacific coast section of the States of Sinaloa and Sonora which well-deserved that designation. The high mountain and central plain was known as Tierra Fria or Cold Country, and the inhabitants in these sections known as Calientes or Frios as the case might be.

These terms and differences were very marked. A good-natured rivalry—sometimes the nature was not so good—existed; a Frio resented being called a Caliente, and a Caliente resented even more strongly being called a Frio. They differed too in appearance and there were certain disparities in their household customs due undoubtedly to the very clear dissimilarity in the temperature of their respective lands.

I think the chief distinctive qualities between the Tierra Fria and the Tierra Caliente lie in their blankets, saddles, and other horse and mule gear; and the protective garments against the brush worn by the *vaqueros.* The saddle used in Tierra Fria is a squat low-cantled, flat, broad, circular-horned affair, and this horn is like a big toadstool cut flat across, about six inches wide. The saddle has a seat leather-covered half-way forward of the cantle. The cinch and latigo rings are set far forward in front of the rider's leg; the right-hand ring is equipped with a broad double strap, punched for the tongue of a large-ring-buckle to which the cinch is woven. The left side is the same, only the latigo is much longer and is run through and over and upon itself twice or three times before it is buckled.

The saddle is furnished with meager skirts. Unless extreme care is used in the arrangement of the saddle blanket the tree is liable to gall the animal. In order to prevent the slipping forward of the saddle, it is equipped with a cropper whose long ends are passed under the tree between it and the blanket or saddle-cloth. The ends of this are divided into two straps and are taken around the horn and made fast to the latigo ring on either side.

The leg protection against brush consists of *chaparreras* made of heavy tanned leather shaped to the leg which has short, narrow straps with many buckles from hip to foot where the *chaparrera* is flared to cover the top and side of the rider's foot.

The headstalls for the animals are not very different in the two sections. In the Cold Country they do not often use the light leather halter under the headstall to which the *cabresto* or halter rope, is joined. The saddle-cover is generally more elaborately decorated, since the lack of saddle skirts makes it more visible, than is the case with his Hot Country brother. The Cold Country spurs are cumbersome and weighty, they have large blunt rowels, and the spur straps hold it but loosely to the shoe of the rider.

The Hot Country rig is far better-looking and more comfortable, to my way of thinking. The saddle-tree is shaped more like our own Western stock saddle of the better kind It is frequently adorned by beautifully carved leather skirts, and these skirts are ornamented by tiger-skin *baquerillos* in combination with carved or pressed leather. The cantle is slightly—yes, rather more than slightly—higher than the saddle-tree of the Cold Country. The horn is long; quite slender of neck and small of head, and there is a more graceful curve to the entire tree.

It is lighter in weight than our Western tree. It is made from the wood of the *guassima* tree. This is very tough and strong and light; from this comes the expression *"aggarrar la guassima,"* to grab hold of the pommel of a saddle. It is easy on the back of an animal. The latigo rings are set quite far back, almost under the stirrup leather so that the cinch when in place comes just about in the center of the lower side of the animal's barrel. It is a single rig and rarely if ever does a self-respecting rider degenerate to using a cropper. In fact with the cinch located where it is, and with the knowledge of saddling, it is not necessary, as a Hot Country tree will remain in place under nearly all normal conditions.

The stirrup straps are broad, double, and with sweat leathers for leg protection. The stirrup is made of wood carefully shaped, and with a hood, more to guard the foot against cactus thorns and brush (which are also copiously supplied with thorns), than to keep the foot from going forward through the stirrup.

The Hot Country does not use the chaparreras. Instead it uses what are known as armas, which are two tanned, pliable cowhides, correctly trimmed and joined by leather lacings end to end in front, at which point is arranged a hole of the right size. Through this hole the horn of the saddle can project when these hides hang down, one on each side of the animal in line with the front legs, long enough to reach well below the bottom of the stirrup housing. With these armas, when they have been pulled back and tied at the waist of the rider in the back by thongs, the *vaquero* dashes through any kind of brush and remains unscathed. That is if he has also a stout buckskin or leather jacket.

His spurs are not cumbersome and are very useful. The spur straps are strong and a double chain goes under the foot better to insure its remaining in place; these chains, however are never tight against the wearer's foot, they hang down from half an inch to as much as an inch at the point of the greatest sag. The rowels are from an inch and an eighth to an inch and a half in diameter with a varying number of points. These are usually blunt; it is very rare indeed to see an animal with a bloody flank or belly. The rowels are set to the spur shank by a strong pin or shaft upon which they revolve freely on the end of the shaft, which is pierced for the purpose. On the outside or right-hand side are suspended two small pear-shaped pieces of steel which jingle pleasantly as the animal moves. They are not, however, only to afford music to the rider and to the animal as you can prove for yourself by trying the following stunt:

Set your animal at a gallop; as you swing down to raise a handkerchief or it might be a silver dollar from the ground, the leg opposite to the side from which you swing down comes up, and the rowel of the spur is hooked against the back of the cantle, which gives you something to hang from. Now, why does the rowel not revolve on its axle and thus break your hold? Because these little jingles have dropped down between the points of the rowel and they jamb against the shank to keep the rowel from turning. So we see that this finishing touch to the work of silver-inlay art which these spurs frequently are, is one of usefulness rather than adornment.

The Hot Country rider has a single narrow strap for a headstall pierced or split, or so arranged that you can slip the ears of the animal through them. This is seldom done. The strap rests on the head of the animal just behind the ears. Under this often very flimsy headstall is a stout halter, loosely fitting with a ring at the back where the halter strap is supposed to be attached. But the Caliente fastens to this his horsehair *cabresto,* which is coiled and which hangs by a leather thong to the pommel of the saddle; when the rider dismounts, this is either tied to some convenient object or the animal is trained to stand when the rope is unslung and the coil laid on the ground.

A *vaquero,* and those others who are much on the trail, will carry two other ropes besides the *cabresto;* one of these is the *reata* (or lasso or *pita,* so-called from *pita, henequen* fiber, from which this rope is made). But it may also be made from plaited rawhide; sometimes, but less often, a twisted rawhide is used. This does not refer to the *reata* used for a pack animal. This rope is coiled and tied to the saddle customarily on the right side just behind the leg of the rider, a little back of the point where the cantle meets the tree. The other rope is the *pial,* which is a short rope worn wrapped about the waist of the *vaquero* and carried only by him. It is used to tie the feet of an animal which has already been roped and thrown.

You may think: "What a lot of space devoted to the description of horse and mule gear. Is that so important?" Yes, indeed! In a country where if you move about at all you must do it either on foot or on the back of an animal, the article upon which you sit, and upon which you live a considerable part of your life and upon the proper adjustment and fit of which depend your travel comfort, is a matter of vast import.

There is another piece of equipment which you will find as useful as the musette bag which we knew to be of infinite convenience in France in 1917-18. This is a morral, which is, in fact, a musette bag, slightly different in shape, made of leather, and it is usually the last thing that goes on the saddle before you mount. This useful article will carry your face towel, your shaving kit, a quart bottle, your lunch, your extra pack of cigarettes, and any number of other requirements for your comfort. Since it hangs in the most handy place possible, from the horn of your saddle, it is an incomparable solace.

If you belong to that section of the human race, you can even fill your quart bottle with water . . . this, however, is considered rather bad form.

Chapter 12

Hunting Peccary

When we were at home for the winter vacations from Sewanee my father employed us for all kinds of different work in and about the mines, to give us practical experience. Those months free from academic study were filled with manifold duties. Nevertheless we managed to have lots of fun between periods of actual work.

I think I was riding the horse known as Calamity on a hunting expedition Conness and I went on with some of our friends during one of these special phases in our years of lessening adolescence. I really ought to have been riding a mule, for the trail was very bad indeed. We were going to Eurique; this was the name of the hacienda and home of our Mexican friends, the Becera family. This family might fittingly be called one of the feudal lords of the Sierras. That is really what certain families in the heart of the deep mountains were, but they lived kindly and benevolent lives in those isolated regions, and did not exploit the peons, as was the erroneous idea usually held by the unknowing.

We crossed the Eurique River many pages ago on our first trip into Batopilas. The Becera hacienda at Eurique village was situated many weary miles farther downstream from where we crossed, and it was a hard day's ride up and over the ridge from our own canyon. We planned to go to the Becera Ranch to hunt deer and peccaries for a few days, and were going from there to spend the week-end in the village of Eurique at the fine old hacienda. There were quite a number of us in our party and I furnished the biggest laugh for the first day's peccary hunt.

They had stationed me at a certain post; no one was near me. I was carrying a Marline Carbine .44, which you probably know has a side ejection. I never knew one to jamb before this particular carbine did that very thing at the precise moment I was trying to have my second shot at a charging peccary. The big old devil broke cover from the tall ototillo grass about a hundred and twenty-five feet from me and he headed directly, determinedly, and very rapidly in my direction. His speed increased when my first shot, fired in a tremendous hurry and a little uphill, succeeded only in irritating his already hot temper by scraping his back. The shell of the carbine did not eject cleanly but stuck in the slot; there I was, so damned scared I forgot all about my six-shooter which was in my belt holster. A pochote tree happened to be very close. I do not remember doing it, but by the time that old boar arrived at the foot of the pochote I was climbing its branches ten feet from the ground. "Now, this is fine," thought I.

My excitement (shall we call it that, in the spirit of charity?) was so intense that I had failed to notice the fact that a pochote tree is entirely profuse in, and totally covered with, spikes accommodated with very sharp points. In my eagerness I had ignored this.

For some fool reason, I still clung to that old Marline carbine and was energetically working on the jambed shell with the point of my knife when I realized all at once for the first time that I was also possessed of a revolver. I knew, even shaking as I was, that I could not miss that old peccary who was valiantly attempting to climb the tree to get at me, and was making circle after circle around it. On his next halt and struggle to clamber up the tree, I leaned over as far as I dared and with the muzzle of my six-shooter not more than four feet from his head, I murdered the wretched beast. It was willful murder and no mistake.

After he was down—and I knew that he was, for a .44 in the head will stop almost anything—I scrambled from the pochote almost as full of spikes as the tree itself. I appeared to be examining the old boar in an off-hand manner when the Kid and Rafael Becera rode on the scene and remarked with ill-suppressed amusement upon my extreme agility. They had enjoyed a perfect view of the whole performance from the adjoining little ridge where they had been posted in case the wild hogs should select that way down into the *arroyo* instead of choosing my ridge. My prowess as a mighty hunter would have been bandied about those two canyons forever and a day if another and yet more absurd performance had not been staged in the afternoon by Rafael Eureuta. This young man was a friend of our host, and had very recently returned to Mexico after graduating from the University of Pennsylvania. He was a few years older than Conness and I. I must have been around eighteen years old.

We did not linger over our lunch, and the four of us were making our way along the slope of the mountain to a place where the dogs were barking furiously. In a steep-sided little arroyo we found, on one side, a cave. Into this cave up an exceedingly precipitous ledge of rock the dogs had chased several big peccaries. They are bad-tempered vicious little beasts. But come to think of it, you really could not blame them for being in a bad humor.

We settled ourselves in the gorge about seventy-five feet from the mouth of the little cave, directly opposite to it. The huntsman climbed the sheer, contracted ledge, placed an armful of dry grass in the mouth of the cave, set fire to it, and waited for about three minutes to see if it would burn well. This was exactly three minutes too long. The peccaries came boiling out of there and the poor devil of a huntsman had to grab the roots of a tree that luckily hung above him. He drew up his feet as high as he could, hanging there by one arm, and struck violently and ineffectually at the hogs with his *machete*. The smoke was stifling him, the flames were singeing the bottom of his pants' legs; to add to his predicament, Eureuta got a bad case of "buck fever" and began pumping his entire magazine of .44's at the peccaries.

The angry animals were thrashing about the dangling feet of the hanging huntsman, and the yells of the poor fellow were enough to wake the seven sleepers, as he implored Eureuta to cease firing. Conness reached for Eureuta and held up the muzzle of his gun when there were yet a shot or two left in the weapon, but Eureuta kept on pumping and pulling the trigger until the missile was empty.

We got three or four of the peccaries. During all this time, they had rolled or scrambled to the bed of the gorge about thirty feet below the place where we were waiting for them. Before we could shoot them for fear of killing the dogs, those wild pigs had disemboweled three. They are ferocious fighters, their tusks are wicked weapons. The biggest one of those we bagged that day could boast of tusks five and a half inches long counting the roots. Just the same I cannot help feeling that they were much better men than we were. We were four, each man armed with a six-shooter, a Bowie knife, and a .44 carbine. We had a bunch of dogs of assorted breeds and they were good hunters, much better than we were. Besides this, we had employed several huntsmen armed with *machetes* and an amount of knowledge not possessed by any of the other members of the party, except maybe Becera, our host.

On the way to the ranch that night, we caught two young peccaries by rolling them in a *serape* as they dashed out from beneath a rock in the bed of the *arroyo.* Two nice little pets we thought they would make. We handled them with greatest gentleness, put them under a big *guacal* or crate. But they plunged about in it all night, going round and round in that four-foot square cage. Next morning we went out to inspect them, and they were as dead as Hector. The Mexicans told us it was practically impossible to tame them. They often did what these two little ones had done, "run round and round their place of confinement until they died of *corraje,* died of rage," as the natives put it.

A young peccary is very good eating if the musk sack is cut out immediately after he is killed. This sack is directly over the middle of the haunch. It is powerfully pungent and will taint the entire carcass in a very short time, making it unfit for food. Broiled peccary is quite palatable, not unlike not too fat domestic pig. Notwithstanding their succulence, I, for one, am willing to do without them as a food supply. That was the last time I ever hunted peccaries, or anything else as a matter of fact. Even deer-hunting gave me very little amusement. When my turn came for vacations, later on when I used to go to the States every two years to rest from work in Batopilas, I greatly preferred other forms of diversion and relaxation, like drinking and eating contests in some comfortable New York restaurant, for instance. Although medical men say that deer and peccary hunting are very good for the liver, did it ever occur to you how few medical men have ever hunted peccaries or deer in the Sierra Madre Mountains?

If my liver ever goes back on me I know it will not be from the good food and wines and company I have enjoyed, but from the roasting heat and pumping heart while climbing steep hillsides, nearly perishing from thirst, fatigue, and heat, trembling to such an extent in consequence that I would have had to put the rifle barrel down the throat of the miserable deer to insure a hit. If I had not been compelled to put in so much time fighting spiders, snakes, centipedes, tarantulas, scorpions and the physically insignificant wood tick and red-bug during a hunting expedition, I might have had time to bag an occasional buck.

Pretty nearly the easiest deer-hunting imaginable was at the big mill where the screens were placed across the aqueduct to catch the leaves and other trash, and to keep the nozzles of the turbines clear. The aqueduct was three miles long, and every now and then a deer would come at night to water there. While reaching his muzzle to drink, he would fall into the ditch and be carried down gradually to the screens; the walls forming the sides of the aqueduct were too high for him to escape. At the screens the deer would be found by the man whose duty it was to clear them of trash at regular intervals; with the assistance of one or two other men and two ropes they would pull the creature from the ditch and take him to the place where there was an arch carrying the aqueduct sprung over an *arroyo.* Here they would release the animal to let him make his way up under the arch to the steep mountain side and liberty. No human being could do otherwise than to free the poor beast when captured under these circumstances.

Deer are every bit as destructive as goats. I have more than once rescued parts of the week's wash from deer as well as from those milk-giving quadrupeds. Deer are raised very easily when they are caught young, but they are regular nuisances at all times. A buck can be dangerous too when he has reached maturity. He is able to strike a wicked blow with his forefoot as well as with his horns. We could always get venison when we wanted it. We would give a hunter some .44 cartridges, loan him a carbine and he would bring a deer to the camp for four or five dollars. That was cheap enough in all conscience, since he had to lug the dead deer on his own back for not less than ten miles and frequently farther still. That beats the labor of hunting him for yourself, that is if you are as poor a hunter as I am.

I almost forgot the best hunt that my brother-in-law Ned Quintard and I ever had. It was away up the canyon in the tall pine forests. In that particular spot there is a lake and a very shallow lake it turned out to be, but we did not know that when we saw it the first time. A lot of ducks were swimming about in the water when Ned and I first glimpsed it. We were both carrying Savage Carbines, .303 I think was the caliber. Since the ducks were very tame, being unused to human beings, we could approach them near enough to shoot a brace in their heads. Our *mozos* had gone on ahead of us en route for camp, and must have been a mile or more on their way. In January at those high altitudes it gets mighty cold. In the late afternoon when the sun is almost gone the air grows chillier still, and those damned ducks were two hundred feet from the shore of the lake. To be obliged to ride two hours longer in wet shoes and the thermometer at freezing was not our idea of pleasure. The bed of the lake might be boggy; to ride into the lake where the ducks were floating would be in order, but the water might be very deep. We were about to mount our animals and abandon the fowl, when along through the pines came a little Indian boy about three feet tall herding a few sheep.

He was not so scared of us but that I could entice him near enough to point out the ducks and to show him at the same time two silver dollars. I managed to convey to him the fact that these shining coins were his if he retrieved the ducks. The little fellow grinned with delight. Stooping down he removed from one small brown foot the remnant of a *guarache* and handed it to me to hold for him while he solemnly waded out, picked up the ducks, and waded just as solemnly back to shore again. The water came up to his knees. By this time Ned was rolling about on the ground emitting peals of rocketing laughter. While I had been intent on the negotiations for the salvage of our game, he had been busily engaged in shooting his Kodak. He had a perfect record of the entire performance and Ned was almost delirious from mirth for he had incontrovertible proof that would afford many a laugh at my expense when we got home, and there would not be one loop-hole for a denial of anything on my part.

The photographs were outrageously ludicrous. He had taken them so that the discrepancy in our sizes was more marked than it actually is between six-feet-three inches and three feet.

That poor little Indian boy handed me in all seriousness that fragment of a rawhide *guarache* . . . his great eyes shone when I gave him the *pesos fuertes,* strong silver dollars. One silver dollar was the price for a fine sheep. His opinion of me for being such a fool *gringo* as to give the price of two fat sheep for two miserable, thin, unpalatable wild ducks the Lord only knows. I do not know what "fool *gringo*" may be in the Tarahumare tongue, but that is what was in his mind I am sure. He dashed off like a streak when he recovered his sandal from me with those two *pesos fuertes* in his grimy little fist, fading out among his sheep in the tall pines.

Ned was responsible for the nickname of "Pud" given me years before this when I was fatter than I was anything else. I mean when that was the only distinctive qualification that I possessed . . . it stuck to me for many years until I grew into the six-feet-three of awkward lankiness which is the only other distinguishing characteristic I have held since.

Chapter 13

Bishops and Football

A visit to Batopilas which caused even more awe and excitement than that of the Governor of the State was the one made by the Bishop of the Diocese, the State of Chihuahua. In its way it was a more notable event, because it meant that children could be baptized by the Bishop and thus go through life with that distinction if with no other. The good people of our camp swept the trail clean and free from stones for a distance of fifteen miles up the valley. There were innumerable arches of green boughs which were not easy to procure although the rains were barely over.

The procession that met the Bishop on the trail consisted of men, women and children, all the population whose duties in connection with the reception in the town itself did not necessitate their remaining at these duties. Forward to meet him and back to escort him fifteen miles each way these devout people tramped; the *Señor Obispo* surely at no other place had received so true and reverential a welcome. The contributions given to him for one good cause or another were rarely equaled from a town of five thousand population. I venture to say that the Bishop had never seen such a well-dressed, cleanly and healthy set of parishioners. That he was tremendously respected there can be no doubt. There is a strong, deeply religious feeling in the Mexican nation which is a characteristic of the people. In our camp many of the men themselves cared but little for attending Mass, some of them did not go at all, but the women were exceedingly devout. They made every effort to instill a belief in the Christ in each of their children.

Their piety was very apparent considering the fact that the old Padre in our town and district was a man of none too churchly habits. He was endowed with an indolence far in excess of that which any of his flock could hope to emulate. This uneradicable belief, deep-seated as it was, in itself demonstrated the undeniability of Jesus Christ. For God knows I have seen devotion and sacrifice made for the Church under conditions where there was, during many years, an absence of contact with priest, religious training, or church service.

Many of the workmen, fathers of a generous number of offspring, whose wives were consumed with anxiety to have them baptized by *El Señor Obispo,* borrowed the needed money from us for new clothes and many other essentials. We were only too glad to lend it to them so that they need have no feeling of humiliation and the dignity of their families could be properly maintained. Marriages were much more numerous during the visit of the Bishop than over a similar period of time ever before. In fact, it became a perfect mania, everybody got married. Couples who had been devoted and faithful husband and wife, who had reared large and self-respecting families under common-law marriages, embraced this opportunity to climax the successful union as husband and wife by having it recorded that they were married by the Bishop. Many lukewarm swains were swept away by the general enthusiasm; others under the effects of this, and the exhilaration derived from other sources, became victims of certain ladies of vast experience, but with heretofore no yen for the married state. Everybody was happy in the general revival of the favorable occasion to express their faith in the Church of Christ and its earthly symbols . . . the bringing up to date, as it were, of these symbols and customs. Certainly it had a beneficial effect upon the community.

I was home on a vacation from Sewanee at this time. I think I was seventeen years old. Some of the young men attended a special Mass on Sunday morning and afterwards saw the baptism of several hundred children . . . the mothers kneeling on the stone floor of the ancient church; the Bishop and his colorful retinue very dignified; the priest delegated to take up the tickets which each mother carried showing that the preliminary details, fees and the like had been complied with; the consternation and misery on the faces of some poor mothers who had come in from the mountains miles away on foot carrying a little child, or maybe two, to be baptized, ignorant that there were any such details and preliminaries to be complied with. We immediately organized a relief corps. There were hurried contributions of all the cash we had with us, we secured more from a convenient store opposite the church. Jesus Hernandez and Rafael Martinez exhibited promptness and efficiency combined with diplomacy, and the situation was relieved. Those poor mothers were lined up and their children baptized after the first and more provident ones had been attended to. The Bishop was elderly and frail. Even though staggering with fatigue he completed the services which consumed the entire morning and part of the afternoon without a let-up.

This demonstration and many others it has been my privilege to witness in my life, and they have filled me with confidence that an atheist, if it be his desire to convert the world to his condition of non-belief in God and His Son Jesus Christ, must be one of two things, maybe both of them, either a person of abysmal ignorance with an immense amount of time on his hands, or just a plain damned fool. Maybe the two states mentioned are synonymous after all.

The Bishop came to Batopilas and left, and the whole affair was an excellent thing. Those who had gone into debt had to practice self-denial in the luxury of the sums of money they had been devoting to their weekly games of chance and to liquor, or cockfighting and the like.

The ladies in the camp of Batopilas are responsible for the church there not being ruins. For years it had been lacking half a roof, but this was remedied. A large proportion of the funds came from the winnings of the weekly games of poker and other card games at the Hacienda San Miguel. There was no fun in winning money from one's friends unless those winnings could be spent on their amusement. The chief amusement was getting tight and raising Hell; so we decided that all the winnings over a period of a year should be put in a fund for the purpose of assisting the ladies of the camp in the new roof campaign. The new roof was a good one and it did not leak. I believe there was not a thing improper in the way part of the money was obtained. I was one of the poorest poker players in the outfit and I felt very proud that my contributions were of considerable size, therefore.

Bishops were no rarity with us since we had been attending the University of the South.

While I am on this subject I want to describe that seat of learning at that mountainous place. It is located on the Cumberland Plateau, and the name of the small village of Sewanee is so closely allied with the University of the South that the names are interchangeable. Before the Civil War this educational institution was established by leading Southern gentlemen and it was heavily endowed.

We three Shepherd boys went to Sewanee because it had become a place of importance in our lives when my sister May married Edward Alexander Quintard, an engineer and chemist who was a graduate of the University. Ned was the son of Charles Todd Quintard, Bishop of Tennessee. After the Civil War, the funds were absolutely depleted, and no more were to be secured from the original sources. This indefatigable Bishop took up the burden and revived the corpse of what had been a richly endowed Southern university. He raised a quantity of money in England where he was very popular. The University was located near the little town of Sewanee because of the salubrity of that climate and the large grants of land donated for that purpose.

When we went there in 1891 there was a preparatory department connected with the University; it was a military school of high standing. You paid for your demerits by walking extras in full uniform on all holidays . . . far too many of my Saturdays and other holidays were thus spent. In 1891 Sewanee's first football team came into existence through the fact that Alex and Elwood Wilson, who were Lawrenceville men, Elwood's brother Buck Wilson, the artist, Jim Wilder and myself had seen the game played; we had indeed played it before our addition to the roster at Sewanee. No one else there had done so. Nevertheless in the fall we trained and worked to such advantage that we had two games with Vanderbilt and were beaten both times.

But we came back at them in 1892. We took Vandy's scalp twice that year. Out of eight games played altogether we lost one to Virginia. That aggregation of "murderers" outweighed us by about twenty pounds to a man. I was sixteen years old and weighed one hundred and seventy pounds, I played right guard. Penton, my opponent on the Virginia team, weighed two hundred and ten pounds and he was twenty-five years old. We played on a field called Island Park in Richmond. From the center of the field to one goal post was a heavy downgrade, the other half was practically level. We held them to 0-0 the first half; we had a very fast light team, and they could not catch us. But when they got us working uphill they absolutely sat on us and held us down. Then they would knock down a few of the line men by well-delivered punches to the jaw, eyes, or nose, push their backs over us for enough touchdowns to run up thirty points in forty-five minutes. When we staggered into the Jefferson Hotel after that memorable game, I said to Jim Wilder our center: "Gosh, Jim, what a face you have got!"

Jim tried to grin and remarked from the corner of swollen lips: "There's a full-length mirror. Have a look in it. That very round, big, yellow and black pumpkin you see in it is you.

That was the year when flying "V's" and revolving wedges were popular, they surely were hard on light teams at best, but when you went against a much heavier team you certainly paid dearly for your sins.

The University of the South when we were there had an academic department, an important theological department, a medical department and one of law. The University was under the direction of the Southern Bishops of the Episcopal Church. Commencements were in June and were colorful affairs. Sewanee was a summer resort; the students were notoriously good dancers and held many Germans, dances, and hops. The beautiful girls in their summer frocks when assisted by the Bishops, the embryo Bishops, and the laymen who possessed gorgeous hoods denoting various grades of intellectual and spiritual excellence, made the old wooded college grounds and the village streets have the appearance of a flower garden among immense oak trees.

It was my good fortune when we were at Sewanee to know and to hear many Bishops deliver sermons—big men, able men. Bishop Quintard, Bishop Dudley of Kentucky, Nelson of Georgia, Sessums of Louisiana, Bishops Beckwith and Kinsolving. The Vice-Chancellor and Chaplain was Father Tom Gailor, who became Bishop Coadjutor of Tennessee in 1893. There was more than one man in the theological department who became Bishop after graduating. Manning of New York, Craik Morris of Louisiana. . . . Theologues, good pals of mine, were Cary Beckwith who for more than thirty years was Rector of St. Phillips Parish in Charleston, South Carolina, Wilkie Memminger of Atlanta, and many more eminent men in the Church. I do not know whether it may have been their early association with me that later inspired them to rise to such dignified heights or not. However, there is more than an even chance that the desire to be as different as possible from the horrible example set them by my worldly self and others may have been involved in their striving for and reaching the more worthy plane to which they have risen.

While I was at Sewanee, supper time maybe at Bishop Quintard's hospitable board, I have frequently listened with devoted and respectful attention in rapt concentration to one of Bishop Dudley's inimitable stories, when he little realized that I was one of those responsible for the neat whitewashed plank fences in the village being all painted up with "SMOKE T. U. DUDLEY'S CIGARS. GUARANTEED BY THE CHURCH."

I recall sitting on the Bishop's front porch one afternoon during Commencement week joining in on the speculation, when my opinion was asked, as to who could possibly have stolen the skeleton from the medical department and hung it on a wire stretched from the highest pinnacle on Walsh Hall to the top of Breslin Tower. The access to the tower and Walsh Hall roof were so blocked that not until some time after Commencement Procession from Convocation Hall to the Chapel for the Commencement Service had passed beneath the skeleton, could the janitor and his many assistants obtain release of the bony relic, nor remove the two large sheets suspended from its feet on which were boldly painted such informative lines as "GO TO PIGGOTIT'S FOR NICE FRESH MEAT." Doctor Piggott was the Dean of the Medical Faculty.

For fear lest the deserving group who accomplished this really difficult feat, perilous in more ways than one, might never be recorded in print, I now after all these years shall give their names: Ned Nelson, Alexander Shepherd, Charlie Van Duser, Arthur Rutledge Young, and John Conness Shepherd assisted by his brother Grant. Thinking it over, I believe that Dump Morris also officiated, for in the words of Darby the Blast "he was in all them things them times."

Chapter 14

Modesty and Other Mexican Peculiarities

I wish it was forty years ago. I would take you into the old Gem Saloon in El Paso, Texas. It was a straightforward bar and gambling establishment with a sort of music hall at the back. There were boxes all around the balcony with curtains. The first time the Kid and I went there we must have been fifteen and seventeen years old respectively. But we were very large for our ages and we ordered our drinks at the bar with a sufficiently sophisticated air to convince the bartender that we were entitled to them.

We really had gone to the Gem to see the music-hall show, but we absolutely had to take one drink and to look over the roulette and faro layouts. That made us a little late in going into the music hall. We walked down the center aisle and an inebriated fool in one of the boxes tried to brain us (or maybe someone else, and his aim was bad), by hurling a couple of beer bottles at us. Unfortunately for him, he missed us and hit the back of the seat in which was quietly reposing a big cowpuncher. This worthy made a few comments best not repeated here as to the ancestry of city dwellers and railroad men in particular, and went directly to the box which the hurler of beer bottles was occupying. From what we heard I judge he came off victorious . . . the offender landed at the foot of the stairs, and shortly afterwards the puncher waved to us as he sat with a quart bottle in one hand and a music-hall girl on each knee.

Those old cowpunchers as a rule were good-humored *hombres,* and carried their poison well. Every now and then when they grew excited they would shoot out a light maybe. But the Lord knows that is a dignified and harmless enough form of amusement if the oil does not ignite and burn the dump down. If you are a fairly good shot you cannot miss a light, even an electric incandescent shows up splendidly over your sight. The *Patron Grande* broke us of this agreeable target practice of shooting at electric lights by charging each and every one of the lights broken at a very high figure to our accounts. We got so really that an electric light stood not a single chance with us.

The natives thought them almost magical when my father first had electricity installed in Batopilas. The first evening the lights were used, *El Patron Grande* was in the *asogueria,* the amalgam room literally, but it was much more than that, because it was there that the retorting of amalgam, the refining of the silver, and the pouring into bullion took place.

Never in their lives had the natives seen or pictured to themselves an electric light. One of the men was told to go out and touch a button to light up the place. Any other person might do what this employee did down in the reduction room that first night the electric light plant was put into commission. He got a box of matches and tried to screw off the glass bulb so he could apply a match to the wire. When the glass bulb refused to unscrew he found that it would unscrew from its socket. He did this, and took the bulb over to the work bench, lifted a Stillson wrench—he knew all about Stillsons—and put the bulb into the vise to hold it while he used the Stillson. There was a pop and a crack. He sprang back from this mysterious thing, fell over a wheelbarrow that was directly behind him, and broke his arm! For a long time afterwards he was known as *"luz electrica,"* electric light.

The electric lights were a great relief from the former coal-oil methods of illumination throughout the big plant and all the other places on the outside of the mines. They had to be clearly lighted since work went on day and night. The coal-oil lamps, and the lanterns of all sorts and descriptions entailed an infinite amount of time and trouble.

We had large locomotive headlights placed at strategic points. A line of electric lights was run into the Porfirio Diaz Tunnel. They appeared so beautiful to the natives that many women and children used to come there solely to look into the tunnel to see *"las luces tan lindas,"* the so-beautiful lights. The throng of admirers grew to be a nuisance and on a certain evening the superintendent said nothing about explosions when the time came to fire a round of dynamite shots inside the tunnel. When these fulminated with a great detonation in the face of the tunnel, the blast of air out at the entrance was so tremendous that the crowd of Mexican ladies had a bad time of it with their voluminous skirts. It was thought to be the height of immodesty to show even so much as your ankle. The women did not wear bloomers in those days. Therefore, the devastation suffered by their modest sensibilities was sufficient to insure their never returning to the mouth of the tunnel again to see the wonderful electric lights. The superintendent did not fail to receive his share of abuse from these outraged females as they took their departure sputtering like setting hens in high dudgeon.

The extreme modesty of the Mexican women was never more apparent than when they were bathing in the river. It was not easy to watch them at this. They carry an ordinary sheet, squat down with the middle of the sheet on top of their heads, spread it out over them, remove all of their clothing, put on an ankle-length cotton slip (all of this is done underneath the tent made from the sheet), then walking down into the river in this squatting position, with the bottom of the cotton slip dragging on the ground about their shuffling feet, they perform their ablutions. No one ever saw so much as the points of one of their toes!

When water is available the people are very cleanly. If their homes are by or near a river of sufficient size they are in the water every chance they can get. The success of the soap factories in Mexico at that time attests to this. The soap came in bars three inches wide, four long, and an inch and a half thick; it was the color of the average home-melted and prepared beeswax and similar in appearance. The laundry women gauged the size of the laundry by demanding, *"Tantos jabones?"* How many pieces of soap?

Some of the women can swim quite well, but with no stroke that you have ever seen. It is done as differently as possible from the way a man does it, because to be regarded mannish in any way whatsoever was very bad form. They do it the way we kids used to call dog fashion. It is the way most kids in my day learned to keep afloat, but about every second stroke they would hump up their middle sections like a porpoise. Since they are not built on porpoise lines, especially as they advance in years, needless to say they are not as graceful as that aquatic animal.

I used to be bewildered by the way they struck the water holding their arms bent with their hands cupped in such a way as to make a sort of booming sound. They did this a great deal. I heard that the custom originated years before along rivers where there were many bends and bush-grown banks in order to warn men, who might also be contemplating a bath, to keep away. Mixed bathing, of course, was not a thing to be thought of for a moment.

When a woman finished washing her clothes in the stream, she would spread them out in the hot sun over a smooth round boulder to dry, then she invariably took her own bath. Wherever this was possible they put in all the time they could spare from their other duties splashing about in the water.

Commencing long before daylight on *El Dia de San Juan,* St. John the Baptist's Day, June 24, the river in our valley—and in all the others where people were living on the banks of the river—was full of men and women bathing . . . but not together. The booming sound I have spoken of made by the women's beating the water would awaken you even though you slept some distance away.

Among the men there were really some very skillful swimmers. Before we had built the bridge to connect the two banks of the Batopilas River, they would give exciting exhibitions of swimming this stream at high water during the rains, which may have been accompanied by a cloudburst up in the mountains. It would come roaring down the canyon piled up twenty feet and more above low-water mark, running like a mill race, very fierce and muddy. There was but one way to reach the other bank before we had built the bridge, which was to enter the river at a favorable spot a long way above the place where you had planned to land on the opposite side, else you would be obliged to walk there, having been swept a quarter of a mile or more down stream.

At its widest the river was rarely more than five hundred feet across, but to attempt to swim it directly would only serve to exhaust your strength with probable disaster. You had to work your way across very cautiously, gaining distance as you were carried down stream. I have seen a man swim the Batopilas during the rainy season with two dozen eggs on his head tied in a bundle, which was held fast by a napkin under his chin, and not break a single one. On some of the streams in the mountains it was customary to use a piece of chilicote wood which is very light indeed, so light, in fact, that a piece of this wood two and a half feet long and only six inches wide will keep you afloat. A hole was bored near one end on the broadest and flattest side and in this a peg was set, this was thick and long enough to grasp comfortably. You held on to this peg with one hand, the chilicote beneath you, and with the other hand and your legs you propelled yourself along. The current would be so swift that boulders of several tons in weight would be rolled under the surface in these unusually high-water periods. When the flood would subside familiar landmarks would have disappeared only to be encountered again hundreds of yards down stream.

A *creciente fuerte,* a strong rise on the Batopilas River, was generally the cause of headaches and extra work, despite the fact that every effort had been expended to make these high waters manageable. The rises came down without warning quickly, and fortunately went past just about as rapidly. But in the short time it lasted, the formidable volume of water coming down the narrow canyon and the precipitous mountain sides could do much damage. It swept everything along with it that was not buried deep in the ground. It meant much extra labor and expeditious work at the hundred-stamp mill—Hacienda San Antonio. What a time it used to give poor old Legs, which was Alex's nickname. He was made manager of that important branch of the business, beginning his work after college. I recall one flood when for fifty or more hours he wrestled with the consequences of one such cloudburst. That meant fifty hours without sleep, notes and messages coming from every quarter, the general trend of which were "When do we get electric current again?" with variations.

Sometimes if the cloudburst was immediately above our unhappy heads, the earth from the mountain side would come down and literally fill up the "ditch," the aqueduct. Then the call would come to all hands, and we would descend upon that mud-filled masonry ditch with several hundred helpers, men with bars and shovels, and we would simply clean it out. It was our custom when we started anything to finish it in the shortest time possible and to do this thoroughly. When you are producing a hundred thousand ounces of silver a month, time means money, particularly if you are paying fifteen per cent interest on overdrafts at the bank. Therefore, we often were at the job for twenty-four or thirty-six hours, working in water and keeping full of energy and joyful spirits by copious drafts of black coffee and *mescal.* You would be surprised what a devil of a lot more dirt you can shovel when up to your belly in water if you are getting a good pull at the bottle every hour and a half.

The river itself cannot cut deeper, for it is on bed-rock. Or rather bed-rock is only a few feet below a covering of boulders, gravel and sand. The banks cannot be cut because they are formed by the same bed-rock. The only wide places are used for the streets; the houses and mills were above high-water mark or else they had been protected by retaining walls several feet thick and high enough to be safe above the danger line.

In a country which has a rainy season and where the crops must be planted before the rains begin so that they may get the benefit of every drop of moisture that falls, where the only green vegetables come during that season, every little piece of the river banks where there is a tiny bit of land above the chance of high water, has a brush fence around it and is planted in corn for roasting ears, beans, tomatoes, calabazas, squashes, and usually some melons. How the people did enjoy that change of diet! Some of the older workmen at Batopilas always took a week off to get their stuff planted. When it was ready to be eaten they would move to the *siembra* with their families, and they would camp at their garden for a week or two. Because very little land was available, they sometimes planted their *siembras* as far as ten miles down the river wherever they could get hold of a bit of earth free from other ownership.

During the rainy season the goats' milk, and on the ranches the cows' milk too, is made into fresh cheese every day. *Panela* is a fresh cheese cake six inches or so across and a couple of inches thick. Everybody was happy to be able to get this fresh cheese. With a piece of *panocha, panela* forms a delectable dish, a bite of *panela* and a bite of *panocha.* When we were children we thought it far ahead of ice cream, the latter not being available.

Goats were greatly respected animals. Except where we put in irrigation in later years at Batopilas, for nine months of the year there was not a sprig of anything green. But directly after the rains started the goats began to give fresh milk in abundance, and they continued to give it, though in lessening quantities all during the balance of the year. First they would eat the leaves and little twigs from the bushes and brush; then the larger branches as far as they could reach; finally God only knows what they could find to eat but they kept on giving milk. The herds were guarded by a very small child and some little cur dogs. The dogs were put with the goats when they were puppies. After they grew up you could not make them happy anywhere else, rain or shine. They would raise Cain at night if anything approached a flock of their goats, and they would fight to the death to protect their charges.

Chapter 15

Two-Legged and Four-Legged Playmates

When Conness and I finished college, Alex had already been at work for at least a year in charge of the Big Mill and Power Plant at Hacienda San Antonio. My first steady job was on the night shift at San Antonio with Alex. Then I was put at San Miguel Mine as Assistant Superintendent for six months, after that I was given charge of the mine. The Kid had his first go at Todos Santos Mine. Then he and our first cousin, Frank Merchant, took over the Porfirio Diaz Tunnel on contract while at the same time they took charge of the Bullion train and ran that. Thus they could acquire change of scene and have a vacation—if you can call riding mule-back three hundred and seventy-five miles, and driving three hundred miles in a Concord stage in sixteen days, a rest. Some persons might call it hard work.

Alex slept at the Hacienda San Antonio while he was in charge of the Big Mill. Conness lived at Todos Santos. He had his cooking and sleeping quarters there, very clean and neat and perfectly comfortable but simple as to furnishings.

At San Miguel Mine I had my home. At the immediate entrance to the tunnel, there was a small two-story building. The lower floor of this, at the level of the tunnel and the track, was used as an office and room where the high-grade ores were stored each night. The second floor I used for my quarters. It was on the level of the road to Santo Domingo Mine, and the building held up that part of the mountain side. I had a plain clean bedroom, on the walls of which hung a gem from the clever pen of Louis M., a comically realistic caricature of old Kemper in the act of braining his daughter with a claw hammer.

This room was separated in two parts by a canvas screen, thus making a dining-room for me where the *mozo,* who walked the mile to the Hacienda San Miguel three times a day carrying my dinner pail, laid out my meals. If they had grown too cold and unpalatable, he would heat them up a bit at the forge in the blacksmith shop directly below. Sometimes I made a change both for the good of my stomach and for my spiritual being. A local woman would provide my meals. She was the wife of one of the miners who ran a little *fonda* where she fed some of the unmarried men.

As a rule we held pretty steadily to some special job that we knew best, yet at times for one reason or another—absence of some one of us, maybe—we had to take over the management of one of the other mines for a period of time. So it was that I had work at various times in each and every mine operated by the company, including the Porfirio Diaz Tunnel. It gave me a fine opportunity to study and better to understand the vein groups and the variety of ores, the difference in these ores; although it may seem strange, in the San Miguel group (all worked through the San Miguel Tunnel) the ores of Veta Grande, Mesquite, Carmen, and San Antonio were very dissimilar in appearance. This was because of the divergence of content and crystallization of the various minerals making up the ores. The ores in the Porfirio Diaz Tunnel group were also distinctive in appearance. To the initiated this variation was very obvious; we could pick up a piece of ore and tell from its appearance which vein it came from, and sometimes these unlikenesses were such that we could even tell from what level on a certain vein that particular piece of rock had come from.

Of course, long before this, the mails were coming in twice a week, and the telegraph came to Batopilas. This made it possible to communicate with the outside world quickly, and we could enjoy this useful voiceless method of contact for sending greetings now and then upon some anniversary occasion to a member of the family who happened to be in the States on vacation or business, or to friends. We could employ the telegraph for hurry-up orders to replace broken parts of machinery and other business matters. We could get all the news bulletins rapidly and promptly when the Spanish-American War came along, much to our delight.

We three sons of my father were burningly eager to go. We were men by that time, although but recently having arrived at that estate. We could speak Spanish like natives, we could ride anything that had four legs, we could shoot accurately, and hardships were nothing to give us any care.

But we *were* needed at the mines at Batopilas.

However, our father, who was a personal friend of General Miles, wrote to that gentleman promptly, requesting that he should tell him frankly if there was any real need for us; if he should send us to enlist would we be put in some outfit that was actually going to get into action in Cuba or any other place where our qualifications and training would make us of value to our country? "They are very useful to me," he explained to General Miles, "and it would cause me much inconvenience to do without them. If they are only going to enter some camp to do the manual of arms, I think there are probably plenty of others who would do that quite as well; therefore, they would benefit neither their country nor themselves."

The General replied that there was no chance for a fraction of the men already there to get into action, and that my father would do better to keep us at work in Batopilas. So that is why we were not actively engaged in the Spanish-American War. I believed that the Rough Riders would have been our meat. There was much friendly, though at times strained, fun-making between ourselves and the Spaniards in the town of Batopilas. We were perfectly good friends, and when the news of San Juan Hill, the destruction of Cerveras fleet and Manila Bay came to us, the Spaniards would receive the information from some friends of theirs in Chihuahua at least twelve hours before we did. It would always be the news of a decisive Spanish victory. Immediately a big banquet would be served and they would have a grand time, with speeches and patriotic songs that would absolutely roast the unworthy *Norte Americano.* We would keep quiet till the news of the true state of affairs would come seeping through. Then in our turn, we would celebrate. How I used to regret that we had not been in it!

Gachupin is the term applied by the Mexicans to a Spaniard living in Mexico. He was not particularly popular with the natives. During the days of the War there was more than one disagreement between the Mexicans and the *Gachupines.*

How truly my father understood his countrymen and their politics is witnessed by his remarks that even with the example of incompetence, unpreparedness, and inefficiency afforded us by the Spanish-American War, we would not benefit by the lesson, but when the next war came, would be found in identically the same predicament. That he was correct I personally can testify. I served in France with a regular outfit, the 2nd Division was made up of the Regular Army and the Marines. It was a damned fine outfit. We went through our part of the war with the most inefficient automatic rifle, which was the French Chauchaut. I am alive today, if that is anything to brag about, because I could shoot a hand gun fast and could shoot it accurately. . . .

But that has nothing to do with the old loyal friends we held in high esteem in the towns of Batopilas, Chihuahua, Mazatlan. Manuel Leony, a hundred and thirty-five pounds of courage, wit, humor, loyalty, and ability. The half-brother Angel, that really superb character. Andrez, the daring, long since gone to his fathers. Jesus, Rafael, Anacleto, all the rest of that galaxy of men, whose virtues were far in excess of their faults. My brothers and I live over those experiences, glad and grievous, which we shared in common, work and play. . . .

I can see you now, my friends, as so often in life I have seen you stripped to the waist in a hot, smoking working; the sweat pouring from us as we suffered with fearful headaches from the powder fumes, kidding the gangs along. Getting out the high-grade ores, cleaning out the drifts or winzes or rise so that the next shift could go ahead. Fast workers? People who use that expression in connection with trivial things know little or nothing of what it truly signifies.

On Saturday night I see you in old Don Luis Muzy's, leaning on the counter drinking the usual toast, *"Salud y pesetas!"* or maybe later that same evening, as we made our leisurely way towards the plaza to listen to the band concert at eight o'clock, stopping in Mendoza's to tease Don Benito, that fine young Spanish gentleman. Don Benito, I say, who about midnight would have reached that stage of alcoholic stimulation when he would always insist on trying to ride the black stallion my brother delighted in. This stallion when he was in a mean humor could buck high enough for his rider to see the roofs of the one-story buildings. We would chat on the way up the street with our other friends sitting on the sidewalks in front of their homes in the sultry summer . . . the older women rallying us about some escapade or other, while the younger ones (damned sweet-looking girls) modestly exclaimed, *"Ah, Mama, no digas eso,"* ah, Mama, do not say that! The young ones while strolling round the plaza in one direction as we sauntered in the opposite, would make mischievous eyes at us, or would not, as the case and the nature of that particular daughter of Eve dictated.

Maybe on that same night, or on some other, with permission from *the Jefe Politico,* we would engage the band after the concert was over, to serenade the sundry homes of the *novias* of the men of our party. By this time we were on horse-back doing stunts for the amusement of the crowd which would be following us about.

As you know, the town was built on the gradual slope of the mountain which at this point was less steep. The three streets in the center of the town were connected by other cobblestone streets which themselves were so very slanting that they might as well be called ramps. Precisely in the middle for a distance of a block the main street was quite wide and on this street the church was built. In order to meet the requirements of the terrain the front entrance of the church was six or eight feet above the street level, and steps went up from each side to a platform with a retaining wall facing the street. There was room on this stone-paved platform for two horses to stand comfortably. On the special evening I have in mind my brother from one side and I from the other, while standing in our respective saddles, rode up these steps. When we reached the platform we turned our horses to face the street. The band came close. The player of the bass drum leaned with his shoulders against the front of the wall resting his weary feet and showing the effects of his many potations.

"Jump him off, *Patroncito,* jump him off!" yelled someone in the crowd. This the Kid did. It would have turned out to be only an ordinary show had it not been for the fact that although the player of the bass drum saved himself from being jumped on, he was obliged to desert his beloved drum. The hind feet of Conness' overmettled stallion went through it. Of course, I know that the horse did not actually turn somersaults, because the Kid stayed on him, but for three blocks I never saw anything in my life quite so fast and furious. Fragments of the drum were scattered far and wide. The horse with his rider came up against a high stone wall at the end of the street.

After this exhibition, the *Jefe de Policia,* requested us to go home. The row caused by the admiring throng of half tipsy followers at the hour of one in the morning was more than the *Jefe Politico* could put up with: messengers were coming to him from all quarters of the place with urgent entreaties to "stop the riot."

Poor dyspeptic Don Luis, one of the successors of our old friend Don Jesus Hernandez, was far more considerate to us than we deserved, when I look back on those nights of *serenatas.* We paid but a small sum of money for permission to hold a *serenata.* The fines collected, generally, for disorders were very few, therefore it was of no especial financial benefit to the town treasury. But how the people did enjoy it all! How the *señoritas* peeped out through the slats of the shutters with which the windows were protected, and from inside iron bars . . . with what an innocent expression of their dark, sparkling eyes they would say to you when next you met, "I understand that you gave a *serenata* last Saturday or Sunday." . . .

Those were magnificent horses, sweet saddle animals that came from Sinaloa. The best of them were from the town of Ahome down near the mouth of the Rio Fuerte. There an Italian, Secannini, of more than usual intelligence and ability, had a big ranch. He was fond of horses and the breeding of them. He imported the finest Morgan stallion money could buy at his price, several thousand dollars. By carefully selecting native mares which showed the most marked signs of the Arab blood that had come to Mexico during the years when the Spaniards brought in good stock, he developed a strain best suited to the climate and conditions with which they had to contend. They were exactly the correct size for the saddle, of splendid conformation, strong, hardy, quick as a cat, and intelligent to the last degree, with gentle dispositions. They were scarcely ever broken until they were four years old, consequently they were long-lived and they never knew the feel of a bit until they were entirely saddle-broke and docile.

A hair-rope halter snug-fitting about the nose was used by the "buster." After this had been done, the horses were turned over to the *arrendador,* whose duty it was to bridlewise the animal; this man settled him to his gaits and habits of good behavior. It was a finishing school and a fashionable one. When the horse had completed his education there you had the opportunity to purchase something that was, in truth, worth buying; something to ride for pleasure and business; something that had been selected as good saddle material from the herd, and set aside, watched from earliest colthood; full of life and ginger. Something in the way of horse-flesh that could just about talk and had nearly twice as much sense as the average *homo sapiens.*

They ran in color from a flea-bitten gray to a beautiful golden sorrel, the latter usually had a partially blazed face.

In the early morning hours of a Monday as about five of us were riding home from a *fiesta* or a *serenata,* I forget which, we stopped for one last one, that always fatal last one, at a store and bar (all the stores sold liquor in any size package, the size of the package being limited only by the capacity of the customer to carry it). This store was of small dimensions; in fact, when the Kid and I had ridden inside and had made our horses put their front feet on the counter, there was no room left except for a foot customer or two. The ceiling was low and our heads, covered as they were by our sombreros, were bent to escape a bump. We drank our last one, our horses removed their feet from the bar, and we backed outside to commence doing stunts.

I owned a beautiful sorrel horse that was much more intelligent than I was. I loved to make him stand on his hind legs and walk about prancingly. But this time I was not timing right, when he reached the perpendicular I failed to loosen the rein and he fell over backwards. Being filled with the fatal last one, I was not as alert as I ought to have been and the side of my head came into contact with the cobblestones with which the little street was paved. Next thing I knew I was in my cot at the Porfirio Diaz Tunnel and my head was all wrapped up in bandages. I got busy at once making up a yarn about having hit my head on the roof of the tunnel while riding out on an ore car. As soon as I could manage it, I staggered out to the corral to see if El Oro was injured. He came trotting to the bars at my whistle, whinnying a welcome to prove to his repentant owner that he harbored no hard feelings.

There was nothing "The Golden One" loved more than to dance down the street when the band played a tune that suited him. You did not have to do or to say a thing to guide him. He followed it first to one side of the street and then to the other, keeping it up until the music stopped, all in perfect time with the rhythm. He had the grandest manners for social events! At a *baile* when it was part of a round-up or some such affair where they danced *al fresco* under a big temporary brush roof, you could ride him beneath the roof, drop the lines on the pommel of the saddle, and El Oro would move about the ground where the dancing was going on in time to the music, in and out among the other dancers, without interfering with a soul. He was the great-great-grandson of the Morgan aristocrat I told you about, the one that Secannini brought from the States; his innate gentle breeding and blood showed most plainly when he was in the presence of ladies.

Once I raised together a black kitten, a spaniel puppy, and a game rooster; they were as friendly and as playful with one another as any three animals could be. When meal times came, old Antonio would put their three plates close together and they would contentedly go to work, but woe betide the cat or the dog if either of them attempted to stick his nose in the plate of the rooster! That one would fly at the intruder and administer on the nose of the offender a crack that often brought forth yowls of pain.

El Oro was a great pal of Moods, the cocker spaniel. They would talk with one another in friendly converse. Moods would sit down in front of El Oro and look up at him head on one side, the horse would stretch forth his golden neck until their noses touched. They would stay in that position fooling for minutes at a time. Moods would lick El Oro on his nose; El Oro would let out a quiet snort.

Moods would turn away his head as though in remonstrance against the rudeness of having received a sneeze full in the face, and they would do it all over again and again and never move from the original postures. Moods was a funny little dog. If he transgressed in any way and you spoke to him in a low reproving tone of voice, he would creep off under your cot and there he would remain until you coaxed him out with melting tones telling him that you were sorry you had hurt his feelings. Poor little devil!

He used to beg me to take him down to the river to throw sticks for him to retrieve, and he would frisk himself into contortions of delight when you said, "All right, let's get some sticks!"

One of the most interesting characters, in his own particular way, who lived in the canyon was Brad. Brad was an engineer, and a good one, in charge of the only other property being operated in the Camp of Batopilas which was not owned by our company. It was a small development. Brad was a good scout, only he was a bit erratic, doing none too orthodox things every now and then when he had been imbibing freely.

Brad lived at the Santo Domingo Mine, a quarter of a mile above San Miguel Mine on the same side of the river. The road was benched into the side of the mountain and was made possible, as a road, by a retaining wall built up about twenty feet, against which rested the sloping, shingled roofs of some miners' houses.

He was on his way home in the early morning hours. We had all been to some dance or other and were making it back to our jobs in time for the Monday morning day shift, hoping to get an hour or two of sleep before we went to work. When we got as far as San Miguel Mine, Jesus Hernandez, who drank very little, and who was my timekeeper, thought he ought to accompany Brad the rest of the short ride to Santo Domingo Mine, because Brad was a great fellow for going to sleep on his mule or horse when in that state of somnolence, and had fallen off two or three times before. So I said good night to them and went to sleep in short order.

An hour later I was awakened by guffaws from Jesus Hernandez and the night watchman. To my rather peevish inquiry as to why this early morning mirth, Jesus informed me that Brad had gone fast asleep riding along, that his mule had stumbled and that Brad had gone from off his back onto the shingled roof of one of the miners' houses below; through this flimsy affair he fell into the middle of the kitchen, where three women were busy over their breakfast preparations.

This violent awakening, his befuddled condition of mind, combined with his being all tangled up in a pile of wood which had come down with him, caused Brad to think that he was being set upon and attacked. Jesus Hernandez had scrambled down the wall to the rescue, he found Brad sitting in the middle of the room waving his automatic (the first of its kind to reach camp), vowing vengeance for the insult offered him and challenging the horrified women to mortal combat.

Amidst the screams of the women, the squalls of the babies, the indignant protests of the men who were at a loss to know how their patron had got into their kitchen, Jesus called attention to the remains of the roof, and he did his best to pacify and quiet everyone because a crowd was collecting.

At last they got Brad on his feet and started homewards. Jesus said that all the way home, Brad was maintaining that he would be damned if he would pay for a new roof, that he had nothing to do with putting it there. "By God, if it had not been there I never would have fallen through it. I have a perfect right to fall off my condemned mule if I want to.

By the way, where is this mule? Because if I was down there with those fool cooks, then my mule must have been down there too," and so forth.

All Brad's friends would remind him of this happening every so often by sending him a shingle all wrapped up in a very elaborate package with "Many happy returns" written on it with flourishes.

Notwithstanding all these gay times I'm writing about, don't think for an instant but that life went on at the mines on the regular twelve-hours-a-day working schedule . . . if you were lucky and did not have to stretch them out to eighteen and even at times to twenty-four. . . .

Chapter 16

The Indispensable Mule

You could buy a saddle-gaited mule now and then in Mexico for one hundred and fifty to three hundred dollars that would make many of the show horses I have seen look mighty dim as far as gaits go. I once owned a saddle-gaited mule that I could never force into a trot even when she was very tired. She would take any horse along at a hard gallop for miles. You could forget all about your reins till you were ready to stop her, and you could do that by your voice alone, if you wanted to. She had a running walk that would carry you for thirty or forty miles as comfortably as a Pullman car . . . much more comfortably than an automobile, for you did not have to think for yourself, nor to be watching out for the other damned fool.

On those horse and mule ranches they watch the young colts with solicitude and choose for saddle animals those that are naturally gaited and also possess other favorable requirements. When the wobble leaves the legs of a young colt, and he is still out on the range, you start him going faster than a walk and if he is naturally gaited he will take to that gait rather than to a trot. If you have competent *vaqueros* you will know very accurately how many of your colts will be available for saddle material.

Our company had two main ranches, El Alamo at Carichic where were kept the stage mules and a few others; and across the ridge between the Batopilas canyon and the valley of the San Miguel River, where there was a good-sized area of foothill with some almost level land, was located El Rodeo where we kept the several hundred pack-mules. This area was formed by a condition resulting from the junction of the three main rivers of the district: the Batopilas, the San Miguel joining it from the east; the Eurique joining these two. They combined, making one river called the San Miguel. Later on in its course, it was joined by the Rio de Oro or Rio de Chinipas, and was known as El Rio Fuerte.

For long-distance riding I personally like an easy trot, but the ideal combination is to have two animals, one of them gaited and the other with an easy trot, and to have them well trained so that they will follow one another keeping together on the trail. Then when you are plum fed up on trot and the old trot-absorption springs are showing signs of re-crystallization you can climb down from your saddle, put it on the pacer and go on for another twenty-five miles all freshened up.

Wherever you have to use mules in the day's work, of course, you must have corrals. Therefore, there were corrals at the two main haciendas. At Hacienda San Miguel were kept some saddle animals personally owned by employees and some the property of the company, also the pack-train of mules used for local purposes. At that place at the end of each month were assembled, shod, and fitted with pack-saddles the mules brought in from El Rodeo to be used for the monthly bullion train. Their stay in the corral at the Hacienda San Miguel was generally from twenty-four to thirty-six hours. In conjunction with the corral at Hacienda San Miguel were the saddle room, the pack-saddle room, and the quarters of the *arrieros* and corral man.

Identification tags were used on all pack-mules; each pack-saddle on the top of the saddle just over the withers had a small brass tag riveted to it, these were numbered serially. A light leather strap went around the mule's neck with a tag corresponding in number. When you had fitted, let us say, pack-saddle number twenty to a certain mule, you placed a strap with the corresponding number about the neck of the mule, and that mule used the same pack-saddle for the complete journey. Not until he was to be returned to the ranch at El Rodeo after his coming back from Carichic was his identification tag removed. This saved much galling that is sure to follow an improperly fitting pack-saddle.

If the mule and the driver are to get satisfactory results the pack-saddle must fit the mule who wears it; therefore, on hand we had never less than two hundred and fifty pack-saddles of a variety and size in order that all customers could be comfortably fitted when they appeared for work. There was plenty of work for one leather worker to keep himself constantly occupied; when he was not busy with the pack-saddles he put in his time in mending the *costalera,* which were leather sacks used for all purposes such as conveying high-grade ores, corn, beans, salt and lime. . . .

At the Hacienda San Antonio, half a mile up the river and on the opposite side from the Hacienda San Miguel, were located the Big Mill and the mouth of the Porfirio Diaz Tunnel; out of the latter the ores were drawn by trustworthy mules for many years until the gasoline locomotive was installed. Here was situated the other corral, the home of these good helpers. There was not much space on that steep mountain side, but by retaining walls a yard was established of sufficient size for all purposes, and a considerable portion of this space was occupied by the corral. It was a stone-walled corral, a masonry wall, high and strong, as all the walls had to be of necessity in the canyon if they were to stand the wear and tear. The floor of the corral was cobblestoned with a place left bare for the animals to roll in. This floor was kept clean, being swept twice each day with stiff brooms.

Is a mule smart? I remember one old veteran of the pack-train who had so much personality she was beloved by all the regular *arrieros,* even if she did give them the trouble to pick up her *aparejo* wherever she had dropped it in the corral at the end of the day's march. In the morning you would put on her pack-saddle, and when her turn came you would put on her load, She was ready and willing to leave at or near the head of the train, be it a small one or one consisting of a hundred or more mules. She was a black mule with a Roman nose, and was fifteen years old when we retired her. You could always locate her, for she never failed to be at or near the head of the pack-train all day long. But she was absolutely sure to be the first mule into the station enclosure at the end of the day's travel, right up front too, at the edge of the portal to have her load removed first. Until the load was taken off she was as patient and well-behaved as any mule could be, but once the load was gone, instead of waiting with the others to have the saddle removed in turn, she immediately sought and found a corner or a corral post and she would get the edge of the *aparejo* against it. Then she would heave and draw in her belly and slip out of the saddle, although the cinch had been plenty tight enough to carry her along all day with no danger of any loosening in the load. She would give herself a vigorous shake, find a suitable spot to have a gratifying roll, shake herself once more, close her old eyes and go to sleep until feeding time.

This story of mules and another and yet another I was telling to a Know-It-All American who came down to Batopilas to have a vacation from the Wall Street atmosphere at the same time I was returning from a vacation in the States to go back to work.

We watched one old saddle-mule attempt to hide away each and every morning. When the man delegated to saddle him would enter the corral, the mule would lower his head and slowly slink into the farthest corner of the corral behind the biggest group of mules to hide. But when he would be discovered, he would consent to be bridled and gave the man no need to throw his rope in order to catch him.

After the noon halt to tighten and adjust the packs and pack-saddles, I showed the fellow the mules that would immediately start out to make their way to the lead at every spot where the trail was wide enough to pass those ahead of them. I pointed out to him five or six special mules who had been the last ones to be loaded and the last ones out of the corral in the morning, which were the first ones always to be in the station enclosure at the evening halt, standing where they would be the first to have their packs removed. There was fierce competition between them to keep the lead, they would race each other wherever there was a level stretch on the trail in order to accomplish this.

I explained to him that once a new mule had made the trip there was never any danger of his trying to leave the trail during the long forty miles to the next station, because this new mule knew that on reaching this place, the load would be taken off, he would be watered and fed, with at least a rest of twelve hours. And I told the K.I.A. American and I showed him much, much more that had come to my knowledge and observation through childhood's and manhood's close association with mules, upon which sagacious beasts the life of the mining camp of Batopilas depended.

And then the poor fool told me that a mule could not think. That only those creatures that walk about on their two hind legs can think. So I picked out a lively young pack-mule for him instead of his usual saddle mule the next morning when we set out. I had him saddled. The man did not know the difference until he got in the saddle and the mule walked about on his hind legs till the rider fell off. After he had recovered from the surprising conduct of what he thought was his gentle saddle animal, and I had dusted him off, his regular saddle mule was brought to him and he climbed aboard. He found that the old reliable moved forward as usual at a nice, easy, ladylike trot. But he still maintained that mules do not think. He could not realize that the pack-mule would rather have its two-hundred-pound pack than to carry a less heavy rider; be free to go along as he pleased eating a bite of grass now and then; drinking from each stream he passed through; having an independent time, than to suffer the martyrdom of being pulled and hauled about by the bit, even though he did have a lighter load, but a load that slipped and slid about on his back for seven hours. It never entered the head of the creature that walked about on his own two legs that the mule was more than willing and anxious to put forth the extra exertion to throw his rider, in order not to be compelled to carry something on his back that he was not familiar with, not to have that damned bit in his mouth. . . .

Like Hell a mule does not think! That pack-mule did exactly what any thinking human being would have done rather than to be obliged to bear that dumb two-legged animal about on his back.

There are many more human beings or two-legged beings than there are mules; unfortunately this discrepancy in numbers is increasing constantly; hence, there are few cases where a mule has been known to run to the doctor. Besides, the doctor does not keep the same careful records.

At El Rodeo we had a ranch-keeper and there after each *conducta* were sent back the pack-mules who had just completed their round trip to Carichic with the bullion, and the return with what we may call the "fast freight." These mules rested here for at least a full month, since there were a sufficient number of them to have an entirely fresh set of mules for the next *conducta.* Now, mules will get galled. While every effort was made to see that they were kept free from any risk of disease, still blow-flies and other sources sometimes produced an infection on some part of their anatomy that spread rapidly, and which would soon, if unattended, cause death.

El Rodeo was not less than twenty-five miles by the trail from the Hacienda San Miguel and it was a steep trail on both sides of the ridge. More than once one or more of the old-timers finding themselves suffering from a bad sore that was spreading would decide to come to the corral at the Hacienda San Miguel to undergo hospitalization. They would arrive at the main gate of the hacienda and await admittance about midnight or early morning, having naturally preferred the cool of the evening for travel as against the more fatiguing heat of the day. They would be admitted by the night watchman at the main gate, a big wide gate of iron bars locked by a chain and a massive padlock. All he had to do was to open the gate, and the mule or mules would quietly walk in and make their way to the corral accompanied by the night watchman who would open the corral gate for them, then notify the corral man that a mule or mules had arrived from El Rodeo in need of medical attention.

But it was not always need for hospitalization that brought them to the corral at Hacienda San Miguel. Some of the mules belonged to the group that were used to do local work during the year, taking supplies to the various mines and bringing down the first-class ores. These mules were fed corn each evening, along with all the hay they could eat. Their terms of duty might be from four to six months when they would be sent to El Rodeo for rest and grazing. Several of the older mules liked their corn so well that a few days or weeks of grazing satisfied them, and the longing for succulent grains of corn would bring them back to the corral at Hacienda San Miguel. There would be little or no use in sending them back to the ranch again, for they would be back at the corral very soon after the man who had taken them returned. This would mean two days' time for the man who had acted as escort.

There is more difference between two particular mules than there is between two particular human beings. Unless you appreciate this you would do better to go home and stick to railroad trains. They may be of opposite color, size; come from ranches miles apart, but be as alike in disposition and in habits as any two things can possibly be. If one mule makes friends with another mule, the two will be positively inseparable. If this is the case, it is preferable to take both of them with you on a trip, or you will find that if either one is able to escape the first night, he or she will beat it to the place where the other one is. Of course, you will be able to take your journey, if you leave them apart, but you will know that you are riding a very unhappy mule.

I told the Know-It-All American about the mules, about fifty of them, who were used in the Porfirio Diaz Tunnel's eight thousand feet of single track. These mules made two round trips and then went to the corral for a rest. Each driver had his own set of mules. They hauled into the big tunnel two ton-and-a-half empty side-dump cars, which were loaded at the chutes and came out of the tunnel at a fast willing trot. There was enough down-grade for drainage purposes, which made the cars come out with little or no exertion on the part of the mules.

Now, when a mule had made his two trips he went to the corral, as I have said, for his regular interval of rest. When his turn came to go back to work in the tunnel he was willing enough to go in to do his "trick" and he would do it agreeably. But just try to make him do more than two tricks . . . or rather please do not try to make him do an extra trick. Because the work must go on, and there must be hauled out hundreds of tons of ore and waste every twenty-four hours. If you should try to use force in order to compel the mule to take a third trip with the assistance of ten or twenty able-bodied men and the expenditure of two hours in time, you might be able to accomplish your object. But the loss of time involved, and the possibility of the hospitalization of a man or two *and* the mule will hardly compensate you for the effort put forth by all concerned and the experience gained.

Got enough about mules? I'm sure you have, but don't think that I am not going to talk a great deal more about them. Damn it! I love 'em!

We know very little about the usefulness and power of man-power as such, when unaided by mechanical power. Suppose a thousand feet or so of wire cable one and a quarter inches in diameter on one of the big spools they wind it on at the factory for shipment is needed in our mining camp. It is ordered; the railroad deposits it at the appropriate point on their line; you get it loaded on a wagon, and you haul it to the end of the wagon trail. Now what? Either one of two things takes place. If you use man-power, a number of men unwind the cable, stretching it along the trail which they expect to traverse. At reasonable distances from each other the men station themselves, put their *serapes* on their respective shoulders. They then get under the cable and walk with it to the destination, reaching there not today nor yet tomorrow, nor even the day after tomorrow, but eventually. As a matter of fact, if those men whose duty it is to have laid out the work are alert as they ought to be, the "eventually" will be just exactly the correct time for it to arrive.

If you use mule-power in place of man-power, you start at one end, making two small coils of the cable; at intervals of about fifteen feet, you make two more coils, and this operation is repeated until you have all the cable unsevered in any place made up into a series or a succession of two coils or rolls, each set of two coils connected one with the other a distance of three feet apart. The coils are made of sufficient cable according to its size so that no single coil will exceed a hundred and fifty pounds in weight, thus making each group of two rolls weigh approximately three hundred pounds.

The *arrieros* line up their pack-mules, one mule opposite to each two coils. These are then placed over the pack-saddle, one roll on each side, and are made fast by the *reata* and the diamond hitch. All the animals are thus loaded, and there you have a gigantic snake of mules as the string thus connected mince their way over the trail.

The first gasoline locomotive ever used underground in that country was employed in the Porfirio Diaz Tunnel, a tunnel drilled through the hardest damned rock that ever was drilled, a grand piece of work. The gasoline locomotive was a queer-looking piece of machinery. A Mayo Indian ran it, he listened to the name of Amado Bobolla, or "Molly." Molly was the nearest the old German mechanic Bill Schwender, who came down to

Batopilas from the factory in the United States to set it up, could get to pronouncing Amado Bobolla.

I imagine to the everyday person in these times who needs a piece of machinery, and who has the money to pay for it, the buying of it and the getting of it to its final destination is a simple matter, even though it should weigh tons. But if you have confronting you the problem of setting it up in a canyon in the Sierras it has a different complexion. A mule load is three hundred pounds and the bed-plate of the engine, for instance, weighs several tons. You ask the manufacturer to have this bed-plate especially cast for you in sections not to exceed three hundred pounds each, and to have them so arranged with lugs that they can be bolted together. That is simple, is it not?

"Yes, but my God, the expense!"

Surely that is true; and you want to be very certain that you have a good proposition that will earn money enough to take care of that additional expense. If you are contemplating any such business in the mountains, be sure to select a man to do your calculating who has had to climb over and through many of them, preferably on the hurricane deck of a mule.

If you want a mule to stand perfectly still, blindfold him. For this purpose and reason each *arriero* carries a *tapaojo,* eye cover. This is a strip of leather about five inches wide and twenty-four inches long, with a loop in the center through which a finger is thrust for convenience in carrying. At each end is attached a double leather *correa,* which makes the lash. When this is knotted at the right point, the strap placed over the mule's eyes with the thongs drawn back behind the ears of a mule, and on its neck, it successfully blindfolds the animal. This blindfold is used when shoeing and so on. The lash is also an unanswerable argument when the animal shows symptoms of lost inclination to moving forward. . . .

We had an American employee who was an elderly man, very circumspect. Came time for his vacation. As often happens, his closest friend was a young fellow, a nice enough youngster, but just that . . . a youngster. Maybe he did have something over the normal amount of the spice of the devil in his make-up. Our old friend had an exceptionally good saddle-mule which he left in the care of the young companion when he went off on his vacation. The mule was ridden with exceeding regularity after dark by the youngster; in fact, so consistently did he ride the animal up a certain narrow street of uncertain reputation to stop at a certain house, that the mule formed the habit, of course, of going to that one particular place at fall of night or any other time.

In about two months the owner returned, and saddled up his mule one evening to ride down town with the rest of the crowd. The mule was true to habit, but he showed a singular lack of judgment; he turned at the fateful corner and despite the rider's most persistent efforts took him to the certain little house with the adobe wall around it, stopped and waited for him to dismount. The beast was indeed so very obstinate about remaining before the house that by the time the animal was convinced that it was not the desire of the rider to dismount, nor even to tarry in that vicinity, a throng of people had collected. Meanwhile the lady of the house posed in an enticing attitude in the gate of the adobe wall, and made uncomplimentary and sprightly remarks about the *viejo asqueroso,* the disgusting old man.

Before the evening was over, we inveigled the youngster into buying the faithful mule he had trained so well, for considerably more than *el viejo asqueroso* had paid for him two years before when he was a perfectly decent creature who kept to reputable streets. What irked the oldster most was the fact that he had been paying attention to a good-looking perfectly respectable young widow. There is no one who relishes a risque tale more than a Batopilense, and he was horribly afraid that the story would be handed on to her.

He was in such a state of relieved anxiety and consequent elation when we had made the trade and the youngster was now the possessor of the mule, that he had his saddle changed immediately to another animal and rode past his true love's house on Tom's little prancing pony, Chupa Rosa—which means humming-bird—solely to establish an alibi. Then he bought wine for the crowd, and took such a quantity of it himself that the widow came near getting him tied up with a promise of marriage before he could get away from her.

Chapter 17

Vacation Journeyings

We have wandered far from El Camino Real, far from the Royal Road, where a paved highway now takes the tourist, artist, writer, to the capitol of Mexico at a rate of speed we thought only birds could attain when you and I started out on this journey. Before I die I must go back to see, via a railroad train, that west coast.. . see El Fuerte, Culiacan, Altata, Mazatlan... I wonder if the shades of my former friends and their faithful mules and hones with whom I have traveled those hot distances will see me and some night speak to me. I would like to take you to Choix on that trip to the west coast, where more than thirty years ago I danced all of one night, drank beer, mescal, novalato rum which they called cognac . . . danced until breakfast time, after I had ridden eight solid hours the day before. After breakfast I saddled up and rode sixty-five miles more to El Fuerte and climbed aboard a mail stage on my way to Culiacan.

A pleasant cool spot was the hotel in El Fuerte kept by old Dona Concha. Her hostelry was a hollow square with a portal all the way around four sides. The courtyard was a big patio filled with lime and orange trees, planted with many flowers of all colors and perfumes.

I enjoyed a good bath in my brick-paved room. There were some big clay ollas with wide mouths from which I had my mozo dip huge gourds full of the cool water which he poured over me for a shower. When I had dressed I sat at a small table in the corner of the portal to sip limeade with something else in it; at this place Don Francisco Torres joined me. Don Francisco Torres, now forty-five years old and getting fat with a prosperous forwarding-agency business.

For many years Don Francisco had been bookkeeper at Batopilas as a young man. When he went to El Patron Grande to tell him that he much regretted it but he would be compelled to leave us because his sweetheart was a young lady of his own home town El Fuerte in Sinaloa, and could not separate herself from her parents, and in order to marry her he must move there to make his residence, he was congratulated and given a handsome wedding present. My father promised him the company's business in the .forwarding of freight for the purchase of corn, beans, lard, onions, great quantities of salt used in the reduction of silver ores by the then popular chlorinization process; leather in immense amounts used in making the zurrones, and other bags for the packing of the high-grade ores; rawhides (for the sulfides of silver after being sewed up tight in canvases were finally sewed into bags of well-wetted rawhides, which when dry it took an axe to and in which covering they went all the way to Aurora, Illinois, there to be smelted down and brought to sufficient fineness to be marketed by the New York Office in the New York market) and many more articles that a company of such size employing over fifteen hundred men requires in the way of things that life and business demand.

That is how it happened that Don "Pancho" Torres and I were having our refreshments together with an affectionate reminiscence of times past, discussions of the future... Lord, what days!

There was I, thirty-eight hours without sleep, having ridden a hundred and more miles and danced all of one night during that time, accepting an invitation to a baile for this night and planning to take the mail stage to Culiacan in the morning. Were we physically fit? God! If I could only live it over again under the same conditions. Young and strong and well-to-do; knowing the people, loving them; able to do any reasonable thing; when under the influence of liquor and a fine horse, a smile from a lovely Sinaloense, able to do many more things that were far from reasonable, by the non-initiated pronounced more than foolhardy... Ah well, an old cripple can at least dream about those halcyon days.

The mozo at Dona Conchita's is sleeping when I roll in from the baile at Don Pancho Torres' home in El Fuerte. I have eaten much, drunken much, danced much, told many pretty girls that I loved them ... which was more than true, I did love all of them. But the mail stage will be pulling out at four A. M. I change into my riding clothes, because nothing else will withstand the dust I am going to encounter during the ride to Culiacan. With a cup of very strong, black coffee inside me, with my mozo and saddle-bags and small steamer trunk, I set forth for the meson from which the mail stage is to start. A rather weary-looking moon dips down to the horizon, is drowned bit by bit in the Gulf of California a short ride towards the right. I am feeling mighty good . . . in love with the world..

"Buenos dias, senores .. . Senor Padre, tambien es madrugador," good morning, gentlemen; Señor Priest, you are also an early riser.

I am happy, I take pleasure in making the disgruntled other passengers exert themselves to respond to my cheery greetings. There are only four of them so far, and I thank God for that. For during the coming hot and sweating hours which are to be my dusty fate in that rocking stage, four are plenty. The Padre, of all the passengers except myself, is the most affable. He exclaims:

"Whom have we here? My good friend Don Pancho with others."

And as I live, sure enough here comes Don Pancho Torres with some friends and a couple of mozos carrying bottles. With merriment and good feeling we all have a drink two or three drinks including the cochero and his helpers. These worthies are called aside by Don Pancho, he tells them what a Hell of a fellow I am and what a friend of his and the like. This means later on if other passengers are picked up on the road. I will be given the seat on the box and will not have the body of a stranger, hot and smelly and sweaty, sitting on my lap.

"Vamonos, senores!" let us go, gentlemen, says our coachman, We scramble in after one last abrazo and handshake; the brake is kicked off; with the "Mula! Mula! Vamonos!" and the cracking of the whip we are away from El Fuerte and heading south.

What the other travelers did for the next few hours until we arrived at the Remuda Station in a small town where breakfast was taken, I do not know, but this individual slept like a top. When we went to the table, you and I, we did full justice to the huevos al ranchero with plenty of good hot chili and coffee to stimulate the digestive apparatus. When you have dashed some cold water over your face and head, dried them the best you can on a tiny clean towel supplied by the fondera, you are ready to clamber aboard the stage with fresh mules all hitched and waiting, to bounce along towards Culiacan. There con el favor de Dios, with the favor of God, we will arrive tomorrow afternoon.

That part of our trip was uneventful; very dusty; none too comfortable; but who cared? We were catching up on lost sleep; we were on our way with plenty of money; after two long years of very hard work underground in the mines what we craved was change.

Culiacan was not a bad town. We would have a day and two nights there to play about in and to become acquainted with new people before taking the narrow-gauge railroad to Altata. At Altata the coastwise steamer would pick us up to take us to Mazatlan where we were to embark for San Francisco. A pretty, nice little city was Mazatlan. We made Culiacan on schedule. After seeing about getting our baggage to the hotel and giving the cochero something to insure him certain relaxation's, into the shady patio through the wide door we go. You put your name down in the book, you order up an extra amount of water with which to get rid of the dust too thick to mention; you climb the deep imposing stone stairway to the second floor; and you are shown into a clean, spacious, almost-cool room.

Ah, but you are glad to wash and wash and wash again! Glad to change into clean clothes. You can hear a band playing somewhere not to far away: the sun is going down. When you have had a glass of beer you are ready and anxious to go out to look the situation over. As you reach the patio there is an attractive woman cutting tuberoses. To your "Buenos tardes, senora," she responds and introduces herself as the wife of the proprietor. This lady has a sister who lives in Batopilas, the wife of Don Torfilo Orduno. Of course, you know him quite well and you now recall that you have a letter for her. You hasten back upstairs to your saddle-bags to get it out; with that accomplished the senora hastens away to read the letter to her husband . . . these people are very clannish, very fond of their relations.

The rattle of the dice says that the cantina is over on that corner of the patio. That is the way to head for. . . cold beer has not been enjoyed for a very long time. The dice box is being worked by two Americans, apparently. One of them is the biggest man you ever saw, the other is quite small with a jovial red face, the kind of face that would not tan although its owner should spend a hundred years in the tropics; it simply persists in peeling, peeling.

"Jim Coley," the big man, "at your service.

"Patrick Flynn," the small one, "at your service.

The former is from San Antonio, Texas, and by birth a Texan with a capital "T." The small one is from San Francisco. One is a salesman of pumps, big pumps like himself. The other, a son of Eriri, as good an Irishman as one ever knew, is the local ore buyer for the Selby people. Both of them are full of fun with a proper capacity for the wine when it is red and the ability to carry it. A pleasure, they said, for them to have an addition to the American population, hence, a welcome like that to a long-lost brother.

"I thought you said you were the only Americans here. What's that sick-looking fellow playing poker over there using a Mexican deck of cards, with the two gachupin card sharps?"

"Him? Oh, yes, I forgot about him. He's a poor unfortunate lunger, came down here for his health. Looks to me as if he was slated. This makes the third day those two have been taking him along. Hell! It ain't right. Reckon I'll be doing what I intended to do last night when this damned Irishman took me out to supper and got me loaded. Drift over, feller, after I get in the game, and watch the fun."

This we did. We witnessed one of the cleverest exhibitions of card manipulations I have ever seen. Coley bought chips; the Spaniards were glad of what they believed to be another sucker. The game progressed, and Coley began losing and overbetting his hand, apparently not liking it from the way he talked. The betting grew heavier in about an hour. The older of the gachupines suggested that the limit should be removed. When buying his chips the sick American had shown a number of bills of large-appearing denominations; in his wallet there must have been nearly five hundred dollars. I thought Coley agreed rather reluctantly to the suggestion of no limit; the sick man shrugged his shoulders, and muttered; "Hell, it might as well be this week as next!" and he agreed. The poor devil was surely a sick-looking man to be going about.

Pretty soon, Coley and the sick man began to win. Every time the deal came to Coley, he, the sick man or one of the others drew tremendous hands, too big, I thought. I caught the eye of the Irishman, he elevated his eyebrow and winked at me; then I knew that Coley was in command of the situation.

Just one hour was needed after that for him to be in possession of all there was on the table. I He threw down his cards. Once or twice one of the pair of card-sharpers had started to say something, but his partner had shaken his head. His own skill with the cards was such that he felt himself to be in command till it was too late.

"Now," said Coley to the American, "how much money have these blacklegs taken from you, you poor damned sick fool?"

"I have lost about five hundred dollars."

"You lost it all right, but it was stolen," commented Coley counting from the money that was before him five hundred dollars, and handing it to the poor fellow. One of the Spaniards sprang forward with abusive language. Firmly I pushed him back in his chair:

"Wait a moment. Easy now on the rough talk, this gentleman has some more to say. If you are vivo, as all Spaniards like you, of course, are, you will take your medicine and keep quiet. You are being addressed by the grandson of the man who invented poker, and he can twist your neck like a pollo, too, if you get him roused."

"Now, you mining man," said Coley to me. "You can talk this language better than the pilot of Christopher Columbus' flagship. Just you tell these men here that many years ago I put away as being useless the old tricks they tried to pull on me. Tell them that every hand I dealt has been dealt crooked. Tell them I'm going to give back to this sick man what was his. I'm taking what I put in the pot in chips, and they can go, and I don't care how damned far they go so long as they don't come fooling around here again while I'm here. What is left is theirs."

It was done as the big man commanded. Those two humiliated Spaniards got up with their money and left. I followed them to the door and when one of them turned to utter a threat vehemently, I opened my coat and pointed to my faja where my Colt .44 was visible, being thrust there as was my custom in the evenings.

"Little man, I do not know who you are, nor where you come from, as for that I do not care. But look at this and remember I am from the mines in the Sierras."

The supper was more than usually palatable because of the letter with news I had brought to mine host from the family away off there in the deep mountains. Coley told us an interesting yarn as we ate the meal and when you hitched it up with the occurrences of the afternoon, it shows that you cannot know too much about any useful thing. Even when Coley was only sixteen years old, he was a big man. It was easy to pass himself off as over twenty-one. He got himself a job as a brakeman on the Santa Fe. He worked for years with the same crew and conductor on freight trains. In those days much more often than now trains had to lie on sidings for hours at a time, especially freight trains; there was no such thing as regular short runs.

Time had to be passed somehow, and the conductor, who was possibly the most skillful and dishonest card player in the Southwest, according to Coley, taught him every trick and crookedness that was known to him. By constant practice Coley became entirely proficient. His immense but supple and quick fingers made the manipulation of the cards simple for him. When he was twenty-eight years old, he left off playing cards for money. Although he tried his best to fight off the temptation to cheat when playing he discovered that the habit was too strong for him, so he quit playing for money. He kept in practice by playing now and then with his special friends and making monkeys out of them "in the effort to save as many innocents as possible from the curse of being sacrificed to the professionals they would undoubtedly come into contact with in life's journey."

Coley had a grand sense of humor, and he was a fine upstanding man, honest and kind. He said he had rarely found his match or superior and he took pleasure in getting into a game with a crooked professional. He loved to make him squirm and sweat and hunt excuses to leave the game when he realized that against himself he had an equal.

We joined forces to make the trip to Altata and Mazatlan. The narrow-gauge railroad that ambled from Culiacan to the port of Altata was the proud possessor of a little train which carried five passenger cars made by converting a flat car into a shed with rough board sides and a roof; there were glassless openings at intervals for windows. The little train was taxed to capacity pulling all the flats it could move on the morning we took our departure for Altata.

A fiesta of several days' duration had attracted many attendants at Novalato. Novalato was a few miles from Culiacan and the crowd had come there to see the sights as well as to visit friends or relatives, before returning home. Their time was up and they took the train to drop off at their home villages along the road to the coast; some of them were going as far as Mazatlan. These residents of Mazatlan were readily distinguishable by their more cosmopolitan clothes, the rouge of the women and the unmistakable appearance and manners of the men. The country women wore the universal cotton frock appropriate to the climate, easily washed; skirts very full, stiff ed with various and sundry high sounding titles, the most popular of which was cognac. It was at this place, at Novalato, we came upon the source of the liquor with which I was familiarly acquainted in the Sierras as cognac.

Coley took me with him when he went to the office and warehouse of the company where the proprietor filled a basket with assorted bottles to fortify us for our coming sea voyage of about fourteen hours. He handed Coley a draft on a house in Mazatlan for a large sum of money. Coley, as I said, sold pumps and he had just installed for the Engenio (sugar company) a set of pumps with capacity so great that they pumped all the water from the river into the irrigation ditches. This was the reason for there being a great deal of sugar and hard liquor in that section. In fact, the result of the drumming of Coley's pumps was frequently felt in the heads of those persons living hundreds of miles away, and being tasted by those whose coffee had to be con azucar, with sugar.

For lunch we were guests of Don Tomas, who held the train an hour in order that we might be able to finish the meal in comfort. It was to this foresight of his that we owed our seats in that conveyance, because he sent four peons to sit in the passenger coach to hold the space until we were ready. Otherwise we would have had to hang on to some projecting plank or something else because there were at least twice as many passengers on the little train as it could possibly hold. We made the regular stops, and a few additional ones to pick up those who had fallen off, or been pushed off; finally late in a sweltering afternoon we reached the coast and were lightered out to the smallest damned little steamer I ever saw permitted on the waters of the ocean without a nurse.

Our captain was a handsome young Mexican in immaculate whites and quite drunk already. By dint of much cursing and yelling in which he was echoed by all the crew and most of the roustabouts on the lighters, interspersed with references to the ancestry of all concerned extending back many generations, we were squeezed on board, the anchor was raised, .and we steamed away across the bar. The last half of the sun vas full in our faces.

Considering the size of the ship there was an uncommonly spacious saloon. When we passengers all were forced to cram ,ourselves into this on account of a sudden violent storm, which came upon us about ten o'clock that night, we could appreciate what a slender bit of room a human being can lye in when he is threatened with the possibility of being washed out to sea. It was the very devil of a storm; soon all were saturated, the waves broke over the bridge, destroyed the glass in the windows of the saloon, or the ports or whatever it is you call them. There were screams from the women, curses from the men, howls from the children, cries of hope, of encouragement, of despair. . . .

We had a clear exhibition of the time needed to slip from times to prayers. When we would be struck by a particularly heavy sea, drenching everybody afresh, prayers and promises or penance filled the air. In the confusion resulting from right many persons had thrown themselves on the floor or seen dashed there willy-nilly. Amidst the struggles of the them to get down onto their knees to pray, I found myself on all fours with two weighty arms around my neck nearly choking me. This state was greatly exaggerated by a quantity if the very cheapest and loudest perfume ever concocted assailing me. The roar of the wind was as summer zephyrs compared to the hoarse bellowing of that old Madam, who as some younger women with her, and who was pouring into my ear a cataract of prayers to all the saints in the calendar. Coley was still standing like a rock, his back against the wall, is pillar-like legs braced with what seemed at least six women hanging to him. This became visible when as suddenly as we had run into the squall we ran out of it, and the brilliant moonlight flooded the interior of the saloon. Of course, we rolled and tossed about for a while, but it was possible to disentangle ourselves and to get out on deck.

"This," observed Coley, "is a very small but a damned fine ship; any ship that with this mob on board can turn over four times and come up with no more water in her than she now has is a boat, young feller, and don't make any mistake about that."

"Want to make me acquainted with your girl chorus? How many do you usually hug at one time?"

"Before this, I have lost pocketbooks. I certainly was not going to give any of those little things of pleasure the chance to get my wallet and escape with it in the confusion and darkness. A couple of them gave indications recognizable by a man of experience of not being entirely overcome by fright. The acquisitive instinct, my boy, is very highly developed in some Christians, and from what I heard inside there I believe that each and every one of them was a very good Christian. Did you ever hear such a thorough knowledge of the calendar of saints? Get out your corkscrew, feller, here is one I saved. . . ."

We landed at Mazatlan only two hours late, and found that beautiful little city all arrayed in gala attire, for it was the "Saint's Day" of the Governor tomorrow and two-days holiday had been declared with bull-fights, balls for all classes, primera, segunda, tercera. This is a very good way to give bailes; there are no fool heart-burnings, no hurt feelings; no pretensions as to the class in which you belong and the corresponding ball you attend.

I presented myself to our agents and bankers, Hernandez, Mendia Y Compania, cashed my drafts, and met the head of the house. He told me that he would send to my hotel invitations to the balk for that night and tickets to the special bull-fights on the morrow. This was to be a very distinguished affair, in that there were to be a professional quadrilla of bull-fighters and for three of the bulls the picadores would be caballeros of the district who would ride their finest horses; and besides this there was to be a roping contest and exhibition at the end of the corrida which should prove very interesting.

We thanked this hospitable gentleman, hurried to the hotel, unpacked our trunks to got out our evening clothes to be pressed while we spent the rest of the hot afternoon watching 'chicken fights. They were about like all other chicken fights, except that these were interstate and the stakes in consequence were bigger than customary . . . anywhere from one thousand to ten thousand dollars. It is pretty nearly as quick a way to win or lose that much money as any I know of; that is, the way Mexicans fight chickens.

I'll have something more to say about chicken fights later. . . .

Chapter 18

Vacation Journeyings Continued

In Mazatlan could be procured the very finest vintages of wines and liquors. When we have enjoyed what might be your choice in these refreshments, we shall go to the Plaza. The municipal or military band is a good one, it plays before supper for an hour or so, and afterwards for a long while. Beguiling girls and women are sure to be walking around in one direction, with their delicate swaying gait, while the men stroll around on a separate path in the opposite. Thus you may admire without offense if you do not make the observation too apparent. You will see some blondes, many with hair of a coppery sheen, and others with that blue-black hair that is so fascinating. In Mazatlan are families with Spanish, German, English, French strains, combined with some of the Indian blood which gives perfection of form, feature, coloring, and grace of movement not to be excelled anywhere in the world.

Being inclined to be lazy, although having had but little opportunity to indulge this taste, and also tired, because Coley and I had been obliged to stand up nearly all night on that wretched boat, we found a comfortable bench on which to revel at our ease in this exposition of melody and beauty. We smoked perfect cigars made from tobacco grown in the Valle Nacional near the town of Vera Cruz on the Gulf of Mexico. A delightful form of entertainment is that custom of music on the Plaza, which is prevalent all over the country. Even the smallest town or hamlet has a band or orchestra; at least twice a week, there is a *serenata* at night or late in the afternoon. I shall not dwell too long on these remembrances . . . the longing to return to those places and those times grows too strong for me the more they are lingered with in memory. . . .

A well-proportioned ballroom, splendid music, well-gowned and beautiful women, who dance the waltz, the schottische, mazurka, with a perfection of achievement. A Spanish gentleman and his graceful partner, when the floor is cleared, dance a *jota,* a rhythmic delight to see. You are introduced, you go to supper, you drink champagne, you dance some more until nearly daylight. But you will not see a man, and God knows, never a woman! show any signs of inebriation. Getting drunk in the presence of ladies in those days in Mexico was not considered good form.

How we did sleep after a cold shower and a rub-down! We nearly overslept, in fact, which would have caused us to miss the bull-fight. This was the best show of its kind that I had ever seen. The *picadores* were mounted on very good horses, not one beast was so much as touched by the bull, which was the original intention in a bull-fight. The *quadrilla* was capital. Maybe it was Cara Chica who did the *espada* work, maybe Ponceano Diaz, maybe any one of several of those dexterous men. I do not recall accurately, so many years have drifted by . . . but it is a fact that he gave a supreme display of his art. The two bulls chosen for the exhibition of the gentlemen *picadores* could not have been better. I confess to shivers of apprehension when the two *caballeros* rode in on their perfect saddle animals, one an iron gray that made your heart swell with admiration, the bay no less beautiful, and admirably well ridden, both of them.

That was a sight to hold the eye and to thrill the mind. A charging bull. The horse head-on like a flash to meet him. The rider with the set lance catches the great bull in the exact spot. There is a straining between them, the pain in the shoulder of the bull forces him to try to back away from it. The horse follows, follows, keeping that even pressure on the lance, side-stepping as the bull does so in order to prevent that animal from slipping from off the lance. The exciting, screaming crowds, shouting *"Viva! Viva!"* At last the game bull, brave, bewildered, exhausted, with stiletto sharp horns, gives it up as a bad job.

Of all bull-fights that kind is the best for skill. Bull-fights vary much, as do baseball and football games. I remember one in Chihuahua that for a demonstration of the brutality that a crowd on pleasure bent may develop exceeds anything I ever saw.

The entertainment in Mazatlan was filled with color and enthusiasm. The Governor of the State was present, his family and his staff. Many hundreds of the representative people of the city and surrounding countryside were there . . . bewitching women old and young, gayly dressed, handsomely dressed. There was a great deal of money, of really substantial wealth, in this part of the Mexican Republic at that time. Some of those present were descendants of *Hidalgos* who had migrated to Mexico from Espanola, and direct from Spain just after the conquest.

How those young *caballeros'* sweethearts felt when the crowd in *El Sol,* the uncovered part of the grandstand, and in the more distinguished *Sombra,* the shaded part, went wild at the exhibition of consummate art and skill of the perfect horses and fine young riders, I do not know, but I remember clearly what a tingling sensation it gave me.

The last act of the show was very good too, although a sort of anti-climax. Three young bulls were let into the arena, full of the lust of life. Two boys twelve and fourteen years of age rode in and roped the pawing, bellowing beasts in every conceivable way, by any one foot, by the horns, whatever combination they chose . . . throwing, tying.

As a token of my appreciation I sent two cases of champagne to the donor of the tickets, to be delivered to him after I had sailed for San Francisco. It was as little as I could do under the circumstances.

On our way out from the bull-fight, at the foot of the stairs, we heard a woman's cry. Looking back I saw an elderly lady pitch and fall forward. Both Coley and I jumped for her; we caught her before she struck the steps below. She was a heavy lady, and we saw that her ankle was injured; we offered to carry her to her carriage.

"Let me have her," said Coley; he picked her up followed by the grateful husband and the family, large and small. We made our way to her carriage a block away. Coley deposited her safely therein. Amidst the exclamations of *"Que fuerza!"* and *"Mil gracias, señores!"* we backed away, sought for, and found a hack in which to drive back to town.

"'What did the lady weigh, Coley?'

"What do you think?"

"Damned near two hundred."

"Just about," agreed Coley; and he had carried her with little or no effort.

"What do you weigh, Coley?"

"Oh, two-twenty-five."

"How tall are you, Coley?"

"Six feet three and a half."

"And all muscle," added I. I was no weakling myself, but this was just a fast whale of a man.

Before bathing and changing our clothes, we were sipping an iced drink when we received a call from a nice little fellow, son of the rescued lady. He brought a message, an invitation from his father with excuses for his non-appearance in person, again to thank us for our kindness and would we "honor his poor house by joining us at dinner the next evening, a dinner given to His Excellency the Governor?" This invitation we *did* have to decline; the good ship *Peru* sailed at noon and we could not delay our journey. Thus ended our stay at Mazatlan for that time.

I think it was on this trip to San Francisco that we came into the Golden Gate only a few hours after the *Rio* had gone down on Mile Rock with nearly a total loss of passengers and crew. It seems very strange now when we have the daily news on shipboard via radio, to recall that the first news we got of anything that had taken place since casting off was when the pilot clambered aboard to take us in at the end of the voyage.

San Francisco was to me the most cosmopolitan city in the United States, but I did not linger there this time, remaining only just long enough to have some clothes made and then quickly went to Evansville, Indiana, where I officiated as best man at the Kid's marriage to Miss Sarah Clifford. It was a gala affair, and they left among the acclaims of the party for a honeymoon in New York and Europe. I also continued on to New York, not with the bride and groom but a day later. Some of the fellows in the wedding party were old Sewanee men, Henry Soper of Henderson, Kentucky, in particular. After we put the bride and groom on the train there was a lot to talk about . . . talking is a dry business if you are mixed up with several southerners, one of them at least a Kentuckian. I will not swear to it, but I think I caught the train for New York the next night.

The habit of wearing long-tailed coats stood me in good stead during my eagerly awaited vacation in that city of delight . . . New York. But it did take me a while to get accustomed to the top hat which I was not used to wearing in Mexico. A top hat is something that I like very much, but it is a "hair shirt" when one has been away from it for two or more years. The first evening of my arrival I hastily adorned my brow with one, and promptly forgot all about it, dashed from my hotel in a hurry to keep a captivating appointment, and sprang into a handsome cab. Naturally my forgetfulness of the topper resulted in its hitting that part of the cab entrance especially designed for the discomfiture of "farmers come to town." It was then too late to do anything about it except to work if off my ears and thank heaven that those necessary appendages prevented its going any farther down on my neck. In the dim light afforded by the cab the article of apparel did not appear too utterly impossible after I had straightened out the telescopic effect and smoothed its ruffled fur. Only when I entered the hall of the place where I was expected to dine, and the dignified butler wearing that frozen martyr expression with a dash of virtuously restrained condescension peculiar to butlers, took the hat from me, did I realize why the crushable opera hat had been invented, and I cursed the individual who inaugurated in that particular era the fashion that an opera hat was not *de rigueur* for all occasions after dark, and that the silk topper was the one and only thing for the theater.

My long legs made it necessary for me to buy an aisle seat whenever that was possible. This helped the silk topper a lot. I always forgot to remove it from its rack where it nestled beneath my seat when someone wanted to pass in or out and always at the most inopportune time. My silk top hat was kicked and dragged about by the trains of stout ladies for a distance of half a row of theater seats to wind up in such a condition of undisciplined furriness that it proved a source of augmented income to Knox. But that was of little comfort to the owner who had to go about in it for the remainder of the night. When I say the remainder of the night I mean that literally.

If you have been away two years or more in a mining camp in the Sierras of Mexico, and you have thirty days' vacation in New York City, the hours there are entirely too precious to waste in sleep, you can do that on the Pullman going back to El Paso. What a grand thing it all is to remember! An enlivening musical comedy with some especial one in the cast; supper afterwards at Rector's or Shanley's or Martin's or any one of a dozen of the old places where there were such honestly good things to eat and to drink; the final satisfaction of breakfast at Jack's, which was the third hearty meal in about nine hours, but which always was devoured with gusto. . . .

These memories have helped me to pass many a weary interval while sitting on a rock by the side of the track in some wet level two thousand feet underground, with a great hunger and fatigue upon me, not having seen daylight for twenty-four hours. There were many emergencies that presented themselves in our lives in the mines that kept us out of bed for three days or more. I often think when I have heard persons complain about the discomfort of staying in bed, how easily they could make it comfortable by simply staying out of it until they were so very tired they had actually to drag their feet. When I hear someone complain: "Why, I was too tired to go to sleep!" I wonder. That condition is not one of being really tired, it is just the first stages of weariness.

But I certainly was not tired when on the way back to Mexico I ran against Coley in El Paso at the Hotel Sheldon, where I was stopping for a few days before continuing to Chihuahua. It was fun to see each other again, and very late that night we dropped into a small barroom on a side street to have a last one before turning in. When we entered, we noticed that the bar was deserted except for a lone individual standing at the far end, facing the door. He caught my attention because of his set attitude, which relaxed when he had scrutinized us. The barkeep moved to the other end and regarded us inquiringly. He beckoned us to move to his position instead of waiting for us to choose our own places at the bar, and spoke to Coley by name. He produced the poison ordered and conversed about everything in general in a jerky fashion. Finally he said softly to Coley:

"You better get out .of here, Mr. Coley. There's goin' to be trouble. Hell will pop around here if the sheriff comes and he is sure to do it. They want that bird over there," with a jerk of his chin towards the lone individual. "That is Blank.' He wiped his bar nervously. "He knows damned well he'll swing as he deserves, and he'll fight it out. He is goin' to mess my place all up sure as Hell."

"Bad egg, eh?" said Coley. "Well, let's have another." He raised his voice. "Come on over here and join us, stranger."

"To Hell with you and your drinks! I can buy my own drinks. And what's more you ain't goin' out o' here ahead o' me to tip off any—sheriff!"

This *bribon* was on my left. I was standing facing the bar and sort of leaning on it with my elbows. But when he started to get nasty I slipped my hand down and took hold of my gun, which I always wore in the front of my waistband when I went out at night. I had this bad egg covered under the edge of the bar, the overhang as it were, and he did not know it till I told him about it.

"You are a bad man, eh? Keep your hands where they are, I've got you covered. Put 'em on the bar. Quick, I say! You are not dealing with a tenderfoot. Now, Mr. Bartender, give this bastard a full glass of liquor and so help me if he don't drink it down, I'll turn him over to the cops. They can take him to the coroner. Frisk him, Coley."

Coley did this with great rapidity and thoroughness, producing a short-barreled .44 which he carried with him to where we were now drinking beer. I was mighty relieved I had not been obliged to shoot the fellow. The sheriff came in; he had been looking through the window and had seen Coley disarm him. The sheriff handcuffed the offender and took him away, thanking us. This bad man was a product of San Francisco and had done-in a defenseless man on the waterfront in that place. He had made his get-away from there to El Paso, where he had expected to cross the Rio Grande into Mexico. Only this very morning, he had murdered a helpless, unarmed section boss up the road towards Sierra Blanca, and had been forced to come back to El Paso.

Coley and I left the little barroom and had some ham and eggs at the Chinaman's before turning in. But I demonstrated again to Coley before we bade each other good night the advantage of a woolen *faja* as against a belt when you want to tote a gun in the only place *to* tote it if you are not wearing a belt and holster . . . and that is sticking in the front of your waistband.

There was a primitive sort of a dance hall on Eutah Street in El Paso forty years ago. Next night having exhausted the possibilities of the better part of town, a citizen of El Paso, a friend of Coley's and myself wandered along from one bar to another till we struck this place that was patronized by all the nations in the town. It was a one-story, adobe structure, plastered on the outside and in, it had the usual two narrow doors, there were a front and a back room with tightly packed earthen floors. The lighting was supplied by coal-oil lamps, one hanging in the center of the ceiling and some in brackets on the walls of each room. We had a drink at the bar, chatted with the proprietor who was dispensing drinks. He seemed friendly enough. He was acquainted with the fellow who was with us, although before this night, we had not the pleasure of knowing him. For some months, it seemed, he had been the guest of the State of Texas for having beaten another good citizen to it one evening. The beaten one became the "late lamented" in short order, and unfortunately for our companion he happened to have been a special friend of someone high up in the administration of the State's governmental machinery.

Those drinks were potent. Because I was a great hand, or I better say a great foot, for dancing any and everywhere in those days, I went into the back room where the dancing was going on. This room was a long one and it was lined with Mexican leather-bottomed chairs locally made. On these chairs were sitting a number of girls and some old women, most of them Mexicans. The girls were all properly chaperoned even though their experience in life was more than extensive; they were quiet and well-behaved. They danced well, and I started in dancing with one of them although her dueña remonstrated with her charge for doing so. She danced very well indeed. I realized that the few lamps at times looked to be a far greater number than I knew they actually were as the motion and rhythm gave the many drinks I had taken another chance to bite in.

The orchestra consisted of harpist, violinist, and *guitarrero* who played almost incessantly; finally they gave out and I took the young woman back to her seat and ordered something for us to drink, not forgetting the orchestra. We had only just begun to sip our refreshments when the *dueña* exclaimed:

"Por Dios, aqui viene y esta borracho!" By the Lord, here he comes and he is drunk!

I turned. At my right elbow was a tough-looking fellow who made a vile remark to the girl. Before I knew what was happening, he had slapped her a resounding whack and knocked her into someone's lap. He whirled toward me all set to go and I landed mine where it would do the most good from my point of view. He went over backwards, but he was quick and agile, he had swayed away from my blow and so was perfectly conscious. No sooner had he hit the floor than he drew a short-barreled Smith & Wesson. I jumped for him and reached for that so-called gun. It was a kind of disgrace in those times to tote that kind of gun and a greater one yet to be shot by the sort of man who would tote one. I was a shade too late to stop his firing it, but early enough to prevent anything serious happening.

He only succeeded in ruining my derby and singeing the hair on my temple.

At this stage of the proceedings the friend came and took the gun I handed him, while I yanked the man to his feet. I let him get his balance, and then operations were resumed. After a couple of punches or so, we carried him out to the street to cool him off, and put his gun back in his hand minus all but the one discharged shell. We started to walk off leaving there, to renew our further diversions.

An enormous policeman hove in sight. The proprietor told him that the drunk on the pavement and some others had a fight outside there in the street; that he had never seen any of the combatants before; he turned to us for confirmation. Of course, we agreed with him, and said that he was undeniably correct. The cop was mad as sin at having a nice nap interrupted by what had turned out to be of no moment, helped the now-returning-to-consciousness slapper-of-women to his feet and took him off. . . .

Chapter 19

Racial Characteristics

On the bright beautiful Sunday I spent in Chihuahua, I saw a queer manifestation of mob psychology. . . .

A bull-fight was planned and arranged for to feature a toreador once very renowned, but whose star was now on the wane because he was growing old. One cannot be a successful toreador after one is past young manhood. They go the way of most popular heroes. Gayety is irresistible to them, they live dangerously and with a feverish earnestness. All kinds of amusements of the most depleting character are indulged in by those physically courageous men who have the guts and dash and perfect synchronization to make them famous bull-fighters.

Although no man loves animals more than I, I must respect a skillful fighter of bulls for his aptitude, his expertness, and his courage. To walk into a bull-ring, to spread a pocket-handkerchief on the ground, to place both slipper-clad feet on that small piece of cloth and then to keep them there while the bull charges, moving the feet not one inch, but weaving the body itself in and out, back and forth exactly enough to make those needle-sharp horns barely miss the thighs or ribs, undoubtedly takes courage.

On this Sunday in Chihuahua there was an immense concourse of people at the *corrida,* it was a spacious *plaza de toros.* The band played a lively air, the *quadrilla* marched in. The occupant of the seat of honor, the Governor of the State, was duly saluted, the bulls dedicated to him.

There were six bulls. They were the very best, full of energy, wild and eager to fight before the *picadores* and the *banderierros* had goaded them to a frenzied fury. They were larger than medium, young, sleek. They put two or three of the *quadrilla* over the barrier several times, so cat-like in their swiftness, so full of the savage desire to kill.

The *matador* did his part well. He killed the first four bulls instantly and cleanly at the first thrust of the sword after playing them so damned close to him that his trousers, tight as they are, and his jacket both were ripped by the creature's horns. Naturally such furious bulls killed or disabled a good many of the poor, wretched horses before the fifth bull was let into the arena. The *toreador* presented himself, stood in front of the stand where the presiding dignitary sat, raised his cap aloft and asked permission to speak. This was granted him; he explained that with deepest apologies he was forced to ask indulgence during the remainder of the performance, he would be obliged to proceed without the *picadores.* He further elucidated that the contractor engaged to supply the horses had failed him and that he now had no more horses with which to continue.

At that, some individual (there is always some moron to do such asinities) started in to shriek objections. "They had paid their money for a fine show. They refused to be cheated!" Before the police could get among them, they had commenced a very pretty riot, throwing the light wooden chairs by the dozen violently into the ring. The bull-fighter retired. The police finally quelled the tumult. The show was declared off, the ring was left with broken chairs, backs and legs strewn about. The bleachers demanded that the old tame bull with the brass knobs on his horns should be turned now into the arena so that the amateur bull-fighters might have their sport, which is customary.

In came the big, slow, old fellow, he began chasing the amateurs here, there, everywhere. The temptation to prod him with the sharp ends of broken chairs was impossible to resist. They got the poor old bull so mad and in such an ungovernable rage that as he charged at a small group he reached one of the men and threw him into the air. The young fellow landed on top of his head. He was apparently unconscious, and his friends dragged him limply to one side of the ring and deposited him against the barrier. In half an hour this amusement was over, the old bull was allowed to retire. Then somebody remembered the young man who had proved the attraction of gravitation with his head. They went over to him as he lay motionless where they had dragged him. After repeated struggles to force him to stand on his feet, he was found to be quite dead, a perfect case of a broken neck. It was all ended now, except for the *toreador,* who was fined all of his gate receipts for non-compliance of contract.

Leaving the bull-fight, we strolled back towards town. Evidences of the Chihuahuenes' fondness for pleasures other than bull-fights, where no attention was paid for long to injuries or even to death, became conspicuous in more than one of the homes we passed where *guitarreros,* an occasional violin, now and then a piano, combined in making music for *bailes* in private homes; impromptu *bailes,* a group sitting about in the *sala,* while some young man with a guitar sang soft, harmonious love songs having to do with eyes, moonlight, soft roses, scented breezes, songs comparing the loved one to some particularly graceful warbler of the bird family. Young men with lovelorn expressions in their dark eyes and languishing postures leaned their shoulders against the bars of deep window seats, while whispering ever so tenderly of love and eternal devotion, *hacienda el oso,* making the bear. And why not? The transition from tragedy to mirth is nothing against a race . . . such men in my experience make good soldiers in the battle of life as well as on the field of battle.

Laughter-loving, courteous, mercurial, swift, tender, fierce, poetical, musical. . . .

Fatigue can be stalled off by sound, rhythmic sound. I cannot explain it, but if you could be with me for a while in a red-hot working where three or four sets of double-jackers were laboring, sweating in actual streams, and could hear the rhythm of their blows accompanied by chanting in unison, you would see for yourself. It is done unconsciously, the men fall into the tone accent almost automatically. When one or two have stopped for a minute or so to swab out the hole they are drilling it is a dramatic pause, there is a sensation of suspense until they start up once more breaking into harmonious chorus.

When the day or night shift would be waiting in groups at the head of the shaft or in some other convenient place for the *poblador* to designate the working to which they were assigned, they would begin a song or rather a sort of chant. In a moment fifteen or twenty of them would join in, and pretty soon all would be singing different parts, and sing them well. It was a pleasure to hear them and was also the cause of some speculation, because none of the men knew anything about music, none of them had ever been taught even the rudiments of harmony. It was just there . . . and their own ears and ideas of a concord of sweet sounds indicated to them what sounds to make in order to blend them into a tuneful whole. A discordant note would be immediately silenced by good-natured gibes such as "How sweetly the jackass brays!" "The young rooster learns to crow," "This axle requires grease," or some similar comparison with a primitive, unpleasant, or dissonant sound.

The Batopilense miners young and old adhered to a universal custom. There was a niche directly inside every tunnel entrance in which a cross was fixed and a constantly burning miners' lamp or a candle kept vigil. In front of this each man would stop and say a short prayer and cross himself. The older generation would frequently collect at the cross until there were some twenty or more congregated there, when they would chant a prayer or a few words of praise, cross themselves and go on into the mines to their work, a mile underground, to do their tasks cheerfully and happily. They were a grand aggregation of *hombres,* young and middle-aged. Quite often a set of two drill men would consist of father and son, and since under the tutelage of the older man the son became more and more expert, he would, in his turn, do a bit more than his share with the sledge in the holes they were drilling, to favor his father.

A *poblador* is a shift boss. Really he was much more than that. A *poblador* is born with the gift; he is the man who points the holes to be drilled, whether these be in a face, a rise, a stope, or a winze. The knowledge of how this should be done in order that each hole drilled and each powder charge exploded will give the greatest effect and break the most rock is an art that many never acquire, even though they be old hands at the game. The *poblador* ought to be a natural leader, one who has come up through the ranks, a strict disciplinarian, but with the right kind of discipline. He may have an assistant or more than one according to the number of the men on his shift. He has under him his peon bosses, who are in charge of those who are shovel men or laborers. The *operario* or drill man is of a higher class than the peon and is a skilled worker.

They liked their work. They were cheerful, contented, happy. They liked to sing, dance, laugh. The Batopilense was a great joker; his repartee was a delightful thing, at times possibly it was a foot or so over the line, but very rarely was it so in mixed company. He was innately respectful to older people and to his superiors. I have indeed known men of forty who would never think of smoking in the presence of their parents; very seldom was the word of the parents opposed; if it should become necessary to point out that the parents were in error, it was done in a very respectful manner. It may not be so now, for I write of an era that has gone into the limbo of forgotten things except by a few old codgers. . . .

The modern mining man little appreciates what the miners achieved in order to get out their gold and silver a hundred, two hundred, two hundred and fifty years before we mined the native silver in that very old camp of Batopilas. The ores from these mines were, of course, world-famous. They were the only ones of the Western Hemisphere until the discovery of Nipissing, which produced native silver in the same amount and form with such varied massiveness and beauty of crystallization.

It was my good fortune to open up a very ancient mine that lay between two we were working. The company from which we had taken over in 1880 had no record of the existence of this ancient mine, nor had we, until my brother-in-law came across an ancient map of the San Miguel Group in the Department of Mines in the City of Mexico. He wrote us about his discovery, we investigated, and sure enough after a good deal of digging, we found what had once been a tunnel entrance. It was plugged up with heavy stalls of pine whose timbers were over fifteen inches in diameter. This tunnel was connected with a shaft to the surface about fifty feet farther up on the hillside, and below the tunnel the narrow little working had been taken down for three hundred feet by a system of short drifts and winzes. There were indications that very rich pockets of pretty good size had been taken out, since in places the working showed considerable magnitude.

We discovered what was of almost as much interest as the possibility of rich ground and these were the ladders and the butts of drill holes. The ladders were of the old native type, which means they were made from a pole fifteen or more inches in diameter with notches cut at regular intervals and at such an angle that when the pole was set against the side of the working, the bottom of the notch would be level and at least eight inches wide, where a man's foot could rest with perfect ease. Ladders of this type were no rarity but we had never encountered any made from timbers of such size as these. The ends of the drill holes—sometimes there was as much as six inches left at the bottom—were four or more inches in diameter. These had been drilled with a *pulseta* drill or jump bar, which is an iron bar six feet long, and on its end was welded a small piece of steel which was afterwards shaped by the blacksmith, usually the miner himself, into a chisel bit, and then tempered. With this tool held near its center with one hand and a little nearer the cutting end with the other the ancient miner would swing it forward against the rock; he would revolve it a little at each blow until with sufficient time and patience the hard rock would be bored to the required depth, scarcely ever more than three-quarters of a yard. When he had succeeded in doing this our determined miner of antique workings came upon his next great difficulty, this was home-made powder, naturally of a very inferior kind. The fuse followed this.

Before the days of paper, corn husks were used as the wrapper for fuses, or the inner bark of a certain tree. The fuses were made in this way: the powder was ground very fine, a small amount of this was rolled in the husk like a very thin cigarette, but no corn husk will average over eight inches in length at most in that country, it is safe to say that it would take six or seven pieces of husk to make a three-foot fuse. These pieces of husk must be stuck together with some sort of glue or paste, the gum had to be secured from a native bush or tree and fashioned into the glue for this purpose. Black powder must be tamped in order to yield any sort of rending force at all; therefore, after the powder charge was put in the hole and the fuse inserted, it had to be tamped. Very fine earth was used, sifted meticulously; this was tightened around the fragile home-made fuse in such a way that it would not be cut nor broken. Sometimes a thin rod of iron was put in the hole, the earth tamped around this and then it was later withdrawn carefully and the fuse inserted in the resulting hole.

When our ancient miner has at last been able to get this far in his labor, we find that while a modern fuse would burn very slowly, thus giving him time to spit his shots and put himself in a safe spot, the home-made fuse flashes almost immediately to the other end when one end has been lighted, therefore, he would be blown to bits every time he lighted the charge or shot. Consequently he would take a piece of frayed rag (we are presuming the work was done before the days of cotton wicking), procure some beef tallow, boil it down and allow it to cool. When it had become quite hard, the frayed rag worked full of tallow was bent around the fuse; it was twisted tightly so it would stick up vertically and the end was pinched into as small a point as possible. He would now be all prepared and I think he would be saying his prayers. Cautiously, I am sure, he would light the very tip end of the fuse and LEAVE! The minute the tallow would feel the veriest breath of heat it would soften, the wick would fall to one side, and the fuse catching fire, an instant explosion would result.

I honestly feel that those old boys were entitled to all the silver they got.

Jesus Hernandez, the son of the old *Jefe Politico* of the same name, grew up with us boys and worked with us. The name Jesus is used in Latin-America as a given name as frequently as Thomas is in the United States. He was working with me the morning we first went into the ancient mine and to this day I can see his nauseated expression when we examined a strange pink growth of what appeared to be of a fungous nature on the foot wall in the little tunnel. We held our lamps close, the peculiar mass seemed to shiver, quiver, move. It did wiggle! What new discovery had we made of a scientific nature? It was a perfect conglomeration of very young bats, each about an inch or a wee bit more in length; there was such an incredible number of them that they covered a space on the foot wall two feet by three. We shoveled them out onto the dump we had made in excavating the entrance to the little tunnel; later in the day a couple of old buzzards appeared to relish them intensely, who thought them, no doubt, tidbits of a rare sort—as indeed they were. Held by the tips of their wings the little creatures were as pretty a shade of pink as you would wish to see; they looked distinctly and precisely the way the devil was generally pictured back in the old days when we believed in devils and punishment after death for earthly sins.

Jesus Hernandez was a philosophic soul. On a certain Monday morning I was sent for to go to him in the hospital; he had been taken there the night before with an eye ruined and a terrific cut on the forehead. It seems that a rival (Jesus was a devil with the ladies) had waylaid him on his way home and had knocked him from his horse with a rock of ponderous size and inflexibility. The surgeon had told me that aside from the loss of his eye little or no damage was done. When I expressed my sympathy to Jesus and said how very sorry I was at having to tell him what the doctor had said, he replied:

"Ah, *mi amigo,* for all there is to see in this town, one eye *es muy suficiente."*

The sight of his remaining eye was evidently unimpaired for he chose one of the prettiest girls in town to make her his wife; it was at *carnaval* time, I think.

When you have a soft-boiled egg, scrambled eggs, an omelette, the shells of the eggs go their own way with a carelessness derived from the mental certainty that they are as useless as any thing could be that makes up the contents of the garbage pail. If you have laying hens, these kind good females will eat them and return you a perfectly good fresh egg having renovated the original shell and made it do duty once more . . . but most egg-users don't raise chickens.

If you had been a citizen of Batopilas in the years that I lived there, and I believe even at this late date, the usefulness of the egg shell was only half completed when it appeared in the role of container. *Carnaval* time came regularly once a year in our camp, just as it does in New Orleans, Nice, and other places in the world, with the culminating international celebration at Coney Island in the sovereign State of New York. Among many other differences in the way these carnivals are celebrated is the use in Mexico of *cascarones*. A *cascaron* is an egg shell, about three-quarters of the entire shell. When the contents have been used, the top of the shell only having been cracked off, there is left a nice little container. These are accumulated during the year; if you are in the business of making *cascarones* for *El Carnaval,* you engage all the neighbors' egg shells and agree to pay for them. You must lay in a supply also of many colored sheets of tissue paper, several of gold and silver tinsel, also colored dyes or paints. *And* a devil of a lot of patience!

When time for *El Carnaval* approaches, you stain or paint with water colors these egg shells in all sorts and varieties of tints. You cut the tissue paper and tinsel into such fine particles that they look, when mixed together, like a pile of many-colored grains of fine sand. Take half a teaspoonful of the paper dust thus made, put it into one of the stained egg shells; paste a little piece of the colored tissue paper over the open end of the one-time egg shell and then you have a full-fledged *cascaron.*

When you go to the carnival ball you carry your *cascarones* with you, when you are strolling or promenading around the ballroom greeting the guests, you crush one of them over a head, allowing the shower of many-colored paper particles to fall on the hair of the lady thus favored. She thanks you prettily, because it is a sign of respect and indeed of affection; I have seen an especially pretty girl so covered with this dust at the end of the ball that you could barely tell the true color of her hair. It is a novel kind of confetti, really.

Not only while at a dance but during calls or at any other opportunity in carnival time this is the thing to do, crush the *cascaron* in your hand as you hold it over the head of the favored one and release the contents.

Like the ichthyosaurus, chaperones have gone out of fashion, but they still roam in Batopilas I am certain, so be sure to devote several *cascarones* to the chaperones. It does not permanently endanger their vision, but it has a strong tendency to make them see things as through a softer and less Grundyish light.

Now, the Mexican is usually a careful person concerning the waste of foodstuff; the beloved and good *tortilla* is made from corn, the wheat flour *tortilla,* however, is not despised, and bread and rolls are also used by the more cosmopolitan of the population. You may say: "What has that got to do with *El Carnaval?*" There is always a big battle on one chosen day during *El Carnaval* between the Abajeños and the Arribeños, the people who live in the down-river part of the town and those who live in the up-river part. The weapons, or better, the ammunition, are flour, white wheat flour; and you can put anyone out of the fight if you are quicker than he may be by filling his eyes, mouth, and nose with handfuls of well-thrown flour. It is very unpleasant, for your hair becomes full of it, it blinds you temporarily, chokes you more than considerably; unless you have the good sense to wear white cotton or linen clothes you look damned funny when you have done your bit in this battle. Once or twice during our years in Batopilas there was a case which caused real suffering, because some simpleton thought to get even with an enemy by substituting lime for flour; if he were identified he got it back with compound interest, be sure of that.

Chapter 20

Accidents

Batopilas was a hard-rock camp. The nature of the ore deposits came at first glance apparently in more or less irregularly arranged *bonanzas* or rich deposits varying in size from ten thousand to a million or more dollars. When drifting and sinking in the effort to discover these rich deposits many holes must be drilled and fired. Dynamite is, of course, the effective explosive. Sometimes we used forty per cent but usually it was sixty per cent.

When a Batopilense celebrates he likes a noisy celebration. During the visit of the Governor to our camp more than one case of dynamite was fired in salutes. It is a very efficient way to fire salutes if you keep sober and are not heedless in the handling. However, if you are not careful you are more than liable to cause as well as to suffer trouble. It was not a rare sight in Batopilas to see a man now and then whose right hand was missing—the outcome of too much enthusiasm in combination with liquor, dynamite, and a Saints' Day celebration.

It is done in this way: You procure a stick of powder, cut it into four pieces; get four short lengths of fuse, about six or eight inches, slip caps on them, crimp the caps. Generally this is done by putting the cap in your mouth and crimping the edge by biting it. Next make a small hole in the end of the dynamite, insert and spit the fuses, and at the exactly proper time you cast it into the air, or some place far enough from those present to avoid endangering them. It is a well-known fact, according to the very best Prohibition authority, that among other devastating effects of alcohol, it distorts the judgment. Therefore, if after lighting the fuse you start in making a speech or otherwise allow yourself to be diverted from the actual situation in hand, when the resounding explosion is over you will find that your hand has also disappeared with the smoke and the noise.

If you want to make a cleaner job, you can use a third or even a half stick of dynamite. But this is not recommended for those not possessed of an above-the-average strong and robust constitution . . . better ask the surgeon.

Dynamite is a strange substance, kind of like a woman in some ways, for they occasionally do not function according to the rules and customs which are supposed irrevocably to govern life. I remember one time a man was sent to the powder magazine which was in a distant and abandoned drift. He was careless with his light and somehow three cans of black powder became ignited and exploded. Within twenty feet of the powder cans were three cases of forty per cent dynamite. The wooden cases were thrown about and scorched, but they did not explode. Not possible? Well, maybe so. But it happened. I was one of the first men to reach the place, and in a thick and nauseating smoke I helped to pick up and to carry out the dead and well-broiled miner who was responsible for the catastrophe. When things had cooled off and the atmosphere had cleared somewhat I examined the spot and the facts were as I stated them.

I have seen a mule—you see I cannot keep away from mules—loaded with four cases of dynamite roll down a steep hillside for two or three hundred feet, scattering the dynamite from Hell to breakfast, and nothing happened. Once, though, I saw a mule do it, and after rolling he dropped vertically a hundred feet. There was a tremendously loud noise . . . that is all we recovered.

When the Chihuahua & Pacific Railroad was built out to La Junta our stage drive was cut down to sixty-five miles. One morning I was waiting there for the train to come so we could load our bullion and go on to Chihuahua. I began chatting with the agent and others. We were leaning against a pile of cases of dynamite stacked on the platform. As the train pulled into the station, we noticed there was an extra passenger coach. This train was of such modest proportions normally that an extra car, especially a Pullman, was an object of particular regard.

"Oh, yes," said the agent, to our inquiry, "that's right, certainly it is a Pullman. It is a special car. He is making a trip over all Mexican railroads."

The bullion was stacked at one end of the platform of the station where the express cars of the train would be. The dynamite cases were at the other end and the wagons were preparing to load it. The observation platform of the private car stopped immediately where we were doing this. A gentleman with a party of friends was sitting on the observation platform and as I glanced up I saw the expression on his face blaze into consternation and fear, he half rose from his seat and gasped out:

"Look out! My God! Look out! Pull the train out. You damned fools, throw away those cigars, you are going to blow us all up.

With this he rushed to the other side of the observation platform and leaped over the rail. He was clumsy, fell, and rolled down the slight embankment of the road. It flashed upon me that the ends of the cases of dynamite had that word stenciled upon them in large letters and that, therefore, this was the cause of all the activity. We ran around the end of the car and picked him up; we had forcibly to restrain him from a sprint across the plains. After some brushing off and other soothing efforts, I prevailed upon him to calm down. I explained to him that there was no danger to the other members of his party who were still seated on the observation platform of the Pullman, and who were regarding him with expressions of combined amusement and timidity. I impressed upon him the fact that the railroad company itself would never have unloaded the dynamite at that spot if there had been any peril in it, any danger of blowing up one of the two trains which it owned. Moreover, the company was entirely aware that the private car with many important persons was attached to that particular train. In fact, that no railroad company could afford to take such a risk. Hence, there was no actual jeopardy.

"But, by the Lord Harry, sir, you were smoking!"

"Well, then we will not smoke any more until we have gone three or four miles up the track."

Eventually I succeeded in getting him back on the train. His poor wife, to whom I was introduced, was half way between tears and laughter. The efforts of the others to refrain from roars of amusement plainly showed him to be a person of great importance, but not of immense sense of humor.

Just like anything else, continually handling dynamite becomes second nature, and you automatically use caution and circumspection in its management. There are men who are such experts in putting and shooting dynamite that, if you had a big boulder in the middle of your drawing-room they could crack it with dynamite and not soil your wall paper. It is all in the knowing how.

One day we were examining an old working, a big stope, to see about putting in some timbers. There were three of us. We felt a shower of small stones and we jumped aside. This shower is generally a forerunner of a larger piece of rock becoming detached and falling. Two of us barely got clear. We expected the other one to be squashed flat as a pancake. In a minute we heard him groan, and we spoke to him. When we could get to him to examine him we found he had a bump on his head as big as an egg, but he had escaped further injury. Three big boulders were holding the slab of fallen rock and he had been able to throw himself prone between them. We had severe labor in getting the slab from off him and extricating him. We were obliged to shoot one of the slabs with dynamite and that took damned careful calculation as to exactly how much dynamite to use in order to crack only so much from the slab and no more, consequently not to let it completely down on him and thus crush him to death after all.

Naturally only a part of the time does one come out unscathed from dynamite accidents. Then it is a nasty business carrying mangled live and dead men on your back up or down several hundred feet of ladders. They will bleed all over you and the odor of human blood has always been repugnant to me. However, if the mine management and discipline are as they ought to be, you will find that at least ninety per cent of the accidents are due to the man's own carelessness and because he has not complied with the laws laid down for his own protection.

One night I was awakened by the night watchman at San Miguel Mine with the word that there was someone hurt in the mines. I jumped into my pants and shoes, ran to the gates, the watchman handed me my lighted lamp as I passed him. I opened both the outer and the inner gates. The messenger from the bottom of the mine told me that so-and-so had been killed in such-and-such a winze by having three charges of dynamite fulminate while he was still at the bottom of the winze.

In I hurried to the mouth of the hoisting shaft. I was informed that the injured man was being carried up the ladder-way on the back of a peon. They thought it best to bring him out that way. It did not take long to do it; as I have told you, those peons could put as much as a hundred and seventy-five pounds on their backs and climb ladders with very little effort. I lit out down the ladder-way. We met the procession and found the "dead man" slightly cut up about the side and back, but quite alive and cheerful, smoking a cigar!

We sent him to the hospital and he was out in a week. Of course, by all the rules he ought to have been dead. Three one-yard shots had gone off in the bottom of the shaft six by ten feet and he was right there in the bottom of the shaft with it.

The reason for his being there was his own laziness. He ought to have secured a new rope from the boss with which to climb the twelve feet to the end of the second ladder. The lower ladder is always removed when the round of shots is to be fired. The hand rope he used was old and frayed, this broke with him and he fell back into the winze. He was slightly stunned, therefore unable to call to his partner on the level above him. This worthy had also disobeyed orders by not remaining at the mouth of the hole until his companion had come out. The injured man was a very wise miner. He knew that the shots were pointed to throw against the foot wall. He scrouged himself into as small a ball as possible, well down in the corner opposite to the shots, and said his prayers.

The charge exploded, breaking three tons of rock, of which only about half a ton fell back onto him. After he had regained his breath and was pulled out from the stuff, he asked for a cigar; this was given him. He remarked, *"Dios es grande!"*

One of our employees had married a Hot Country girl and went there to bring his family back to camp. On his return he told me about a colonization scheme that was going on at Topolobampo on the coast of the Gulf of California, not far from El Fuerte. This port of Topolobampo is entirely landlocked, very deep, an uncommonly good natural harbor. The colony of Americans there was unsuccessful and we got two or three fine young fellows from that place when they had to leave there to seek employment elsewhere. I had a sad experience with one of these boys. He worked for us a number of years in charge of a shift on the Big Mill. But he grew tired of it and wanted very much to get into the actual mining end of the game, so *El Patron Grande* sent him up to me at San Miguel Mine.

For a few days I took him about with me to familiarize him with the mine, and then one day I sent him up to a level eighty feet above tunnel level where we had a working in light silver.

I went about my own affairs; going into the shaft I jumped the skip and was dropped down to the fourteenth level where we also had silver. I had been there scarcely twenty minutes when a peon came running into the working where we were getting ready to fire a round of shots, with the word that "Don Gustavo has fallen down the *chorrera*." This is the chute through which ore is thrown to the tunnel level.

We ran to the skip and were hauled as rapidly as might be to the tunnel level. As I went by the chutes at the hoist, I called off all the car men to follow me and sprang out towards the main tunnel. When I got there to the chute I had another demonstration that *Dios es grande*. We carefully removed the gate of the chute; I had two of my car men to hold back the ore with their shovels, and I climbed in only to find Gus lying on top of what was the very last few carloads of ore the chute held.

There were still several carloads of rock caught up above me and it would require but the slightest jar to start it sliding down on us. I got my hands under the boy's arms, strongly braced myself so that we would not slide down with the rock as a sufficient amount was drawn off to enable me to pass the now unconscious Gus, very bloody and breathing heavily, out to the waiting men, feet first. This we managed to do, and we rushed him out of the mine; there the doctor was waiting for us with a stretcher. He gave Gus a hurried examination and had him taken to the hospital. Gus did not remember a single thing about any of it afterwards. The only words he uttered were, "For God's sake get me out of here!" when he heard my voice.

He had rolled eighty feet down the chute. He must have been walking in a sort of dream ever to have stepped into it, for it was a hard feat to accomplish even if you had set your mind on doing it. A lucky thing it was for Gus that a loaded car was just about to be dumped as he got there, for the car man had paused to let Gus pass before dumping the ore and he had been a witness of the fall. If it had not taken place in this way Gus would have been covered by tons of rock, because we would not have drawn off that chute until the next day. There would certainly have been the devil's own time to find him and to get out his body, or what was left of it. As it was, Gus stayed in hospital only about two weeks.

But at my special request he was not returned to the mine. I did not consider him noticeably qualified for this kind of work.

Bullion Shipment—About 30,000 Ounces Fine Silver. Each bar weighing from 60 to 65 pounds.

Chapter 21

Fighting Cocks in Mexico

In Mexico a cock-fight is a legitimate pastime and is conducted openly and aboveboard. The atmosphere surrounding it is more like that which used to exist in Ireland and even in certain sections of the United States before the "purists" began to clean things up.

The training and heeling of cocks for fighting is an art that few understand. It was really an art, the man who was an expert in tying a knife on a chicken was one who was in high demand. The *ammarrador* had to know his business. There was as much care in the training of cocks as there is in training for a prizefight in the United States. The chicken is a courageous bird and fights for his life. One of them is always killed and very frequently both combatants die in the ring. It is nothing like so ignominious a death as to have his neck wrung to serve for Sunday dinner. When you possess a chicken that has weathered three or more fights you have a marvel, few reach this number of fights. He is thus proven unusually good at fighting and is put out for breeding purposes, the resulting chickens for which he is responsible are birds of value.

In Mexico the gaff as we know it is not used. The weapon is a double-edged, minute saber as sharp as a razor both as to edges and point. I have seen a doctor perform a neat operation with one when his regular tools were not available. They vary in length from two inches to three and are shaped and balanced and of appropriate weights to suit the particular cock, his size, weight, general conformation, and style of fighting. The natural spur is cut off leaving a stub less than one half inch long. The *botanilla,* which is the pad with a hole in it to fit over the spur-stub, is made of the finest chamois or buckskin. Around the hole two or three thicknesses are added so that it makes a pad three-quarters of an inch square with the hole exactly in the middle. The ends of one thickness are long enough to overlap when placed around the leg of the chicken. It is made with the utmost care and the weight is very slight.

On the end of a fine twisted silk or cotton cord is a loop which passes over the spur-stub, is wrapped twice about the center, once or twice between the spur-stub and the edge of the *botanilla* above, and the same below the spur-stub.

The knife, the *navaja,* is now produced having been skillfully chosen from a selection of twenty-five or more, which every owner keeps to fit the requirements of this especial cock. What would be the hilt, if this knife were a saber, is at right angles to the blade and projects like the letter "U," the saber going from the base of the "U." This is slipped up over the spur-stub and settled firmly and evenly on the *botanilla,* then made fast by wraps around the leg and *botanilla.* Finally after it has been pointed with exactitude it is secured tightly by the last few wraps of cord.

A leather scabbard is fitted over the *navaja* in order that the bird may not cut himself or the person who looses him into the ring. This tiny scabbard remains in place until just before the cock is released; after he has been released no one except the judge can touch him until the fight is either won or lost. The rules are very strict and are rigidly enforced. The judge must also be an expert. Those who release the cock, the trainer, the *ammarrador,* must know their business if they are to win any fights.

Now, a game chicken must be as tame as a pet dog. During the training he is staked by an especially arranged leash, and this leash is always fastened to the leg which takes the knife. The trainer gives him his food and exercises him, allowing at stated intervals a "go" at another rooster about twice a week for a short tussle. In the meantime, he exercises the fowl in dodging and turning and striking by holding another chicken in his hands and playing this other chicken with him, thus teaching him to jump and to strike at different angles and distances from the ground.

I have had a game chicken spring up to strike another one that I was holding as high as my shoulder. The strength in the blow of a trained cock is sufficiently powerful to leave your knuckles numb if he hits your hand. If he is tame and accustomed to being handled he will not be startled nor made nervous when he is put in the ring surrounded by the tumult of noisy, shouting onlookers. You always match your chickens according to weight, unless they weigh over six pounds. From that weight upward they are what is called *tapados,* or free for all comers.

All this may give you an idea of what it takes to keep a string of fighting gamecocks in training. It is an exact and a nice science.

There is no bird more beautiful than a chicken when ready for the cockpit; that is, the way they train him in Mexico. He is always in complete and full feather, not one of them is out of place nor missing. You may not know it, but the big stiff feathers in the tail of a rooster keep him from being knocked over backwards. He goes backwards spreading his tail, and each feather acts as a part of a fan-shaped prop.

Game chickens once were the cause of my spending forty-eight hours *incommunicado* in the public school building in Batopilas, which was used as a substitute for the regular jail for two reasons. First, the jail was too full. Second, it was lousy and ill-kept and the old *Jefe* did not want anyone whose unfavorable comments would receive attention in the office of the Governor in Chihuahua to have personal and undeniable experience of conditions.

This *Jefe* was not a native of Batopilas, but had been sent to our camp for some political debt owed him from the City of Mexico. We will call him Don Bombardioso Cogñaqueño because he was bombastic and he was too much addicted to the sipping of cognac. He was tall, about sixty years old, wore a long beard, which with the hair on his head he kept dyed a glossy black, because he was a dog with the ladies . . . or thought he was.

Don Bombardioso was a devoté of the cockpit, and he believed that he knew more about the sport of chicken fighting than anyone else in the world. He challenged my kid brother Conness and me to hold a main, a *pelea de gallo,* on the fifth day of May. There were to be five fights; four matched for weight, and one *tapado,* making five in all. Five hundred dollars for the winner of the main, the majority of five.

This *Jefe* did not like us. He had it in for all Americans. He brought this dislike with him to our town. We had always been perfectly respectful to him, but he was not partial to the conditions in Batopilas where all our workmen were contented, their respect for us as individuals and for the organization which had made their lives much easier than was usual in a mining camp, being so very apparent. He also realized that he was actually second in command to my father in the town and in the minds of the majority of the population; also he himself was unpopular. As the Batopilense reasoned, was he not an outsider? Did we not have citizens every bit as capable as he to be *Jefe?* He did his best to make trouble for the company and was instantaneously squelched in his efforts by the Governor of the State. All of this, added to his probable defeat on the fifth of May, which was a day of rejoicing, a national holiday, made the cockpit crowded to overflowing, and was almost more than he could endure.

The great day arrived. Old Don Romulo Rocha was the *asentista,* the judge, at the chicken fight. I was appointed to release the cocks belonging to Conness and me and the *Jefe* was to do the same for his. All went well until the very last fight. We had won the first four, and Don Bombardioso was boiling. His temperature reached a height causing him to try twice to interfere and pick up his bird when it became entangled with the other cock in the pit. This, of course, is strictly against the rules; once the cocks are loosed in the pit, no one with the single exception of the *asentista* being allowed under any circumstances to touch them.

The first time he tried this, I was polite, but firmly remonstrated with him. The second time he sprang forward and stooped to grab hold of his bird, I pushed his shoulder. He sat down hurriedly and in no dignified manner. The watching crowd howled its appreciation. A bystander aided him to his feet. He made a mighty struggle to welch on his contract, and we agreed—"If he thought that anyone claiming to be a *caballero* could do such a thing."

Confidential orders were given to the Chief of Police to see that one of the policemen should do something that would "compel one of those *gringos*" to strike him, and then the fun would begin.

Old Macario, the Chief of Police, had known us since we were small boys. He had a friend in us when he needed funds, or hospitalization for himself or family, or for any policeman or prisoner in jail who got sick or was injured; he had been hard ridden by the new martinet of a *Jefe.* What, therefore, was more natural than that he should quietly caution us what we had to expect!

But it all supposedly blew over, and we thought everything had been forgotten, since we obeyed the warning Macario had given us—to keep away from the town for a while.

Two months had passed, and we believed the whole affair lost in oblivion. Bill Kirby-Smith and I were returning kind of late from down river one afternoon where we had been inspecting some prospects that were being opened up. We came through the town and passed the home of a friend. An impromptu *baile* was in progress; our friend, who was a wild youngster, came hurrying out when he saw us and insisted that we come in. He urged us so eagerly that we agreed, but not being dressed for dancing we only went into the refreshment room to have some beer. Within half an hour we said good-bye. As was customary, I let out a yell in the street and a *"Viva, Sarachito!"* the name of the young friend whose hospitality we had enjoyed.

Then I walked over to my horse, took my spurs from my *mozo,* and stooped to adjust them to my feet. At that precise moment, a policeman ran up to me and using obscene language reached for his gun. Of course, I hit him. I knocked him down and extended my hand for my own gun which my *mozo* was holding. I had left it with him, because it is exceedingly bad form to enter the home of a friend wearing a gun or spurs. The Chief of Police hurried to the scene. He ordered the cop away and told us to go home and "Be good, please." Bill Kirby-Smith had leaped across from where he was about to mount his horse, gun in hand. I had some difficulty in convincing him that the best thing to do was for us to obey Macario, that he was our very good friend and that we really ought to follow his advice.

Alex was then General Manager, and next afternoon he sent for Bill and me. We went down to the Hacienda San Miguel and he showed us a letter from the *Jefe,* in which he stated that we had been guilty of a serious offense and were to come to his office in the town to pay a fine of one hundred dollars each. We went to the *Jefatura,* which was on the second floor of the building, and there the old rascal proceeded to read me a lecture. I told him:

"I am here at the request of the *Jefe* to pay a fine for having struck a policeman who without cause grossly insulted me. But, with the *Jefe's* permission, I am not here to be the recipient of a lecture on good behavior from the *Jefe.*"

He further told us that it was not a matter of a mere fine. (Although he had accepted the one hundred dollars from each of us and had given us each a receipt for it.) He informed us that we were to be incarcerated until a decision should be reached as to our ultimate sentence by himself, the *Jefe Politico.* I knew that all this was the bunk, of course. But I saw, and Bill did too, that the only exit from this upstairs room was filled with *pelados,* armed troops, and their bayonets were fixed. I agreed to be incarcerated. I didn't want too much trouble nor to make any move to place me in a position where he could say with truth that I had resisted an officer in the performance of his duty. We were escorted to the public school. It was vacation time and the building was empty. This was a nice structure adjoining the jail. Passing my *mozo,* who had been holding our horses, en route to the "jail," I told him to tell my brother that Bill and I were *incommunicado.*

Almost at once we were supplied with comfortable cots and bedding by some of our sympathetic friends in the town and as soon as supper time came we were served, from the same source, with more delicacies than we could eat. The jailer handed us nice little notes of joking condolence. So much for the lighter side of the affair.

On his way to the Hacienda San Miguel, my *mozo* spread the news. He met some of the day shift from San Miguel Mine and the Porfirio Diaz Tunnel, and told them. They ran back to the mine and soon from both places they had organized a hundred or more miners under the command of the two head men, and had started for the town to take the damned jail, to clean up the police, and to free us from durance vile.

But not so vile. Bill and I were in separate rooms, to be sure, but at that moment we were engaged in consuming all sorts of good things to eat.

Fortunately my brother Alex and my cousin Dr. Merchant were in the act of mounting their horses to go to the telegraph office to wire the true facts to the Governor of the State at Chihuahua. They hastily crossed the river and were able to intercept the army of angry miners and to explain to them that their efforts would cause no end of trouble and difficulties to all concerned. Alex received word from an influential citizen that the entire business was a frame-up, that he could accomplish nothing locally, for the *Jefe* was saturated with cognac and was, besides in a very ugly humor, refusing to listen to anyone. My brother was further informed that a garbled account of our conduct had been sent to the Governor the night before. This report stated that I had fired six times at close range upon the Chief of Police, but fortunately had missed him.

Good old Macario had refused to confirm this by a sworn statement at the request of the *Jefe.* First, said Macario, it was not true; secondly, anyone, although not a witness of the occurrence, would know it was false; and thirdly, there were many persons present who would swear that my gun and belt were still held by my *mozo* when it all took place.

Alex sent a true statement to the Governor. This gentleman had telegraphed the contents of the *Jefe's* telegram to one of the leading citizens of the town with the request that it should be confirmed or rejected. A prompt rejection was wired to the Governor with the additional clause that the claims were false on the face of them, because the sender of the message knew that it would be an impossibility, if I had fired six times at close range at any man, for that man still to be walking about the streets uninjured, as the Chief of Police was doing at that precise instant. The Chief was also willing to "deny the whole thing as being a fabrication and that under no conditions could he see me, whom he had known since I was *muy pequeno,* do anything unkind to him . . . unless it were to make him drink more liquor on occasions than might be good for him, but that he would leave it to the judgment of the Señor Gubernador if that was an unkindness."

Some of the "Gang." Con and Grant Shepherd, Louis Mohun, Frank English, Tom Shepherd, Gilbert Geiselhart, Ed Stevens, "Dick."

Chapter 22

Thieving Silver

About the year 1898 a renegade labor-union cast-off came to Batopilas and instigated a campaign. We said nothing but left it to the men. For a few days about ten per cent of the miners stayed away from work; suddenly they all came back. The older men knew that nowhere in that part of the world was the worker so well taken care of, and they went to the Chief of Police, took council with him, and abode by his advice. He was their friend and had been a former companion.

Of course, the Chief could not take action officially, but he intimated to the old miners that they ought to call upon the trouble-maker in a body and suggest to him that the miners were entirely satisfied in their work and with their pay; that they had no intention of supporting a lazy good-for-nothing; that they certainly were not fools and they realized that the company had given them fair treatment. The Chief further instructed them to let the cast-off union man know that their Patron was their friend; that he provided them with a good hospital; that he let them have money when it was needed in emergencies; that he charged them no interest, allowing them a long time in which to repay it; that unless this newcomer was in a position to duplicate or to improve these conditions he would do better to go away. This he did. That was the last as well as the first we ever heard of him or any other labor agitator. It was a joke for a long time among our men.

"To think," they used to say, "the poor fool believed that the Batopilense was such an *inocente* as to be taken in by such a *tonto.*"

Although the men were faithful, in every group of employees there are a certain proportion who will take the easiest way. . . .

The ores from our mines were what is commonly known as high grade; therefore much watchfulness had to be exercised to prevent them as well as the silver itself, while in the various processes of reduction from the crude ore state to the refined bullion, from being filched. We had a group of trusted employees, native and foreign, who kept themselves on the thinnest edge of readiness to combat the ingenuity of those who hoped to add to their wages (in a few cases they succeeded in doing so) by stealing small amounts now and then and carrying them out of the mines on their persons. Some of the methods are worth relating—there is no knowing when you may be reduced to working in a silver or a gold mine, and with this knowledge of how to secrete the precious metal you might make enough on the side to cover your monthly installments on the radio or the electric ice-box. Say, for instance, you wear your hair quite long, and while you are turning the drill steel and it is cutting through rich native silver ore, you clean your hands to rid them of the mud caused by the cutting of the drill-bit moistened by the water you squirt from your mouth into the hole; if you succeed in cleaning your hands by wiping them on your head the long hair will get full of mud. When you go home, and wash your hair in a basin, you will find that there remain in the basin, fine particles of silver: after you become expert at it you wall be able to run it up to as much as fifty cents worth a day. If you are diligent this will increase your weekly income about three dollars.

Suppose, on the other hand, you are wearing the native sandal made of heavy sole leather. If you exercise patience and skill you can insert the cutting edge of your sheath knife into the edge of the leather, preferably on the inner side under the instep. Gradually as you work this edge back and forth to split the sole leather, you will have an opening not much wider than the blade of your knife; thus you make a pocket into which you can put an ounce of native silver that you have secured by pounding up some of the rich ores and blowing the powdered rock away, leaving the heavier silver.

Another way is to forego your dinner. Never mind if you are hungry; if you will take your dinner of hash or frijoles into the mines in a porridge bowl with corn *tortillas* laid on top to prevent the contents from spilling, the whole thing wrapped in a clean napkin, and can go without eating it after working hard all day, you can put the filched silver in the bottom of your bowl. You can replace the tortillas on top of the hash or *frijoles;* look sick as you reach the mouth of the tunnel to be searched; tell the gate keeper and searcher that you did not eat your dinner because you had a *dolor muy fuerte* in your stomach, and you may get away with it. But you will stand a slim chance indeed if old Don Romulo Rocha or Ramon is on the job.

There are other very unique methods, but the ones I have told you about will be plenty to start on. Oh, yes, there is another trick you might attempt. However, it is scarcely worth while because you would have to establish a reputation as a *macouchic* smoker. This is a very inferior tobacco. Learning to smoke it is in itself an ordeal that badly shakes the system of the uninitiated. Tie up in the corner of your bandanna handkerchief a handful of *rnacouchic* and mix the fine silver with the *macouchic* before you come from the mine. But Don Romulo is so very expert that he may smile subtly and say:

"What heavy tobacco that is! Let me look at it; I am, as you know, an expert on tobaccos."

He will do the same thing with your cigars, so do not waste any time hollowing them out and charging them with silver. I have watched that fine old fellow, Don Romulo Rocha, search hundreds of men and I honestly believe that he intuitively knew, when they stepped up to be searched, just who did and just who did not have contraband silver on him. Many of the mines were superstitious about Don Romulo. When he had been tipped off by the mine boss—which used to happen rather often—that so-and-so would probably make an effort to pass him with some stolen silver, he would wave the man back into the tunnel a few feet until he had finished with the others of the group. Then he would call the culprit and say:

"I am surprised and hurt that you should have attempted to do this. Give me the silver. Appreciate the fact that I do not expose you to the rest of the men as a rascal and a thief."

That old gentleman was a student of psychology, he could have given cards and spades to some of the persons who write books on the subject.

But taking all things into consideration and the temptations these miners were subjected to, there were comparatively few who tried to steal. As a matter of fact, at first they did not look at it in that light. "Has not *Dios* put it there to be taken from the earth and to be used by mankind? Did not my own labor actually bring it forth?"

An old woman, Juana, put one over on me. I never did live it down because I was supposed to be tolerably wise about such things. She showed up at the mine one day to draw her pension (her son had been killed at the mine some time before) with a hunk of ore, a good-sized piece and very rich in black silver, sulfide of silver. Juana would not tell me from what place this ore had come, but said that, for a reward, she would show me the place.

"Well, Juana, you know what the rules are about that; if this proves as you say you will be well-fixed for the rest of your life."

I settled matters so I could go with her the next day, Saturday and have two men accompany us with an outfit to remain for two days, to shoot a few rounds of dynamite in the vein this rich ore was supposed to have come from. Very early in the morning I sent a *mozo* with a saddle-mule for the old woman, dispatched my men with the pack-mule, telling them to go ahead and that I would catch up with them on the trail. This I did after putting in the shift on Saturday morning and signing the payroll. The superintendent's O.K. was necessary for the money to be delivered to the paymaster. Off I went in high expectation.

About twelve miles up the river I overtook the cavalcade; we turned off, and continued upward into a very bad trail that led to God knows where. I noticed that Juana had a good-looking young Indian girl with her, she too was mounted on a mule. After we had arrived at the place where Juana insisted that the vein was located, I knew that she had misrepresented things to me, and that the only object in the expedition was the twenty-five-dollar store credit I had arranged for her. The good-looking young Indian girl had been brought along as a sacrificial offering to appease my expected wrath.

It was growing dark when we reached this place, but I emphatically affirm that any old woman who had endured the ten hours' ride on a mule over those trails as Juana had done for twenty-five dollars store credit, did not deserve too rough handling.

At break of day I had a look at the supposed vein; there was a seam of decomposed porphyry; I sampled it and traced it for some distance. There was no possible hope that the rich sample she had used as a bait could have appeared in the formation in that section, and I gave Juana a mild reproof. To the Indian girl I gave five dollars so that her hard journey would not prove a total loss, warned Juana that if she took the five dollars away from the girl I would have her put in jail, saddled my beast and lit out for camp. I got back to the mine in time to have a shower, eat my supper, and get to town in time not to miss the circus showing there on Sunday night, which was a rare event in our camp.

Being well-lubricated when the evening was a little older, we were having *menudo* in Manuela's and I told our crowd, in an unguarded moment, about my fruitless quest into the mountains. I had to buy wine and more wine and then some more wine! Old Juana cost me more than a hundred dollars.

I sent word for Juana the following week to come and tell me where she had got that piece of ore. I was informed that Juana could not come to see me then, that she was getting married. Thus the necessity was explained for my contribution taking the form of an order on the company store. Further inquiry revealed that the man she was marrying was a powerful Mayo Indian, who was known to be infernally lazy but more than commonly attractive to the ladies . . . so much so indeed that he could afford to indulge his talent for being the most indolent devil in camp. I knew now who had done the thinking-out of the plan, and I sent a note to my friend the judge.

Bright and early one morning up comes the old girl accompanied by her former lover, now her husband. He was all rigged out in new store clothes. I knew that unless I landed him now, both Juana and I would be the losers. I took the fellow aside and told him: "You *sin verguenza,* what did the judge tell you yesterday?"

"He told me, *Patroncito,* that if I did not pay that store order he would put me in jail."

"Right," said I. "Get your good clothes off. Go into the mines on the day shift. I have already told Don Manuel where to put you to work, and that work will be good for your soul. Old Juana may support you by taking in washing after you have paid off that twenty-five dollars, but until that time you work on Number eighteen level where it's hotter than the hinges of Hell . . . or you go to jail."

"I will go to work, *Patron,*" agreed the Mayo.

I learned that the Mayo had picked up that ore sample in the town dump and had cracked off the worn edges with a hammer so that it would look like a comparatively newly broken piece of ore. Further investigation revealed that Don Ignacio Ramirez had received this sample from a friend many years before while he was in Chihuahua, and the Lord only knows where it came from in the first place. It had landed on the town dump after a house-cleaning at Don Igancio's All these investigations and things took time and my best Secret Service methods.

I got the dope about the sample's reaching the dump from Don Igancio's lovely daughter while sitting out a dance one night in their garden, where the scent of the orange blossoms and the light of the moon tended to soften the sting of what that wretched piece of ore had cost me.

The Batopilense is a great *chalan* and *pullista,* which being interpreted means a great chatterer and "ragger." But this ragging was a sort of play on words something like punning with, a rule, a risqué tone and very witty. So that condemned piece of ore cost me much more than a couple of hundred dollars, what with the good-humored raillery and banter which grew less as time went on but which never wholly ceased.

Chapter 23

Comestibles

There was a custom in our time in Mexico, I hope it yet prevails, of serving *menudo.* This is a tripe stew accompanied with a red sauce of *chili colorado,* very hot. It took place mostly from one in the morning on until daylight, and certainly was a life-saver for those who were overalcoholized. It surely straightened you out. All the *fonderas* specialized in this. There was one old woman, Doña Anselma, a vigorous soul, whose *fonda* was noted for a *menudo* that was particularly efficacious and palatable. Her long table would seat as many as twelve and on Saturday and Sunday nights it was always working to capacity.

Rafael Diaz was a tall young miner, very pleasant in appearance. With some others he came into Doña Anselma's one night; there were two big *ollas* of *menudo* simmering on the hot coals in the corner. Rafael was observed to approach one of these while the old woman's back was turned. This Rafael loved a practical joke, and being well-stimulated added to this rather questionable taste in amusement. Coming along the street on his way to the *fonda,* he had been a witness to the fact that although a cat may be quick, the hind feet of a mule, at times at any rate, are even more alert. A miserable and unfortunate cat, chased by an equally wretched dog, had tried to escape by climbing the hind legs of a mule which was peacefully sleeping in front of the house where its owner was disporting himself with wine. . . .

Now, the hind legs of a sleeping mule are something to be treated with respect and consideration. If you must play with them, awaken the mule gently first with kind and soothing words uttered in melting tones of voice. This was not done by the perturbed feline. The resulting effect to the cat was the loss of her nine lives at one fell swoop, when propelled by the mule's instantaneous and best efforts she sailed across the street crashing against the wall of a stone building.

"Pobre gatito! poor little cat!" murmured Rafael in his sympathetic soft voice as he lifted the limp form by its skinny tail. "Come with me, we will yet find a way by which you can enliven the existence of others although yours has ended."

As I said, Rafael came into Doña Anselma's; there was a slight flip of his hand as he neared the *ollas* of *menudo.* The table was surrounded by a full quota of customers. The hostess with smile and jest proceeded to ladle out the big, deep soup plates full of the succulent life-giving *menudo.* Suddenly a strange and awful change transformed the face of Doña Anselma. . . . hanging across the ladle was the furry carcass of one of the most repulsive, squashy, dead cats ever beheld by man.

The screech emitted by the horrified Doña cannot be depicted in print, the language she used would be prohibited in the mails. And when the cat which she hurled at the table of expectant guests landed smack in the face of an able-bodied drunk who, awakened from his serene slumbers by her screams, raised his unsuspecting head to see why he had been so rudely disturbed, the fight started.

When the police reached the scene they were convinced that there had been a fierce cutting affray, for in the dim light the combatants were apparently covered with blood. *Chili colorado* splashed indiscriminately on white suits gives exactly that impression. Old Anselma was eventually soothed, explanations entered into. Rafael, whose white clothes were still immaculate, had absented himself early in the fray, and was quietly ordering a drink at a cantina a few doors away. He was heard to remark:

"La vieja Anselma is too irascible to carry on a restaurant business as it ought to be conducted. I, for one, intend to transfer my patronage elsewhere."

Rafael, by the way, was one of the most perfect double-jackers in the camp. I doubt if you could find a better one anywhere. When that boy began to swing an eight-pound sledge you got true poetry of motion, rhythm, and timing.

Menudo was only one of many delicious Mexican foods. I have already spoken of the young goat stew made by the wife of the station keeper at Teboreachic. Young goat is every bit as tender and savory as is young lamb, in fact it is hard to detect the difference between the two.

Huevos al Ranchero are a favorite with me. You may use olive oil or *manteca,* hog fat, in which to fry plenty of green peppers and onions, and salted and peppered to taste with plenty of *chili colorado;* when these are cooked to a nicety, put your eggs lightly on the top of the cooked mass and allow them to poach, as it were.

It was great fun on a Saturday or Sunday night to saddle up and ride down town to have some kind old *fondera* make us a nice supper of *sopa de chili verde con queso.* This is a soup, as its name implies; it is made with green *chili* and cheese. We will have served with it a big platter of hot *enchiladas* and a bottle of good claret. It is best to send her word an hour or two before we are coming so that she will not be hurried in preparing the supper, for you are too hungry to wait.

If you have never had the opportunity to eat a plate of good *sopa de queso* you do not know good food. The first time this conjunction of circumstances comes your way do not hold back. The *enchilada* is made from uncooked *tortilla* in which is wrapped a delectable combination of finely ground and highly seasoned meat or chicken with plenty of chopped olives; then it is fried. After it has been cooked this way, the *enchiladas* are laid side by side in a pile three or four inches thick and covered with grated Mexican cheese, which is somewhat like Parmesan but not quite the same, and lastly they are enveloped in a sauce made from finely chopped onions, *chili colorado,* olives, and a few other enticing-tasting tidbits. You put them on your plate two piles at a time or even more if your companion eats fast. With your fork you cut off about a fourth and proceed as customary. When you get this far you need no further instructions from anyone.

I am so fond of *enchiladas* I forgot to tell you how to make the *sopa.* Procure as many green peppers as you think you can eat, cut them around the pepper in pieces about half an inch wide, stew this in enough water to cover it and yet to allow it to have some juice. When it is about done, put in the cheese, not grated but cut into small bits about half an inch square; allow this to simmer until the cheese gets soft. You will find that the dry Mexican cheese will not melt as rapidly as does our yellow American cheese. Take your spoon in your right hand. . . .

If there are no spoons, take your *tortilla,* tear this into four equal parts, and use each quarter as a scoop, eating the scoop when desired or when it becomes too soggy and soft to function as a scoop. The *sopa* being related to the international soup should be eaten as a first course as custom demands. It is perfectly proper to drink some of the claret with this kind of soup, the rest with the *enchiladas.* If you do full justice to these two comestibles there will be no roast.

Frijoles are beans. And *frijoles* prepared and seasoned by a good Mexican cook make a delightful dish. The same thing may be said of the white army bean when prepared by some French women cooks up in the Vosges. It is apparently not so much the bean itself as it is the artisan who manipulates it. Whatever a great artist paints, is a picture that looks like something. The poor artist turns out exactly what the poor cook does . . . "just beans."

While we are on the subject of foods, let me introduce you to the best spinach in the world, which is not spinach at all. It is a weed which springs from the earth to bless the stomach of man at the start of the rainy season, and, therefore, can be enjoyed for only two or maybe three months during the year. I shall not attempt to instruct you how to cook it, for you never could do it in an aluminum pot or frying pan on an electric stove. It has to be done by a Mexican woman squatting down over a small wood fire, cooked in a baked-clay *olla,* with the knowledge of the right soupçon of onion, lard, and salt to make it what it should be. You need not look over your files of the *Homemakers' Magazine,* no one has ever advertised *quelite* as a vitamin-filled food; I do not believe that *quelite* ever heard of a vitamin. Transportation has been very bad down there and the vitamin, like a lot of other modern things, has probably not reached into the country as far as the Sierras.

The Mexican is interested in food simply and solely as food and the pleasure it gives his mouth and his belly. He is an ignorant cuss and has no particular use for color schemes and such things in food; he would undoubtedly tell you: "What is the use of color schemes in food? Foods are only helpful when consumed, and who the Hell sees what is in your stomach?"

One occasion, when I was a young man, we had been having a very bad time on the trail, as I accompanied the *conducta* into Chihuahua. It was the rainy season, and we had been delayed by roads heavy with mud, swollen streams, bad crossings, and all its concomitant ills; our grub had given out when we reached El Fortin tired, harassed, hungry. We were twelve men on this especial trip with the stages of the *conducta.*

The proprietor at El Fortin greeted us with the news that he had nothing to sell us but dried beef and some frijoles, but that his woman would make us some *tortillas*. No chickens, no eggs, no young pigs, nothing but the eternal *carne seca* and *frijoles*. He did have some *tequila* and with that potent drink to sustain us, we got our three teams of fourteen mules under shelter and fed. By that time our reliable old cook Antonio had concocted a stew of dried beef and *frijoles,* which we promptly demolished. The *carne seca* was particularly tough and tasteless, but we paid it scant heed at the time, only thankful enough for anything to fill the empty void.

Early in the morning of the next day, we were refreshed and pulled out from El Fortin. I took with us a poor devil with a sore foot who wanted to get to Chihuahua for medical treatment. I gave him two or three smokes and a drink of *tequila*. He asked me if I did not find the *carne seca* which mine host at El Fortin had sold us rather bad. Knowing that this question had something behind it I agreed that it was worse than usual. I asked him where it had come from.

"*Carne de burro,* meat of a donkey," he answered with a wag of his head. "And not only that," he further volunteered, "but a dead burro."

"Naturally it had to be a dead burro or else how could it be made into *carne seca?*"

"Yes, that is quite true," he agreed. "But it is a sin to sell anyone the meat of a donkey who died of a disease; and these eyes of mine saw what a very sick donkey that was when he died."

It seemed to me to be time for a big drink. Though I rarely ever took one before breakfast even in those robustious years, that morning, on account of the rains and the burro—well, you know how such things are.

There used to be quite a business in Mazatlan in the livers and certain other parts of sharks (seems to me it was the fins) to be sold to the Chinese in San Francisco. The sharks were caught by the natives there on the coast. I had the opportunity to see them at this doubtfully safe occupation one time. Some of the shark fishermen were in dug-out canoes and those canoes appeared to me to be very narrow ones. I was told that only an Indian could possibly navigate them and not turn over. Although I have been in many places of danger and have seen a great number of other people in like predicament, I never got anything but an unpleasant thrill from it.

When Bob Wagner and I, in a seaworthy boat of ample proportions, watched those Indians hook a seven-foot shark and work him up the edge of that little dug-out canoe, and then club him to death, it was borne in upon me that if it took courage to do this, I was entirely confirmed in the doubt that had always been mine as to whether I possessed any of that particular brand of moral excellence. Each of the canoes was manned by two Indians; as soon as the shark was hooked, one of the men deserted his own line in order to devote his time and energy to working the canoe with his paddle while his partner attended to wearing out the shark. The fishing for these sea beasts was done off the mouth of the harbor at Mazatlan where there was a very respectable swell, and the way the two men would handle that infernally difficult situation was a thing to arouse the greatest possible admiration and respect.

What would have taken place had both men hooked a shark at the same time, I will let you imagine. When I asked that question of our boatman, he shrugged his shoulders with a *"Que sepa Dios,"* God knows.

The men had no poles, no reels, no refinements of any kind, and when the shark ran (or whatever you call it when he leaves that especial locality), the men paid out the line with their bare hands. I saw one fellow break it gradually by holding the line down to the bottom of the dug-out with his foot. He wore a *guarache* it is true, but the line was almost smoking hot as it paid out over the gunnel of that old piece of a onetime monarch of the forest. Of course, it was a heavy line. They exhibited wonderful skill, really, in adjusting their weight to the necessities that arose in order to keep the canoe right side up. While they were very earnest in their work and exchanged a shout of some evident import one to the other now and then, there was no apparent haste nor excitement about any of their actions.

I made a trip one time on a little steamer whose forward hatch was filled with dried shark, or fish, or some other sort of sea-faring animal. Most of the voyage was made in very calm weather, and we got the air movement from the bow to the stem with no relief for many days. The old hooker sweated out her eight or nine knots an hour and I wondered what the Chinese would do with the cargo when it finally was delivered to them in San Francisco. 'Way up in the bow was the only spot one could get any air that was not seventy-five per cent contaminated.

Habits and customs in foods are as varied as the thoughts that inspire them. Misinformation as to the wishes of the poor *peon* in Mexico for different food from what he had was rife at one time in the publications in the United States. One thing among the mass of erroneous information is vivid in my memory. It was to the effect that the writer had come in contact with two poor women, grinding their *nestamal,* which is something like our lye-hominy (or samp or big hominy—it is all the same). The women were grinding the *nestamal* preparatory to making their tortillas from the paste obtained in this way. It is done on a *metate,* a flat stone especially shaped for that purpose with the aid of another smooth stone somewhat like a short rolling-pin. In an earthenware pot the *frijoles* were cooking. To the inquiry as to what they were making, and finding that it would be bread: "What, no flour? No wheat flour with which to make your bread?" "No, ah no! we never see flour, all we have is corn and beans. Meat we have every now and then."

Now, that may sound perfectly dreadful to those who have never seen nor eaten a *tortilla,* some people shudder at the thought of corn bread. If you tried to make Mexicans and Indians—except a small proportion of the city dwellers—live and work on a wheat-bread diet they would kick like a couple of bay steers. The *tortilla* and the *frijoles* with their *queso,* and a small quantity of meat now and then, keep them in excellent health. Where there is irrigation, and, as I have said, during the rainy season, they have vegetables. This food is what they like (do not the Afghanistans eat sour mash from mare's milk?), what they have been brought up on. Frequently in bad years, our company paid as high or higher than six dollars a bushel for corn and had it imported from the United States in order to keep our people contented, which they would not have been if we had supplied them with wheat flour. They will gladly pay more for corn with which to make their beloved *tortilla* than to make and cook wheat *tortillas*.

It was not only misinformation about food that went to readers of the press in the United States. Once I boarded a train at Chihuahua en route to El Paso, Texas, and ran into a couple of men I knew from the States who were on their way home. They introduced me to a lady also on her way back to the States after having made a tour of Mexico. She was a very plump lady, and excessively wrought up over many annoyances she had encountered in Mexico. One thing that was burning her up was the difference in foods between her Ohio home town and those of Mexico, which food was not prepared properly.

Her chief complaint which gave her no rest was the clothes worn by the poor *peon* in Vera Cruz and the surrounding countryside. The poor *peon* went about in a pair of cotton pants, or long, loose drawers, a single cotton shirt, a rough straw hat, and a pair of *guaraches*.

"It was simply appalling," she stated. "And oh, the heat! It was so hot I nearly suffocated, I almost died, dreadful, dreadful!"

This last grievance gave me my chance. I asked her if the poor *peons* in their cotton drawers seemed to be suffering from the heat as she had done.

"Oh, no, they didn't seem to mind it at all."

"Then, my dear Madam, when you make your next trip into Vera Cruz why not try wearing a pair of cotton drawers and a cotton shirt? I am sure you would not suffer nearly so much from the extreme heat."

"You are utterly disgusting," was her offended reply.

I made my escape marveling at the attitude of mind shown by many travelers in the criticisms they make of the food, customs, clothes, beliefs of the natives in the countries in which they are touring.

Another thing that struck me as peculiarly insular and provincial, this time in a supposedly cosmopolitan man, was something that occurred in Chihuahua on a certain day when I was going to the States for a vacation. I made a date with two or three friends to meet me at the hotel, after I had changed my traveling clothes, in order to have an aperitif before I attended a formal dinner at the splendid home of Ambassador Creel. This gentleman had been in the Banco Minero when I was unloading the bullion there and had invited me to dine with him that night.

At the hotel I changed the riding clothes in which I had traveled from Batopilas, and went into the *patio* to join my friends. I found them chuckling with mirth. They introduced me to a New York mining engineer who had just arrived on the train from New York, and he was all dressed up in a complete riding rig.

"What was the joke?" I asked Alberto when we had settled down at the table in the jockey club across from the Plaza.

"When you came down the steps into the *patio* in a tail coat and a top hat, this little stranger said, 'I say, look at the tenderfoot, who in the world can he be?' And," continued Alberto, "he is all ready for the ride of fifteen miles behind Father's best team of English carriage horses; fifteen miles to Santa Eulalia tomorrow when he goes to meet Bill who is selling him his mine. He was all dressed up like you saw him when he got off the train this morning, only then he had a big six-shooter strapped on him and was carrying a Winchester .44."

"Where are they now?" but he did not hear me.

"Here is a ticket to the theater. Meet us there after the dinner. We will have some fun, and make you miss your train tomorrow. There are dancers from Spain tonight, and they ought to be worth seeing."

I tell this seemingly trivial incident to show how strangely ignorant some persons are about other people and other places. This man was a mining engineer, supposedly having had a wide experience, he was over thirty years old, from New York City, had come all that distance to purchase a mine at Santa Eulalia, which was a carriage ride from Chihuahua. Chihuahua, a city of thirty-five thousand population, was the junction of two railroads. It was more than two hundred years old, through which and around which the Lord only knows how many millions of dollars had come and been produced and had been paid to stockholders of two continents. Yet this person thought that because another man dressed appropriately for a formal dinner he must be a tenderfoot.

Why, Hell! Some people even in those days dressed for dinner in Chicago! If he had been at our camp on an anniversary of some sort, I suppose he would have yelled bloody murder and thought that all of us were insane when he found us dressed in tail coats. If he had had a Scotch and soda that came direct from Scotland in special fifteen-gallon kegs, he would have thought that he was dreaming!

Chapter 24

El Patron Grande with Angels and Calamity

The *Patron Grande* was the kindest and the most charitable man I have ever encountered in more than sixty years wrestling with what we call life. He had an ample field in which to practice these characteristics in the mining camp. In the first fifteen or twenty years of our existence down in the Sierras occasionally old tramps of non-native parentage would wander in. Sometimes it would be perplexing to the last degree to discover their nationality until they had forced upon them a bath, a haircut, and a clean outfit of clothing from the skin out, and then we would be able to decide with which geological age and continent they had been connected.

Very early in the game these wanderers were called "angels." Dad always said that it was necessary to take them in, "because who could tell whether we might not be entertaining one of the winged divines unaware?" This was confusing for a long time to my kid brother and myself when we were small boys, for we could not tie together the idea of angels as we had been taught to conceive them, and these battered dirty old wrecks.

One of them we called "Roses" and he was never known by any other name. Over a period of years he made us many visits. He would come into camp worn with fatigue, thin, dirty, hungry. He would leave whenever he pleased after a few months, clean, well-dressed, rested, fattened. He acquired the name of Roses one night when he reached the front gate to the Hacienda San Miguel very drunk and singing lustily. He loved, when he had acquired this stage of exaltation, to quote Shakespeare and other authors, correctly or otherwise. The night watchman and my uncle Sam Young (who was a sort of general superintendent of the whole hacienda at night) escorted Roses to the rooms over across the corral where he slept, endeavoring to pacify him in order to prevent his disturbing those of us whose windows overlooked this lower level.

Thanking their lucky stars that he had at last succumbed to their efforts they laid him on his bed and left him to his alcoholic slumbers . . . as they fondly hoped. But no! Out of his room Roses flung himself screaming: "Sit down, Tommy. Sit down I tell you! Listen to me while I tell you that this world ain't no bed o' roses!"

Again my Uncle Sam, who was a gentle man, ably assisted by the night watchman, strove by kind words and calming tones to quiet him. But Roses was adamant in insisting in a whiskey voice again and yet again that this life was no bed of roses.

"Sam," this voice was that of my father, it was an impressive sound. It trembled a little and this denoted high steam pressure, a tone of voice thoroughly understood by all. "Sam, knock that old cockroach on the head and drop him over the river wall."

Absolute silence prevailed. Presently Roses turned toward his sleeping quarters whispering hoarsely: "What did I tell you, Tommy? This world ain't no bed o' roses. No one around here appreciates Shakespeare. They ain't even up to the lesser poets."

When Roses paid his first visit to the camp he must have been around fifty years old, he was over sixty when he passed from our ken to, I hope, that bed of roses he constantly talked about when he had finished his bottle of *mescal.* He was a wizened-up old man. I have not a doubt that to his diminutive size could be attributed the fact that he had not long ago been exterminated by someone. He was a fearful pest. The event I have just narrated occurred in the early hours of a certain Monday morning, and when my uncle reported to *El Patron Grande* before turning in for his sleep, my father said to him:

"Sam, why in Hell do you take so much trouble with that old reprobate? Why don't you knock him on the head?"

"Because, brother-in-law, every Sunday night you WILL read the Church service to all of us and insist on my singing beautiful Christian hymns. [Uncle Sam had a fine voice.] Last night you laid especial stress on the chapter which has to do with charity. What you read in the way of prayers and chapters from the Holy Book evidently penetrates deeper with some of your listeners than they do with the lay-reader himself."

The arrival of one of Dad's angels was as much of a calamity as the possession of a horse by that name almost turned out to be. My father was a large man, six feet two in height; when he reached his early fifties he had accumulated some extra pounds; not fat, but a big man. He weighed about two hundred and thirty pounds. It was not a simple matter to find a riding animal that was up to his weight and other requirements. Uncle Jack helped me one day in making a trade of my ill-mannered pony for Calamity. We paid something to boot, for Calamity was a strong good-sized horse, well-gaited. Very soon after he came into my possession I went back to school at Sewanee, and father began using him and liked him; he was riding Calamity when he came near to having a fatal accident. This near tragedy broke us from giving any name to our saddle animals which might have a sinister meaning.

One of the many pieces of work that was put through at the camp by my indomitable father was the more than three-mile aqueduct of solid masonry built along the side of the canyon. For many feet the leveling was done through hard rock, in some cases short tunnels from thirty to a hundred feet had to be driven. Regular inspection of the work was made; when it was possible to do so the party on inspection and pleasure bent would ride through the aqueduct itself, since its floor made a very acceptable roadbed. On one afternoon my father was mounted on old Calamity and had ridden about half way through the longest of the tunnels where the light was dim. A drunken Indian arose suddenly from the floor where he had been asleep, directly under Calamity's nose. The horse, of course, reared in fright, and threw my father's head against the jagged rock of the roof, giving him a nasty scalp wound which nearly caused his death after erysipelas set in.

I can never forget the feeling of accessory before the fact that was mine when at school in the States I received word of this accident. Was I not the owner of the animal? Had I not acquiesced in my uncle's bestowing the name of Calamity upon him? As a matter of fact Calamity looked it, though that was more on account of his Roman nose than of any meanness of disposition.

Quite often while the work of Porfirio Diaz Tunnel was under way and the heavy masonry work of the Hacienda San Antonio was under construction, the *Patron Grande* accompanied by his son-in-law Walter Brodie would walk the half mile to the tunnel on a tour of inspection. Walter was responsible for that engineering feat. Neither of these gentlemen was inclined to tote a big gun; they usually slipped a small revolver, generally a .38 into their hip pockets. This habit caused Mr. L. H. Stevens, the vice-president of the Company, to send them each as a present a hammerless Smith & Wesson safety. It had a plate on the stock that you were supposed to squeeze as you pulled the trigger, else it would not fire.

One afternoon they were walking to the tunnel on such an inspection when that great piece of work was nearing completion after heart-breaking months of hard times and tribulation. They were about half way there, when a vicious-looking dog darted out at them from a small *jacal* on the mountainside. At the same instant each man drew his little gun and aiming, pulled the triggers and pulled the triggers till they could pull no more, but never the sign of an explosion. Along came a small boy who shied a rock at the vicious beast. This worthy defender of the home fled to the protection of his refuge, the little tyke grinned at the *Patron Grande* and his son-in-law, and went merrily on his way.

I believe the laughs they got from the oft-repeated story was worth hundreds of dollars in doctors' bills and medicines. Both guns were turned over to Marshall Willis who gave them a good soaking in oil and a thorough cleaning. The gentlemen went to the upper *patio* privately afterwards and fired the guns a time or two for their own inward satisfaction.

My father inspired a strong feeling of affection and one of deep-seated respect in his workmen. The only drawback to a complete one hundred per cent sympathy was his Spanish. It was a bit out of the ordinary and difficult to understand. Thus it became a habit whenever possible for one of us who knew what he would be trying to say to be present or within hearing of what was said, so that the *mozo* to whom instructions had been given could slip to the *patroncito* unknown to the *Patron Grande,* and ask him to translate the order. Many times I would come to the main office and see a poor *arriero* standing there scratching his head with a lost-soul expression wondering what in the world he was to do. Then I would go into the office and tell my father that so-and-so had not understood him exactly and would he repeat to me the instructions and I would translate them to him.

"What?" my Dad would say. "Another damned fool who don't understand his own language? Well, I don't blame him, I don't either."

We all caught our bit of Hell now and then. It was usually justified. I recall Clemo particularly in this connection. He was an old Cornish miner and he was a corker when it came to putting in timbers. The only trouble with him was that he did from time to time get beyond his normal condition of alcoholic stimulation and then his work was not so good. On the other hand, if he became entirely sober he was no good at all. So long as he kept to, say, a quart of *mescal* about every ten hours, he was in fine shape. He taught many of us more than a little about timbering.

Every Sunday morning at ten o'clock the mine superintendents and sometimes their assistants would come to the main office to have individual chats with my father. After this was over, we would all assemble in the big main room around the large table where old Domingo had already deposited a tray covered with sandwiches, cakes, and things . . . not forgetting the Scotch whiskey and the sparklet siphon. For twenty years, every Sunday the *Patron Grande* would turn to old Clemo and say:

"Come on, old man, have a Scotch and soda with us."

"Oh, no, Governor, thanks. I don't believe I will have one today."

"Oh, come on and try it!"

"Well, sir, if you insist I will take a small one."

He would seize the tumbler in his huge fist, taking the bottle in the other, then would engage all of us in deep conversation; before the tumbler got so full that one could see the whiskey above the edge of his hand, he would put the bottle back on the table and shoot what was apparently a quantity of water into the Scotch from the sparklet siphon. With a graceful "Your health, Governor!" he would absorb all but about half the contents of the tumbler in one gulp. Then he would say: "If you do not mind, I would like a little water. I never could stand liquor without water."

There are fifty-two Sundays in a year, sometimes more; I am willing to gamble that old Don Guillermo Clemo never failed once in the ritual and I actually believe that he thought he fooled all of us each and every time. Once or twice the *Patron* would glance at us and apparently forget to urge old Clemo when his turn came. After a perceptible pause, the old fellow would say: "Well, Governor, if you insist, I believe I will," and he would put on the same show not one whit abashed. Just the same, the old Cornishman was all there. Many times working with him in some damned hard piece of timbering job I would thank my stars that I need have no fear that anything wrong would escape him.

Because in all companies there is a director who is always a perpetual suggester, and faultfinder, our company was no exception. My father had a letter from ours telling him that he believed there was a superabundance of sons, sons-in-law, nephews and brothers-in-law on the payroll. This director received a reply by telegraph from my father to the effect that if he could supply others who would do the same amount of work on the same salary, please to send them down to Mexico. He wanted it to be very plain that he, the *Patron Grande,* was ashamed to employ trained men to whom he was obliged to pay so small a salary for the quantities of work turned out, but that the company could not pay larger salaries unless the stockholders would agree to an annual assessment. The suggester was formerly a native of Scotland, and had more than once been cautioned for disturbing the peace by squeezing the eagle on the dollar until he screamed; therefore, we heard nothing further from him on the subject.

Most of the directors of the company played the game. But it was only natural that because at the beginning a couple of very big bonanzas were taken out, the uninitiated among the stockholders could not understand why this heavy production could not be a constant one. They could see no logic in the explanation that these rich bodies of ore lay distances apart and were hard to find, that there was hard rock to be broken, and many other difficulties to be overcome before another one could be reached. These first bonanzas were the reason for many headaches; they caused a prodigious error in calculating what might be regularly expected in the future. Therefore, the improvements were started, the cost ran into the millions, no sufficient capital subscribed to cover them. Hence the mines had to take over this burden from their regular monthly production. This resulted in a strong desire to take advantage of any big production era to sell the property.

We had no objection, for we felt that we could use our share to as good a purpose and could not have to work nearly so hard in some other part of the world. All this resulted in visits upon three separate occasions by representatives of syndicates who came to investigate and examine the mines with the object of buying the property. The Spanish War killed one opportunity to sell; the Boer War killed another; and the Madero Revolution settled the affairs of Batopilas.

A party of these experts direct from London spent a Christmas with us. An English engineer came with them whose reputation and experience embraced South Africa, Canada, and God knows where! He arrived in Batopilas as second in command, the real underground man, one of those supermen, as it were. He could look into and through hard rock and tell you all sorts of things which you found to be wrong after you had laboriously broken the ground and weeks later had come to the place where these things, according to his X-ray eyes and supernatural intuition, were supposed to be.

Por mis grandes pecados it was my misfortune to be in charge of the particular mine upon which he elected to make his first examination. After a preliminary talk with him I was duly impressed with his vast experience and superior knowledge. "For," said I to myself, "this man would not talk so high, wide and handsome unless he was as good as he says he is. Otherwise he would be shown up *pronto.*"

Commencing on Monday I was to take him over all the old workings of the old San Miguel as well as those below tunnel level. This job, if it was to be a real one, would entail a couple of weeks. The old workings were a thing of real magnitude, especially since all the ladder-roads except one main set had long ago been taken out to be used in the present development.

I explained this to him at great length. I asked him to give me a week to arrange a semblance of ladder-roads, else we would be compelled to do a great deal of climbing up and down ropes. Most of the veins were of a dip that permitted climbing hand over hand while partially walking on the foot wall, but it would be a tiresome business. Unless one was used to such things it would be dangerous because we would have to cross stopes which were several hundred feet high and where a misstep would result disastrously.

The English engineer ridiculed me and said: "Of course, if you are afraid to do it as it now stands, why, I will wait till you prepare the ladder-ways, but certainly there is no need to do so on my account." Then he recounted to me some of his extraordinary exploits in the mining field. So I shut up and let it go at that.

We were all ready for him on the appointed morning. I had engaged to accompany us two of my best climbers who knew every working in the mine, and we went in.

I had tried to prevail upon him to put on one of the cheap straw hats we were using, because one can safely stick the hook of the miners' lamps then in use through the bent-up hat brim. This he refused to do, saying that he never needed to use but one hand when he was climbing and, therefore, could carry his lamp in the other. I had looked askance at his stiff new boots, which were not only uncommonly heavy in the soles, but were laced up tightly. Since I had told him before what I considered the best thing for him to wear on his feet for the work in hand, and had been severely snubbed for my pains, I refrained from further suggestions and we entered just as he was.

We went up the old ladder-road to the five hundred foot level, called by the name of some saint or other, the invariable custom of the Mexican miner. Before reaching this level I knew by his awkwardness that we were in for it, but I hoped that he would learn something about how best to do it by watching the men who were ahead of him. Wherever it was possible, these men from then on climbed and swung about to put ropes in places for hand-holds. With laborious exertion we crept along and had reached a point by noon where we would be able to get to tunnel level by going down a hundred feet, and there we could have our dinner. Long ago the visiting engineer had lost his lamp and was in a fearful sweat nearing collapse from fright and exhaustion. Thankfully he agreed to my suggestion about getting to tunnel level to have our dinner.

I said: "Will you go ahead or shall I'" He gasped out: "Let me go ahead!" He did so, his feet slipped, he hung suspended by his hands. This was a matter easily remedied, all he had to do was once more to place his feet on the foot wall, let his buttocks hang down with his legs at right angles to his body, and thus gradually work them down, while he let go the rope in a hand-over-hand manner. But he was through and could only pant and hang there. I had to climb over him, get my shoulders under him, and by degrees we worked ourselves the hundred feet down to tunnel level.

We had dinner outside.

After a rest for digestion, I said: "We can go back now and finish our investigation."

He swelled all up and told me that for the present he had seen all that was necessary. So help me Bob, that is the last we saw of him at San Miguel Mine except on tunnel level, where he spent two or three days fooling about to establish an alibi.

The same thing happened at the other mines. We had a perfect set of maps which were absolutely up to date. He had access to the records of the Assay Office for the ore values of mill-runs for twenty years and the bullion records. He really had a much more comprehensive and completely thorough record than he could have made himself in a million years. His report was so very flowery when it was submitted by the chief of the expedition to my father as a work of art, that the *Patron Grande* after he read it refused to send it to anyone.

"The report is entirely misleading. You have theorized as to ore values and credited possible returns that twenty years of actual work showed were impossible. The lower grade ores would never average what your report claims for them."

"Well, but did you or did you not want to sell the property?" blustered the chief of the expedition. "Did you or did you not arrange to have us make this examination?"

"I did not," stated my father. "I knew absolutely nothing about any of it until I heard from New York that they had overtures from an English company saying they might be interested in buying the property. The Board of Directors agreed that they would send engineers down here. My figures on the books are a true record of twenty years, and they are good enough to sell the property on. I will readily agree for you to copy these figures since they are without embellishment. But I will be eternally damned if I will endorse even by silence such fool statements as those that have been made by your engineer and O.K.ed by yourself. I do not think that any of you know enough about mines and mining to warrant your having a position in my mines even as an assistant to any single one of my superintendents or mine bosses."

As I have intimated previously, my father was a forceful man.

He had instituted a company store among all the other things. If this had not been done the native and the *gachupin* storekeeper would have raised the prices of all commodities to such a height that it would have been impossible to give a man a living wage, and at the same time to keep the mines in operation with the price of silver where it was.

Wise President Diaz gave permission to have the company store established at the camp, being satisfied in his own mind that my father was interested in the welfare, physical, mental, social, moral, of our workmen. Our plan was to stock the store with everything from bread and beef to needles and shoes. When a man went to work on Monday morning his family could draw an order on the store for the sum that his half-week's earnings would be. This insured sufficient food and other necessaries for the week. Thus we did not care nor did his family suffer if the miner blew the balance of his wages received on Saturday night on *monte* or *mescal*.

It was an innovation; there was some grumbling in the beginning but being of a philosophical race they soon appreciated the advantages of a well-fed family. The results obtained in general health and improvement in other ways were truly remarkable and gratifying. The company was in a position to buy in large quantities and thus to obtain lower prices; we sold as close to actual cost as it could be done; the proposition worked out successfully, even though it was a great nuisance to my father and much extra trouble. The company considered it best to return to the old system after trying out the store for a few years, but after making a general inquiry among the men and their families as to how they felt about it, such a howl went up against any change, and requests to keep to the present method to save them from their town merchants were so urgent, that we decided to keep on with the store.

Often under the old way when a workman was paid off on Saturday he would reach home with little or none of his pay left. This would mean a hungry, therefore discontented, family; it would mean that the man showed up to go to work on Monday morning with an empty belly and no lunch. Now, these two sources of irritation are detrimental to a good day's work, there is a strong tendency towards becoming quarrelsome . . . and that means trouble. Or it would mean his getting in the clutches of some native or Spanish storekeeper who would cheat him to the Nth degree. The storekeeper would be a tiresome problem on pay day to the company hanging about the pay-window waiting for the workmen to be paid off. Under our store system, there were no empty bellies, there was greater contentment, health, cleanliness, and a well-clothed community. I quote from the policy of my father's friend, the clear-seeing ruler, His Excellency Don Porfirio Diaz. . . . It is much more difficult to interest a contented family man in any change such as a revolution may bring to them, than to interest a discontented man. The greatest reasons for discontent are an empty belly and idleness. Work and a full belly make things run along smoothly.

Chapter 25

Death of El Patron Grande

In the late summer of 1902 my father died. At the time I was at the country place Bleak House in Washington still confined to my bed after a severe operation.

Notification came to us of the serious illness of my father, and my mother immediately set out on that long and trying journey to Batopilas escorted by my cousin, Dr. Merchant.

She made a very rapid trip; everything was done by our good friends in and out of Mexico, officials and others, to speed her. But my father had passed on before she could reach him.

As soon as the surgeon permitted me to travel, I returned to Batopilas; this was in October, I think.

My father's body had been placed in a tomb on the mountainside above the *hacienda* where he had established a small cemetery: there also had been entombed two infant grandchildren.

It was my mother's desire and that of the other members of the family that his body should be finally laid to rest in Washington, the place of his birth and the scene to which he had devoted the earlier portion of his life. Washington was the place where he had unselfishly built up, against unscrupulous and violent opposition, the nation's capital, preventing its removal to some interior section of the country, by which move the traditions and desires of the patriots who had founded the nation would have been discarded in order to satiate the greed of those politicians who came on later, after all the hard work had been done—those politicians who wished to take to themselves the benefits which would undoubtedly accrue to the town and who might have been able to grab off the plum by use of crooked political schemes.

A heavy casket is a difficult object to be transported across one hundred and eighty-five miles of the Sierra Madre Mountain trails, There was but one way that this could be accomplished and that was on the shoulders of strong and devoted men.

And so it was done.

In the doing was manifested the true respect and affection this community of Mexican citizens held for the man who dedicated all of his magnificent abilities and all of his time for twenty-two years to building up a business which employed as many as fifteen hundred men; who paid them a minimum wage of one dollar and a half a day for unskilled labor; who protected them by preventing unfair advances in the cost of the necessities of life; who gave them and their families free hospitalization and medical attention; who founded and established a happy and contented community of approximately six thousand souls.

We came to the conclusion that it would be necessary to have the carrying cradle for the casket so arranged that two men could support it at the same time at each end, and two on either side . . . thus making eight carriers. The Mexicans are accustomed to conveying loads on their backs and shoulders; they are very remarkable in this way. They fold their *serape* in such a manner that when they are hung on the *necapal,* which is a short broad leather strap with the ends connected by leather thongs, the strap placed on the forehead, the *serape* will form a pad on the shoulders at about the level of the top of an Infantryman's combat pack. The handles of the carrying cradle rested on these pads formed by the *serape,* and the carriers moved forward at a steady walk.

We had five sets of eight men who worked as a unit, each set matched as nearly as possible as to size; the groups relieved one another at intervals of twenty minutes to half an hour while in motion. Thus there was no loss of time on the trail and the casket was placed on the ground but once during the day's march of thirty-five miles, and this was when the noon rest was taken and food eaten.

We made the one hundred and eighty-five miles on the regular *conducta* pack-train schedule . . . that is, in five days.

It is not a task that would appeal to most men even for good pay; to be compelled to march thirty-five miles each day over rough and narrow mountain trails for a distance such as that trip consumed. Yet when it became known in Batopilas among our workmen that the journey was contemplated, many, many times the number of men needed, volunteered to carry the casket. They were careful to specify:

"Without pay for the trip. Solely for the desire to demonstrate the respect and affection for *El Patron Grande* and *Doña Maria* his wife, who had in all ways done so very much for us and for our children."

Had it not been for the many years of experience and the smooth-running organization developed at Batopilas, to make such a journey would have been next to impossible. As it was, we managed it on the regular fast-mounted travel schedule and with little or no trouble.

The pack-train with the beds and the food set out ahead of us the first day, with sufficient start to enable them to be already installed at the end of the day's march at the Station, with the supper well on its way towards readiness for those of us who followed with the casket. More than forty men, of course, require a great deal of food and good substantial food. Fresh beef had been arranged for by the station keepers who had been advised by my brother Conness that this must be on hand. Old Antonio Navarro, one of the most faithful and sure, was in charge of the kitchen.

On the second morning of the journey, my brother Alex and I and the carriers with the casket started shortly after day break; before we reached the point where we took our midday rest of an hour, the pack-train overtook us and passed. At the rate of travel they could maintain, they were at the station at least an hour before we arrived. And thus for five days the cortège moved forward until the last morning. We set forth on that morning long before daylight, because we had not only to reach Carichic early in the afternoon but at that place we transferred to the wheeled transport, and had to drive an additional sixty-five miles. It is safe to say that by trail and by wagon we covered ninety-five miles on that last day.

While we were crossing the mountains, in order that those who were one day in advance of us might know that all was well and that we were keeping up with the schedule, once or twice after reaching our night stopping place we secured a runner from the station keeper. Maybe this messenger would be one of his own sons on horseback. This one would leave immediately upon our arrival at the station to travel fast to the next one ahead where he would arrive some time before midnight. He would have a note from Alex containing the news of our progress and with a reassuring message for my mother. This note was delivered to Conness as soon as the messenger reached the station, and he would give it to my mother in the early morning when that brave lady awakened.

During this her last trip across the Sierra Madre Mountains, in the same manner as on many of her former ones, my mother was carried the greater part of each day's journey in a chair. This was made feasible by arranging a wicker rocking-chair with handles such as were employed in the sedan chair of olden days. Eight good men trained to such work bore the burden two at a time with frequent changes. And this more than tiresome trip was in this way somewhat alleviated for the ladies.

Comparatively few men have ever trudged thirty-five miles a day for five consecutive days in succession, and the feat performed by those fine faithful souls who carried my father's remains across the Sierra mountain trail can be but little appreciated. Always cheerful, never a complaint, never an attempt to shirk when their turn came to assume the burden . . . it was one example from out the vast number of others which I had been a witness to since early childhood that endeared the Mexicans, especially the Batopilense, to all of our name and race.

I suppose it is natural that at times there comes a homesickness for the land and for those people which is almost too strong to be resisted. A yearning which forces one, for the time at least, to regret that circumstances prevent the return for one's few remaining years to the place where was passed early youth as well as a great part of one's manhood.

My mother and other members of the family left under the escort of my brother Conness one day ahead of us; arriving at Carichic they rested for a day at the home of our good friend Don Ignacio Ortega. Alex and I with the casket were met by the largest wagon just beyond El Alamo ranch.

We drove from there into San Antonio, the railroad station, that same day, where a private car was waiting for us. By the time my mother and the others of the family reached there, the casket was settled in its position in the observation end of the car where it rested until we arrived in Washington.

There was an interlude at Chihuahua while we were being transferred and attached to the regular north-bound Mexican Central train. There we received visits of condolence from representatives of the families of my father's devoted friends—Don Luis Terrazas, Don Enrique Creel and his charming wife, Don Antonio Prieto, Don Juan Creel, and many, many others, not only Mexican but other foreign friends. Quantities of flowers of every kind imaginable were brought to the train, and put in the private car.

The trip to Washington was uneventful, and on arrival there an impressive cortège escorted my father's remains to Rock Creek Church, where they temporarily rested in the tomb of a friend, until my father's mausoleum was constructed, in which they now lie with those of my sainted mother.

Batopilas Mining Company's outfit (La Conducta) ready to start. Chihuahua.

Chapter 26

Batopilas without El Patron Grande

It was not all beer and skittles during the thirty-odd years of mining the precious metal in Batopilas. Silver went 'way down in price; there was a heavy floating debt and the overdraft allowed by the Banco Minero in Chihuahua was overreached. But before matters hit the absolutely fatal spot at any one time, we would run into a bonanza of greater or less extent, and sometimes in the very last two weeks of the month, at the end of which the bullion would leave for Chihuahua, we would knock out anywhere from fifty to a hundred thousand dollars. One month we took out four hundred and fifty thousand dollars worth of silver. At various times we had run into debt with the bank for around eight hundred thousand dollars and paid it back all from a few months' production.

After my father died, we had been going through a trying financial time. Our credit was not as good as his had been; we were the younger generation and had not proved that we could move mountains as he had done.

My much-beloved brother-in-law Ned Quintard had died suddenly in Washington while we were on the road with my father's remains. Alex had been made general manager at the mines. On a certain afternoon instructions were sent me to report to him at the Main Office. When I got there I found Conness also at the Hacienda San Miguel, and we were informed that the Banco Minero now refused to permit us the overdraft of sixty thousand dollars which had been agreed on, unless we would send them that much as well as a pretty large additional amount in bullion at the end of the month.

Dios es grande! It chanced that the previous night I had showed up in a small working some signs of native silver. This ground *ought* to prove productive. I personally was satisfied in my mind that it would do so. We decided that we could telegraph the bank that we would meet their demands.

We met them.

By the end of the month we sent out a little over one hundred thousand dollars worth of silver bullion. This was the beginning of the bonanza which paid off all the floating debt and more besides during the next twelve months. If I am not mistaken, and I believe that I am not, the debt was eight hundred thousand dollars or thereabouts. This example is cited to demonstrate the richness of the ores of Batopilas and also that we worked plenty hard to get them out.

We had no air drills then. On the tenth of the month we began to take out one hundred thousand dollars in twenty days. We were in a small narrow working, badly ventilated; the ore showed up right down at the foot of the face.

Did we work! We drilled and shot round after round of dynamite in powder smoke so thick that in order to see the head of the drills we had to hold our lamps within a foot of them, and even closer. God! the headaches! No headache is more intense than the one produced by dynamite fumes. Days, nights, days, nights, no sleep except what we could snatch back in the drift every now and then for maybe an hour lying alongside the tracks.

Alex worked far too long and far too hard without a vacation. Finally we prevailed upon him to take this long-deserved change. I took over the management during his absence. He was unavoidably detained two or three times on his journey back to Batopilas from the East, and the last delay was caused by high rivers in the mountains from unusually heavy rains. He had his family with him and could take no risks. Of course, I could not leave the mines before his return. There were some appointments in New York City, of great personal importance to me, which I had been forced to postpone several times by telegraph. The persons with whom the appointments had been made became insistent and almost unpleasant about my procrastination in getting there. New York residents who abide in that city in comfort and financial ease, and who can arrange matters for months ahead, sometimes are a trifle hard to reason with.

At last Alex reached the camp after great inconvenience to himself, in order to make it possible for me to turn things over to him and get away in time, by dint of utmost speed, for the appointments in far-away New York.

He arrived at Batopilas almost exhausted in the early morning after having ridden nearly all night. I turned things over to him (there were innumerable details to clear up), and got away from Batopilas at two o'clock the next morning. I left the camp in a downpour of rain, knowing that the Arroyo de las Huertas, three miles up the river and directly above the dam, had risen very high. I must be obliged to swim the Arroyo, which was two hundred yards wide at that point.

I took some lead-animals with me so they could spell each other, two pack-mules and one saddle-mule. These I sent ahead of me with my loaded pack-mules the afternoon before. Alex and I had a farewell stirrup cup at two in the morning, I bade good-bye to him and some of the boys, and accompanied by my old friend Angel Gill who insisted on going with me as far as the Arroyo de las Huertas, I set forth already weary and anticipating tiresome traveling.

I was riding a powerful sorrel *macho.* A *macho* is a male mule. This animal was a *burrero,* the opposite cross to the usual mule-producing cross. He possessed a good bit of his donkey mother's stubbornness with an endurance and strength that was almost supernatural. His sire was a stallion of excellent blood; this *macho* was as strong as a steam engine, courageous, and could swim like a Newfoundland dog. We got to the Arroyo de las Huertas and found it pretty high. I said good-bye to Angel, rode up the bank as far as I could and started into the rolling, swirling current. The minute we got into the water where the depth made the *macho* swim, I slipped from his back, caught hold of his tail and we made a safe landing without being swept down into the Batopilas River. This would have been, to express it mildly, inconvenient, because we then would have been in the body of the water formed by the dam and it was still pitch black dark.

The *macho* and I shook ourselves, I had a pull at my bottle, and we went on to get dried out by the sun, for the day cleared as we advanced.

We climbed the hill out of the Canyon onto the trail to Teboreachic Station, which you will recall is the last night-stopping place on the trip coming over the trail towards Batopilas. Here the *macho* and I joined the pack-mules and the *mozos* with the spare animals. We were all of us outside a big meal very quickly, I with plenty of hot strong coffee, and had two hours' rest. Off again then, mounted on a fresh animal en route to La Laja seven hours' ride away. At La Laja there were four hours' rest and sleep. Seven more hours of riding brought me to Pilares, but before reaching that place I had had to swim the Eurique River. At Pilares I had two hours of rest and moved forward once more.

In good time I reached Gauhochic and found the river fordable. *"Dios es grande,"* I said, because when that river is high you absolutely cannot fool with it—exactly below the ford the stream is enclosed by precipitous rock walls with no other bank for many miles. We fed there and moved on . . . at any moment the river might come down upon us, there was no time for rest. If the river rose it would lose me forty miles and the trip must be made on schedule. The stage would lie waiting for me in the early morning, and if there were no delay whatsoever I would be able to make the train at two p.m. at San Antonio Railway station and thence to Chihuahua in time to catch the Mexican Central out that same evening en route to El Paso.

I did a hundred and eighty-five miles in the saddle in fifty-two hours. With no margin to spare I made my connections. After I boarded the Southern Pacific Railroad train in El Paso, I had the first opportunity to shave, bathe and change to a costume more appropriate for travel on the Sunset Limited . . . a truly de luxe means of transportation, especially when contrasted with the last fifty-two hours.

I had to walk through two Pullmans in order to reach the drawing-room which I had reserved by telegraph. I was certainly a tough-looking customer, and I received some startled and disapproving glances on my way through the Pullmans the hotel porter lugging my two big bags, I following unshaven, hollow-eyed, still wearing the clothes in which I had left camp, my six-shooter strapped around my waist.

There were some ladies from the East on the train with their husbands on their way home from a trip to California. The earthquake and fire at San Francisco had just devastated that city. Among the passengers was Miss Kathryn Gray the actress, who was returning post haste to the East to fill an engagement. She had made a dash across the continent to San Francisco at the first news of the catastrophe, because her mother was there at that time. I was introduced to Miss Gray and at dinner that night she informed me that I had been the cause of no little speculation on the train after it had drawn out from El Paso. She heard that a disreputable-looking person had got on the train there, and that he must be secreted somewhere on board, since he had not been seen afterwards; he had gone into the drawing-room from which I had emerged later.

It was not until the conductor had told one or two of the passengers that I was the disreputable-looking specimen, that often in this part of the country a haircut, a shave, a bath and a change of clothes produced the same result had they been relieved of apprehension.

I was far from well; had been suffering for a long time from malaria. I saw a doctor in New York who had been highly recommended to me. Among many other ailments he found that my heart was affected; that I was on the way to a dangerous condition of anemia; that I should dose myself with the most immense quantities of various kinds of medicines, go on a strict diet, refrain from anything alcoholic to drink except one pint of Burgundy at lunch and another after dinner. I paid the doctor, I even thanked him. I drank the Burgundy, I like good Burgundy. To that I added many other forms of liquid refreshment, and ate everything delicious that I could buy at Martin's, Delmonico's, many of the hotels, and all the good after-dark places. In sixty days I was slightly over normal in weight and I could push over a house. . . .

Chapter 27

General Porfirio Diaz

Some years ago, it was popular to declare Porfirio Diaz possessed of all the worst attributes possible for the Chief Executives of a nation to be afflicted with. But if you have lived in a country from the age of five years, from 1880 to 1911, during an era—according to the press of those days and some of its politicians—when it was a hotbed of disorder, peonage, corruption, and a thousand other civic ills; when you yourself have traveled the country, have known hundreds of its people, spoken the language as fluently as you do that of your native country; when you yourself, I say, have never in your life come into contact with a single one of those frightful abuses attributed to Mexico and the Mexicans at that time, but have seen a nation advancing in every way as rapidly as did our own Southwest, you are filled with amazement and a boiling sense of injustice.

Without hesitation, I say that General Porfirio Diaz gave the Mexican nation an era of order and of good government far above anything that we can approach now. There were fifteen million souls in Mexico. There were about fifty different tribes of Indians, each having its own dialect; among many of them only a decided minority could speak Spanish. Inaccessibility was the principal feature of the country.

Not only our company but many others made regular monthly bullion shipments, which ran in value from one hundred to two hundred thousand dollars. These same pack-trains which carried the bullion brought back to the mining camps from fifty to a hundred thousand dollars *in currency* for payrolls. I have already described the journey and the terrain over which the trips were made. In thirty years only once was an attempt made to hold up one of them—that was the monthly *conducta* from the mines of the Pinos Altos Mining Company—and it was unsuccessful.

It was not until the despotism of President Porfirio Diaz was overthrown that our company ever lost a bar of silver or a dollar of payroll money. The great liberator, that oppressed Francisco (Pancho) Villa, stole thirty-eight thousand dollars worth of silver bars and buried them in the *patio* of a house in Chihuahua. He was afraid to convert them into cash, and later when this leader was not so strong in power we recovered the treasure.

All this talk about peonage! How many people knew that the word "peon" in Mexico means an unskilled laborer, a pick-and-shovel man.

It angered us more than once to hear verbal statements from, and to read accounts by, persons who believed that General Diaz made no efforts toward establishing schools or inaugurating sanitary and health reforms.

In the year 1885 I attended a School Commencement at that small mountain camp of Batopilas three hundred miles from a railroad in the very heart of the Sierras, and it was as well conducted as any that could be found anywhere at the same period.

More than forty years past the smallpox epidemics among the Indians and the town inhabitants were nearly eradicated in this way: every medical man anywhere and everywhere in the country was supplied with vaccine and ordered by the Government to vaccinate any and every citizen. The Indians feared any such innovation with a fervent and superstitious terror; the doctors were given a detail of police and soldiers to capture the prospective victims and to hold them while the vaccination took place. When they came to town, they were grabbed and held fast in abject dread and mental torment while the doctor performed.

Our surgeon at this time, Dr. Merchant, rode a big white horse. I remember one Saturday afternoon watching him galloping down the street, El Calle Principal, with soldiers in hot pursuit of ten Tarahumare Indians on foot, and as many more mounted on their small ponies and burros, fleeing in desperate fear of their lives. They made a frantic effort to escape while the unsympathetic populace shouted in delight, encouraging surgeon and police and Indians indiscriminately. The poor wretches were captured at the edge of town; someone headed them off. There they were surrounded and for the good of their souls and bodies they were firmly held and the surgeon cleaned and scraped and inoculated.

This piece of work was accomplished in so thorough a manner that the scourge of smallpox became practically unknown. Since this brutal despot abdicated and since Mexico entered into the era of true democracy and brotherly love, there has been one scourge after another, which took hold of uninoculated unfortunates who grew up during the latter enlightened years, and which have left entire villages as inanimate as did the Boche some of the French areas.

The general situation in Mexico about the year 1883 when General Diaz was President was chaotic and lawless. But he was astute and strong; he knew men. He knew what the moral and psychological attitude of the *pronunciado* and bandit was. He selected in each district a courageous man, one who was known to be a person of quick action with offensive weapons. This individual was ordered to organize a posse, well-mounted and well-armed.

The leader was called a *Juez de Cordada,* or sheriff, with the power of life or death under certain conditions. The *Juez* was notified that lawlessness was out of fashion; he and his posse were to make such affairs unpopular; this was to be effected as quickly as might be; they were to take care not to double-cross the Diaz Government, because then, in their turn, they would receive immediate liquidation. Within three years Mexico was as safe as a church. These *Jueces de Cordada* had been compelled to execute fewer criminals than would have been expected. They had no chance at all if they were caught red-handed, no trial, nor a bail, nor an appeal, nor any other demoralizing refinement enjoyed in the higher civilization. The culprit was shot down when he was captured or while he was fleeing. Sometimes he was made to flee and then shot down.

Terrible? Well, maybe. But they gave a murderer, a ravisher of women, a thief, exactly what he had been giving to others . . . and those others had been helpless, law-abiding citizens.

The enemies of General Diaz used to claim that many innocent men were killed in this way. Diaz answered that "innocent men had no business in that bad company; that the State is greater than the individual; that no State can prosper unless there is internal peace; that internal peace is not possible where there is no discipline."

President Diaz was a man of enormous courage. His courage carried him through a series of years filled with violence and disorder and enabled him to bring peace and advancement. His courage held back the hand of many assassins and would-be assassins. There was a little malcontent in Mexico who was an anarchist, an anti-anything-decent if he could make a dollar from it. He was a paltry thing. More than once this fellow was warned and his anarchistic sheet was suppressed. But he refused to believe in moderation and kindness shown him; therefore, after a while he was escorted to the Rio Grande where he crossed into the United States and established himself in California. Before long, the authorities there had him incarcerated for his anarchistic activities. He was not really even an anarchist. He was simply a dangerous little beast practically demented, but he was the type who inspired other cowardly morons to assassination. After a while he was freed and joined the campaign against General Diaz, who was the president of a nation friendly to the United States; he was, in truth, a friend to the United States of America. Magazines published grossly erroneous articles about all this and a thousand other matters. These were profusely illustrated, and showed among other pictures the floggings of peons. But these floggings were not photographs, they were pen-and-ink drawings.

Among the prominent men who came to the fore during the days that General Diaz was bringing order from chaos was the Honorable Enrique Creel, who was at one time Ambassador to the United States. Mr. Creel was the man who had organized the Banco Minero in Chihuahua and developed it into a strong and useful institution. He was a close personal friend of our family and he used to tell many interesting events concerning the early days in Mexico, when, as a small boy, he would make trips with his father. Those trips were regular journeys by wagon trains in order to secure goods which were used in trading with Mexicans in the interior of the country, Chihuahua being the distributing point.

Mr. Creel had a favorite story about the first pair of little boots his father bought for him—it probably was in San Antonio, Texas, where they were procured. Those little boots had brass toe caps and a red patent leather ornamental piece let into the front along the top. Mr. Creel said that his joy in the possession of them was so very intense that he suffered agonies with chafed toes and heels for many days rather than not keep them on his poor little feet so he could strut about and show them off.

When I was a little boy myself, this always seemed strange to me . . . a man of wide and varied experience and taste, a man who had seen much, accomplished much, possessed much, extracting infinite pleasure in recounting the story about his first pair of boots.

Mr. Creel, God rest his soul; was probably one of the most brilliant and able financial brains of his time. He was one of those patriotic and capable Mexican gentlemen with whom General Diaz surrounded himself. They ought to have been left alone to solve the difficulties of their own nation. . . .

Chapter 28

Twenty Thousand Dollars Worth of Dirty Clothes

Sandy was not the only cook at Batopilas; among many others we had a Chinaman who ran the general mess at Hacienda San Miguel, he was very dependable. Charlie Sing was as honest as any man could be. He never held out a penny of the money given him with which to purchase supplies and other foods, nor did he allow his "boys" to do it either. He had a harder time trying to keep his fat Indian wife in bounds than he did his helpers. This wife suffered from a horde of relations—or rather Charlie did the suffering—who were properly lazy; they positively hated to think that with the sister married to a source of supply such as Charlie by all the rules ought to have been, they could not eat as often as they wished without humiliating themselves by manual labor. One of them said to Charlie one day when the Chinaman had relieved him of a hunk of beef:

"You *Chino sin verguenza,* starving your wife's people! What right have you to take this meat from me? It does not belong to you, and it will not cost you a cent."

The fat wife became more than poor patient Charlie could put up with; he came to me in grave distress. I called in the worthless devil who was paying his attentions to her at the time, and told him that if would leave for the Hot Country and present himself before Don Pancho Torres with the letter which I would give him, that Don Pancho would pay him fifty dollars in cash. I told him that if he failed to do this, he would undoubtedly be taken up as a vagrant and be put to work on the streets with the other loafers. Thus Charlie was eased from the burden of the lover of his fat, worthless wife.

In gratitude Charlie did particularly well for a long time and there were very few complaints about the eatables. But one morning I went in to breakfast, and found our old foundry-man with one of Charlie's ears in each mighty hand beating a tattoo with Charlie's head on the stone wall.

"Hey, Kauffman! Lay off Charlie, he is the only cook we've got!"

"Boss," said Kauffman solemnly, "look at this!" lie shoved me the saucer on which his coffee cup had been resting, in which two enormous cockroaches were lying. "I told this damned Chinaman," continued Kauffman, "that one cockroach would be all right. But I'm damned if I'll stand for two in one cup of coffee."

We went out to the kitchen and slapped Hell out of the three boys there, Charlie's helpers, and promised them more unless they confessed who had done the cockroach trick. The youngest of the kids was a decent enough little rascal; he blurted out,

"Nepomecino did it. Nepomecino is a cousin of the dear wife's lover now for long a time in la Tierra Caliente. For revenge upon Charlie because of his treachery to this dear cousin, the departed lover, Nepomecino did the trick."

The too devoted relative got a licking and lost his easy job as Charlie's helper in the kitchen. Next time I saw him he was packing a *zurron* at Todos Santos Mine . . . and very good it was for him physically, mentally, and morally. The boss there was very just but he would stand for no foolishness. If a man could be made out of Nepomecino the difficult piece of work would be accomplished there in the shortest length of time. Often these healthy boys like Nepomecino, who had a mean streak, also possessed a brand of courage which when it was brought forward largely submerged the mean streak, and the result would be a good workman, endowed with qualifications which we cultivated in the field in which he appeared most apt.

As an example of the lawlessness of the Mexicans which was talked and written about so very much by untraveled-in-that-country individuals as well as the press during the regime of President Porfirio Diaz, there were three American bandits who held up the Mexican Central train one time between the towns of Torreon and Jimenez. The express messenger on the train attempted resistance and was badly wounded, I think he died. His statement was very clear that three men held up the train and he gave a pretty good description of two of them. I think he shot the third man—I cannot exactly recall that fact . . . I have seen a lot of dead men since then. At sixty-odd one's memory is none too lucid on unimportant past events. I am only interested in this because of the reasons indicated, and because from this incident and the efforts of one of the hold-up men to escape, we had a good joke on old Kauffman.

Kauffman was on the road from San Miguel Mine to the Hacienda San Miguel—he had been examining an old steam hoist at the mine—and overtook a man who had evidently come down the trail from El Parral which came into the cart road between the bridge and San Miguel Mine. This individual was very palpably an American of distressing appearance, dilapidated shoes, sore feet, a hungry look, needing a shave the very worst way, to say nothing of some clean clothes. It was an almost unheard-of thing for an American to walk into our district in that condition, but it had occurred a few times. Kauffman's curiosity was aroused. He deduced, from replies to his questions, that the fellow had left El Parral a few months past with saddle-and-pack animals bent on prospecting the Sierra Madres. He had not found a mine and he had not become suddenly astoundingly rich . . . as happens in the movies and fiction magazines. . . .

He had lost himself. He wandered and scrambled about, finally he managed to get onto the El Parral trail sans saddle-mule and pack-mule. He had experienced a very bad time. Even though he did have a little money with him, he could find no one from whom he could buy anything to eat till at last he had come upon a pack-train on the way back to El Parral. From these people he had bought some food, and had learned that there was a mining camp two days farther on. The mining camp was, of course, Batopilas.

"Another damned tenderfoot," thought Kauffman. But since hospitality is customary in that part of the world, Kauffman took him to the hacienda after stopping at the store to get him some clean clothes. He had a bath, a shave, and turned out to be a presentable young man about twenty-five or so. His baggage consisted of a little bundle of dirty clothes that he was anxious not to relinquish.

Everybody had about as much to do as he could attend to comfortably, and no one could waste time on the affairs of other people. Therefore, it never occurred to us that this stranger could be in any way connected with the more or less recent hold-up on the Mexican Central Railway. A job at the mill was found for him; he had been working about a month contentedly enough when on a certain Sunday afternoon old Macario, the Chief of Police, came to call on the general manager, with a description of the man who was wanted in connection with the hold-up.

It had been reported that this man had got as far as El Parral in his efforts to leave Mexico, but from there he was supposed to have gone into the mountains. Since there were only a very few trails he could have followed, and these had been searched without results (no passage or arrival of any strangers whose presence was not explainable) the authorities were checking up, and this fellow was the only person unaccounted for. The general manager acceded the reasonableness of Macario's attitude, consequently the young stranger, West we called him, was sent for. Of course, he repeated the first story he had told us, and to give him credit, he never varied it a hair's breadth. This in itself to the mind of a Sherlock Holmes would have damned him. But it seemed to meet the requirements as far as Macario went, and the description the Chief brought of the possible culprit did not tally with West's appearance.

Following the custom, Alex, who was then general manager, ordered some drinks for refreshment, and he passed around some cigars. At this point West asked to be excused to get his pipe because he did not smoke cigars. Macario gave his consent, the drinks arrived; but after a reasonable length of time, West did not.

Alex suggested to Macario that they should go to see what had happened, it all looked pretty phony to him. West's room was at the very end of the long portal of the inner quadrangle, it had a window opening on an alley or passageway from which, via a cobblestone ramp, the upper level of the hacienda could be reached. The room was empty.

A hurried inquiry and a general search were made with no satisfactory outcome. Macario decided that West had made his get-away, and hastened to town to organize a posse, thoroughly convinced that West and the hold-up man were identical. Darkness had fallen at the time when West had gone to get his pipe, therefore, there was practically no hope of being able to do anything about it that same night. But the trails leading from the town were covered.

Supper time at the mess was lively with discussion about the matter; Kauffman was gibed and questioned about how much his split had been; how in the world it could have happened he had not known that West's bundle of dirty clothes which he could not bear to be parted from was worth twenty thousand dollars; whether he was accessory after the fact, and so on *ad nauseam.*

"That twenty thousand dollars," growled Kauffman, would have finished paying for my ranch out near Guerrero. Old Kramen and me could have laid off and took it easy. Well, that's what you get for doin' a good act."

West was captured after all. He shot a woodsman, who, inspired by the reward offered, had attacked the bandit with a knife, the poor fool, and for his pains had stopped a .44, thereby acquiring some experience if nothing more. West was held in jail in the town after being brought there from Sinaloa, and he was still there when the town was captured during the Madero revolution. He was released with all the other prisoners, which was the usual manner of doing such things. I believe that he joined with the revolutionists and became quite a leader in a small way. But I do not think they ever regained the balance of the hold-up money. Sometimes I doubt that he had it in his possession. With that much cash as a stake in those days, a man of any intelligence whatever and with only a bit of experience, having time to study the maps of the section, would have worked out some scheme by which he could have made himself very hard to catch.

Poor old Kauffman! He was able by and by to develop that ranch of theirs to a point where the production of potatoes alone was giving them a fine annual income. They were shipping several carloads yearly and there was a never-failing good market for potatoes. When Pancho Villa got busy, old Kramen was murdered and every single thing they owned that could be carried off was confiscated, and all the buildings were burned. A nice place completely destroyed.

Kauffman was a splendid man, exceedingly accomplished in his profession of foundry-man. When he was in a hurry he would use a three thousand six hundred pound engine bed plate as a model from which to cast a duplicate. Not every foundry-man when he has no time to make a wood model can swing the engine bed plate up on his crane and then lower it into the mold, and sneak it out delicately enough to leave a perfect matrix in which to pour his molten iron.

The mess hall and kitchen for the foreign and native employees was reached by a wide *cantera* stone stairway which spanned the aqueduct from the second level or terrace to the first level below; this was at the up-river side of the Hacienda San Miguel. There were three dining-rooms, that nearest the stairway was for the foreign employees, next came one for the natives; then the several rooms used by the cook and his waiters and helpers. There were generally from eight to ten foreigners who held different positions of trust—usually one mining engineer whose duty it was to keep the maps up to date and to make all necessary mine surveys; the bookkeepers, a senior and a junior; an assayer (chemist); head machinist; and last but not least old Kauffman.

I will call over some of these able men as best I can with my jaded memory. They were a self-reliant aggregation; they had hard jobs, at times very galling, but said little about it . . . if it were possible to do it they succeeded. Many of those with whom we first worked have passed on. I will wager that in heaven where they are enjoying their just rewards they are frequently called on to help out, for they were grand men in emergencies.

After the Jack Ogden era there was Frank English, a damned fine bookkeeper. Frank was like a bank, there was no use maintaining that he was wrong when you were in the red at the end of the month . . . he always had the irrefutable and damnable evidence of the necessary I.O.U.s to back up his statements.

In the same essential profession in rotation there was Jem Smith, a good fellow, now dead. Then came White, who for many years has held a prominent position with the Government doing things with figures to make the careless watch their steps. Gilbert Geiselhart was the boss machinist who owned the bull terrier, of whom more anon. Old Bill Schwender, who first assisted in making the gasoline locomotive and gasoline hoists at the Weber works in Kansas City, later came down to Batopilas to set them up and to show us how to make them start and go. If Bill played out after a brief spell of fourteen hours at work, all he needed to freshen him up for another go was a couple of quart bottles of beer and a few sardine sandwiches.

Then there was George Bryan who came to Camp to secure lucrative employment the same time Clarence Foreman and Gus Morehouse did, when the Topolobampo colonization scheme died. And Louis Mohun who got fed up on Batopilas and never came back there from a vacation in the States. He is buried somewhere in Las Filipinas. He did a hitch in the United States Infantry, achieved a lot of good and valiant fighting. He was promoted to a Lieutenancy from the ranks as a result of his being a real *hombre* on the field of battle. He was bumped off by a Moro out in the jungles, and his commission waiting for him in Manila! But so men are, and there's no use in regretting anything . . . much. *Le tocó a Luis,* it touched Louis, and his mortal remains are a long way from where he was born.

Ned Moffat, chemist and assayer, whom I first met when I was at Columbia University in 1896, with whose assistance I absorbed large quantities of Wurtzburger on Hammerstein's old roof and other places of joyful memory. Skipper Wells, Coyote Yeandall, but Coyote, the darned rascal, should have been enumerated along with Frank English, for he did a bit of that work himself. He came to Batopilas via Sewanee. Old Bill Kirby-Smith, bless his heart, was there for so many years, had become so much a part of the landscape I nearly forgot him, but he was generally at one of the mines and wound up at San Miguel as superintendent. Later on Bill's brother, Eph, and Louie Loew came along.

More than once in my life have I noted that as one becomes very familiar with a landscape even a prominent feature by its very familiarity may be not seen at times. Among individuals in Batopilas whose life was so identified with the affairs of the company was E.W.A. Jorgensen. He was Assistant Secretary, Secretary, Chief Accountant, and lastly, if I am not mistaken, Treasurer. He was a great deal more which cannot be set down here. For he is a modest man. He spent by far the greater part of his time in the New York office of the company, but there were many trips that he made to Batopilas. I myself have done many journeys with him across the Sierras. That is a pretty darned good way to size a man up. "Jorgie" was one of the nicest traveling companions that any man ever had.

The ones I have touched upon were the old standbys for years, but there were others who did not last so long. There was Todd who hit camp as engineer, straight from the Scottish Highland via the Royal School of Mines, a true Scot. I will never forget the day that haggis in cans which he had ordered especially from Scotland came into camp. They had spent many months of delay en route and had probably reposed during part of them in a very hot warehouse in the city of Vera Cruz. As a special treat Todd had some of the cans of this delectable haggis opened one night at mess. . . .

Only one other time did the mess hall go through an experience of so foul a stench, this was when Geiselhart's white bull terrier discovered and attacked a skunk which had secreted himself in the fireplace behind some green pine branches on a warm Christmas day.

It was fortunate that Christmas dinner had not yet been served. We bribed a *mozo* to take the dog off and scrub her with hot water and soap using a deodorizer supplied by the doctor. After the room had been whitewashed twice, the brick floor scraped, and every particle of the woodwork washed and repainted, we could return to it as a dining-room.

I have in mind one particular late afternoon when Todd and I were hurrying back to Batopilas from some prospects we had been examining near the San Miguel group. We made our camp for the night in a nice grassy plot on the bank of a small stream after a hot and very annoying day. We had killed some good-size rattlesnakes during the day, and I hate snakes. So did Todd. After supper we spread our blankets and went to sleep. I was dead to the world, when "Bang! Bang!" I came up standing to find Todd doing likewise, but he had his smoking gun in his hand and was blazing away at a spot a few feet from us where my saddle, now plainly visible in the brilliant moonlight, lay with bridle and halter rope over the pommel.

"There it is," cried Todd. "Hells bells, I do believe I missed it!"

"Missed what?"

"The snake, the damned rattler. I see his head sticking out from under the edge of your saddle."

I walked over with quiet tread, and found with burning indignation that what Todd had taken for the head of a rattlesnake was the elaborate, costly and finely made button on the end of my horsehair halter rope. I also discovered that he had placed three .44's in my favorite saddle-tree.

"Just for this, I'm damned if we don't saddle up right now and light out of here to utilize this moon to illumine our way home. *Vamonos, muchachos, aparejan las mulas, vamos de aqui, o no sea este Escocez nos afusila como tigres o elefantes!* Let us go from here, or maybe this Scotchman will shoot us for tigers or elephants."

Chapter 29

The Kid and Villa

The Kansas City, Mexico and Orient Railroad, building out in a generally southwesterly direction, reached a locality where they established a station which was christened Creel. This made it possible for our company to shorten the journey by pack-train to three days instead of five, and did away with the wagon haul entirely. To accomplish this, and to gain a saving in distance, to avoid very broken country, it was necessary to construct a small suspension bridge across the Eurique River, where this sometimes turbulent stream had been kind enough to cut for itself a narrow gash with nearly perpendicular sides in the rocks of the Sierras. Here by utilizing wire cables (I think it was my brother-in-law, Walter Brodie, who pulled it from his wonderful hat of experience), a very creditable suspension bridge was constructed. As far as I know it is still in use. This must have been somewhere around 1907 or 1908. Walter was more or less of a magician when it came to difficult mining engineering problems; just as Ned Quintard was a wizard at solving problems of how to make rebellious ores yield their values, of telling you just what ore values really were.

The suspension bridge was put together with some of the cable we had taken into camp on the back of the noble and patient mule. There it was given a happier life in the good fresh air and sunshine, instead of being wound and unwound in a dark, deep mine shaft where it was all daubed up at frequent intervals and made sticky by having a combination of tallow and resin smeared on it to keep out the rust and to prevent wear and tear. The wire rope was stretched and securely anchored, a good plank floor was laid, and the sides were boarded up a sufficient height to keep the mules from looking over the edge, realizing where they were, and going over in giddiness and fright.

The Kansas City, Mexico and Orient Railroad was a good idea, but it was never completed for reasons that we will not go into here, because what I would say would undoubtedly be contradicted. I made a trip one time, when that railroad was in process of construction, on a private train filled with prospective investors in the securities of the road. The line had been completed into Texas as far as San Angelo. San Angelo was formerly known as Fort Concho.

In the club car they had an informal reception when we were at San Angelo, at which function were one or two of the oldest inhabitants. One of these, among his many comments, said:

"Yes, gentlemen, I don't think you will find many persons now living who were here before I came to this place and went into the ranching business. I came here with my brother in 1883."

"Well, sir," replied Mr. Stillwell, "there is a man right in front of you who was here three years before you came to old Fort Concho."

"Ha," grunted the oldest inhabitant dubiously, "I sure would like to meet up with him."

"You have," continued Mr. Stillwell, pointing to me. "That is he over there," and he went on to explain.

"Well, and so you are one of that family. Well, well, that is something to talk about after all these years! Why, when we first came here, they was talkin' about those folks from Washington, D.C., who went through here on their way into Mexico. I say, that was some trip for a tenderfoot to make, and I sure always did admire that man. He had plenty of courage to take a family across this country in them days. I am proud to know you, young feller. Say, Mr. Stillwell, why don't you take your crowd down into Mexico that way now? I'll rustle you the teams and damned if I won't go too!"

There were no seconds to the idea.

We drove all over the small settlement out to the old fort buildings, which were still standing, although not in use. In imagination I once more saw the three-year-old Kid with his small stick on his little shoulder trudging toward fancied destruction while the marching troops advanced to pass in review before their commanding officer on old Fort Concho parade ground.

Now the Kid had grown to impressive size, abilities in all his endeavors, and respected manhood. He had a meeting with Pancho Villa at Carretas when this worthless one was living on that section of the country, and developing into the grand patriot that newspapers and others who knew nothing whatsoever about Villa or his misdeeds were building up into a great hero.

Francisco Villa knew quite well who our tribe was, and he knew my young brother. The Kid was a competent horseman, pistol and rifle shot; he stood six feet three in his stockings; weighed one hundred and ninety pounds. There was nothing sticking to his ribs but the very hardest and most efficient and experienced muscle; he possessed a pleasing personality. The Mexicans who knew and worked for him loved him with a devotion not frequently met with. In fact, his position in the estimation of the inhabitants of the sections where his work placed him was one rarely found and much to be desired.

After the Madero revolution started, Conness kept some work going in an effort to develop several small properties out in the vicinity of the old Cusi district. Ojos Azules was in this district. With the advancement of the revolution, the size and importance of the internationally known Pancho Villa swelled with much rapidity. His increase in magnitude and undeniable presence as something actual on the landscape may well be compared to that of a fat mule who has died on the trail, and been subjected to the hot sun of the locality. You soon can see him and smell him from a great distance.

The Kid was making his way into Chihuahua; he rode into Carretas one afternoon accompanied by a couple of his *mozos* and a pack animal or two. He had been there only long enough to wash his face and sit down to supper, when into the town rode Villa with a big bunch of followers. Villa swaggered into the main room of the *meson* where Conness was eating his supper and sat down opposite to him. He had had a few drinks and was bombastic and offensive in elaborating upon the fact that "he was a big mad bull who gored whom he pleased and had to account to no one for his goring." The Kid is a very quiet, a very silent man . . . this kind is the most dangerous.

Villa hated all *gringos,* but he knew exactly who this *gringo* was and he also had no particular amount of guts. When he performed his own shooting and killing, which was seldom enough, he needed all the breaks so that this pastime would be a perfectly safe one to be indulged in by Don Francisco Villa.

The Kid looked him steadily in the eye; that same Kid had a damned mean eye to look into when he felt that way. He then serenely informed Villa that if Pancho started anything it would, of course, result in his, the Kid's, being killed; but he was positive that Villa was aware of the fact that he himself would go first, and that the news of the Kid's death would be transmitted to Villa by some of Villa's many followers in Hell or wherever it was he would be residing when dead. Villa knew that the Kid was right, that when it came to a draw this *gringo* had him beat a mile, so he decided to laugh it off and be a good friendly boy scout. The Kid went on to Chihuahua that night.

I have jumped forward at least thirty-five years or more from the time when you first met the Kid. About three years after you first saw him on the parade ground at old Fort Concho in Texas, one day when my uncle reached Chihuahua with the bullion train from Batopilas, there appeared in that city a tall, nice-mannered, snappy colored man. He approached my uncle and asked for a job at the mines; he knew about mules and horses, spoke some Spanish, was in every way a promising possibility. Out he went to the Sierras. Charlie Robinson (you see I told you there would be more about Charlie later on) proved to be willing, a truly desirable character, and was soon established as night watchman at the main entrance to the Hacienda San Miguel.

Pretty soon Charlie married a seamstress who sewed for our family and in due time two boys and two girls were born. The older boy went to school in the town and became a good mechanic, carpenter, and electrician. The younger boy went to school, too, at times and developed into an errand boy for me at San Miguel Mine. He had his share of paddlings, well-deserved ones they were, by the Yard Boss. In the course of time the soldierly father of these two boys died after a good, faithful, worth-while service; under his dark skin Charlie Robinson was a very fine character.

Came the revolution. It was impossible for the company to continue to operate the mines, because it was impossible for us to get in supplies. Villa attended well to that. This rich property after all those years of very profitable operation shut down and some fifteen hundred men were thrown out of work. That is exactly what Villa wanted. It enabled him to recruit his army to a greater number and that with men from the mining camps . . . a much higher type of man than those he had hitherto been able to obtain.

Among the element thus recruited was this youngest son of Charlie Robinson. We will call him Roberto. By his enterprise, dash and soldierly bearing (inherited from his father; Charlie had been in the 10th U.S. Calvary, a noncommissioned officer), Roberto was soon promoted to a Lieutenancy. He was in command of a detachment of men rustling mules and horses for Pancho Villa out in the Zulouaga Ranch section, with headquarters at the splendid old ranch house.

Now, it so happened that my kid brother succeeded in getting his wife out of Mexico and across the border into safety. He decided to return to that section of Mexico to do a little development work in a quiet way on what looked like some good silver-lead stringers. Of course, he was taking a chance, he knew this. He knew that very soon he would have to leave Mexico for good and he thought he would do enough prospecting work on this piece of property so that when he did have to flee across the border to wait for the Mexican situation to clear up, he would know whether these leads were worth keeping in mind for the future or not.

The veins looked good. He had just about made up his mind to stop work, cover under, and light out for the border, some three hundred miles north of him, when his herder came into the camp scared to death. The herder told him that his horses and mules had been grabbed by some of the revolutionists, and herded off to the Hacienda Zulouaga where the bandits had their *remuda* headquarters.

Now, let us jump from Conness' prospecting camp to the Remuda Station of Villa's *revolucionarios* at the gate of the Hacienda Zulouaga. There we find Lieutenant Roberto inspecting a group of recently brought-in animals. Among them standing out very conspicuously from all the others were a long-maned, jet-black stallion and a couple of bay riding mules.

"Where did you get those?" asked Roberto with an interested expression.

"From a *gringo's* camp about fifteen miles from here."

"Ah, ha," said Lieutenant Roberto to himself. "Those are the animals belonging to one of my old *Patroncitos* from whom I and my family for many years received nothing but kindness." He turned to the herder: "Put those animals aside by themselves in the small calf-corral. When this has been done, come back here to me."

These instructions were carried out, and when the herder and Lieutenant Roberto were alone, the following orders were given:

"Well after dark, you and one of your men are to take those animals back to the place where you found them. You are to say to my old *Patron* that I return these animals to him so that he can ride north at *once* on the pressing business that he knows of."

Not a bad story when you realize that it was made possible because an excellent colored soldier in self-defense had been forced to kill an undesirable character, a murderer, away back in about 1886 near a United States Army Post close to the Texas border. The sheriff of the place had been glad enough to be relieved of the necessity of shooting, or being shot by, the murderer. After he had a talk with the Post Commander he decided that the culprit, our Charlie Robinson, had gone over the Rio Grande the same night as the killing.

The sheriff anticipated the crossing by only eighteen hours. In no way did he interfere with the crossing, and that is how Pancho Villa happened to have a lieutenant in his army whose father had once worn the chevrons of Uncle Sam's.

Ojos Azules is important to the history of the Pershing expedition into Mexico when our Government sent that able General to chase Pancho Villa. They took good care to limit the chasing to certain areas and they were not kept secret, so that all Villa had to do when too closely pursued was to run over the border line and there to finger his nose at the Pershing expedition. This, of course, made a laughing-stock of our troops and handicapped them so much that any useful result of the affair was patently nullified from the start. At Ojos Azules very early one morning, the Cavalry of General Pershing came upon a camp of the Villa troops, where they made a very satisfactory retaliation for the ambushing and shooting up which these Villa troops had given our cavalry a short time before. This was the high-water mark of the Pershing advance; I have heard that Ojos Azules was out of bounds, but I do not know. However, I do know that the troops of the United States have always given mighty good accounts of themselves wherever they were.

It used to amuse and disgust us to hear and to read what the wise ones of the press said about Francisco Villa. Actually he was a very low type of vagabond bandit. If he ever killed a man personally you can rest assured that the dead man was in a position where he had no show. I feel sure that Villa shot a great many of them in the back. All the romantic stories of his having gone wrong in the beginning because of evil done to his family and of the rape of his sister by an officer of the Rurales Army, are all bunk. He was a rascal before the Madero revolution gave him an opportunity to gather together, as a starter, a group of equally disreputable villains. He was a petty horse-and-mule rustler; this trade was the most dignified one he was ever engaged in, in the way of rascalities. When he had cleaned out the foreign clement during his heyday as a military leader he robbed the native shopkeeper, then the native rancher and the native agriculturist, leaving them all utterly destitute. Francisco Villa and a relative of Madero stole and sold into the United States thousands of head of cattle from the Terrazas herds alone, simply leaving no animals at all.

After the second year of his regime, the people at large were so damned sick of the revolution that if they had been given the chance they would have welcomed the interference of anyone who would have relieved them from the depredations of that "patriot." Things got so bad they had to make some sort of deal with him. They gave him a fine ranch near El Parral and a large sum of money to make him be good. He was about through anyway; it was better politics at the time than to bump him off. He had milked that part of his country dry.

Villa graciously accepted the offer; when later he was ambushed and killed as he rode to town in an expensive automobile, he was only paying back for one of the many outrages and killings he had committed or caused to be committed for the sake of personal gain by murder and robbery . . . but always under the guise for military necessity. It was this thief, this murderer, this ravisher of girls, who was honored by the United States Government in detailing a special envoy, a United States Government representative, to accompany him and to see that his murders and depredations were reported in a proper and official light. The moving pictures glorifying Pancho Villa as a persecuted son of the soil did a very grave damage to history for the coming generations.

Chapter 30

Tampico

In 1914 I was offered a position by an oil company in Tampico. This was in the great and beneficent era of freedom from the despotism of General Porfirio Diaz. Our mining operations had perforce ceased.

I needed a job and I needed it badly. The oil company needed men who knew the Spanish language and the Mexican people. Securing oil leases was a complicated racket in the Tampico oil region. The company I was approached by had only one man in the field. I got a wire on Friday in New York where I then was. I accepted the offer, and sailed the next day in a small freighter.

There were precious few sailings to Tampico in those days. Affairs were more than a little unsettled; a part of the confusion could justly be attributed to some of the politically whirring brains in the United States.

The little ship *Camaguey* cast off and went down the river with so great a load of tank iron that the dirty, but fortunately quiet, river was much too high on her sides. There were only six passengers including myself. Being a good sailor I slept well and ate more than my share as I usually do on shipboard. She was pretty steady, being so heavily loaded that she would not or could not rise to the swells. She simply forced her way through them, tunneled them, so to speak. Even though the well-deck was constantly under water and the superstructure continuously soaked by spray, the ship rode smoothly.

The morning we were off Hatteras and blowing hard, the old Scotch engineer, being colossally grouchy, finished off his none too complimentary remarks by the statement that he had been going to sea for thirty years, and this was the first time he had ever sailed in a _____ anvil!

In truth, the *Camaguey* was almost that on the trip to Tampico. There were few ships available and there was a crying need for tank iron. She was loaded full with flat sheets of that metal.

We made a short stop at Vera Cruz, and then on to Tampico. My efforts to find out from conversations in the *cantinas* and other such bureaus of information what was going on were fruitless; the only news was that furnished by the government press, for the town of Vera Cruz was in a state of siege by the *revolucionarios* . . . don't ask me which! You asked questions, you heard answers, you enjoyed, or rather participated in, drinks bought to inspire the emitting of intelligence, and you returned to your ship with a quantity of misinformation. Some of the knowledge obtained did have the merit of vivid imaginary tales and romancings.

One old fellow gave me the startling tidings that the people of the United States had been incensed by the injustices to Mexico perpetrated by the President and Mr. Bryan to such a degree that one had been mobbed and that an attempt had been made on the life of the other! He was much pleased by this exhibition of friendship for Mexico, and we had another drink and cried *"Viva Mexico!" "Viva Los Estados Unidos del Norte!"* This was perfectly safe, because we were sure that both of these geographical areas still existed.

I was sorry to take my leave of the gentleman, because I could have afforded to buy a few more *cognacitos;* and it was refreshing to meet a man who had found the philosophical state of mind where, since it was useless to try to talk sense or to act sensibly, the only thing left to do was to drink whatever could be procured, eat when possible, and give an occasional *"Viva Mexico!"* if a Mexican was doing the buying or to substitute the United States if that was what was needed.

Of course, we saw a number of American warships and others lying about; when we came opposite to the mouth of the Panuco and sailed up that stream we also saw two United States gunboats tied to the wharf in Tampico. I asked a gob:

"What the Hell are you doing here?"

"Damned if I know," he replied. "It ain't bad here."

He was conversing in execrable Spanish with a pretty, shapely *mujercita,* she was assisting with yet worse English, and I thought to myself:

"I reckon he's got the right idea. Why worry about fool actions you are not responsible for?"

I reported to the manager of the company in Tampico. He told me my first duty would be to convey more than a hundred thousand dollars in cash for the payroll around to the several camps. This was to be done via the Panuco River and its tributary streams in a fast speed launch. So far he had been unable to obtain passes from the Mexican military commander, who had refused passes to all companies during the past few days.

I was also instructed to go to the lease room or library and to study two or three leases so as to acquaint myself with the forms used. This I did for a few days. I would go at night to the company mess where I slept and ate. This mess consisted of two floors of a big old residence about four blocks from the office of the company. It was about half a block from the corner of the plaza and the soldiers' barracks, El Quartel.

One afternoon as I was walking home, I took a stroll toward the docks and noticed that the American gunboats had cast off and were going down stream. At supper I commented on this fact to the manager, said I thought this disappearance act was a damned funny thing. The feeling against the Americans was growing more torrid daily; if there ever was any need for the presence of the gunboats to protect Americans and American property it would surely be within the next day or two, for things were about ready to break.

"That is exactly what the consul thinks," was his worried answer. "But what makes you think so?"

"Oh, just a hunch, and the information I have acquired in the *cantinas* and cafés where one picks up a bit of stuff if he makes out he is drinking more than he actually is, and if he knows his onions."

"But I feel that you are mistaken," said the company manager, so I let it go at that.

This manager, by the way, did not know a single word of Spanish, he had been at this particular job but a short time past because he had made a good record in the Pennsylvania oil fields. He was a good man, he knew oil. I did not envy him his job with its responsibilities in a situation where no definite stand or policy was taken by his government, nothing but contradictory and vacillating notes being exchanged, and where punishment had been threatened again and yet again with none forthcoming.

It was no wonder that the masses in Tampico were strong in their belief that the "colossus of the north" was yellow and would never take any real action; strong in the belief that they would be absolutely safe in going ahead; confident that if the United States ever did make a military attack Mexico could easily whip the *cobardes,* the cowards.

A Captain of Mexican Infantry told me one night in a *cantina* that they were all set to cross the border at two points, and that it would need no longer than one week to move an army into the City of Washington and take over the United States Government.

He was ignorant and very foolish, of course. He based his calculations on the fact that "Surely you have plainly shown that you are afraid to fight, therefore that the Mexican fighting man could move across your defenseless country at will."

I tried to explain to him that we would undoubtedly fight; that while we might not be able to do much against such ably led troops as those he commanded, not all Mexican troops were so excellent as his. Therefore, there might be considerable trouble in their reaching Washington in so short a time as a week.

"Fight!" he exclaimed. "Fight! *Por Dios,* what makes you think Wilson and Bryan will fight? Have we not insulted you time after time recently? And what do you do? You send ships with orders not to shoot under any provocation. Then you send over another *bombadeo de notas; cartas,* letters! Who was ever hurt by a bit of paper no matter what was written on it?"

The day following the one that saw the gunboats go down the river to join the ships lying off the mouth of the harbor, as I was sitting in the lease room poring over a lease, in came the manager; he informed me hurriedly and a little excitedly:

"They have landed and are fighting in the streets!"

"The Hell they have! This is a small town and I have not heard a single shot."

"Not here," he said, "in Vera Cruz. Here we are at the mercy of these people. The gunboats have gone and the Fleet doubtless had orders to do nothing for our protection. We must get all the office force up to the mess hall and this money too. More than a hundred thousand dollars in cash is in that safe."

By that time, he had the safe open and had extracted two bundles of money done up in sealed packages, unmistakably packages of money. The larger one he handed to me, and the smaller one he gave to one of the other employees. I suggested that a newspaper should be wrapped about these bundles and I did this to mine, trying to make it as careless looking as possible.

"What shall I do with this when I get there?"

"I'll be there before you will. I will put it in the safe we've got there. It is a better one than this one here. I want you to go by the hotel. Go round the block and go into the side entrance. Blank got in last night from up river, tell him to report to the mess hall if trouble comes. We will have a better chance there than we would have at the hotel."

I left. I went round the block as the manager told me and walked back toward the main street and in the side door of the hotel, which was on the corner. The front entrance was on the main street. I don't remember what the name of that main street was now.

I heard shouting, calling:

"Que mueren los gringos!" and the like.

I called at the desk and asked for Mr. Blank. He was not in the hotel at the time. I agreed with the manager of the place that it would be better to get his front doors ready to close and to prepare a group of his male guests to be ready for trouble.

In preparation for a possible siege, I went over to the newstand and bought a box of cigars and some cigarettes. I walked to the front door of the hotel carrying my valuable and less valuable packages on my arm. I had my raincoat thrown carelessly over them, and . . . Good Lord! I stepped exactly in the path of a tumultuous mob of angry Mexicans all sweated up and yelling all sorts of death to *gringos* and their ancestors.

There I was, scared as a rabbit. But self-preservation usually crops up strong in the unworthy, and I walked out of that hotel as if nothing in the world were wrong. Halting, I lighted a cigarette and advanced steadily through the very middle of that enraged crowd towards my corner two blocks away.

The mob had not quite yet reached the necessary temperature when any single one of them would have made the first pass at me. Certainly *then* all would have been over in truth. I should have been well messed up at the least, and the company would have been out of a nice piece of money.

But *Dios es grande!* Except for being cursed as a *gringo* and damned for a coward and such abuse, I got through the crowd and up the street to our corner. I am sure I made that half block to our door in one long jump. I don't recall anything about it really. I only remember that I knocked vigorously at the door, made myself known, was admitted, and went up the stairs, feeling the cold sweat running down my back. Tampico was hot as Hell, but I was in a frigid state when I reached our landing.

I went into the main room. I turned over the package of money to the boss and reported that Blank was not at the hotel.

"No, Blank is here," replied the manager of the company. "But where is the fellow with the other bundle of money?"

"How in Hell should I know where he is, you god-damned fool? He left with you, didn't he? Why ask me where he is? To Hell with you and your _____ company, and your lousy money! So long as I did not lose what I was responsible for, I hope you lose a million or two; God knows you can stand it!"

Maybe this was uncalled for. But under certain conditions of heat and pressure I am inclined to pass from the polite to that other state, call it what you may feel inclined. I had never before been subjected to insult where I was in a position of being helpless to retaliate. . . .

Now, I regretted more than ever the confiscation of my two guns when we came into port at Tampico and went through the customs. In all likelihood we were going to be greatly in need of plenty of firearms before morning. Most of the firearms that we had were nearly worthless. You could readily understand our probable need by going to the window and observing the riotous gang, hearing the discharge of firearms and the shouts and screams of *"Que mueren los gringos!"*

That night we kept guard from the windows in the upper story. I think it was about midnight when it looked very much as if we should have to leave this place, cross the street and get up on the flat roofs of the opposite houses to make a trial at diverting the attention of the mob which was trying to break into the hotel. If there had been no women and children to be endangered in the hotel, we would have welcomed this opportunity to do a little fighting. There was a group of fairly well-armed men inside, they were barricaded efficiently, and there could have been a magnificent clean-up on that rabble, what with the shooting we could have given them from the rear.

The captain of the German ship in the harbor now took a hand and told the commandant of the town that if he did not disperse the mob, he would land his marines and machine guns and clear the streets. This brought immediate action from the Mexican commandant. His cavalry, mounted on their scrawny ponies, dashed out from El Quartel on the corner and into the throng. With the flats of their sabres, and sometimes the edges, the streets were cleared, and the gang scattered to all parts of the city, where they stayed for that night at any rate.

We had the Germans to thank for the prevention of a great loss of life which otherwise would certainly have been the outcome. Our chagrin and mortification were not lessened by the fact that our own ships with sailors and marines aching to go were at the mouth of the river, but were not permitted to protect their own nationals. The gunboats had been withdrawn lest their presence might incense the Mexicans.

They had already landed that same day and had taken Vera Cruz, but we did not know it then. The troubles in Tampico, where a greater number of Americans were living and working, were directly due to this landing at the other and less important port, indeed I doubt very much if there were any Americans living at Vera Cruz.

All Americans were then ordered to present themselves at the dock with clean shirts, a change of underwear, toilet articles, nothing more. This order was obeyed. On arrival at the dock we found that a yacht flying the German flag and a tramp steamer flying the British flag or vice versa, were loading the refugees, taking them down the river and out to sea to join the Fleet, where they were being put on the warships.

The unmarried men, particularly the tougher and more experienced ones, were held to the last. They sat on a pile of lumber and other freight on the quay awaiting their turn. We were to act as rear guard if, while the loading was going on, the mob, now collecting across the vacant square opposite to the customhouse, should try to rush the refugees.

Toward the last our Consul arrived at the pier. He had his American flag folded neatly and placed under his arm, was arrayed in immaculate white linen and a Panama hat. He ostentatiously passed through the milling mass of angry Mexicans, behaving in a truly creditable manner, and putting on a very dignified show. Although he was damned and cursed, no one put a hand on him. This gave us a slight compensation for the humiliation we were enduring and had endured. We were glad that under the eyes of foreign sailors he manifested that Americans could carry off any situation as well as anyone, when not under immediate orders which held us back and mortified us.

Our own turn finally came. We were taken down the river, and passed en route very close to a Mexican gunboat. The excited and mostly quite drunken crew had the time of their lives shouting obscenities at us.

Our destination was the old *Cyclops.* We clambered aboard, something over three hundred able-bodied men sore as crabs. We were so very sore that a little while later, when we were boarded by a Sergeant of Marines with a notebook who told us that a ship with the Army Landing Force had been disabled and would not, therefore, be off Tampico in time, and that the Fleet Commander was asking for volunteers for a landing party that very night, he had more than two hundred names just as fast as he could write them.

You can well imagine how thankful we were when we received word that during the afternoon we would be taken off to other ships and be given arms.

We waited; then we waited some more; and then it got dark and we laid down and slept anywhere we could find a space. The old *Cyclops* was a good sturdy collier; but she was a damned poor passenger ship.

Daylight came, and there we were. A swallow of very bad coffee, a spoonful of beans on a slice of bread, was the breakfast. There were no plates and the porridge bowls in which the coffee was served went from hand to hand. This was our ration without change until we landed in Galveston, Texas. It rained every night. There was no shelter for most of us. Were we damp and uncomfortable when we got there!

In Galveston we were denied the privilege of debarking. The United States Government was willing to give us a clean bill of health. They needed the *Cyclops* with her coal to join the fleet at once. But the quarantine officers of "the sovereign State of Texas, By God, sir!" were not willing.

We passed yet another night on that filthy old collier. Came dawn; a couple of cutters pulled over from one of the warships; selected the side away from the shore. Soon a hospital detachment was on board us with a couple of stretchers. In less than thirty minutes they came up from below with these stretchers and something on them covered with sheets.

"What about it?" we asked the medical attendants. "Those men dead?"

"Naw. A couple of 'smokes' with the smallpox."

We gazed at one another in consternation. We decided we were due for quarantine. We hope so certainly; that would beat the old *Cyclops* all to Hell as a place of residence. But no, along about ten o'clock came the Texas authorities and soon we were declared clean. The ship docked; we went ashore.

I had no clothes, little money. But I knew that the manager and those others who had been more fortunate than we had been in the way of ocean transport were in Galveston. I started to make a round of the hotels. By this time, I knew a little about the crowd I had been working for. Therefore, I did not select the best one at which to make my first inquiry. I made a bull's-eye the very first shot.

I went to my room, had my clothes off and was in a tub of hot water in less time than it takes to tell it; sent the bellboy out to get clean underwear and things; while my suit was being scoured, pressed, and promised for the following morning, I ordered up enough supper for two. I put this away and slept for twelve hours—*on a bed.*

At the breakfast table the manager asked me if I would wait over a few days to return to Mexico with him and two other men on the force. The rest of them were going home. Of course, I agreed. A job was a job in those days even at a salary of less than half of what I was accustomed to receiving. Later on that same day, I was advised that we would not be returning to Mexico right away, and that our services were, therefore, no longer required. We would receive a month's pay; our traveling expenses to point of departure would not be paid to us, because we had not completed our two years' contract.

"What about our baggage?"

"That will be returned to you as soon as possible."

But I, for one, was not willing to agree to that. I pointed out to the manager that he would indeed pay my expenses back to point of departure since it was not through my fault that I was back in the States before completion of the two years' contract. That I intended to have the amount of money due me or to demand payment from the President of these United States. Or the Secretary of State. And that I was wiring to Washington about it right away, giving full particulars!!!!

It broke his heart, but he paid our very small and just claim. It was better for him that he did so, because the press was employing large type about this time concerning the whole affair, and reporters dogged one's footsteps.

Months afterwards when at last I received my trunk it contained absolutely nothing at all, and I paid express and other charges to the tune of nineteen dollars. . . .

THE END

Glossary

ABRAZO	To embrace a friend upon meeting or departing. A modified embrace, not a lover's death hold
ADIOS	Good-bye
ADOBE	Sun-dried mud and straw brick, usually about is 15 x 10 x 4 in thickness
ALACRAN	Scorpion
AMIGO	Friend
AMMARRADOR	One who ties the knife on a chicken which is to fight
APAREJO	Pack-saddle
ARRENDADOR	One whose profession is to train a saddle animal to the bit, to make him bridle-wise, to settle him in his gaits, the person who takes the animal over after the buster has done his first part of breaking
ARRIERO	Driver of a pack-mule
ARROYO	Creek
AZUCAR	Sugar
BAILE	Ball, dance
BANDERILLA	A short rod with small gaff in end. Much adorned by short streamers made of tiger skin or goat skin with hair on, hangs down at back of saddle, on either side. 30 inches long to 36 inches on either side of animal. An adornment, sometimes contains hidden pockets acting as would a saddle-bag
BANDERILLERIOS	Bull-fighters who place the banderillas
BAQUERILLO	Saddle adornment made from tiger skins or long-haired goat skins. Fits over end of saddle-tree behind cantle, like saddle-bags, hangs down on both sides to or a little below line of animal's belly
BARRANCA	Gorge
BIEN	Well
BIENVENIDA	Welcome
BOTANILLA	Chamois or buckskin pad that goes around the leg of chicken about to fight and upon which the U of the knife rests
BRIBON	Rascal
BURRO	Donkey
BUENAS TARDES	Good afternoon
BUENOS DIAS	Good day
CABALLERO	Gentleman
CABRESTO	Halter rope, generally horsehair
CAMPO SANTO	Cemetery (holy ground)
CANTINA	Bar, drinking place
CARABINA	Carbine
CARAMBA	An exclamation
CARGA	Mule load, is used to indicate 300 pounds weight which is the accepted load for slow freight when mules are used. You pay so much freight for a carga of 300 pounds
CERRO	Mountain
CHILI	Red or green bell pepper. *Chili verde* is green, *chili colorado* is colored (red)
CHIMILCO	Small shop or store
CHORRERA	A chute in a mine through which ores or waste flow from upper to a lower level, also used to indicate a small waterfall
COCHE	A carriage or a stagecoach, hack. In some provincial districts a pig is also called a *cochi*
COCHERO	A coachman, a stage driver
CON	With
CONDENADO	One who is condemned, one who is damned. Used as an equivalent of damned, or damn you
CONDUCTA	A train of mules or wagons which transport bullion
CONDUCTOR	Boss of a bullion train, mule train, or wagon train
CONQUISTADOR	Conqueror
CORRAL	Fenced-in enclosure in which animals are kept
CORREA	Thong of leather
CORRIDA	A bull-fight (*corrida de toros*)
DOLOR MUY FUERTE	Very strong pain
DON	Mister
DOÑA	Married lady
DUEÑA	Chaperone
EL ESPADA	The bull-fighter, he who uses the sword, the head of the group (the *quadrilla*)
FAJA	Sash worn about the waist in place of a belt, it is quite long
FIESTA	An occasion of festivity. A day devoted to religious ceremony first and festivities afterwards
FONDA	Eating place

FONDERA	A woman who runs an eating place
FORMAN	A command to form
FORTIN	Small fort
FRIJOLE	Kidney bean
FUERTE	Strong
FUERZA	Strength
GATO	Cat
GOBERNADOR	Governor
GRACIAS	Thanks
GRANDE	Big, large; principal one
GRINGO	Term employed to designate usually a North American or an Englishman, generally the former
GUAYAVA	Fruit somewhat resembling a pear in shape but not in taste
HACIENDA	The group of buildings at which is established the headquarters of a big ranch. A very large ranch may be made up of several haciendas. There are *haciendas de beneficio,* which is used to indicate the place of the buildings, the machinery, and so forth where ores are treated and values extracted. You may have a Concession Minera (mining concession) on which you have an *hacienda de beneficio*
HOJA	Leaf, used to designate the roll of corn husks used for cigarettes
HOMBRE	Man
HIDALGO	A Grandee of old Spain
HUERTAS	Gardens. where vegetables are raised, also a small irrigated farm
HUEVOS AL RANCHERO	Fried eggs garnished with a sauce made from green peppers, onions, and *chili* powder
INOCENTE	An innocent person, also one who is a little lacking in the upper story, quite a young child. A fool
JACAL	Small flimsy house, palm roof, sides of interlaced small sticks plastered with mud
JEFE	Chief
JEFE POLITICO	Political chief, unusually indicates mayor of a town
JEFE POLICIA	Chief of Police
JEFATURA	Office of the Jefe
MACOUCHIC	Very inferior grade of tobacco sold in bulk used in a corn husk cigarette (*Cigarro de hoja*)
MATA	Plant or a small tree
MATADOR	Bull-fighter who actually kills the bull
MACHETE	Heavy broad-bladed cutting knife or sword. Where the country possesses few or no large trees and there is underbrush it takes the place of an axe
MEDIA	Half a quart (pint bottle)
MEDIO	Half of anything. *Medio real,* half a *real.* A real is $12^1/_2$ cents.
MENUDO	Literally small piece; very often used to designate a certain stew made of tripe cut in small pieces with *chili colorado* highly seasoned
MESCAL	Distilled colorless liquid made from juice of maguey plant
MESON	A hostelry, a place where there is cheer for man or beast.
MESA	Literally a table, also used as a tableland
MIL	Thousand
MOCHO	A person lacking a member, one-armed, one-legged, one-fingered
MONTE	Gambling game played with cards. *En El Monte* means out in the bush
MOZO	Man-servant
MUCHACHA	Girl
MUJER	Woman
MUY	Very
MUY HOMBRE	Very much of a man, a very strong man, a courageous man
NAVAJA	Small knife, knife used on chickens when they fight
NOVIA	Woman who is affianced or newly married
NOVIO	Man who is affianced or newly married
OLLA	Earthenware jar, for holding water, etc.
PADRE	Father, either of a family or a church
PATIO	Central garden in a house that is built about four sides of same
PATRON	The big noise in a business, the proprietor
PATRONCITO	Small person, the son of the patron
PECADO	Sin
PECADOR	Sinner
PELEA DE GALLOS	A chicken fight, cocking main
PEQUEÑO	Small
PEON	Laboring man, not a slave, unskilled laborer

PESO	Weight, a dollar
PICADOR	Bull-fighter who uses lance and rides horse.
PINTA	Term used in indicating certain colors in the ores in the Batopilas district
PISO	Story of a house, whether first or second floor
PISTOLA	Pistol
PLAZA	Small park or square usually there is a bandstand; also *plaza del mercado,* a market square
POBRE	Poor
POLLO	Young chicken
POR DIOS Y LA SANTA VIRGEN	By God and the saintly Virgin
POR MIS GRANDES PECADOS	For my great sins
PORTAL	A covered porch, a first floor, covered, outside the corridor
PRONTO	Quickly
QUADRIILA	The group of bull-fighters making up the team for any particular bull-fight
QUE	What or that
QUE MUEREN LOS GRINGOS	Death to the *Gringos*
REATA	Rope of any material, a rawhide *reata* for roping or the reata for tying on the pack on a mule
REAL	Used sometimes to indicate a town. *Vamos al real.* Let us go to the town. 12½ cents in money
RIO	River
SALA	Parlor
SALUD Y PESETAS	Health and money
SANTOS	Saints
SEÑORITA	A young lady
SERAPE	Blanket worn in cold weather over the shoulders
SERENATA	A serenade; music on the plaza is a *seranata*
SIEMBRA	A place where seed has been planted, *Mi siembra,* my garden
SOMBRA	Shade
SOMBRERO	Hat
SIN VERGUENZA	Person without shame, it is a fighting term
TAPADO	Covered up. usually indicates a rooster of 6 pounds or more; a heavyweight, free for all.., Is not matched for weight
TARANTULA	Large black spider, with very long hairy legs, not nice to look at nor to have about the house, poisonous. Plenty of liquor will relieve the bitten person, however, from any permanent disability from its bite
TEQUILLA	Liquor distilled, alcoholic drink, plenty of virtue
TOREADOR	Bull-fighter
TODOS	All
TONTO	Stupid one
TORO	Bull
TORTILLA	Corn cake made from *nestamal,* which is a paste from the grain corn prepared as we prepare the corn for lye-hominy
TUERTO	One-eyed
UN	One (masculine)
UNA	One (feminine)
VAMONOS	Let us go, come let us go
VAQUERO	Cowboy
VIEJA	Old woman
VIEJO	Old man
VIVA	Live. Exclamation of high approval when it is used followed by the name of the person or thing or place. "Long Life To _____." A female may be *viva,* bright, full of life so may a female mule
VIVO	I live. If I am bright while living, I am vivo. To tell a person to be *vivo* is to tell him to be very much on the job, also to act promptly or quickly without delay
ZURRON	Leather sack carried on the back; capable of containing 150 pounds of ore. Wider at the top than at the bottom, to insure easy emptying of contents. Is used with a necapal, this is a leather strap 4 inches wide which goes around the forehead and extends back on each shoulder and is attached to either side of the zurron about one third distant from the bottom towards the top

Basic Travel Tips for Copper Canyon

To obtain a visa, the traveler must have a proof of citizenship which may be a passport, birth certificate, voter's registration or draft card. A complete Spanish-English dictionary is highly recommended. Automobile insurance and visas are mandatory.

In recent years Mexico has had various credit card only fees and deposits on private vehicles driven into Mexico on tourist visas. These change from time-to-time so be prepared.

Water — As with all travel outside the U.S. and worldwide, *all* water must be boiled for safety. Recommended is bringing five to ten-gallons of drinking water *only* and a separate, refillable jug for washing and cooking purposes.

Food — With the exception of major towns, food is generally limited to eggs, range-fed beef, tortillas, beans, potatoes, coffee and soda pop. These items can be obtained just about anywhere.

Gas — Only major cities have "extra" gas (about 85 octane). In the mountains *Nova* (very poor regular gas) is available at infrequent intervals. Fill the tank at every opportunity and keep a 5-10 gallon reserve in cans. Poor quality gas is probably the worst problem encountered in visiting the parks.

Tires — Recommended are five new tires and an excellent spare.

General Travel Advice — Everything in this book is in the best Spanish tradition, *alineamiento aproximado,* and in the best English tradition, "subject to change without notice," so keep your thinking cap on at all times, talk to everyone you meet, ask questions, and have the greatest adventure of your life!

Extensive travel in Mexico and South America has shown that one can survive on a vocabulary of less than 200 Spanish words. Here are the most important words and phrases for travel in northwest Mexico.

please - por favor
where is? - ¿donde está?
road (or trail) - camino
town - pueblo
hotel - hotel
restaurant - restaurante
house - casa
falls - cascada
canyon - barranca
mountains - montañas (sierra)
high - alto
low - abajo
store - tienda
let's go - ¡vámanos!
river - río
meal - comida
north - norte
south - sur
east - este
west - oeste
lake - laguna/lago
mission - misión
you - usted
we - nosotros
I want - Yo quiero
I would like - Me gustaría
meat - carne
eggs - huevos
beans - frijoles
bread - tortillas
potatoes - papas
auto oil - aceite
gas - gasolina
ice - hielo
water - agua
more - mas
very hot - mucho calor
very cold - mucho frio
pretty - bonita
Indians - indigenista
why - ¿por qué?
what - ¿qué?
where - ¿donde?
when - cuando
who - ¿quién?
much - mucho
thank you - gracias
you're welcome - por nada
How much does this cost? - ¿Cuánto cuesta?
bathroon - baño

Numbers

one - uno
two - dos
three - tres
four - cuatro
five - cinco
six - seis
seven - siete
eight - ocho
nine - nueve
ten - diez
twenty - viente
thirty - treinta
forty - cuarenta
fifty - cincuenta
sixty - sesenta
seventy - setenta
eighty - ochenta
ninety - noventa
one hundred - ciento
one thousand - mil

Weights and Measures

U.S.	Metric
Distance	
1 mi	1.61 km
5 mi	8.05 km
10 mi	16.09 km
30 mi	48.27 km
50 mi	80.45 km
80 mi	128.72 km
100 mi	160.9 km
Length	
1 in	2.54 cm
5 in	12.7 cm
10 in	25.4 cm
1 yd	0.914 m
5 yd	4.57 m
10 yd	9.14 m
Weight	
1 oz	28 g
5 oz	142 g
10 oz	283 g
1 lb	0.45 kg
5 lb	2.25 kg
10 lb	4.5 kg
Capacity	
ounce	.0296 l
pint (16 oz)	.4739 l
quart (32 oz)	.9463 l
gallon (4 qt)	3.78 l
10 gallons	37.8 l
Temperature	
Fahrenheit	Celsius
100°	38.5°
80°	26.5°
32°	0°
0°	-17.8°

Bibliography

Sierra Madre

Unknown Mexico, Carl Lumholtz, M.A. Charles Scribner's Sons, New York, 1902.

Chihuahua: A Guide to the Wonderful Country, Richard H. Hancock, University of Oklahoma Press, 1978.

Mexico's Copper Canyon Country - A Hiking and Backpacking Guide to Tarahumara Land, M. John Fayhee, Cordillera Press, Inc., P.O. Box 3699, Evergreen, CO 80439, $12.95, 1989.

Native Americans

Cycles of Conquest, Edward H. Spicer, The University of Arizona Press, Tucson, AZ, 1962.

Rarámuri, A Tarahumara Colonial Chronicle 1607-1791, Thomas E. Sheridan and Thomas H. Naylor, editors, Northland Press, Flagstaff, AZ, 1979.

Tarahumara of Mexico: Their Environment and Material Culture, Campbell W. Pennington, The University of Utah Press, Salt Lake City, 1963.

Tarahumara - Where Night Is the Day of the Moon, Bernard L. Fontana with photography by John P. Schaefer, Northland Press, Flagstaff, AZ, 1979.

People of the Desert and Sea - Ethnobotany of the Seri Indians, Richard S. Felger and Mary Beck Moser, University of Arizona Press, Tucson, AZ, 1985.

Semana Santa in the Sierra Tarahumara: A Comparative Study of Three Communities, John C. Kennedy and Raul A. Lopez, University of California Press, Berkeley and Los Angeles, 1981.

Missions — Sierra Madre

Spanish Jesuit Churches in Mexico's Tarahumara, Paul M. Roca, University of Arizona Press, Tucson, AZ, 1979.

Earlier Jesuit Missions in Tarahumara, Peter Master Dunne, S.J., University of California Press, Berkeley and Los Angeles, 1948.

Railroad

Destination Topolobampo, John Leeds Kerr with Frank Donovan, Golden West Books, San Marino, CA, 1968.

Rails, Mines and Progress: Seven American Promoters in Mexico 1867-1911, David M. Pletcher, American Historical Association, Cornell University Press, 1958 (also Batopilas and Mexico general).

Flora

Biotic Community of the American Southwest - United States and Mexico, David E. Brown, Editor, University of Arizona Press for the Boyce Thompson Southwestern Arboretum, P.O. Box AB, Superior, AZ, 1982.

Fauna

The Grizzly in the Southwest, Documentary of Extinction, David E. Brown, University of Oklahoma Press, Norman 1985.

The Wolf in the Southwest, David E. Brown, University of Arizona Press, Tucson, AZ, 1963.

Harper and Row's Complete Field Guide to North American Wildlife (Western Edition), Harper and Row Publishers, New York, 1981.

A Field Guide to Mexican Birds, Rober Tory Peterson, Edward L. Chalif, (Audubon Society and National Wildlife Federation) Houghton Mifflin Company, Boston, 1973.

Baja

The Magnificent Peninsula, Jack Williams, H.J. Williams, P.O. Box 203, Sausalito, CA, 1986.

Camping and Climbing in Baja, John W. Robinson, La Siesta Press, Box 406, Glendale, CA, 1983.

Mexico - Culture - History

Mexico, Kal Muller and Guillermo García-Oropeza, Insight Guides, APA Productions Prentice Hall, Harrap Lansdowne, 1984.

El Fuerte - Gateway to Copper Canyon

by Emilio Kifuri

El Fuerte, Sinaloa, is a popular gateway for boarding the train into the sierra to enjoy and appreciate an outstanding canyon itinerary with abundant natural, cultural and colonial Mexican historic attractions. The El Fuerte River, with contributions from the waters of the Batopilas, Urique, Verde, Septentrion and Choix Rivers, descends westward from the sierra and feeds a vast river valley basin. Following the building of several dams that enable the irrigation of large tracts of land, this fertile area has become a major crop producer and the "breadbasket" of Mexico.

The Mayo Indians are native to Sinaloa and Sonora and are named for their territorial Mayo River. They speak Cahita, a dialect of the Uto-Aztecan Language, and are closely related to the Yaqui Indians. They cultivate corn, chiles, squash, pick abundant wild fruits and harvest fish. Their colorful ceremonies, which may continue for several days and nights, contain sacred elements of both their native culture and Catholicism, featuring the "Deer Dancers", Pacolas and Matachin Dancers. The Mayo carve decorative masks which are usually available for sale.

Nearby, on the banks of the river, sits an archeological site with well over 200 petroglyphs containing anthropomorphic, zoomorphic and geometric images including a large fox with a spiral tale that we have affectionately named "El Presidente." Relatively ignored in a country with many archeological treasures, little is known of this site. If this treasure were located north of the U.S. border, it would undoubtedly be extensively studied by scientists and have a federal or state governmental designation with a visitor center visited by thousands.

The name El Fuerte means "the fort", and was named by Spanish explorers who first arrived in the area in 1533 and built the first settlement in 1564. The colonial history includes famous names like Diego de Guzman, de Niza, Coronado, de Ibarra, and de Hurdaide. El Fuerte legends include the incredible story of Cabeza de Vaca, who was shipwrecked off the Florida coast and wandered for eighteen years, facing nearly impossibly adverse conditions. de Vaca finally stumbled onto Spanish soldiers some thirteen miles from El Fuerte.

After several settlements were built and later abandoned, in 1610 a fort was completed for protection from fierce Indian raids. Jesuit Missions were built in the surrounding areas and later, with the discovery of rich deposits of silver and gold in the sierra, El Fuerte flourished, becoming the banking and supply center for the sierra mines. The troops of Pancho Villa suffered a defeat by the federal army in El Fuerte. The bullet marks can still be seen on the Palacio Municipal.

The El Fuerte River and the surrounding hills offer a vast variety of plant species in Tropical Riparian Forest and Tropical Decidious Forest, with numerous flowering trees and other flowering shrubs, vines and cacti. This tropical forest is almost exclusively animal and insect pollinated with trees and plants producing attractive flowers to draw suitable pollinators. Examples of flowering plants are: Cardinal Flower, Scrubby Cassia, Lupine, Morning Glory, Scarlet Salvia, and Sunflower Bush. The trees lining the banks are Montezuma Cypress, Cottonwood, Fig, Gumbo Limbo, and Willow. The hills are covered with Organpipe and Giant Cardon Cacti, Tree Morning Glory, Elephant Tree, Palo Verde, Amapa, Sabal Palm and Kapok.

Mexico is one of five countries in the world with the greatest biological diversity resulting from a complex topography that produces a great variation of habitat in a unique geographical location between the continents of North and South America. Located in the meeting of Nearctic and Neotropical zones, Mexico has 1029 species of birds, more than the combined total of the United States and Canada. The El Fuerte area is a birding hotspot with relatively common sightings of endemic and rare species including: Bare-throated Tiger-Heron, Fulvous Whistling-Duck, Solitary Eagle, Rufous-bellied Chachalaca, Elegant Quail, Northern Jacana, Green Parakeet, Military Macaw, Mexican Parrotlet, Lilac-crowned Parrot, Squirrel Cuckoo, Lesser Roadrunner, Colima Pygmy Owl, White-eared Hummingbird, Plain-capped Starthroat, Eared Trogon, Elegant Trogon, Russet-crowned Motmot, Strickland's Woodpecker, Great Kiskadee, Social Flycatcher, Black-throated Magpie-Jay, Sinaloa Crow, Happy Wren, Black-capped Gnatcatcher, Golden Vireo and Yellow-winged Cacique.

In summary, there are few places on earth with as much variety of flora and fauna or with more interesting archeological and historical artifacts. Your memories of El Fuerte will be a treasure you carry with you always.

This text is provided courtesy of Emilio Kifuri • Columbus Travel • 900 Ridge Creek Lane • Bulverde, TX 78163-2872 • (830) 885-2000 • (800) 843-1060 • Fax (830) 885-2010 • www.canyontravel.com